Storage Area Networks

FOR

DUMMIES®

2ND EDITION

by Christopher Poelker and Alex Nikitin

WILEY

Wiley Publishing, Inc.

Storage Area Networks For Dummies®, 2nd Edition

Published by
Wiley Publishing, Inc.
111 River Street
Hoboken, NJ 07030-5774

www.wiley.com

Copyright © 2009 by Wiley Publishing, Inc., Indianapolis, Indiana

Published by Wiley Publishing, Inc., Indianapolis, Indiana

Published simultaneously in Canada

WILEY

About the Authors

Christopher Poelker has been in the field of computer technology since 1974. Chris was an electronics engineer in the U.S. Army, and tried to stay out of trouble by hiding in tanks while installing laser range finders and computer-aided ballistic trajectory systems. After leaving the service, Chris went to school in New York City at good old Control Data Institute and was hired as a field engineer by Digital Equipment Corporation. In his spare time, Chris started his own software company, developed databases, and became a Microsoft MCSE and instructor. Chris worked for Digital for 18 years until it was bought by Compaq, where he stayed on as a StorageWorks systems engineer until joining Sun Microsystems in 2000. Chris left Sun to become a consulting storage architect for Hitachi Data Systems and became the district storage manager for HDS in New York City. In 2006, Chris left HDS for FalconStor software, where he now works as the Vice President of Enterprise Solutions. Chris has designed and implemented storage networks for many of the Fortune 100 companies in the U.S. and around the world. In his spare time, Chris sometimes speaks at industry forums, writes magazine articles, and has acted as the SAN expert at SearchStorage.com.

Alex Nikitin, currently a systems expert at HBO, has logged in 15 years in the Information Technology industry. Alex has worn many hats in this industry, ranging from application programmer and network administrator to the ultimate responsibility over large server farms, and storage and backup solutions for some of the world's top financial and pharmaceutical companies. Alex and Chris worked together at Hitachi Data Systems in New York, where Alex was the "go to" guy for difficult storage designs and implementations. Prior to joining HDS, he also spent time growing the install base of Storage Area Networks as a Professional Services Consultant for EMC Corporation, implementing SAN solutions for various companies, large and small, on Windows NT/2000, Solaris, HP/UX, AIX, and Linux platforms. Seemingly always cast in a storage-centric capacity, his career has focused on caring for and reliably delivering vast amounts of storage to his user community.

Dedication

Christopher Poelker: To my sister Nancy, whose love and friendship meant the world to me.

Author's Acknowledgments

Christopher Poelker: I would have never been given the chance to write this book if it weren't for my friends at TechTarget, who used to run the SearchStorage.com Web site: Michelle Hope and Maryann Tripp. These two wonderful women were the reason I was introduced to Melody Layne and Susan Christophersen of Wiley Publishing, who made the first book possible, along with Teresa Artman, who spent many a long night copy-editing the manuscript and making up for my horrible writing skills. (I should have paid closer attention during eighth-grade English!) For this second edition, I would like to thank Kyle Looper and Kim Darosett for their patience during deadlines when my day job was getting in the way of keeping this edition on track.

I'd also like to thank my partner in crime and co-author, Alex Nikitin, who again saved my marriage and my duty as a father to my children by taking over some of the load and helping me crank out some of these chapters. Alex is one of the best storage guys I have ever had the privilege of working with.

Thanks also need to go this time to FalconStor software, for letting me proceed with this project and letting me play hooky now and then to crank out a chapter or two. Thanks to ReiJane Huai, Wendy Petty, Wayne Lam, Alan Chen, Tom Strumpf, Bruce Sasson, Joanne Ferrara, and everyone else at FalconStor who filled in or helped me out to give me time during the writing of this book.

Special thanks to all the folks who taught me most of the things I know about storage: my brothers, Lenny Poelker and Greg Poelker, who are a heck of a lot smarter than I! Also to my mentors: Wayne Lam, Wai Lam, Stanley Qin, Irving Moy, David Shyu, Cartic Vengkatraman, Gene Chesser, Steve Sicola, Paul Kruschwitz, Jimmy Wu, Raymond Tong, Paul Mitchell, Mike Mendola, Jo McCausland, John Lallier, Nick Sinish, Brian Rice, Steve O'Rielly, Catherine Brown, Frank Cizin, Leonard Hayward, Charlie Mulrooney, Paul Poon, Don Thatcher, Tony Merschdoff, Jeff Sinisgalli, John Fonseca, Marty Citron, Al Catalano, Tom Lindemann, Roland Song, Pierre Dansereau, Mike Pierro, and most of all, Kevin Shumacker, whose help over the years I could never repay. Thanks to Ken Garnau, Nancy Berliner, and Charlie Santana for help with the mainframe stuff, and everyone I ever met from Brocade/McData, and Emulex.

Tom Clark and Robert Stout, Nancy Jennings, and John Dorl from the original Nishan systems were a big help with helping me figure out SAN extensions, (especially Tom's books!), and Mark Farley's book was the first I read on SAN and still is one of the best. (I guess I learned things the hard way, by just doing it.)

Finally, thanks for the support of my family: Deborah, my wife, for being a single mother again while I was writing the book, and of course, my children Cole, Chris, and Rachel for all their support and being the wonderful people they turned out to be.

Publisher's Acknowledgments

We're proud of this book; please send us your comments through our online registration form located at http://dummies.custhelp.com. For other comments, please contact our Customer Care Department within the U.S. at 877-762-2974, outside the U.S. at 317-572-3993, or fax 317-572-4002.

Some of the people who helped bring this book to market include the following:

Acquisitions and Editorial

Project Editor: Kim Darosett

Executive Editor: Steven Hayes

Copy Editors: Barry Childs-Helton, Susan Pink, Kathy Simpson

Technical Editor: Michael Vannette

Editorial Manager: Leah Cameron

Editorial Assistant: Amanda Foxworth

Sr. Editorial Assistant: Cherie Case

Cartoons: Rich Tennant
(www.the5thwave.com)

Composition Services

Project Coordinator: Patrick Redmond

Layout and Graphics: Samantha Allen, Reuben W. Davis, Melissa K. Jester, Christine Williams

Proofreaders: Broccoli Information Management, Amanda Graham

Indexer: Broccoli Information Management

Publishing and Editorial for Technology Dummies

Richard Swadley, Vice President and Executive Group Publisher

Andy Cummings, Vice President and Publisher

Mary Bednarek, Executive Acquisitions Director

Mary C. Corder, Editorial Director

Publishing for Consumer Dummies

Diane Graves Steele, Vice President and Publisher

Composition Services

Gerry Fahey, Vice President of Production Services

Debbie Stailey, Director of Composition Services

Contents at a Glance

Table of Contents

Introduction

Welcome to *Storage Area Networks For Dummies,* 2nd Edition! The first edition was the book we wish was around when *we* were trying to learn about this stuff! We tried to take a fairly mundane topic and make it a fun read so you could get up to speed on storage networking as quickly and painlessly as possible. This second edition is written in the same spirit as the first.

When the first edition was written in 2003, very few books on storage area networks (SANs) were available. The books that were available were very narrow and extremely technical in focus. They were about as fun to read as the directions for setting up a DVD player. Although more books about storage networking are available now, most are still very technical and about as fun to read as the U.S. tax code (nothing against accountants here!).

Over the years, this book has become the standard bearer in keeping the subject concise, simple, and fun, and has now been updated to include all the new cool stuff and changes that have occurred since the original printing. Let's face it — most folks typically look for a fast and easy way to get information; you want the information you *need* to know, and not everything there *is* to know, so this second edition uses that same point of view common to all of us poor slobs who need to make a SAN work with no budget, no training, and no time. So don't worry, be happy — and just have some *fun!*

About This Book

The mission of this book is to help you find your way around while exploring the topic of storage area networking. The book is dedicated to individuals who, for better or for worse, have been tasked with designing, implementing, configuring, or troubleshooting a storage area network. We hope that the information here will enable both the beginner and the moderately expert storage professional sort through the ins and outs of a SAN. We use familiar language to demystify the technology and translate the jargon as necessary. You'll discover how to choose the right hardware for the job, design a SAN by using the best practices in the industry, connect everything to make it work, and troubleshoot the SAN to fix problems when they occur.

You also get to delve into the hard stuff — the stuff that many companies pay expensive consultants for (who have usually just read a book like this just before they were hired!), so be brave, and we'll do our best to make this painless. If you want to understand what a SAN is and what it does, you've come to the right place. Everything you should need (or want) to know about storage area networks is here in one location.

Foolish Assumptions

We have one or two foolish assumptions about you, the reader of this book:

- ✔ You are responsible for or have worked with computer storage before.
- ✔ You might want to continue working in that field of endeavor.
- ✔ You want to find an easy way out of your networking storage problems so you can get home and play video games, watch TV, and drink beer with your friends.

We also assume that you don't want to become an instant expert. You want to know just enough to be able to speak intelligently on the subject matter but also know when it's time to call in an expert.

This book tries to you get past all the little details that get in the way of understanding a subject by using a real-world approach. We didn't create the technology; we just know how to make it work because we've been in the field for more years than we care to say. This book tries to impart just enough good info to help you make your stuff work — and to understand enough to know when someone is misleading you or trying to rip you off. The best defense is a good offense.

Conventions Used in This Book

We want you to understand all the instructions in this book, and in that spirit, we've adopted a few conventions.

When you hit a chapter in which we ask you to do something, you will be prompted by a numbered list. The numbers in the list are the order of the steps that you need to take to accomplish the task at hand. Just follow the steps listed, and everything should be just fine. If you need to enter something on the keyboard, we ask you to *type* it. If you need to use your mouse, we ask you to *click* it. That's all there is to it.

How This Book Is Organized

This book is designed as a reference, so you don't have to read the book cover to cover. Just look in the Table of Contents to find the topic you're interested in and start reading. If you're unsure of some of the acronyms you've been hearing out there, check out the Cheat Sheet at the front of this book for easy reference.

The book is organized in seven parts.

 ✔ **Part I: SAN 101:** This part covers the basics of storage area networks, including what you need to know if you're going to buy a SAN, build one yourself, or have someone build it for you.

 ✔ **Part II: Designing and Building a SAN:** This part of the book handles all the fun stuff, such as how to add more storage to your servers and how to connect everything and get it running. It also covers what you need to know if you already have a SAN in place or need to know how to use it or set it up properly.

 ✔ **Part III: Using Advanced SAN Features:** If you've always wanted to know what the heck a snapshot copy was, this is the place to find out. This part also covers advanced topics such as backing up your data, which will help you get more bang for your buck out of your SAN.

 ✔ **Part IV: SAN Management and Troubleshooting:** Every now and then, something goes bump in the night. This part shows you how to manage and troubleshoot problems when they occur as well as how to avoid having to face those problems in the first place.

 ✔ **Part V: Understanding the Cool Stuff:** This part covers the cool new advances in storage area networking since 2003, such as storage virtualization, data de-duplication, and advances in data protection and replication such as Continuous Data Protection (CDP). You find out how to use these technologies to help you save money and become more productive and better prepared when trouble happens.

 ✔ **Part VI: The Part of Tens:** This part includes ten reasons to use a SAN and ten reasons *not* to.

We've also provided a bonus chapter titled "Outsourcing SAN Solutions" that you can download from the book's companion Web site at www.dummies.com/go/sanfd2e.

Icons Used in This Book

To help you get the most out of this book, we've placed icons here and there. Here's what the icons mean:

Next to the Tip icon, you can find shortcuts and tricks of the trade to make you more productive without even realizing it.

Where you see the Warning icon, tread softly and carefully. It means that we've been burned by this already and don't want you to have to learn the hard way, as we did.

Stuff marked with the Remember icon is like jotting a note to yourself in a class. Make an effort to bend the ear of the page so that you don't forget it.

Okay, we probably put too many of these icons in the book. But what the heck . . . sometimes trying to explain this stuff is like writing a book on *Brain Surgery For Dummies*. We need to point out the details at times so you don't end up with a migraine.

Chapter 1

The Storage Area Network

This chapter is dedicated to helping you get a handle on what a storage area network (SAN) is, the basics of how one works, and whether one is right for your needs. You'll discover all the parts that make up a SAN, the things that make one run, and who actually makes all the different parts that you can buy. Putting a SAN together is somewhat like putting together one of those high-end stereo systems; you have many components and many different manufacturers to choose from. This chapter helps you choose the ones that suit your needs and create something that you can be proud of.

These days, becoming proficient with SANs can mean a major boost to your career. Perhaps you're bored to death in your current position and would like a change of pace. SAN administration is one of the highest-paying jobs in Information Technology (IT) today. If you add storage area networking to your résumé, you may find your phone ringing off the hook as headhunters vie to offer you a six-figure income (hey, might as well dream big).

Defining a SAN

First, the basics. In today's terms, the technical description of a SAN (Storage Area Network) is a collection of computers and storage devices, connected over a high-speed optical network and dedicated to the task of storing and protecting data.

In a nutshell, you use a SAN to store and protect data. A SAN uses the SCSI (Small Computer Storage Interconnect) and FC (Fibre Channel) protocols to move data over a network and store it directly to disk drives in block format. Today, that high-speed network usually consists of fiber-optic cables and switches that use light waves to transmit data with a connection protocol known as Fibre Channel. (A *protocol* is a set of rules used by the computer devices to define a common communication language.) More and more, regular Internet protocol (IP)–based corporate networks, and even the Internet, are being used as the network part of a SAN. IP networks that are already in place can be used by other storage connection protocols such as iSCSI (internet Small Computer Storage Interconnect) to move and store data.

Using a network to create a shared pool of storage devices is what makes a SAN different. A SAN moves data among various storage devices, allows sharing data between different servers, and provides a fast connection medium for backing up, restoring, archiving, and retrieving data. SAN devices are usually bunched closely in a single room, but they can also be connected over long distances, making a SAN very useful to large companies.

Many of today's SAN components are pretty much plug-and-play. To create a simple SAN, you just connect all the devices together with cables, and off you go. Creating larger SANs with many storage switches can become complex, though, and that's the reason for this book: to give you a handle on what you need to know about large, complex SANs.

Fiber versus Fibre

No, it isn't just a snooty way of spelling *fiber*. (Well, okay, not *only* that.) Networking geeks use the *fibre* spelling (reversing the *er* to *re*) to refer specifically to fiber-optic cables used in a SAN. The idea is to differentiate SAN cables from the optical cables used in other networks (such as TCP/IP Networks). That's because SAN devices use a different language to communicate with each other than do the devices in other networks. This is why the main protocol used in a SAN (snooty or not) is called *Fibre Channel*.

All network protocols are divided into layers, like a layer cake. All the layers in the cake are logically tied together into a *stack*. Each layer of the stack provides different functionality, and each device in the network uses the stack like a language to communicate with other devices in the network. The bottommost layer of the stack is hardware-based (as opposed to software-based), and thus is referred to as the *physical layer*.

The physical layer consists of tangible hardware stuff such as cables, switches, and connectors. This is where the fiber-optic cables are. On top of the physical layer are the software layers that make up the *protocol stack*. In a Fibre Channel SAN, those layers make up the *Fibre Channel* protocol.

Each type of network uses a different protocol to handle data. The Internet, for example, uses a protocol stack called the Transmission Control Protocol/Internet Protocol (TCP/IP). The physical layers of both Internet and SAN can transmit data as light pulses over fiber-optic cables — which (as you might expect) makes the data move nearly as fast as light. The only difference between regular fiber-optic computer networks such as the Internet and a fiber-optic SAN is the protocol and the switches used by the devices to talk to each other over the network. SANs use the *Fibre Channel* protocol and Fibre Channel switches, and the Internet uses the *TCP/IP* protocol and Ethernet switches. Fibre Channel was developed to move data really fast between computers and disk drives; TCP/IP (or "Internet Protocol") was developed to move files over long distances between computers.

How a SAN Makes Computing Different

Using a SAN can really change how you think about computing. In the past, there was the *mainframe*, which was a gigantic computer that could run all the programs in a large business. All the computer stuff was gathered in one place called a *data center*. All the storage that the mainframe needed was directly connected to it. Everything was located and managed as a single, large entity.

The PC revolution changed a lot of things. Everything started to spread out. Data was moved off the mainframe and stored in server computers. The servers were then dispersed throughout the enterprise to bring computing power closer to the actual users. The servers became connected by a network, called a *local area network,* or LAN. This was cool because now the computing power was spread out and made more available to end users. Eventually, LANs were connected to create the Internet.

Networks enabled people who used computers in far-flung places to communicate and share information with each other. In business, problems arose when inter-networking finally took off. A great deal of data was now being stored with no effective way to manage it all. Managing all the scattered data dispersed throughout the network became a nightmare.

Because all data storage was located inside each individual server, you had no effective way to efficiently allocate storage space between all the servers. Sure, users could share files over a LAN, but you still needed a way to share access to physical disks, rather than using dedicated disks inside every server. Hence the advent of the SAN.

Since the original TCP/IP network protocols used in a LAN (Local Area Network) were built to move and share files, they had no built-in way to directly access disk drives. As a result, very high-performance applications needed direct access to *block-based* disk drives to move and store data very fast. (Data is stored as blocks on a disk drive.)

Disk drives in a SAN are stored in a dedicated storage device called a *disk array*. All the servers connect to the storage device over a high-speed network using the Fibre Channel protocol, which enables very fast access to disks over a network. Using a SAN gives businesses shared and consolidated access to data storage — available to any server connected to the SAN.

Putting a SAN in place makes individual server computers less important and more peripheral to the data stored in the SAN. After all, the data is what is important to your business. If you lose a server, you can buy a new one. If you lose your data, it's "Adiós, amigo" for your business.

Understanding the Benefits of a SAN

The typical benefits of using a SAN are a very high return on investment (ROI), a reduction in the total cost of ownership (TCO) of computing capabilities, and a pay-back period (PBP) of months rather than years. Here are some specific ways you can expect a SAN to be beneficial:

- **Removes the distance limits of SCSI-connected disks:** The maximum length of a SCSI bus is around 25 meters. Fibre Channel SANs allow you to connect your disks to your servers over much greater distances.

- **Greater performance:** Current Fibre Channel SANs allow connection to disks at hundreds of megabytes per second; the near future will see speeds in multiple gigabytes to terabytes per second.

- **Increased disk utilization:** SANs enable more than one server to access the same physical disk, which lets you allocate the free space on those disks more effectively.

- **Higher availability to storage by use of multiple access paths:** A SAN allows for multiple physical connections to disks from a single or multiple servers.

- **Deferred disk procurement:** That's business-speak for not having to buy disks as often as you used to before getting a SAN. Because you can use disk space more effectively, no space goes to waste.

- **Reduced data center rack/floor space:** Because you don't need to buy big servers with room for lots of disks, you can buy fewer, smaller servers — an arrangement that takes up less room.

- **New disaster-recovery capabilities:** This is a major benefit. SAN devices can mirror the data on the disks to another location. This thorough backup capability can make your data safe if a disaster occurs.

- **Online recovery:** By using online mirrors of your data in a SAN device, or new continuous data protection solutions, you can instantly recover your data if it becomes lost, damaged, or corrupted.

✔ **Better staff utilization:** SANs enable fewer people to manage much more data.

✔ **Reduction of management costs as a percentage of storage costs:** Because you need fewer people, your management costs go down.

✔ **Improved overall availability:** This is another big one. SAN storage is much more reliable than internal, server-based disk storage. Things break a lot less often.

✔ **Reduction of servers:** You won't need as many file servers with a SAN. And because SANs are so fast, even your existing servers run faster when connected to the SAN. You get more out of your current servers and don't need to buy new ones as often.

✔ **Improved network performance and fewer network upgrades:** You can back up all your data over the SAN (which is dedicated to that purpose) rather than over the LAN (which has other duties). Since you use less bandwidth on the LAN, you can get more out of it.

✔ **Increased input/output (I/O) performance and bulk data movement:** Yup, SANs are fast. They move data much faster than do internal drives or devices attached to the LAN. In high-performance computing environments, for example, IB (Infiniband) storage-network technology can move a single data stream at multiple gigabytes per second.

✔ **Reduced/eliminated backup windows:** A *backup window* is the time it takes to back up all your data. When you do your backups over the SAN instead of over the LAN, you can do them at any time, day or night. If you use CDP (Continuous Data Protection) solutions over the SAN, you can pretty much eliminate backup as a separate process (it just happens all the time).

✔ **Protected critical data:** SAN storage devices use advanced technology to ensure that your critical data remains safe and available.

✔ **Nondisruptive scalability:** Sounds impressive, doesn't it? It means you can add storage to a storage network at any time without affecting the devices currently using the network.

✔ **Easier development and testing of applications:** By using SAN-based mirror copies of production data, you can easily use actual production data to test new applications while the original application stays online.

✔ **Support for server clusters:** *Server clustering* is a method of making two individual servers look like one and guard each other's back. If one of them has a heart attack, the other one takes over automatically to keep the applications running. Clusters require access to a shared disk drive; a SAN makes this possible.

✔ **Storage on demand:** Because SAN disks are available to any server in the storage network, free storage space can be allocated on demand to any server that needs it, any time. Storage virtualization can simplify storage provisioning across storage arrays from multiple vendors.

Finding Out Whether a SAN Is Right for You

Though SANs can offer many advantages, they aren't for everyone. If you own a small business and use just a few computers to keep it going, using a SAN is probably overkill for you. Sometimes the cost isn't justified by the benefits. The more servers you have in your organization — and the more data that you need to store — the more benefit you'll see from a using a SAN. Prices have come down a lot since the first writing of this book, but storage networking equipment isn't cheap. For example, a single high-performance host bus adapter (more about that later) can cost more than a thousand dollars; a storage switch can cost tens of thousands.

A good guideline that we use is what we call *The Rule of 16*. If you have 16 or fewer servers, using a SAN probably doesn't make sense. (Of course, you may still benefit from a less expensive NAS- or iSCSI-based solution, which we touch on later.) You can easily manage 16 or fewer servers with one person, and data-storage needs shouldn't be that high. If you use more than 16 servers, or servers that run large databases, you're a good candidate for a SAN. If you're responsible for hundreds of servers, using a SAN will probably dramatically reduce the cost of managing data.

Who should use a SAN?

You should use a SAN if you work in a large organization (more than 16 servers, or servers that run large databases) in which data management or data backup is becoming a problem. (By *server* here, we mean the hardware you buy to run your applications. When it runs your applications, it is the "server" part of a client/server implementation.) Your servers might be running out of disk space all the time, and you might have no room left in the servers to add disk drives. A business in this server pickle is a typical SAN candidate. You might have way too much data to be backed up or restored in a timely fashion. Using a SAN can fix that, too.

The following checklist details the types of server resources, both software and hardware, that should be included in a SAN:

- **Database servers:** Oracle, Sybase, SQL, DB2, Informix, AdaBase, and other databases love to make use of the extremely fast disks in a SAN.

- **File servers:** Using SAN-based storage for Windows or Unix computers acting as file servers lets you expand your file-server storage resources quickly, makes them run better, and improves overall management. Specialized devices called NAS (Network Attached Storage) servers can supply shared access to stored files over a standard TCP/IP network.

✓ **Backup servers:** Connecting all your servers (including backup servers) to a SAN enables you to back up your data through a SAN rather than through a LAN — and SAN-based backup is dramatically faster.

✓ **Voice/video servers:** Voice and video servers tend to push large amounts of data very quickly. That's what SANs are built to do.

✓ **Mail servers:** Using SAN-based storage for mail servers enables quick restoration of data in case of corruption or viruses. It also lets you back up your mail servers faster, and you can use clusters as mail servers.

✓ **High-performance application servers:** A SAN's capabilities benefit applications for managing documents, scientific computations, customer relationships, billing, data warehouses, and other high-performance business functions.

Who should not use a SAN?

You don't really need to use a SAN if your organization is small (16 servers or fewer) or where data management, application performance, or backup is not currently a problem for you.

For that matter, the technology you have may *not* be a good fit with a SAN. Here's a checklist of the types of servers that should *not* be included in a SAN. Such servers are usually better off staying on their internal disk drives; they don't benefit from SAN-based storage (which is also more expensive):

✓ **Web servers:** Computers set up as Web servers don't usually have large storage needs; they're usually connected to larger servers that run the databases from which Web pages are automatically built. Although Web servers are good candidates for NAS, database servers can make better use of SAN disks.

✓ **Infrastructure servers:** Server applications that handle the chores of network infrastructure — such as Domain Name Servers (DNS), Windows Internet Naming Servers (WINS), and Domain Controllers (DC, PDC) — are better left on the server computers' internal disks. They don't need a lot of disk space, and their performance requirements are minimal.

✓ **All desktop PCs:** Personal computers are not good SAN candidates because they usually connect to corporate servers for any applications that require high performance. Those corporate servers, however, *could* use a SAN.

✓ **Servers needing less than 10GB of storage:** Face it: Internal storage is cheaper than SAN storage. If your server has no performance problems and will never need more than 10GB of storage space, leave it alone.

✔ **Servers that don't need fast access to data:** If performance is good already and you don't mind maintaining the server separately, don't bother hooking it up to a SAN.

 ✔ **Servers that have to share files:** Such servers are better off connected to a Network Attached Storage (NAS) server. NAS servers store and transfer data as files, and not blocks of data, so they don't need the high-speed Fibre Channel protocol used in a SAN. NAS devices are best for file-based uses such as user home directories and shared documents.

Dissecting a SAN (The Four Ps)

We divide this section into four parts, which we call *the four Ps* — namely the parts, protocols, players, and platforms you can choose from when creating a SAN. We don't go into all the gory details because it would take up too much space here and most likely be better for bedtime reading (you're getting sleeeepy). We just give you a general overview of the following:

 ✔ **The parts:** All the hardware you use to create a SAN; the switches, cables, disk arrays, and so forth

 ✔ **The protocols:** The languages that the parts use to talk to each other

 ✔ **The players:** The folks who build the parts

 ✔ **The platforms:** The computer applications that benefit from using SAN

The Parts of a SAN

It's most convenient to imagine the parts of a SAN in three layers. The top layer is the *host layer,* which includes the server computers and everything that goes into them. The middle layer is the *fabric layer,* which includes all the cabling and switches that connect everything. The bottom layer is the *storage layer,* where all the storage devices are located.

The host layer

The major components in this layer are the servers themselves, the host bus adapters (HBAs, which include a part called the Gigabit Interface Converter, or GBIC), and all the software running on the server that enables the host bus adapter to communicate with the fabric layer.

The host bus adapter (HBA)

The server connects to the SAN through a *host bus adapter* (HBA) — an I/O adapter card that fits inside your server and connects it to the fabric layer.

The Gigabit Interface Connector (GBIC)

The Gigabit Interface Converter (GBIC) is where the cable plugs into the HBA card. Every HBA has a GBIC that snaps into an opening in the card or is soldered to the card. The openings in the GBIC extend out the back of the server so you can plug in the cable. The GBIC houses the laser and electronics that convert the data inside your server into light pulses that travel over the cables. GBICs are used not only in the HBA, but in every device in the SAN. Anywhere an optical cable has to be plugged in, you find a GBIC.

Fiber-optic cables

Fiber-optic cables are unique in that they are really part of all three layers in a SAN (such as the GBICs where the cables are plugged in). These cables, which connect everything in a SAN, use glass fibers to transmit light waves from one device to another. You can use one of three optical cable types, depending on the distance between connections and the wavelength of light used to transmit data. (See Chapter 2 for more information.)

The fabric layer

The *fabric layer,* or the middle layer of a SAN, is the actual network part of a SAN. The *network* — where all the cables are connected — is also where you find hubs, switches, gateways, and routers, which tie all the cables together into a logical *and* physical network. Its components include

- ✔ **Hubs:** A *hub* is a simple electronic device that physically connects the cables into a logical loop of cable. This is why hub-based SANs are called SAN *loops.* The hub has connection points — *ports* — where the cables get plugged in. These ports use GBICs to connect the cables to the hub. In a hub, the light coming in from a cable can pass through the hub to a device connected to another port. The light travels around the loop to each port in the hub. Because hub ports are connected in a loop, only one device can communicate through a hub at one time.

- ✔ **Switches:** A *switch* is a smart electronic device that physically connects cables. Switches are the heart of a SAN network. This is where a lot of the intelligence resides. The switches reliably route your data from the host layer to the storage layer.

Think of a switch as working like a telephone switchboard operator. Every incoming call gets connected to its destination over the wires in the switchboard, and the operator knows which wire to plug in where to make this happen.

✔ **Gateway**: A gateway (also referred to as a *bridge*) is a smart electronic device that physically or logically enables devices to communicate over one protocol to talk to devices that use a different protocol. For example, an iSCSI gateway can connect hosts that use the iSCSI protocol to storage devices that use the Fibre Channel protocol in a Fibre Channel SAN fabric.

✔ **Router**: A *router* is another smart device that physically or logically routes data between two individual networks.

The storage layer

The *storage layer* is where all your data resides on the SAN. This is the layer that contains all the disk drives, tape drives, and other storage devices, like optical storage drives. The storage layer's devices include some intelligence, such as Redundant Array of Inexpensive (or Independent) Disks (RAID) and snapshot or other data-replication technologies to help protect data. The capabilities of the storage devices can affect what you can do with a SAN.

Storage arrays

A disk is a disk — two disks are (okay) a couple of disks, and an *array* of disks is just a bunch of disks (also called a JBOD) all located in the same place. But a *storage* array adds extra intelligence to the controllers within the array — which allows you to do cool stuff like RAID, so it's no longer just a bunch of stupid disks. The intelligence built into the storage *controllers* in the storage array is what enables this additional functionality.

A *storage array* is a big box that has a bunch of disk drives in it, running smart code called *firmware* that makes it more intelligent. Of course, you could go to a computer store and buy a bunch of hard drives, but how would you connect them to your server? Today's storage arrays use fast, dedicated microprocessors to run complex software that makes them more useful than they'd be if you just connected a bunch of disks to your servers. (More on storage arrays in Chapter 2.)

The storage arrays connect to the fabric layer with cables that run from the devices in the fabric layer to the GBICs in the ports on the array. Many types of storage arrays are available, but they come in two basic flavors: modular and monolithic. Both these types use built-in computer memory to help speed up or *cache* access to slow disk drives; each uses the memory cache differently. Memory is expensive, so the more expensive monolithic arrays usually have more cache memory than modular arrays. Here's a closer look.

Modular arrays

Modular arrays have fewer port connections than do monolithic arrays; they usually store less data, and connect to fewer servers. They're designed so you can start small, with only a few disk drives, adding more drives to the array as your storage needs grow. Modular arrays come with shelves that hold the disk drives. Each shelf can hold between 10 to 16 drives, depending on the model and manufacturer. Modular arrays usually fit into industry-standard 19" racks, so you can have all your servers and SAN disks in the same rack.

Modular arrays are perfect for smaller companies looking to install a SAN on a limited budget. They're also good for large companies with many remote offices, because they are much cheaper and smaller than big monolithic arrays, so they can be placed into smaller offices. Modular arrays almost always use two controllers with separate cache memory in each controller, and then mirror the cache between the controllers to prevent data loss. Most modern modular arrays have between 16 and 32GB of cache memory.

Monolithic arrays

Monolithic arrays are those big, refrigerator-size collections of disk drives you see sitting next to mainframes in a data center. These disk arrays are loaded with advanced technology that almost always prevents them from going down. Monolithic arrays can accommodate hundreds of disk drives, can store data for a lot more servers than a modular array can, and usually connect to mainframes. Monolithic arrays have many controllers, and those controllers can share direct access to a *global* memory cache (up to hundreds of gigabytes) of fast memory. This method of sharing access to a large global or *monolithic cache* is why these arrays are also called monolithic.

Modular versus monolithic in large-scale enterprise use

At larger scales of operation, modular arrays are often used as *midrange arrays* and monolithic arrays are often used as *enterprise arrays.* The main difference here, however, is functional: Although some enterprise-class arrays *can* be modular in design, they can also connect to and store mainframe data (which a modular array usually can't do). Typically enterprise-class monolithic arrays are much more expensive, and have better built-in redundancy features that make them extremely reliable.

Whether modular or monolithic, each array type has its advantages and disadvantages. Modular arrays are generally less expensive but can handle large-scale workloads if you add enough disk shelves or controller shelves to do the job. When you add controller shelves, you get more horsepower. When you add more disk shelves, you get more storage.

Modular arrays are designed from the ground up to be extremely fast when connected to just a few servers. If you need to add servers, you just buy more controllers. Many companies like that kind of flexibility. Monolithic arrays, on the other hand, can be connected to mainframe computers. They also usually have many more physical ports on them to connect to the SAN, allowing many more servers to use the array. Many companies use monolithic arrays to help consolidate more storage into less space without losing performance when servers are added. Monolithic arrays are almost always more expensive than modular arrays, but you get what you pay for.

The SAN Protocols

As mentioned earlier, a protocol is a type of computer language used by a computer system to communicate with other devices. By *language,* we don't mean a programming language. It's more like a set of agreed-upon methods — a way for computers to communicate so they can cooperate in moving data over the network.

Each type of computer device uses a different protocol to communicate with other devices. After two devices find a common language, they establish a communication session by greeting each other with a friendly exchange of code called a *handshake.* In effect, they have a conversation to find things out about each other and to negotiate the best or fastest way to communicate.

There are two major protocols (languages) used in Fibre Channel SANs: the Fibre Channel protocol (used by the hardware to communicate) and the Small Computer System Interface (SCSI) protocol (used by software applications to talk to hard drives). Here's a closer look:

- ✔ **Fibre Channel protocol:** This is the language used by the HBAs, hubs, switches, and storage controllers to talk to each other. The Fibre Channel protocol is a *low-level language;* it's the means of communication between actual hardware components, and not between the applications that run on the hardware.

  Actually, two protocols make up the Fibre Channel protocol: Fibre Channel Arbitrated Loop (FC-AL), which works with hubs; and Fibre Channel Switched (or FC-SW), which works with switches. (Chapter 2 has more on the Fibre Channel protocols.)

  Fibre Channel is the building block of the SAN highway. It's like the road of the highway, where other protocols can run on top of it, just as different cars and trucks run on top of an actual highway. In other words, if Fibre Channel is the road, then SCSI is the truck that moves the data cargo down the road.

- ✔ **SCSI protocol:** This is the language used by SAN-attached server applications on the server computers to talk to the disk drives. This protocol lies on top of the Fibre Channel protocol.

This book is focused on Fibre Channel-based storage networks, so we only briefly touch on other protocols such as iSCSI (the SCSI protocol used over an IP network rather than a Fibre Channel network) and the Infiniband-based protocols (such as iSER and SRP) that can also be used to create a high-speed storage network. Infiniband itself can be a whole other book; it's used increasingly in GRID computing — connecting many low-cost servers over a high-speed network to act like one *very* fast computer. Storage is always the slowest part of any computer, so using a high-speed SAN with a GRID is essential. NASA and the CIA use GRID computing networks to gather and analyze massive amounts of data.

Even though most storage array manufacturers now use Fibre Channel disks in their storage arrays, the disks themselves still use the legacy SCSI protocol to communicate with applications over the Fibre Channel network. All the SCSI messages are *encapsulated* (packaged) into the Fibre Channel protocol. It's kind of like writing a letter to your dear Aunt Sally. (Aunt Sally is your disk drive here.) You write a letter (your data) and address the envelope (a SCSI block) to Aunt Sally (your disk). You want it to get there fast, though, so you put the letter into a FedEx package (you encapsulate the SCSI block in the Fibre Channel frame) and send it off. The Fibre Channel switch in the SAN opens the FedEx package (Fibre Channel frame), looks at the original address on the envelope (SCSI block), and sends it along its merry way at light speed to Aunt Sally (your disk).

How SAN devices communicate

Using English as a metaphor, think of a typical protocol conversation like this:

HBA in the server: "Hey! How are you? I'm in this server, and I'm trying to find a disk drive to store this data. Who are you?"

Switch: "Hi. I'm a Fibre Channel switch. I see that you can speak Fibre Channel. Let's talk using the new version 2 dialect, okay?"

HBA in the server: "Okay. Look, do you know of any good disk drives I can use to store the data?"

Switch: "Sure, according to your address, I've been authorized to give you access to a drive on my Port 3. Would you like to speak with her? Remember, SCSI drives speak a different language. Do you speak SCSI?"

HBA in the server: "Nope, but the server's application does! Thanks. I'll have him send you all the data using the SCSI protocol. Can you forward this to the disk?"

Switch: "Done deal. Hey, SCSI drive on Port 3, here's a message for you!"

At this point, the session is established; the switch now passes SCSI messages through to the disk drive. The drive acknowledges the messages and does what the server tells it to do.

All Fibre Channel devices work this way. The language for communication with storage devices is SCSI. Fibre Channel is just the FedEx way of getting it there faster, like a postal deliverer running at light speed. SANs work by giving the SCSI protocol a free ride on top of the Fibre Channel protocol to make communication happen much faster.

The SAN Players

The *players* are the companies that are the driving force in the SAN industry. Hundreds of companies are selling SAN equipment these days, each selling products that fit into a particular niche. You can break the players down into the different types of products that they sell. Some companies can sell everything you need, including servers. Server companies sometimes buy other companies' products and resell them as their own. (Most of us can't be good at *everything* these days.) You can get a listing of companies that develop products for SAN from the Storage Network Industry Alliance (SNIA; www. snia.org), a consortium of companies all working together creating standards for storage area networks.

The SAN Platforms

The *platforms* are the types of servers that can benefit from using a SAN and are appropriate for SANs. As indicated earlier in this chapter, not all servers should be hooked up to a SAN.

The operating system running on your server requires a driver. A *driver* is a small bit of software (detailed in Chapter 7) that enables the HBA in the server to talk to the other elements in the SAN. Some operating-system platforms support HBA drivers; some don't. You might need the latest version of your operating system to use a SAN if earlier versions don't support the needed drivers. For example, older versions of Windows NT, such as Windows NT 3.51, don't support SAN drivers. The same is true for older Apple-based networks. If you're running later versions of Unix or newer Windows server environments, you should be fine.

Three types of server platforms are good to use in a SAN: big, fast Intel- or AMD-based servers; big, fast servers that can run the different flavors of Unix; and mainframes. No surprise that these are the more expensive and powerful systems that need to store a lot of data. Most server platforms have drivers that allow them to be hooked up to a SAN environment. Whether doing so makes sense depends on the type of application running on it and the amount of disk storage that the server needs. Here are the *minimum* operating-system versions you can include in a SAN:

- Microsoft Windows NT 4.0
- Microsoft Windows 2000 or later
- Sun Solaris versions 2.6 or above
- HP-UX version 10.2 and higher
- IBM AIX version 4.2 and higher
- HP Tru64 Unix version 4.0F and higher
- HP Open VMS version 7.2 and higher
- Novell Netware version 4.11 and higher
- SGI IRIX version 6.5 and higher
- Sequent DYNIX version 4.5 and above
- All the various flavors of Linux (such as Red Hat, SuSE, and their cousins)
- IBM OS/390 Mainframe MVS, or Z/OS

Always check with your SAN vendor to find out whether the disk array you're purchasing supports the operating systems you're using.

Applications that benefit from a SAN

Most applications running on a server would benefit from faster access to the disk drives that the application is trying to use. Using a SAN instead of disks inside the server not only makes disk access faster (SAN disk access is at light speed) but also makes managing those disks much easier. If you're building a SAN, this list is a guideline for choosing servers to hook up:

- **Any server-class computer running a high-performance application:** By *server class,* we mean anything with at least lots of memory (2 to 4 GB or more) and a fast Intel, AMD, or Reduced Instruction Set Computer (RISC)-class processor. (**Note:** This *isn't* the kind of chip you'd find in your normal desktop-type PC, Web server, or infrastructure server such as a DNS or domain server.)

- **Any server computer with expanding disk-storage needs:** Using a SAN makes it easy to allocate more storage to a server without having to bring the server down.

- **Any database-type application server:** Databases require very fast disk access. A SAN can provide this kind of fast disk access.

✔ **Any backup server:** Backup servers have tape drives or disk drives connected to them to back up your data so you can restore it if your disks crash. Using SAN-connected tapes or disks to back up your data relieves the strain of backing up your disks across your computer network — and also makes backup happen much faster. Backup servers benefit greatly from SANs; backup moves a *lot* of data.

✔ **Any virtual-server solution:** Server virtualization makes it easy to make one physical server look and act like many servers. Server virtualization software or hardware benefits from the performance a SAN offers, and by the ability to share the external storage among the virtual machines. (More on virtualization for both servers and storage in Chapter 15.)

Applications that require a SAN

Only a handful of applications actually require the use of a SAN. These are usually newer applications, designed specifically for SAN capabilities:

✔ **Cluster applications:** *Cluster applications* are created by tying a group of servers together via a fast network and then allowing those servers to access the same disks' storage where the application is installed. This allows for very scalable and highly available applications; if one of the servers fails, another server in the cluster can pick up where the first one left off. GRID computing (mentioned earlier in the chapter) is another example of applications that need a SAN to work right. Common cluster applications are IBM HACMP (www.ibm.com), Solaris Cluster 3.0 or above (www.sun.com), Compaq/HP TruCluster (www.hp.com), Oracle Failsafe Cluster (www.oracle.com), Oracle Real Application Clusters (www.oracle.com), Microsoft Cluster Server (MSCS) (www.microsoft.com), HP MC/Serviceguard Clusters (www.hp.com), and Novell Netware Cluster Services (www.novell.com).

✔ **SAN backup applications:** SAN-based backup software is optimized for using SAN hardware. The backup software includes intelligence that takes advantage of what SAN offers. When using SAN backup software, you can back up your data directly over the SAN to a tape drive, which makes backup run much faster. Common backup software that has this capability includes Veritas NetBackup (www.veritas.com), Tivoli Storage Manager (www.ibm.com), Veritas Backup Exec Enterprise Edition (www.veritas.com), CA ARCserve with the SLO option (www.ca.com), Legato NetWorker (www.legato.com), and CommVault (www.comvault.com).

✔ **Server-virtualization solutions:** *Server virtualization* hardware and software such as VMware, Virtual Iron, Microsoft Hyper-V, Egenera, and others need the disk-sharing capability of a SAN (especially fail-over for applications between physical servers), and they also gain from the performance benefits that a SAN has to offer.

Chapter 2

SAN Building Blocks

*T*his is a pretty heavy-duty chapter. We dig deep into all the things that make up a storage area network (SAN) — the nuts and bolts of what's inside SAN storage arrays, and the network components that tie it all together. Read this chapter to find out what RAID means — and to see how it's used and the benefits you get from it. You get a look at how the components used in a SAN interact, and at the methods of connecting the components together.

SAN Components and How They're Used

In Chapter 1, we cover what we call *the four Ps* of storage area networks: parts, players, protocols, and platforms. The parts section can be broken down into three distinct layers: the host, fabric, and storage layers. (See Figure 2-1.) The following sections describe in more detail the components that make up the layers of a storage area network, along with where and how they're used.

In Figure 2-1, you can see the different layers in a SAN. Figure 2-2 depicts how all the components are physically and logically tied together through all the layers so information can be transferred from the host layer, all the way down through the fabric layer, to the disks in the storage layer.

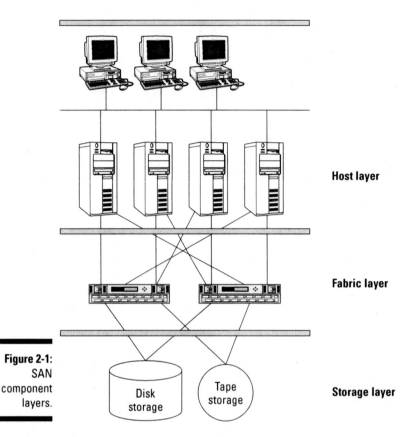

Host layer

Fabric layer

Figure 2-1:
SAN
component
layers.

Storage layer

When an application in a server needs to store data in the SAN, it sends the request as a write-request command to the operating system. The operating system then gathers up the data and the command and sends the request through the host bus adapter's software driver to the host bus adapter (HBA) itself in the server (more about the HBA in the next section).

The driver converts the data into a format understood by the HBA hardware. The HBA driver hides all the complexity of what's going on in the SAN from the operating system. The Basic Input Output System (BIOS) in the HBA hardware houses the intelligence that makes the HBA function. The HBA uses the intelligence in its BIOS to move the digital data to the gigabit link module (GLM). The GLM converts the data from digital ones and zeros into a serialized bit stream to be transmitted over the optical cable as pulses of light. The optical Fibre Channel cable connects the HBA in the server to the gigabit interface converters (GBICs) located in the switches that make up the fabric layer of the storage network.

The GBICs convert the optical light pulses back into digital data so the switches' *firmware* (a specialized type of low-level operating system used in intelligent devices) can read the address information with the Fibre Channel frame to see where the data is destined, and then route the data through the switch to the port that connects to the proper storage device. If there is more than one switch between the host and the storage, the data may need to be converted back and forth between its digital form and analog-light-pulse form several times. Whenever this happens, it takes a little bit of time — a *hop* (yup, the data hops between the switches).

The GBIC on the other switch port then reconverts the data into light pulses that it transmits over the optical cable that connects to the storage array controller. Once at the storage array, the data then travels through the storage array controllers to the RAID generator. (RAID is short for Redundant Array of Independent Disks). The RAID generator creates parity information for the data so the data can be recovered in case of disk failure. The data is then routed over an internal optical or copper cable to the disk drives in the array.

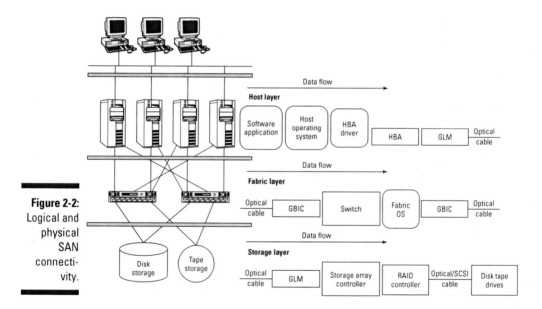

Figure 2-2:
Logical and physical SAN connecti- vity.

The disk drives are connected to the array with either an optical Fibre Channel cable — or a copper SCSI, SATA, or SAS cable, depending on what type of drives the array manufacturer uses in its array. SCSI drives use the SCSI inter- face, using copper cables to connect the drives. Fibre Channel drives use an optical interface and connect to the storage array with optical cables. Some newer storage arrays can mix and match drive types on different shelves.

Newer drive-interface technologies — such as Serial Attached SCSI (SAS) and Serial ATA (SATA) — offer improved capacities and lower costs than older SCSI (and lower than some Fibre Channel–based drives). Fibre Channel drives are still the standard in larger, more expensive, high-capacity storage subsystems (more about those later in this chapter).

The Host Layer

The *host layer* of a SAN consists of the servers and the components that go into them — all of which enable the host (server) to be physically connected to the SAN. Only a few components make up the host layer:

- ✔ **Host bus adapter (HBA):** This card, placed in a slot in the server, contains all the hardware and firmware you need to interface with the server's operating system.

- ✔ **Host bus adapter drivers:** The software driver interfaces with the operating system on behalf of the HBA hardware and firmware. It enables the server's operating system to communicate with the HBA and (therefore) the devices in the SAN.

- ✔ **Gigabit Interface Converter (GBIC):** The GBIC houses the lasers, and is where the cable connects to the HBA.

- ✔ **Cables:** The cables actually work at all the layers, and connect the HBA in the server and all the other devices in the SAN together.

Host bus adapters

The *host bus adapters (HBAs)* are the intelligent devices used to connect the servers to the fabric layer. The host bus adapter fits into a slot inside your server and, through the use of software drivers, allows the server's operating system software to communicate with the external storage arrays in the SAN.

Anatomy of a host bus adapter

The HBA's intelligence resides in both software and hardware. The server uses a driver (a small, specialized bit of software code, usually written by the HBA vendor) to allow the host operating system to communicate with the HBA. The driver contains all the commands the server needs to communicate with a specific device — in this case, the host bus adapter. The HBA also contains a small bit of software called *firmware* — located in a computer chip on the adapter called the *BIOS chip.* The BIOS is the brains of the HBA; BIOS firmware can be updated to give the HBA new functionality.

Updating the BIOS firmware is simple. HBA vendors include software utilities that can be used to update the firmware. Most vendors' Web sites offer drivers and firmware that you can download. Follow the steps in the manual that comes with your HBA for instructions on how to use the BIOS firmware's update utility to update the BIOS.

The transmission cable is connected to this card via a Gigabit Interface Converter (GBIC), which is either fitted into a slot or soldered onto the card itself. The cables are inserted into the GBIC in the adapter. The HBA uses "driver" software running on the operating systems to allow the operating system to work with the disks in the SAN.

The HBA vendors usually create the driver software for the operating system platforms they support. The software driver, installed after the operating system is loaded, is the magic that enables different operating systems to participate in a SAN. If no driver software is available from any of the HBA vendors for a particular operating system, that operating system can't be used in a SAN. As an example, older PC operating systems such as DOS or Windows 95, or Apple's original MAC OS may not have drivers available for SAN connectivity. Virtually every server-class operating system (Unix, Windows server, Linux, and so on) has SAN drivers available.

Gigabit gadgets: GBICs and GLMs

Storage area networks deal with huge amounts of data all the time — not only storing it but moving it around at near-lightspeed. To make this happen, a device called a *Gigabit Interface Converter* (GBIC) — inside the switches and other devices in the SAN — converts billions of digital bits into light pulses to be transmitted over optical fiber. The GBIC is formally known as a *transceiver*; it can be a transmitter *and* a receiver. In older HBAs, the transmission device was called a *Gigabit Link Module* (GLM), which was a replaceable module in the HBA that was expensive to manufacture. These days, most HBAs use a GBIC that is either removable or soldered directly into the card. (You'll still see GLMs referred to now and then; sometimes vendors even use the terms GLM and GBIC interchangeably.)

Presently there are two kinds of GBICs, defined by the wavelength of light that the laser inside generates: *short-wave* and *long-wave*. Long wavelengths of light can travel farther than shorter wavelengths, which affects the type of GBIC you choose:

- **Short-wave:** Utilized for connecting devices with distances between .5 meters and 500 meters between devices. The laser frequency (wavelength of light emitted) operates between 780 nm and 850 nm (*nm* stands for *nanometer*). You need a short wave GBIC in your HBA if your SAN storage is fewer than 500 meters away (most SAN storage is within a couple of feet of the server). Short-wave GBICs are the most common.

✔ **Long-wave:** Utilized for connecting devices between 2 meters and 10 kilometers apart. The laser frequency (wavelength of light emitted) operates at 1300 nm. You need a long-wave GBIC in your HBA if the SAN storage is more than 500 meters away from your server. Newer long-wave GBICs can handle connections of up to 100 km (kilometers) away.

Today's GBICs include the tiny laser or light-emitting diode (LED) that transmits light across the cables. Every GBIC (or, for that matter, the older GLM) has two connections: one for transmitting data and one for receiving data. The core of every fiber cable is a very long, thin strand of glass. Every Fibre Channel cable has two strands. One strand is used for transmitting data and one is used for receiving data. (See Figure 2-3.)

No, we didn't suddenly get creative about spelling *fibre* and *fiber*. Glass "fibers" are used in the cable, and "Fibre Channel" is the protocol used to transmit data over those glass fibers in the cable.

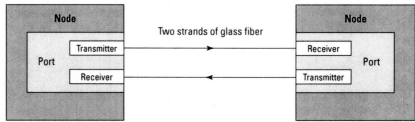

Figure 2-3: Fibre Channel full-duplex data transmission.

The capability for simultaneous, two-way data transmission is known as *full-duplex* data transmission. This is a good thing to have because you can transmit and receive data at the same time, which means that things can go twice as fast.

Data coming from the SAN enters the server from the cable into the GLM in the HBA as light pulses. The GLM converts the light pulses back into the digital data stream that your server understands. The GBICs inside the hubs and switches in the SAN receive the light pulses from the server's GLM and convert the light pulses into a format that the switches and hubs understand. The GBIC itself can both transmit and receive data. The connector on the GBIC where the optical cable fits in will be either an SC or LC connector:

✔ **SC connectors** are the original optical-connector design used in SANs. They're larger than LC connectors; you find them in SANs that operate at the older speed of 1 Gbps (1 gigabit — 100 megabytes — per second).

✔ **LC connectors** are smaller, second-generation connectors used in SANs that operate at the faster speeds of 2 Gbps (equal to 200 megabytes per second), 4 Gbps (equal to 400 megabytes per second), 8 Gbps (equal to 800 megabytes per second, and 10 Gbps (equal to 1000 megabytes per second, or a gigabyte per second.)

When the term *Gbit* is used to refer to data-transfer speed, it means the same as the standard unit of measurement *Gbps* (gigabits, or billions of bits per second). Now, that's a *lot* of bits to move in a single second!

The Fabric Layer

Common devices found in the fabric layer of a SAN can include SAN hubs, SAN switches, data routers, protocol bridges, gateway devices, and cables. The *fabric layer* is the actual, tangible network part of the SAN: All the stuff in the fabric layer of a storage network moves data — usually from an *initiator* (a source component, typically the HBA port in a server) to a *target* (a receiving component, typically a port on a storage device).

Understanding storage fabrics

Even a simple word like *fabric* takes on more than one meaning in the world of SANs:

✔ The *fabric layer* ("the fabric" for short) is storage geek-speak for the hardware in a traditional storage area network, specifically one that uses Fibre Channel components and storage.

✔ A *storage fabric* is a set of organized, connected storage devices on a network of interconnected switches that can be accessed by servers. A storage fabric is created when one or more Fibre Channel switches (as many as 239) are connected and used in a SAN.

✔ A *switched fabric* consists of all the switches in a single storage fabric.

✔ A *SAN fabric* consists of *all* the individual switched fabrics in a SAN.

A SAN can have more than one switch, and more than one fabric; in fact, most use at least two fabrics for redundancy. A single switch can be the only switch in a fabric, or a single fabric can have many connected switches. When switches are not connected together, they constitute individual fabrics, and even get their own *fabric IDs* (identifying numbers set inside each switch).

Large-scale, complex SAN fabrics are possible (Chapter 8, for example, discusses connecting multiple SAN fabrics together to create a global SAN).

A *storage network* (which is not the same as a SAN storage fabric) can be created using existing network cards and switches; it doesn't need any SAN switches to work. A simple storage network can be created by using simple iSCSI software drivers on the servers over your existing TCP/IP network, and then tying these together with iSCSI-capable storage arrays. An even simpler method is to dedicate a NAS device to sharing file-based storage.

To keep it (relatively) simple, we can list some commonly used terms here:

- **SAN:** Storage area network, which uses SCSI blocks to transmit data over a Fibre Channel–based network.

- **NAS:** Network Attached Storage, which uses CIFS protocol(Common Internet File System) for Windows servers, or NFS (Network File System) protocol for Unix servers to transmit files over a TCP/IP network.

- **Switched fabric:** One or more switches in a SAN that uses the Fibre Channel protocol.

- **SAN fabric:** One or more switched fabrics in a SAN (each with one or more switches) using the Fibre Channel protocol.

- **Storage network:** One or more storage devices connected together over a network.

SAN hubs

SAN hubs are connection points; they connect the host bus adapters (HBAs) in your servers to storage devices, to which they share access. Using a hub as the connection point creates a *Fibre Channel loop*: You run a fiber-optic cable from the server to a port on the hub and another fiber-optic cable from the hub to the storage device. This arrangement (for example, the small SAN shown in Figure 2-4) allows shared access to a disk array.

A *hub* is like a single loop of wire with connection points on it. Each device connects to one of those points, and each device takes turns transmitting data on the loop. (See Figure 2-5.) Each device has to take a turn on the single wire, which can transmit only one thing at a time.

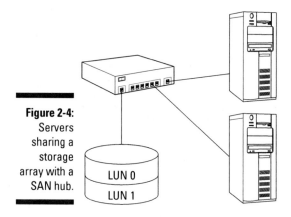

Figure 2-4:
Servers
sharing a
storage
array with a
SAN hub.

Hubs use a particular version of the Fibre Channel protocol (see the section "Protocols used in a Fibre Channel SAN," later in this chapter) called *Fibre Channel Arbitrated Loop,* or FC-AL: The devices arbitrate for access to the loop so they can communicate with other devices attached to the loop. The FC-AL protocol handles that arbitration. Devices connected to a hub share the total bandwidth of the hub.

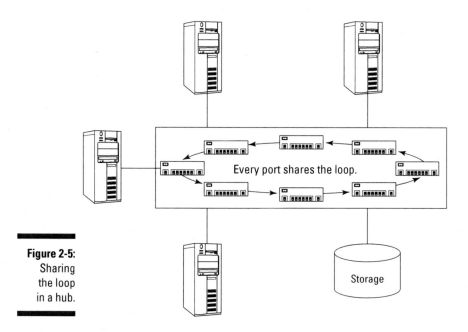

Figure 2-5:
Sharing
the loop
in a hub.

Hubs typically run at lower speeds than switches. If a SAN hub runs at a total bandwidth of (say) 100 megabytes per second, no device connected to the hub can exceed that speed. Congestion can further reduce speed of data transfer as more devices are connected to the hub and try to communicate. Hubs usually provide 4, 8, or 12 ports per hub, and can be connected (called *cascading*) to enlarge the size of the Fibre Channel loop — up to a limit of 126 device ports. No more than 126 devices can participate in a single FC-AL loop.

When a device is added to a hub, every device connected to the hub is affected because each new device must interrupt the other connected devices to arbitrate for a loop address. This interruption can cause problems for servers transferring data to disks. That's one reason, especially since the advent of SAN switches (more about them in the next section), that hubs are rarely used anymore in SANs. Switches are normally used to share disk arrays in a SAN because they're faster than hubs — and shared access to disks needs to be fast.

But switches are also more expensive than hubs, so a common use of hubs is to give servers economical, shared access to tape-storage devices (which are much slower than disks) — usually for backing up data. Sharing the Fibre Channel loop bandwidth through a hub works fine for data backup to tape (for an example, see Figure 2-6).

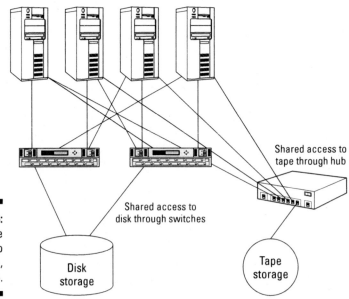

Figure 2-6:
Separate
backup loop
to tape,
using a hub.

Shared access to
tape through hub

Shared access to
disk through switches

Disk
storage

Tape
storage

Using a dedicated HBA in each server to connect to shared tape storage through a hub offers several advantages:

✔ **Greater efficiency:** You can do backups over the SAN while keeping your backup traffic separate from disk traffic.

✔ **Less cost:** Hubs are inexpensive, especially in comparison to buying a backup tape drive for every server. Using a hub to move tape backup traffic off of a SAN and onto its own separate network could also free up SAN bandwidth for other production applications.

SAN switches

SAN switches are used as central connection points for the devices in a SAN that require disk access. You attach a Fibre Channel cable to the GBIC on the HBA in the server and connect the other end to a GBIC port on a switch. The storage array gets connected the same way. A *switch* is, in effect, a bunch of wires connected together which enables every device on every wire to talk to any other device at the same time. When a switch can transmit data across all wires at the same time, it's known as a non-blocking switch. (See Figure 2-7.)

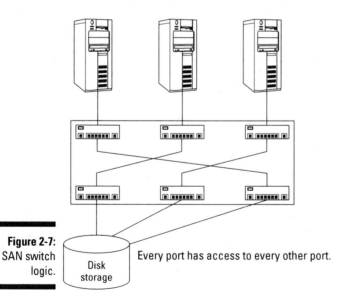

Figure 2-7:
SAN switch
logic.

You *could* connect servers to storage in a SAN with just one switch, but two switches are normally used to prevent a single switch failure from bringing down the entire SAN. Figure 2-8 shows a simple SAN fabric that uses two switches to connect a server to a storage array. Note that the server has two host bus adapters, each connected to a separate fabric switch. This creates two basic fabrics (one switch is used per fabric) through which data can travel to get to the storage. The switches in Figure 2-8 are not connected, which separates data traffic and prevents a failure in one switch from affecting the other switch. As your SAN grows and you add more servers and storage, you simply add more switches to each fabric. (See Figure 2-9.)

When SANs first started shipping, the only devices on the market that could handle Fibre Channel connections were hubs. Since then, Fibre Channel switches have been developed, their prices have rapidly dropped, and they are now the standard. (Hubs are rarely used for disk access anymore.)

Switches allow every device connected to the switch to communicate simultaneously. This allows for each device connected to a switch to have a dedicated link between itself and the device it is talking to on another switch port.

You connect switches to create large SAN fabrics. Most SANs today are implemented using two separate fabrics, as shown in Figure 2-9. This is done so that normal maintenance can be performed on the switches one fabric at a time.

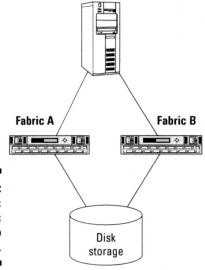

Fabric A   Fabric B

Figure 2-8:
A basic
SAN fabric
using two
switches.

Disk
storage

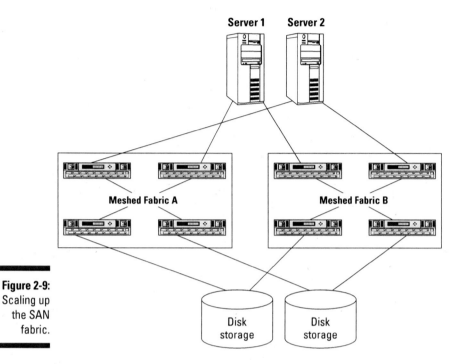

Figure 2-9:
Scaling up
the SAN
fabric.

Standard modular (midrange-class) switches

SAN switches come in many flavors, from 8 ports up to hundreds of ports per switch. Most modular-class SAN switches come in the 8-, 16-, 24-, or 32-port varieties. (See Figure 2-10.) The term modular switch usually means a self-contained switch that cannot be expanded, and has a fixed port count of fewer than 64 ports. Larger, multiple-port modular switches are increasingly available; as physical connectors get smaller, modular switches will likely contain more ports.

Figure 2-10:
Eight- and
16-port
modular-
class
switches.

16-port switch

8-port switch

Using modular switches is a good way to create a small SAN. Two 16-port switches give you a SAN that provides 32 ports for connecting servers and storage. If you use two host bus adapters in each server, and use two ports from each switch to connect your storage, you can connect as many as 14 servers in your SAN. To scale this up for more connectivity, you can connect more modular switches to create larger fabrics, or you can use larger modular switches or director-class switches. As a best practice, it's always a good idea to leave a couple of switch ports available for further expansion.

Modular switches create high availability by creating fabrics of switches with fewer single points of failure. If one switch fails, data can be automatically re-routed to another path through the fabric. Individual modular-class switches are not as fault tolerant as director-class switches, but connecting multiple modular switches into a fault-tolerant fabric can be just as effective (though not as fast) as using a director-class switch.

Director-class (enterprise-class) switches

Director-class switches are larger and more expensive than modular switches. (See Figure 2-11.) You will usually find director-class switches at the center of very large switched fabrics. Directors are used as the core of large switched fabrics because they not only have many more ports than modular switches but also are built to almost never go down. You can usually perform normal maintenance on a director switch without having to take it offline. You can even replace parts in a director switch without powering it off.

Most director-class switches use *port blades* that fit into a frame. Port blades are used so that you can replace the blade if a failure occurs. You can replace a blade without powering down the switch. Director switches also come with dual-processor blades. The processor blades are the brains of the switch. If a processor fails, the other one takes over automatically. This makes director-class switches much more fault tolerant than modular-class switches. Because director switches use ports on individual blades, you can start with just a few ports and then add more blades to scale up to hundreds of ports on a single switch.

Figure 2-11: Director-class switches.

128-port director   64-port director

When large SAN fabrics are created, director-class switches are usually used. Directors can also be used as stand-alone fabric elements for SAN designs in which latency is not tolerated. (*Latency* is the time it takes to move data between two points.) Director-class switches have the features that make them an excellent choice as core switches for very large fabrics. (See Figure 2-12.)

Figure 2-12 shows a *core-edge* SAN design, using director-class switches at the core and modular switches at the edge. The modular switches at the edge connect to your servers, and the core switches connect to the storage array. If an edge switch fails, it affects only the devices connected to it. If one of the core switches fails, it affects half of the entire SAN. This is why director-class switches are used at the core.

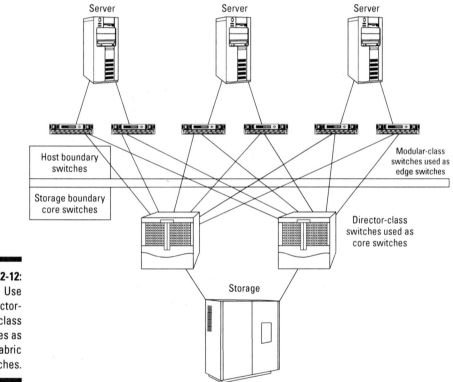

Figure 2-12:
Use
director-
class
switches as
core fabric
switches.

Data routers

A *data router* is a different beast altogether. It is a device used as a bridge to connect SCSI devices to Fibre Channel devices in a SAN, or iSCSI connected-servers over an IP network to a Fibre Channel SAN. (Note: Other terms that many people use interchangeably for data routers are *gateways* and *bridges*.) For older SCSI disk drives and tape drives to participate in a SAN, some way to connect them is needed. The data router usually has a Fibre Channel interface and one or more SCSI or iSCSI interfaces to connect both types of devices to one another. (See Figure 2-13.)

The data router can also provide intelligent bridging, enabling the servers in the SAN to see and address older SCSI disk and tape drives connected to the data router. (See Figure 2-14.) Using a data router enables you to re-use older tape and disk devices in a SAN environment.

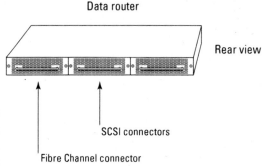

Data router

Rear view

Figure 2-13:
Data router.

SCSI connectors

Fibre Channel connector

Another use of data routing and bridging is to use a bridge to connect iSCSI-based hosts on an IP network to an already existing Fibre Channel SAN. Using iSCSI to Fibre Channel bridging enables you re-use FC storage devices for the storage in an IP-based iSCSI SAN (see Figure 2-15).

If you want to check out some high-end uses for intelligent data routers and appliances in a SAN environment — such as data protection, de-duplication, and virtualization — see Chapters 13, 14, and 15.

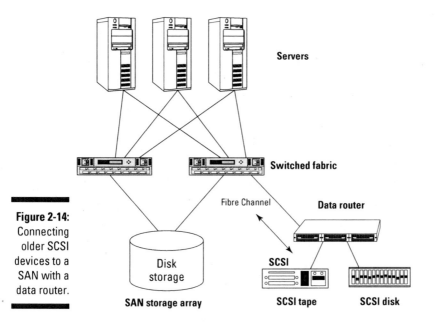

Figure 2-14:
Connecting
older SCSI
devices to a
SAN with a
data router.

Servers

Switched fabric

Fibre Channel

Data router

Disk
storage

SCSI

SAN storage array

SCSI tape

SCSI disk

Heterogeneous SAN Environment

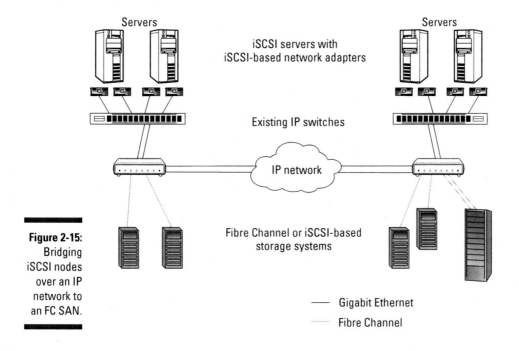

Figure 2-15:
Bridging
iSCSI nodes
over an IP
network to
an FC SAN.

Servers

Servers

iSCSI servers with
iSCSI-based network adapters

Existing IP switches

IP network

Fibre Channel or iSCSI-based
storage systems

—— Gigabit Ethernet

—— Fibre Channel

Cables

Cables are the physical links that connect everything in a SAN together, and therefore are used in every layer of the SAN. When Fibre Channel was first introduced to the market, the only cables available were made from copper. Due to the nature of how Fibre Channel data transmission works, using copper cables limited the distance between devices in the SAN. The industry adopted the use of fiber-optic cables to dramatically increase the speed and distance that data could travel between SAN devices. Copper cabling is now very rarely used in SAN fabrics.

SANs can use any of three basic types of fiber-optic cables; each type uses a different size glass fibre core, measured in *micrometers* (one-millionth of a meter, abbreviated with a lowercase Greek letter mu): 9μm, 50μm, and 62.5μm. The type of cable — and the wavelength of light it uses during data transmission — determine how far the devices in a SAN can be from each other. The most common cable type used in SANs today is 50μm *multimode (MM)*, which can carry different frequencies of light (in wavelengths).

For some reason, all Fibre Channel SAN cables are usually orange, maybe because it makes them easy to see. You can purchase 50μm MM Fibre Channel cables in lengths from 3 meters to 500 meters. The 500-meter length is the maximum distance you can go with this type of cable. Most SANs are built using 15- to 20-meter 50μm multimode cables. Unless you have an unusually large building, we doubt you will ever need the 500-meter version.

Light is generated from the GBIC in multimode environments by using a light-emitting diode (LED) at a wavelength in the range of 850nm (850 nanometers, that is, billionths of a meter). The light emitted from a multimode LED is not as powerful as a single mode laser, so using multimode provides for a safe working environment. The cables used in multimode environments also use a larger-diameter glass core, which makes it easier for the light to get into the cable (see Figure 2-16).

The size of a fiber-optic cable's core matters, because although the 50μm is larger, it has problems with light reflection and refraction, and therefore can only be used for distances below 500 meters. The smaller core 9μm cables are not as affected by these technical issues, and can be used for much greater distances.

When 9μm cables are used to transmit data over long distances, they're called *dark fiber cables.* That's because you cannot see the laser light being transmitted with the naked eye, and if you ever *did* look into one of these cables, it would fry your eyeballs! Be VERY careful, and heed all the warnings printed on the cables when handling 9μm cables.

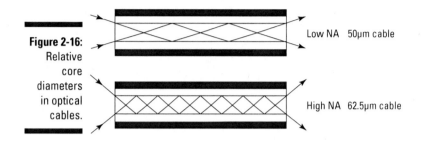

Figure 2-16:
Relative
core
diameters
in optical
cables.

Low NA   50μm cable

High NA   62.5μm cable

In a *single-mode* environment that uses only one type of cable, a powerful laser in the GBIC emits light in the 1300nm range — which is a much higher wavelength than that used in multimode environments.

Never, *ever* look into the end of a 9μm SM cable. You will end up damaging your eyes, even though the light generated by these high-powered lasers is invisible to the naked eye. Although you could see the red light at the end of a multimode cable, don't look into those cables either. (*Not looking into an optical cable* is a really good habit to develop.) If you want to make sure a cable is transmitting light, use an optical tester instead.

Because the laser light that uses them is more powerful, single-mode optical signals can travel much farther than multimode signals.

A few years ago, 62.5μm cables were the most common type of optical cable used in TCP/IP networks (the type of network used for the Internet). Some newer buildings had these types of cables pre-run through their structure as they were built. You can re-use these cables in your SAN, as long as you stay aware of their distance limitation (200 meters). We recommend standardizing on a particular cable type. It's not a good idea to intermix 62.5μm and 50μm cables in the same fabric; the core sizes in the cables are different, and connecting them can be a real pain. If it's not done properly, you can experience signal loss at the connection.

The 9μm cables are normally used for long-haul distances, which means you are probably trying to connect two buildings. The 9μm cables require the use of single-mode lasers in the GBICs in the switches and GLMs in the HBAs. These are high-powered lasers that send light farther through their smaller-core cables. Not only is the source of light more powerful than that used in multimode, but the core of the cable is also smaller, so the light doesn't bounce around inside the cable and get absorbed as it moves along. (See Figure 2-17.)

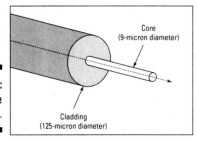 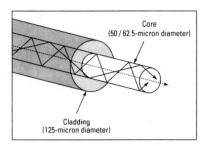

Figure 2-17:
Cable core
sizes.

The smaller the glass core of the cable, the more direct path for light to travel.

Use the following chart to see how the diameter of the cable and the wavelength of light can determine distance. (See Table 2-1.)

Table 2-1	SAN Cable Matrix for Different Cables and GBICs		
	50μm Multimode Cable	**9μm Single-Mode Cable**	**62.5 μm Multimode Cable**
Type/ Wavelength	50 μm	9 μm	62.5 μm
	Short wave Multimode	Long wave Single mode	Short wave Multimode
	850nm**	1300nm	850nm
Distance: 1Gbit	.5m to 500m	2m to 100Km	.5m to 300m
2Gbit	.5m to 300m	2m to 100Km	.5m to 150m
4Gbit	.5m to 150m	2m to 10Km	Not Used
8Gbit	.5 to 150m	2m to 10Km	Not Used
Bandwidth	100–400MB/sec†	100–400MB/sec	100–200MB/sec

*A micrometer is one-millionth of a meter. μ=micro, μum=micrometer

**nm =nanometer, which is a wavelength of light

†MB/sec = megabytes per second

As you can see from Table 2-1, the distance that light can travel over an optical cable is determined by the core size of the cable and the wavelength of light used. The smaller the core, the farther light will travel. If the core is too large, the light bounces around too much inside the cable, and some of the light gets absorbed by the *cladding* (the outer wrapping of a fiber-optic cable) around the core.

Cable-connector types

As mentioned earlier in the chapter, the two types of connectors used on the optical cables in a SAN are the SC type and the LC type. (See Figure 2-18.)

Port density increased with
LC connections

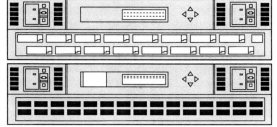

Figure 2-18:
A sample
GBIC with
SC cable
connec-
tions.

Switch with SC
connectors

Switch with LC
connectors

Cable connectors come in two different types. An *SC connector* (SC stands for Subscriber connector) is the standard optical connector for 1Gbit Fibre Channel. An *LC connector* (LC stands for Lucent connector) is standard for 2Gbit and 4Gbit Fibre Channel cable. The connector types determine what type of cable end you need.

The SC type was the most common connector used in original SANs, but this is changing as more components become available that can handle 4Gbit to 10Gbit speeds. The smaller, denser LC connectors are replacing SC connectors so switch manufacturers can pack more ports onto a single switch.

SAN ports and port naming

In general hardware terms, a *port* is the place where you plug in your cables; in software terms, a port is where the data goes. In SANs, the hardware components used to connect cables to ports are GBICs.

Though you'll hear *port* and *GBIC* used interchangeably, here's one way to keep them straight: The GBIC is the physical connector, and the port is the logical name that the SAN uses to identify where the GBIC is connected.

Ports have different names depending on how they're used with each device in a SAN — that is, a port's name depends on its *mode of operation.*

Basic SAN port modes of operation

The port's mode of operation depends on what's connected to the other side of the port. Here are two general examples:

- ✔ All hosts (servers) and all storage ports operate as *nodes* (that is, places where the data either originates or ends up), so their ports are called N_Ports (node ports).

- ✔ All hub ports operate as *loops* (that is, places where the data travels in a small Fibre Channel loop), so they're called L_Ports (loop ports).

Switch ports are where it gets tricky. That's because switch ports have multiple personalities: They *become* particular types of ports depending on what gets plugged into them (check out Table 2-2 to keep all these confusing port types straight). Here are some ways a switch port changes its function to match what's connected to it:

- ✔ Switch ports usually hang around as G_Ports (global ports) when nothing is plugged into them. A G_Port doesn't get a mode of operation until something is plugged into it.

- ✔ If you plug a host into a switch port, it becomes an F_Port (fabric port). The same thing happens if you plug in a storage array that's running the Fibre Channel-Switched (FC-SW) Protocol (more about this protocol in the next section).

- ✔ If you plug a hub into a switch port, you get an FL_Port (fabric-to-loop port); hub ports by themselves are always L_Ports (loop ports).

- ✔ When two switch ports are connected together, they become their own small fabric, known as an E_Port (switch-to-switch expansion port) or a T_Port (Trunk port).

- ✔ A host port is always an N_Port (node port) — unless it's attached to a hub, in which case it's an NL_port (node-to-loop port).

- ✔ A storage port, like a host port, is always an N_Port — unless it's connected to a hub, in which case it's an NL_Port.

If that seems confusing, it used to be worse. Believe it or not, different switch vendors used to name their ports differently, which confused everyone. Then the Storage Network Industry Association (SNIA) came to save the day and standardized the names you see in Figure 2-19.

If you want to get a good working handle on what's going on in your SAN, use Table 2-2 to find out what the port names mean after all the plugging-in is done.

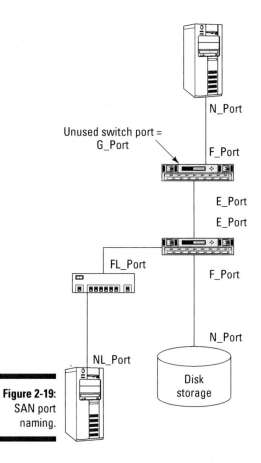

Unused switch port =
G_Port

N_Port

F_Port

E_Port

E_Port

FL_Port

F_Port

N_Port

NL_Port

Disk
storage

Figure 2-19:
SAN port
naming.

Table 2-2		Basic SAN Port Modes
Port Type	*Location*	*Associated Topology*
N_Port	Node	Point-to-point or fabric. (*Point-to-point* means without any hubs or switches in the middle.)
NL_Port	Node	Node connected to an arbitrated loop.
F_Port	Fabric	Fabric port.
FL_Port	Fabric	Fabric to loop port. A Fabric connected to a Fibre Channel Arbitrated Loop.

(continued)

Table 2-2 *(continued)*

Port Type	Location	Associated Topology
L_Port	Loop	Hub port on an arbitrated loop.
T_Port	Fabric	Trunk port between switches.
E_Port	Fabric	Standard inter-switch link connection.
G_Port	Fabric	Unused switch port.

Protocols used in a Fibre Channel SAN

Protocols are, in effect, an agreed-upon set of terms that different computer devices use to communicate with one another. A protocol can be thought of as the common language used by different types of networks. You'll encounter three basic protocols in the Fibre Channel world:

✔ **FC-AL:** *Fibre Channel-Arbitrated Loop Protocol* is used by two devices communicating within a Fibre Channel loop (created by plugging the devices into a hub). Fibre Channel loops use hubs for the cable connections among all the SAN devices. Newer storage arrays that have internal fiber disks use Fibre Channel loops to connect the disks to the array, which is why they can have so many disks inside: Each loop can handle 126 disks, and you can have many loops in the array. The array uses the FC-AL protocol to talk to the disks.

Each of the possible 126 devices on a Fibre Channel loop takes a turn communicating with another device on the loop. Only one conversation can occur at a time; the protocol determines who gets to talk when. Every device connected to the loop gets a loop address *(loop ID)* that determines its priority when it uses the loop to talk.

✔ **FC-SW:** *Fibre Channel-Switched Protocol* is used by two devices communicating on a Fibre Channel switch. Switch ports are connected over a backplane, which allows any device on the switch to talk to any other device on the switch at the same time. Many conversations can occur simultaneously through the switch. A *switched fabric* is created by connecting Fibre Channel switches; such a fabric can have thousands of devices connected to it.

Each device in a fabric has an address called a *World Wide Name (WWN)* that's hard-coded at the factory onto the host bus adapter (HBA) that goes into every server and every storage port. The WWN is like the telephone number of a device in the fabric (or like the MAC address of a network card) When the device is connected to the fabric, it logs in to the fabric port, and its WWN registers in the name server so the switch knows it's connected to that port. The WWN is also sometimes called a WWPN, or World Wide Port Name.

The WWN and a WWPN are the exact same thing, the actual address for a Fibre Channel port. In some cases, large storage arrays can also have what is known as a WWNN, or World Wide Node Name. Some Fibre Channel storage manufactures use the WWNN for the entire array, and then use an offset of the WWN for each port in the array for the WWPN. I guess this is a Fibre Channel storage manufactures way of making the World Wide Names they were given by the standards bodies last longer. You can think of the WWNN as the device itself, and the WWPN as the actual port within the device, but in the end, it's all just a WWN.

The *name server* is like a telephone directory. When one device wants to talk to another in the fabric, it uses the other device's phone number to call it up. The switch protocol acts like the telephone operator. The first device asks the operator what the other device's phone number is. The operator locates the number in the directory (the name server) in the switch, and then routes the call to the port where the other device is located.

There is a trick you can use to determine whether the WWN refers to a server on the fabric or a storage port on the fabric. Most storage ports' WWN always start with the number 5, and most host bus adapters' start with either a 10 or a 21 as the first hexadecimal digits in the WWN. Think of it like the area code for the phone number. If you see a number like `50:06:03:81:D6:F3:10:32`, its probably a port on a storage array. A number like `10:00:00:01:a9:42:fc:06` will be a servers' HBA WWN.

✔ **SCSI:** The *SCSI protocol* is used by a computer application to talk to its disk-storage devices. In a SAN, the SCSI protocol is layered on top of either the FC-AL or FC-SW protocol to enable the application to get to the disk drives within the storage arrays in a Fibre Channel SAN. This makes Fibre Channel backward-compatible with all the existing applications that still use the SCSI protocol to talk to disks inside servers. If the SCSI protocol was not used, all existing applications would have needed to be recompiled to use a different method of talking to disk drives.

SCSI works a bit differently in a SAN from the way it does when it talks to a single disk drive inside a server. SCSI inside a server runs over copper wires, and data is transmitted in parallel across the wires. In a SAN, the SCSI protocol is serialized, so each bit of data can be transmitted as a pulse of light over a fiber-optic cable. If you want to connect older parallel SCSI-based devices in a SAN, you have to use a *data router,* which acts as a bridge between the serial SCSI used in a SAN and the parallel SCSI used in the device. (See "Data routers," earlier in this chapter, for the gory details.)

Although iSCSI and Infiniband protocols can also be used in storage networks, the iSCSI protocol is used over an IP network and then usually bridged into a Fibre Channel SAN. Infiniband, on the other hand, is used over a dedicated Infiniband network as a server interconnect, and then bridged into a Fibre Channel SAN for storage access. But the field is always changing: Infiniband and iSCSI storage arrays are now becoming available, but they still use either an IP or IB interface rather than FC.

The Storage Layer

The *storage layer* contains all the disk and tape arrays used to store your data. In this chapter we focus on disk storage arrays, because we cover tape subsystems in more detail in Chapter 9, which covers backing up your data to tape, and Chapter 14, which covers continuous backup to disk. (See Chapter 1 for more about the differences between storage-array types.)

Storage arrays: Storing your data

Storage arrays are the devices that contain all those spinning disk drives where your data is actually stored. In a SAN, you cannot simply hook up a single drive to the network. In a SAN, the disk drives are always packaged inside intelligent storage arrays. They come in varying sizes, colors, and capabilities. Some are fairly inexpensive; others can cost a million dollars or more. Storage arrays all have one thing in common, though. They all use disks drives to store data. They are called arrays because inside them are a lot of individual disks arrayed together to form larger redundant arrays of independent disks (RAID). Suppose that you have a 100GB disk drive in your computer and you're running out of space on it. To add more storage, you can buy another 100GB drive . . . maybe even two.

Now you have three drives of 100GB each. In a dedicated storage array, those three 100GB drives can be combined to let your computer (in effect) see *one* 300GB drive instead of three 100GB drives. That bit of magic is called an *array of drives.* If you stripe your data across all the disks when you write to them, and then add another disk with a copy of the data, you have a RAID set of disks that is protected from failures. If you take that to the next level and put a couple *hundred* drives in the array, you can make (in effect) really *big* hard drives called Logical Units. A storage array can make a lot of little drives look like a few big drives. But the *real* difference between computers with internal hard drives and dedicated storage arrays is that the disks in the storage array can be *shared* among all the computers connected to the SAN.

Explaining Redundant Array of Inexpensive Disks (RAID)

We're old-timers in this field. Back in the day, as they say, RAID used to stand for *Redundant Array of Inexpensive Disks.* Today the term has been updated to Redundant Array of *Independent* Disks. That's kind of strange, in our opinion, because disks are a *lot* less expensive then they used to be. We still use the old term because we think it still applies. Either term can be used, and people will still know what you're talking about.

RAID is a way of grouping individual physical drives to form one bigger drive called a *RAID set.* RAID can make many smaller disks appear as one large disk to a server. The RAID set represents all the smaller physical drives as one logical disk to your server. The logical drive is a *LUN,* or Logical Unit Number. (More on LUNs later and in Chapter 7.)

RAID benefits

Using RAID has two advantages: better performance and higher availability. Thus, it goes faster and breaks down less often.

Performance is increased because the server has more disks to read from when data is accessed from a drive. Availability is increased because the RAID controller can recreate lost data from a failed drive by using the parity information. (*Parity information* is created while the data is written to the disks.) The server accessing the data on a RAID set never knows that one of the drives in the RAID set went bad. The controller recreates the data that was lost when the drive went bad by using the parity information stored on the surviving disks in the RAID set.

Drives can be grouped to form RAID sets in a number of different ways — *RAID types* — which are numbered from 0 to 6. The numbers represent the level of RAID being used. Read more about these levels in the upcoming section "RAID types." RAID levels 0, 1, and 5 are the most common methods of grouping drives into RAID sets because they give you the best variation of redundancy and performance. Since RAID 6 uses two parity drives, it's a bit slower than the other RAID types, but is normally used when data loss is out of the question.

Combinations of RAID types can be used together. For example, you can create two RAID 0 sets and then combine the RAID 0 sets into a RAID 1 set. This will essentially give you the performance benefits of RAID 0 with the availability benefits of RAID 1.

The RAID type that you should use depends on the type of application that you're running on your server. RAID 0 is the fastest; RAID 1 is the most reliable; RAID 5 is a good combination of both; and RAID 6, since it uses multiple parity drives, is best when long-term archiving is more important than performance.

RAID types

Following is a description of the different types of RAID that are most commonly used in SAN storage arrays. Not all storage array vendors support all the various RAID types. Check with your vendor for the type of RAID that's available with the vendor's storage.

✔ **RAID 0:** RAID 0, called *disk striping,* comprises all the data spread out in chunks across all the disks in the RAID set. RAID 0 has great performance because you spread out the load of storing and retrieving data onto more physical drives. The more physical spindles you use to store and retrieve data, the more I/O operations per second you will get. You see, any given physical disk can give you only a maximum of around 150 I/O operations per second. This is because of the physical latency of moving the data on the spinning spindles under the read/write heads on the disk (called *rotational latency*), and the physical act of moving the heads across the spindles (called *seek time*). Having more disks to spread out the load multiplies the speed at which you can access data. Because no parity is generated for RAID 0, you have no overhead to write data to RAID 0 disks. RAID 0 is good only for better performance, not for high availability, because parity isn't generated for RAID 0 disks. RAID 0 requires at least two physical disks, but is usually implemented as a group of three or more drives. (See Figure 2-20.)

RAID 0: Disk striping without parity

Figure 2-20: RAID 0 data is striped across disks.

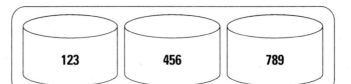

The number 123456789 is broken into chunks and spread across multiple disks.

✔ **RAID 1:** RAID 1 is called *disk mirroring*. All the data is written to a minimum of two separate physical disks, which essentially are mirror images of each other. If one of the disks fails, the other can be used to retrieve data. Although disk mirroring is good for very fast read operations, it's slower when writing to the disks because the data needs to be written twice. RAID 1 requires at least two physical disks. (See Figure 2-21.)

RAID 1: Disk mirroring

Figure 2-21: RAID 1 data is mirrored between drives.

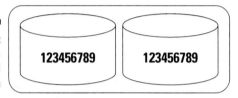

The number 123456789 is written to two disks.

✔ **RAID 1+0:** (or RAID 1+0, also called *RAID 10*) uses a combination of disk mirroring and disk striping. The data is either mirrored first and then striped (see Figure 2-22), or in some instances, striped first, and then the stripes are removed. You can do this in two ways: striped mirrors or mirrored stripes. Mirroring striped sets accomplishes the same task but is less fault tolerant than striped mirror sets. The reason for this is if you lose a drive in a stripe set, all access to data must be from the other stripe set because stripe sets have no parity. RAID 0+1 requires a minimum of four physical disks.

Figure 2-22: RAID 0+1 known as (RAID 10) data is mirrored and striped.

RAID 0+1 (RAID 10): Striped mirror sets

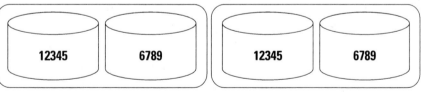

The number 123456789 is broken into chunks and spread across multiple disks; then the disks are mirrored.

✔ **RAID 2:** RAID 2 is no longer used.

✔ **RAID 3:** RAID 3 uses a dedicated parity disk to store the parity information generated by the RAID controller, separating the parity disk from the actual data disks (instead of striping it with the data, as in RAID 5). This RAID type isn't currently used very much because it performs poorly with many little requests for data, as in database applications. RAID 3 performs well under applications that just want one long, sequential data transfer. Applications such as video servers work well with this RAID type. RAID 3 requires a minimum of three physical disks. (See Figure 2-23.)

Figure 2-23:
RAID 3 data
is striped
with dedi-
cated parity
drive.

RAID 3: Striped data with dedicated parity disk

The number 123456789 is broken into chunks and spread across multiple disks;
parity information is stored on a dedicated disk.

✔ **RAID 4:** RAID 4 is very similar to RAID 3, but the difference is a wider stripe (block level) while RAID 3 uses bit-level striping. Although now less common, RAID 4 is still used in NetApp disk arrays.

✔ **RAID 5:** RAID 5 uses disk striping with parity. The data is striped across all the disks in the RAID set along with the parity information needed to reconstruct the data in case of disk failure. RAID 5 is the most common method used because it achieves a good balance between performance and availability. RAID 5 requires at least three physical disks. (See Figure 2-24.)

RAID 5: Striped data with "striped" parity

Figure 2-24:
RAID 5 data
is striped
with striped
parity.

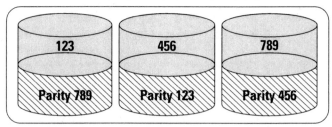

The number 123456789 is broken into chunks and spread across multiple disks;
parity information is also striped across the disks.

✔ **RAID 6:** The chance of a disk drive failure increases over time. When you need to store data for long periods on disk, RAID 6 can be used to prevent data loss, even from double-disk failures. RAID 6 uses two parity drives to reduce the odds of data loss. RAID 6 is the worst performer but the most reliable. (See Figure 2-25.)

✔ **Adaptive RAID:** Adaptive RAID lets the RAID controller figure out how to store the parity on the disks. It will choose between RAID 3 and RAID 5, depending on which RAID set type performs better with the type of data being written to the disks.

RAID 6: Doubles the number of parity drives

Figure 2-25:
RAID 6 data is striped with double parity.

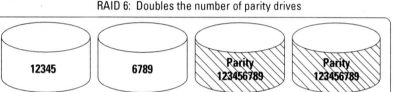

The number 123456789 is broken into chunks and spread across multiple disks. Parity information is stored on two disks to protect from double disk failures.

Logical Unit Numbers (LUNs)

A *Logical Unit Number* represents the storage space in disks that are assembled into a RAID set. A logical disk can be created either from all the space in the RAID set or just from a slice of the space, called a *partition*.

Disk partitions

A *disk partition* is a slice of either a single drive or a slice of a RAID set. The disks inside a disk array are first arranged into RAID sets and then sliced up into partitions. The partitions are then assigned a LUN, and the LUN is assigned to a server in the SAN. (See Figure 2-26.) Think of a partition as the layers in a layer cake: A partition represents each layer of the cake. The LUN is the name of the layer, which is represented to the server.

In Figure 2-26, you can see how a single spindle is partitioned into three separate partitions and assigned to two servers. You can also see how a RAID 10 set is partitioned into LUNs of equal size so that each partition can be assigned to one or more servers.

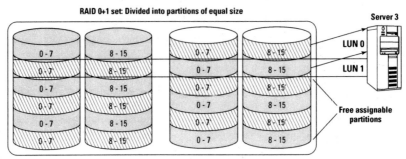

RAID 0+1 set: Divided into partitions of equal size

Server 3

LUN 0

LUN 1

Free assignable
partitions

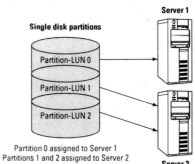

Single disk partitions

Server 1

Figures 2-26:
Single disk
partitions
and RAID
set parti-
tions with
LUNs.

Partition-LUN 0

Partition-LUN 1

Partition-LUN 2

Partition 0 assigned to Server 1
Partitions 1 and 2 assigned to Server 2

Server 2

You can use partitions to more effectively dole out your storage in smaller slices, or layers, to your servers. Suppose that you have a 73GB disk inside a modular array. Your server may need only 20GB for its application. If you use the entire disk as a LUN, you're wasting the space that's not needed by the server. If you partition the disk into three partitions of 24.3GB each, you can create three LUNs from the disk partitions, assigning each LUN to a different server in the SAN. (See Figure 2-27.)

You could also assign both LUNs to the same server to be used for different purposes. For instance, you could use LUN 0 to store your programs and LUN 1 for your data files. This way, when you want to back up your data, you need to back up only the information on LUN 1, because you can always re-install the programs themselves back onto LUN 0 if the drive fails.

See Chapter 7 for more on how to create RAID sets, partitions, and LUNs.

Because of the considerable differences between storage arrays, deciding which one is right for you depends on how many servers you have and how much data you need to store.

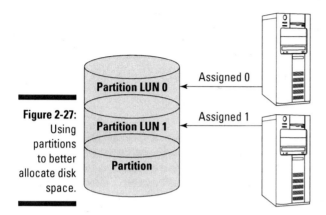

Figure 2-27:
Using
partitions
to better
allocate disk
space.

Understanding storage-array classification

Storage arrays can be classified by type, which also usually means size. The first type is *monolithic* arrays. They're the big, expensive boxes with all the redundant features in them that make them good candidates for use with expensive mainframe computers. Monolithic arrays can have hundreds of storage ports, and have all the internal goodies like massive amounts of cache memory to accommodate a lot of servers accessing data at the same time without performance issues occurring. The internal features are also duplicated; if one part fails, another takes over. Monolithic arrays are also used with mainframe computers, so they're usually found in the large data centers of big corporations. Monolithic arrays require a raised floor, conditioned power and air, and multiple large-amperage 3-phase electrical connectors. Monolithic arrays cannot be used in the general office environments, only in data centers.

The other type of storage arrays consist of the smaller boxes, called *modular* arrays. Modular arrays cannot connect to mainframe computers. The ability to connect to and store mainframe data is usually what sets modular and monolithic storage arrays apart. Some modular arrays have many of the same redundancy features that their big monolithic brothers have, but modular arrays have limited cache memory and port connectivity, so they can't connect to as many servers as a monolithic array without degraded performance. Modular arrays can still be used in large data centers, but they also work just as well in smaller departments or remote offices.

You have two approaches as to how to store your data here. Either centralize everything into big powerful monolithic boxes, or spread everything out across many individual modular arrays. If you have mainframes, you have no choice; you need the big guys. If all you need to connect are a few Windows NT or Unix servers, then the modular approach might be right for you. However, if you have many servers (say, more than 16 to 32), and zero downtime is a priority for you, then use a monolithic array if you can afford to. If you have fewer than 16 servers, then staying with internal storage in the servers or using a less expensive modular array may make sense.

Modular versus monolithic

As discussed in the previous section, the two types of storage arrays are modular and monolithic. Modular storage arrays use controllers that are separate from the disks. Modular arrays usually come with two controllers. If one controller fails, the other one automatically takes over. The controllers are housed in a shelf that is powered separately from the disks. The disks are housed in shelves and connected to the controllers with either optical or copper cables, depending on the type of drives used. Monolithic arrays use disks that are assembled inside the array frame. The disks are connected to the many internal controllers through large amounts of cache memory.

Monolithic (Enterprise)

Monolithic arrays, those big powerful boxes with tons of disk storage in them, are so called because they come in big cabinets, and can sometimes look like the monolith from the movie *2001: A Space Odyssey.* (See Figure 2-28 for an example of a monolithic array.)

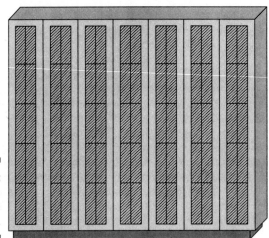

Figure 2-28:
Monolithic
storage
array.

Monolithic storage array frame

Mainframe computers are the computers that run massive and essential information networks such as the stock market, airline reservation and traffic control systems, and hospitals. These systems need to stay up all the time, or somebody (or lots of somebodies) gets in major trouble. These boxes also use a feature called *Phone Home,* from which the storage array performs a self-diagnosis and calls the manufacturer if it discovers a problem with itself. The manufacturer can then dispatch an engineer to fix the problem before you're even aware that anything is wrong.

Monolithic storage arrays include redundancy features so that if any part goes bad, another one automatically takes over for the failed part. Such features as these are needed for high-availability solutions. These boxes hardly ever go down and are often guaranteed to be available to use. Monolithic arrays have tons of cache memory, which is shared between all the devices connected to the array. Whereas modular arrays can come with 8GB to 32GB of cache memory, monolithic arrays can come with 128GB or much more. The cache memory is used to reduce the need to read data from physical disks, which makes things run faster. Monolithic arrays also usually come pre-loaded with very intelligent *firmware* that allows users to manage their data more efficiently. (More on storage firmware features in the advanced chapters of this book.)

Modular (Departmental)

Modular arrays are usually cheaper than the monolithic arrays. Modular arrays are just that: modular. You can start out with just a controller shelf and a single shelf of disks. You can then increase it to its maximum capacity. (See Figure 2-29.)

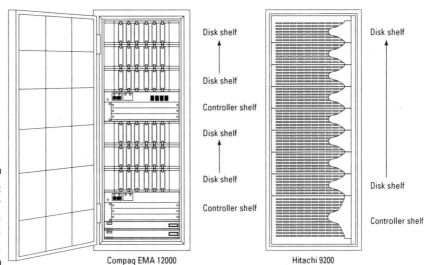

Figure 2-29: Modular storage arrays use shelves.

Disk shelf

Disk shelf

Controller shelf

Disk shelf

Disk shelf

Controller shelf

Disk shelf

Disk shelf

Controller shelf

Compaq EMA 12000

Hitachi 9200

These arrays are great for smaller companies or for smaller departments of larger companies. You can start out small and inexpensively with a modular array, growing into it by adding more disks or controller shelves when your data needs grow. Some companies use modular-class arrays as their enterprise standard. If your company doesn't have mainframes, then you can use modular arrays as the basis for all the storage in your enterprise. You can scale by adding controllers for performance or disks for capacity.

Some modular arrays include functionality, such as Phone Home, that is similar to the big boxes (see the previous section). Some even have the same redundancy features of the more expensive boxes, although these are usually add-on options. It's just like buying a car: You automatically get four wheels and an engine, but the cup holders cost extra. Check with your vendor to see what options are available for your particular array.

Why Cache memory makes a difference

A *cache* is a bunch of very fast memory — just like, but faster than, the memory in your server.

The cache memory is used by the storage array to store your data before it gets sent to the disk drives. This is good, because storing data in memory is much faster than storing it on disk. (Memory runs *much* faster than spinning physical disk drives.) As soon as your data hits the cache, the array tells the server that sent your credit-card number that the array has safely received the number, and the server can now move on to something else.

The more cache memory the storage array has, the more it can store in cache, and the faster it goes. This makes your servers run faster, too. If the server needs the same data again, it's already in the cache; thus, the server doesn't have to wait for the disk array to move the data up from the disks before it can perform another operation on the data.

Think of it like this. You're watching the Super Bowl with your friends and you have a cooler full of beer next to the couch. Someone just grabbed the last beer, so now you have to pull yourself away from the game and walk over to the refrigerator to get more beer for the cooler. As luck has it, the refrigerator is also empty, so now you have to get into your car and drive to the nearest convenience store (not impaired, of course) to stock up. You're grousing all the way there because you're missing the best part of the game.

Think of the cooler as your server's memory, the refrigerator as the storage array's cache memory, and the convenience store as the disk drives. It's much faster to store beer in the cooler or in the fridge than it is to drive all the way to a convenience store every time you want another frosty.

The differences between SAN-enabled storage arrays

This stuff is really technical, and you don't need to know this. If you're looking to buy a storage array, though, it might help you figure out what's important and what's not.

Some storage arrays use a data bus architecture, and others use a data switch architecture as the internal data paths inside the array itself. On a *bus architecture* array, only one thing can happen at a time per bus. On a *switch architecture* array, multiple things can be going on at the same time. Think of a bus-based array as being like a narrow road on which only one car can travel at a time. Think of a switch-based array as being like a superhighway interchange where cars can come and go as they please. The technical term for this is a *non-blocking architecture*.

The same holds true for computer networks. A *hub-based network* allows only one device at a time to use the hub; a *switched-based network* allows each device to access the switch simultaneously. A switched-based design is inherently faster than a bus-based design. The first of the following two figures shows the slower, bus-based architecture; the second shows the faster, switch-based architecture.

Just keep in mind that a switch architecture can handle many more servers connected to it without impacting the I/O performance of the other servers accessing the array. Switches are inherently more scalable than buses.

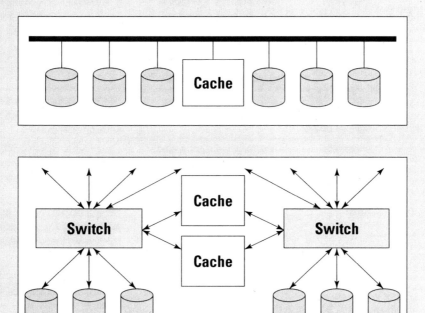

Most SAN storage subsystems also have a high-availability feature called *mirrored cache*. With this, the data actually gets written to two cache memory banks simultaneously inside the array. A mirrored cache protects the data in the event of a cache failure because two copies of the data are always available.

Congratulations: You made it through SAN Anatomy 101. Table 2-3 offers a handy summary of the parts of a SAN and what they do.

Table 2-3	Summary of SAN Components	
Component	**How It Works in the SAN**	**Typical Benefit**
Cache memory	Used in differing amounts in both monolithic and modular arrays to help performance	Can provide a dramatic boost in I/O performance for applications
Fibre Channel protocol	Used as the language of communication between devices in a SAN	Very low-latency and dependable protocol for optical connectivity to block-based storage devices
Gigabit Interface Converters (GBICs)	Contains the lasers, and converts the digital data into the light pulses that travel over the SAN	Depending on the type of GBIC and the wavelength of light used, can transmit data over very long distances very fast
Host bus adapter (HBA)	Placed inside the servers, it enables the server to communicate over the SAN	Used to transmit data over the SAN at speeds up 800MB/s
Modular (mid-range-class) storage arrays	Normally departmental-level data storage	Scalable to match the data needs of a mid-size business or large enterprise
Monolithic (enterprise-class) storage arrays	Normally enterprise-level data storage, and mainframes	Can provide very reliable centralized storage resources for up to hundreds of servers
RAID	Used in the storage arrays to create the parity data needed to recover from a disk failure	Provides a high performance method of protecting data as it is written into the storage arrays in the SAN
SAN hubs	Provides connectivity for up to 126 devices using the FC-AL protocol	Great for connecting up older tape devices to the SAN for backup
SAN switches	Provides the basic fabric connectivity, and is the core of the SAN fabric	Enables many devices to communicate at great speed at the same time

A good SAN not only has good hardware, but also good software to efficiently manage it. Storage-management software platforms includes tools for usage reporting, provisioning, data backup, data mirroring and replication, and hierarchical storage management (HSM). The reports tell you what can be thrown out to save disk space and also let you know *who* is using the storage for *what*. The backup software moves what's needed to tape storage for safety. HSM software and mirroring migrates old data to less expensive storage or tape, and data replication makes sure your data is safe in a local disaster.

Chapter 3

What Makes a SAN Go

1 n this chapter, you discover how the devices in a storage area network (SAN) communicate with each other. Building a SAN is similar to building any other kind of data or voice network; it has three phases:

✔ Making the physical connection between all network devices with cables

✔ Initiating the directory in the network so the devices can find each other

✔ Enforcing the set of rules (that is, the protocol) so each device knows how to communicate on the network

Understanding how all these pieces fit together in a storage network is useful when something goes bump in the night. If you have to troubleshoot a problem in a SAN, knowing how it's *supposed* to work will help you figure out why it's broken.

Networking Basics

In computing, a *network* consists of two or more elements (devices) connected over a common medium (usually a cable) and a process (or protocol) for transmitting data from a sender to one or more receivers. Pretty simple.

When you were a kid, did you ever try to create your own little phone network by using a string to connect two paper cups? Although it was probably a bit hard to hear your friend on the other end, the "phone" actually worked. The vibrations from your voice were transmitted over the string (the medium) to the paper cups (the devices), which allowed your friend to hear your voice, and you took turns talking and listening (the protocol); taken together, the cups and string were really a simple network.

Okay, that was fine for only two people, but what if little Johnny across the street also wanted to play? You *could* always tie on another string and paper cup — but if all three of you spoke at the same time, distinguishing one voice from another would be really hard. Not only that, but string probably didn't transmit vibrations very well. If more kids were going to play, you needed a better way.

Electrical engineers figured out that using copper wires to carry electrical signals through transmitters and receivers worked a lot better than string and paper cups. In a common telephone handset, the *transmitter* is the little device you speak into that converts your voice into the electrical signals that get sent over the wire to someone at the other end. The *receiver* converts the electrical signals representing your voice back into the vibrations that the person on the other end hears as your voice through the handset speaker.

Today's phone networks tie together billions of people. With all that talking going on, every conversation has to be intelligently routed to the person you are trying to call. The intelligence is implemented as a *protocol* — a set of rules that all the devices follow. It's a common language for the devices, if you will; it lets all those conversations take place without getting jumbled. The phone *network* is nothing more than a well-organized bunch of wires and switches connecting all the phones together, but with intelligence built in to control how everything works.

Telephone networks for voice communication operate very similarly to the Internet for computer communication (in fact, part of the Internet still uses phone lines). In storage communication, the network is made of servers and storage arrays (the devices) connected together via optical cables and switches (the medium) — and the rules for communicating between the devices (the protocol) is Fibre Channel. Everything together makes a storage area network, or SAN.

Moving Data at the Speed of Light

Using copper as a network connection medium has its limitations. First, copper is heavy; the poor guy who runs all the cables gets a real workout. Second, electrical signals traveling over copper wires lose strength when they have to traverse long distances. At intervals, signal regenerators or amplifiers have to boost signal strength to get the data all the way to where it's going. No wonder that using copper cables as a connection medium for a storage network puts a limit on the distance you can have between devices.

SCSI (small computer system interface) cables are commonly used to connect disks to application server computers, and they can't be more than around 25 meters long to do that job. And then there are security issues: Copper-based networks such as Ethernet are easy for hackers to tap into if they're looking to capture data or disrupt the network.

The geeks found a better way: fiber optics.

Fiber-optic cables use light pulses to transmit information. Light can travel *very* fast, which makes it a great medium for data communications. Light travels at around 300,000 kilometers (300,000 km) per second in a vacuum. Fiber-optic cable, using a core made of tiny strands of glass, slows light down a bit to around 200,000 kilometers per second because of the impurities in the glass — but it still carries data faster than any other solid medium.

Fiber-optic cables are made by surrounding a long strand of very fine glass (called the *core*) with a plastic coating (called the *cladding*). The light travels through the strand of glass, and the coating prevents the light from escaping through the sides of the cable (see Figure 3-1).

Bottom line: You can push tons of information over a fiber-optic cable at a speed not much slower than the speed of light. No wonder today's phone networks use fiber-optic cables instead of copper cables wherever possible to increase efficiency. Fiber-optic cables also proved to be reliable and speedy as the backbone of many high-speed networks, so they also became the medium of choice for moving data over high-speed storage networks.

Fiber-optic cables are used in most storage networks. Because storage networks use the Fibre Channel protocol to transmit data, the cables are also called *Fibre Channel* cables to set them apart from other optical network uses, such as when used in telephone networks or other computer networks. (Maybe the guy who came up with the name "Fibre Channel" was French? Whatever.) Fibre Channel cables are the ones that use (logically enough) the Fibre Channel protocol for data communication (as detailed in Chapter 2).

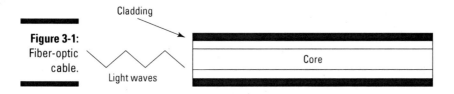

Figure 3-1:
Fiber-optic
cable.

Bandwidth

Moving data from a fast server to its hard drives requires a lot of bandwidth. The *bandwidth* of any network connection is, essentially, how much data can be passed over the cable in one second. The actual physical limits of how much data can be pushed over an optical network haven't been determined yet, although some tests have shown that speeds over 1,000GB per second are possible. That's a lot of data. In storage networks, the more efficient the "pipeline" (that is, the bandwidth), the faster the data can be moved to disks. For the network to keep up with today's fast hard drives, you need a fast network. That's one reason fiber-optic networks are used in a SAN.

To store information, the computer uses a series of eight bits, or one byte of data. A byte is eight characters of data; it takes eight bits to make a byte. The letter A is stored on your computer as a byte of data. If you could pull apart your hard drive and look at the way the letter A is stored as ones and zeros, it would look something like this: 00000101. The letter A is stored using eight bits.

In data-communication networks, bandwidth is how many bits of information per second can move across a particular link. In data storage networks, bandwidth is described by how many bytes per second can be moved across a particular link.

Megabit (Mb) refers to 1 million bits. (Note the lowercase *b*.)

Megabyte (MB) refers 1 million bytes. Note the uppercase *B*. There are eight bits in every byte, so technically, it takes 8 million *bits* of data to equal one mega*byte*. This all gets kind of confusing, so if you just remember that the gigabit number of a Fibre Channel cable correlates to its speed — in hundreds of megabytes per second — you should be fine.

The original Fibre Channel devices were developed to move data at a rate of 100 megabytes per second as the optimal speed. This speed is correlated to a communication speed over the network as *Gigabit (1Gbit) Fibre Channel*. A 1 gigabit network can move approximately 100 megabytes of data per second. This speed has been increased and the most commonly used speed is 400 megabytes per second today, which is known as *4Gbit Fibre Channel*. Fibre Channel devices able to push 8 Gbit and 10 Gbit or 800 to 1000 megabytes per second are now showing up. Another highly advanced protocol known as *Infiniband* has very low latency (that is, the time required to access or move data) and can achieve speeds over 20 Gbit (2000 MB/s). Infiniband uses copper or optical cables to transmit data between devices in high-performance networks, often those made up of powerful supercomputers.

Fibre Channel Protocols

Networks use a *protocol* as the language that each device on the network understands so the network doesn't become a Tower of Babble. Each device using the network needs to speak a common language. Think of it this way: If everyone in your neighborhood spoke a different language, communicating with each other would be virtually impossible. If you pick up the phone and call someone in France, you'd better be able to speak French or your conversation won't get very far.

And just as different dialects of the same language can be spoken in different parts of the same country, so can different protocols be used by similar devices to describe the same thing. Take United States English vernacular, for instance. If you were in a grocery store in New York and wanted something to put your food in, you'd ask for a bag; if you were in Georgia, you'd ask for a sack. Both mean the same thing but are called something different depending on where you come from. Computer networks and storage networks have a similar need for all the components to speak the same language so they can communicate effectively.

The process of using a protocol is similar to how the telephone network operates. Wires coming into your house connect your phone to the telephone network. The only way you know you can use that network to make a call is when you hear a dial tone. No dial tone, no call. Therefore the dial tone in a phone network acts as the basic protocol (between you and your phone) for understanding whether a connection can be established. When you use a cellular phone, you still hear a dial tone, but cellular phones use a completely different type of network. So the dial tone acts as the signal that lets you know that the basic network is functional and a call can be placed. A dial tone on a phone network is a basic signal, no matter whether it's a copper wire network or wireless network.

When you dial a number and someone picks up the phone on the other side, a higher-level language comes into play; which one it is depends on the country you're in, and on the country you're calling. In France, the language would be French; in the United States, the language may be English; and so on. The spoken language over a phone network works at a higher level than a basic dial tone. The dial tone serves as a *low-level protocol* that lets you know the network is working. The spoken language serves as a *higher-level protocol* that you can use to get things done. Many higher-level languages can be spoken over a phone network; the network doesn't need to understand the higher-level language for the network to work.

The phone network itself just provides the transport mechanism for moving the spoken words from one place to the next. All you need for a conversation to be successful is that the people on each end of the network understand the same higher-level language being used. The same holds true for computer networks. Each device on the network needs to understand the same higher-level language for a conversation to take place between devices.

Continuing with this analogy, in a storage network, the underlying "dial tone" is the Fibre Channel protocol. The "spoken language" that your applications use to talk to the hard drives is the SCSI (Small Computer System Interface) protocol. The SCSI protocol, as a "higher-level language," is layered on top of the Fibre Channel protocol "dial tone."

Two types of "dial tones" (that is, protocols) are used in Fibre Channel storage networks:

 ✔ Fibre Channel-Arbitrated Loop (FC-AL) protocol helps establish data communication in network loops, which are created by connecting the devices with hubs.

 ✔ Fibre Channel-Switched (FC-SW) protocol helps establish data communication in the SAN fabrics created by connecting devices with switches.

The arbitrated loop

FC-AL, or Fibre Channel-Arbitrated Loop protocol, is the Fibre Channel language used by hubs. Connecting servers and storage together by using a Fibre Channel hub creates a Fibre Channel arbitrated loop. It's called an *arbitrated* loop because only a single device can send a signal across the loop at any given time. Each connected device must *arbitrate*, using the FC-AL protocol, for access to the loop.

Each device connected to the loop through the hub has to share the bandwidth of the loop — and only one device can use the loop at a time, waiting its turn to use the loop (similar to taking turns to talk when using paper cups and a string!). A maximum of 127 devices can be attached to a single loop. The inside of a SAN hub looks like a single piece of wire wrapped around to create a loop. Because it's only a single wire, only one device can use the loop at a time (as shown in Figure 3-2).

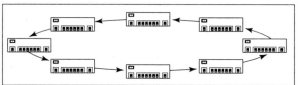

Figure 3-2:
SAN hub
design.

Every port shares the loop.

The loop protocol defines how each device should act when trying to use the loop to connect to other devices in the loop. This is the defined etiquette of how each device connects to and uses the loop.

Loop addressing

Using the string-and-paper-cup analogy from earlier in the chapter, you have to designate in what order each person connected to the string should speak. The easy way would be to use a number system. Person 1 talks first, followed by Person 2, and then Person 3. Each person would listen for his or her number to know when to reply. That's roughly the way the Fibre Channel loop protocol works. Every device attached to the loop is assigned a loop ID number when it's plugged into the hub.

Loop IDs are assigned a number from 0 to 126. Remember: No more than 127 devices can co-exist in a single loop. Each device takes turns talking on the loop using the loop ID as its priority. If your loop ID is number 1, then you go first. Algorithms make sure that everyone gets a turn. This way, loop ID 1 can't hog the loop.

To loop or not to loop?

The Fibre Channel loop was the first method used to connect servers to storage in a SAN. In SAN historical terms, this is similar to the primitive method of telephony using string and paper cups. Everyone shares the string — or in this case, the loop — so only one device can transmit or receive on the loop at a time. Fibre Channel loops are still around today because they're reasonably cheap and they get the job done.

The Switched Fabric

When you connect two switches in a SAN, you create a *switched fabric*. SAN switches tend to be much smarter than SAN hubs because a switched fabric can contain many more devices than a loop can. Whereas a loop can have a maximum of 127 devices connected to it, a switched fabric can contain thousands of devices.

Switches are sometimes called *nonblocking* devices: That is, each device can communicate with another device without having to wait its turn. The inside of a switch is designed so that multiple physical connections exist between each port and every other port on the switch. (See Figure 3-3.)

Figure 3-3:
A nonblock-
ing SAN
switch.

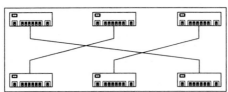

Every port has access to every other port.

Multiple conversations can happen through a switch simultaneously. Conversations are routed between the devices connected to the switch ports using the FC-SW protocol. If you connect two switches to create a fabric, the protocol lets the switches discover each other, allowing communication to happen across switch boundaries. This connection between the switches is an *inter-switch link* (ISL). By using the FC-SW protocol, any device connected to any port on any switch can communicate with a device on any other switch port. For example, the server in Figure 3-4 that is connected to Switch 1 can communicate with the storage connected to Switch 2 by using the ISL between the switches.

You can create very large switch fabrics. Thousands of devices can be connected through switches, and switches can be connected to make very large fabrics. And because communications between those devices can all happen at the same time, SAN switch fabrics are very scalable. This is also why SAN loops are going the way of the dodo. Using a fabric rather than a loop in a SAN makes more sense for some practical reasons:

✔ A fabric can be designed to allow you to nondisruptively add more switches to expand the network.

✔ Switches can be added to expand the network without affecting what's currently happening in the fabric.

✔ The rest of the switches in the fabric automatically discover each new switch and any devices connected to it.

You're probably wondering how the FC-SW protocol handles all this. Back to the old phone-network analogy again (see the next section).

The fabric protocol

Because so many more devices can be connected to it, more control is needed over what's going on inside the fabric. SAN fabrics can contain thousands of devices — so they need some type of service that can handle the discovery of new devices and switches being added to the fabric.

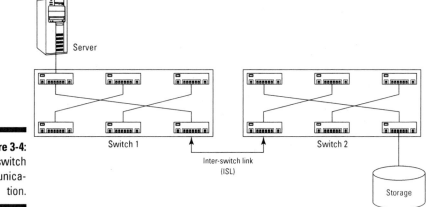

Figure 3-4: Inter-switch communication.

Server

Switch 1

Inter-switch link (ISL)

Switch 2

Storage

Other considerations include these needs:

- **Effective routing of conversations between devices:** Without an efficient mechanism to route communication sessions between devices (and to determine the proper devices to participate in the sessions), the storage network would be a jumble of corrupt data.

- **A listing service:** This is akin to a telephone directory, ensuring that devices can find each other in the network.

- **Data security:** You need to be able to effectively separate components of the system that shouldn't know about each other and keep the data safe on its journey.

The FC-SW protocol handles all these tasks by using a database that's shared among all the switches in the fabric.

Again, think of the telephone service to your house as an analogy: Your phone is connected to a telephone network, and millions of other phones are connected to the same network. To locate another person's phone, you look up his or her phone number in the directory listing (the database). When you dial that number, the network routes your connection to the other person's phone (the routing in the switches). After you're connected, the network gets out of the way and lets you communicate until you hang up the phone and the network then terminates the connection.

Now suppose that a fabric contains 20 switches. A server device on Switch 1 needs to use a storage device on Switch 18. Using the FC-SW protocol, the server would ask the switches to look up the address of the storage device in the directory service of the fabric (called the name server). If the server has enough rights in the security database to use the storage, the switches would then route the server's connection to the correct port on Switch 18, creating a communication session. The switches keep this connection open until the server hangs up; the connection is then terminated.

Fabric addressing

The addressing scheme used in SAN fabrics is quite different than that in SAN loops. A fabric can contain thousands of devices rather than the maximum 127 in a loop. Each device in the fabric must have a unique address, just as every phone number in the world is unique. This is done by assigning every device in a SAN fabric a World Wide Name (WWN).

What in the world is a World Wide Name?

Each device on the network has a World Wide Name, a 64-bit hexadecimal number coded into it by its manufacturer. The WWN is often assigned via a standard block of addresses made available for manufacturers to use. Thus every device in a SAN fabric has a built-in address assigned by a central naming authority — in this case, one of the standard-setting organizations that control SAN standards — the Institute of Electrical and Electronics Engineers (IEEE, pronounced *eye triple-e*). The WWN is sometimes referred to by its *IEEE address*. A typical WWN in a SAN will look something like this:

20000000C8328FE6

On some devices, such as large storage arrays, the storage array itself is assigned the WWN and the manufacturer then uses the assigned WWN as the basis for *virtual WWNs,* which add sequential numbers to identify ports.

The WWN of the *storage array* is known as the *World Wide* Node *Name* or WWNN. The resulting WWN of the *port* on the storage array is known as the

World Wide Port *Name* or WWPN. If the base WWN is (say) 20000000C8328F00 and the storage array has four ports, the array manufacturer could use the assigned WWN as the base, and then use offsets to create the WWPN for each port, like this:

20000000C8328F01 for port 1

20000000C8328F02 for port 2

20000000C8328F03 for port 3

20000000C8328F04 for port 4

The manufacturers can use offsets to create World Wide Names as long as the offsets used do not overlap with any other assigned WWNs from the block of addresses assigned to the manufacturer.

When it comes to Fibre Channel addressing, the term WWN always refers to the WWPN of the actual ports, which are like the MAC addresses of an Ethernet network card. The WWPN (now forever referred to as the WWN for short) is always used in the name server in the switch to identify devices on the SAN.

The name server

The name server is a logical *service* (a specialized program that runs in the SAN switches) used by the devices connected to the SAN to locate other devices. The name server in the switched fabric acts like a telephone directory listing. When a device is plugged into a switch, it logs in to the switch (a process like logging in to your PC) and registers itself with the name server. The name server uses its own database to store the WWN information for every device connected to the fabric, as well as the switch port information and the associated WWN of each device. When one device wants to talk to another in the fabric, it looks up that device's address (its WWN) in the name server, finds out which port the device is located on, and communication is then routed between the two devices.

Figure 3-5 shows the name server's lookup operation in action. The arrows show how the server on Switch 1 (with address 20000000C8328FE6) locates the address of the storage device on Switch 2 (at address 50000000B2358D34). After it finds the storage device's address in the name server, it knows which switch it's located on and how to get to the device.

When a network gets big enough to have a few hundred devices connected to a bunch of switches, the use of a directory listing inside the fabric makes sense.

The switches' name server information can be used to troubleshoot problems in a SAN. If your device is connected to a switch but doesn't get registered in the name server table, then you know that the problem is somewhere between the server and the switch; you may have a bad cable. (See Chapter 12 for more SAN troubleshooting tips.)

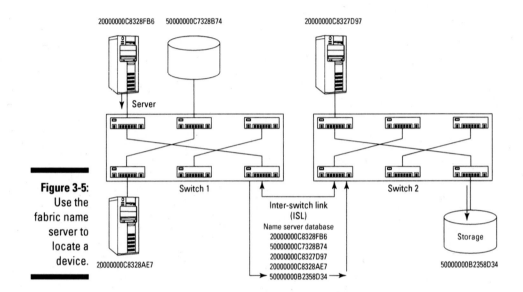

Figure 3-5:
Use the fabric name server to locate a device.

Chapter 4

What Makes a SAN Stop

*T*his chapter deals with the things that can give you grief with your SAN. Sometimes it's Murphy's Law — *Anything that can go wrong, will go wrong, and when it does, it will be at the worst possible moment.* Sometimes you'd swear it's gremlins — those little magical creatures that make your socks disappear from your clothes dryer and cause all those funny engine noises in your car. When it comes to computer systems and networks, these guys work overtime. If it seems your computer's hard drive is likeliest to crash only after a long work session, just before you save your work, on a weekend, when no support is available and you were working on a brilliant movie script with a deadline tomorrow . . . well, you get the drift.

So here's where you get a handle on how to steer clear of Murphy and the gremlins during the implementation of your storage area network (SAN).

Discovering What Causes SAN Problems

Yup, even though all those storage vendors out there will tell you that implementing a SAN is the greatest thing since sliced bread and will save you billions of dollars in decreased downtime, the inevitable !*#^* still happens. Sure, using correctly implemented SAN-based storage will save you tons of money over the long run — and keep your applications running longer and faster — but you still have no control over Murphy. Sooner or later, some dope is going to trip over one of those orange fiber-optic cables and pull out the connection to your disks. And yeah, someone is gonna spill his soda into the switch that just happens to connect the computer that runs your nuclear power plant. (Just kidding. I hope.)

So what can you do to help minimize the effects of Murphy and the gremlins? What can you do to help keep your SAN up and running all the time? Basic things to watch out for are

- **Poor design:** Improper bandwidth, latency issues, congestion (over-subscription)

- **Cabling problems:** Inconsistent labeling practices, damaged cables, wrong cables, signal loss, patch-panel problems

- **Unsuitable drivers:** Wrong drivers, outdated drivers, unfriendly driver interaction with other software, missing drivers

- **Using the wrong storage for your needs:** Using the wrong RAID types for your applications, storage performance issues, cache issues, and so on

- **Inadequate planning:** No change control, lack of testing before implementing, device interaction, operating-system issues

- **Untrained people:** Incomplete training, poor vendor support, pushing projects with limited resources, no SAN team

- **Incomplete management software:** Neglecting to set up the right alarms and notifications for when things break, or failing to get people and procedures in place to monitor and respond to problems

We cover each one of these in more detail throughout this chapter.

Preventing Poor SAN Design

Designing a small SAN is simple. You can design your own SAN just by using the information contained in Chapter 5 of this book. If you have your storage vendor do it for you, just check out the design yourself by reading Chapter 5 and this chapter to make sure that no mistakes have been made. (Trust, but verify!)

Things to look out for in a bad SAN design are inadequate bandwidth, too much distance between system components, excess latency (the time it takes to access or move data) and congestion (over-subscription of inter-switch links or storage ports). Other considerations include

- Getting the right cables for the job

- Using active or passive connections appropriately

- Choosing reliable and cooperative equipment vendors

- Making wise hardware purchases

Bandwidth

Bandwidth is essentially a measure of how much data your storage network can handle every second. The speed of SAN components are measured in *gigabits* per second, which is shortened to Gbps, with a small "b" for bits. Every one Gbps is equal to 100 megabytes per second, which is shortened to MBps, with a large "B" for bytes. (A *byte* is equal to 8 bits.)

You can get SAN components that run at 100 megabytes per second (1 Gbps), 200 megabytes per second (2 Gbps), 400 megabytes per second (4 Gbps), 800 megabytes per second (8 Gbps), and soon 1000 megabytes per second (10 Gbps). One thousand megabytes per second is equal to one *gigabyte* per second, which is one billion 8-bit bytes per second, which is *really* fast. SAN vendors are nice, and they like to make things easy for you (was that a blatant enough schmooze?), so they make all the faster stuff backward-compatible with the slower stuff. So what's the problem? Well . . .

Everything in the network path always slows down to the speed of the *slowest* part in the path.

Theoretically, you could have a very fast SAN switch, hooked up to a cheetah of a host bus adapter (HBA; see Chapter 2 for details), but if the storage comes with 2 Gbps ports, that's all the speed you're going to get. Period. If you spend the extra money to buy an HBA that's built to run at the faster speeds, then everything from that HBA all the way down to the storage must *also* be able to run at that speed.

Sure, you could use 4 Gbps (or even 10 Gbps) core-switch connections for trunking inter-switch links (more about trunking later in this chapter), put those links between the core switches, and then put 2 Gbps switches at the edge — if you can afford such a hot-rod setup. But it's still better to have all the components matched and operating at the same speed.

Not having enough storage bandwidth for your applications can make your server seem sluggish. Bandwidth problems can be the cause of frequent time-outs, cause your system to hang, and cause a host of other assorted gremlins to show up and make your life miserable.

The best practice for good bandwidth design is to

✔ Use parts that are all the same speed.

✔ Use the speed that your applications need.

For example, if you're just running a word processor over the SAN, then you don't need 4 Gbps Fibre Channel parts.(In fact, you wouldn't even need a SAN!) On the other hand, if you're running on-demand video applications for a chain of hotels, then you definitely require the extra speed of 4 Gbps-to-10 Gbps SAN parts.

Making sure that everything runs at the same speed helps avoid wasting your money on fast parts that can't be fully utilized, or inviting bandwidth problems by using slower parts in a fast network. Meanwhile there's an upgrade "gotcha" to consider: In the near future, as faster speeds start coming out, most 1 Gbps and 2 Gbps SAN components will start to disappear from the market. Make sure that any storage array you purchase comes with *at least* 4 Gbps ports and can run in a 4 Gbps SAN, or is at least upgradeable to new, faster ports as they become available.

Too much distance between components

Distance issues can be the cause of all kinds of flaky intermittent gremlin-type problems. Hop back to Chapter 2 to review Table 2-1, which covers the type of cables to use as well as what kind of Gigabit Interface Converter (GBIC) goes with which type of cable. (GBICs are where the little lasers hang out. You need either a short-wave or long-wave GBIC, depending on distance.) Use that chart as your bible when deciding on how far your servers can be from your storage.

Here's a classic example: A SAN that uses 50μ multimode cables connecting 1 Gbps devices can have no more than 500 meters between each device native (without using expensive SAN extension gear). This means you can have 500 meters between your server and SAN switch and another 500 meters between the switch and the storage. That's pretty far. But if you use a lot of patch panels for your fiber-optic cables, you might be close to the edge of how far you can go, even though you're nowhere near the distance limits of the cables.

Patch panels are devices that consolidate cable connections into one place. Patch panels are very useful for keeping all your cables nice and neat, off the floor and away from clumsy folks' feet. (Read more about patch panels in the upcoming section "Macro- and micro-bends, and the patch-panel pain.")

Using a patch panel, however, limits your distance because of signal loss from the connection. Think about it: The *core* of a fiber-optic cable (where the light travels through) is made of a tiny thread of glass. Whenever you splice an optical cable together with a patch panel (or any other way), you're not going to get the glass in the core to line up perfectly with the core of the other cable. This means that light is lost at the splice (see Figure 4-1).

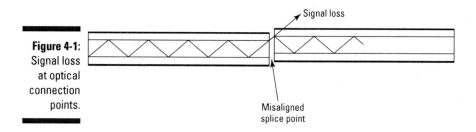

Figure 4-1: Signal loss at optical connection points.

Signal loss

Misaligned splice point

Normally, SAN storage is located in the same room as the servers that connect to it. Most of the time, the distance is no more than a few dozen feet, even though the cables may be longer. (A commonly used cable length is 25 meters, although you can buy 50μ cables in lengths from 3 meters to 500 meters.) Although patch-panel connections can cause some signal loss, if you stay within a few hundred meters, you should be fine. You aren't likely to have a room that is more than a few hundred meters in size. If you do, bless you; you're doing very well for yourself.

Signal loss for optical networks is measured in decibels (dBs) . Using a patch panel, the maximum allowable signal loss is .5 dB (point-five decibels) per connection. This means that the total allowable loss when using a patch panel, together with the host and storage connections, is about 4.0 dB. Using 50μ multimode cables, you lose about 4 dB per kilometer. Using 62.5μ cables, you lose about 4.5 dB per kilometer. That's why the distance specs are different between the cable types. As a rule, try to keep signal loss at 4 dB or less across all connections when using either 62.5μ or 50μ cables.

Every connection counts; the fewer you need, the less signal you lose.

Excess latency

Latency is the time needed for data to travel from point A to point B. In a SAN, latency can be caused by too much distance between a server and its storage array, or by too many *hops* (connections through switches) between your servers and storage.

Hops slow down your data

Connecting a server through one switch equals one hop. Each hop adds approximately one millisecond of delay through the fabric. If the SAN is designed poorly, your data might have to traverse multiple switches (hops) to get to its assigned storage. One to two hops is normal in a well-designed SAN. The more hops your data needs to take, the more latency you get.

Distance slows down your data

Latency can also be caused by distance. Believe it or not, this has to do with the speed of light. Light travels through a vacuum at about 300,000 kilometers (km) per second. Through a fiber-optic cable, light travels at about 200,000 km per second. Thus light traveling 10 km takes around 50 microseconds. You can figure latency of the speed of light through fiber-optic cable at around 1 millisecond for every 200 km when using good cables.

A millisecond delay may not seem like much, but combine this with the signal loss you get through every connection and the (worst-case) 1ms it takes to get the data through each switch, and it all adds up to a significant slowdown. In fact the Fibre Channel protocol (FCP) defines four steps, or two round trips (at least 2ms) before every I/O can complete, so the speed of light actually becomes the limiting factor in moving data through fiber-optic cables over long distances.

Congestion

Congestion occurs when there is not enough bandwidth to move data over a SAN connection. Congestion can happen when two high-performance applications are sharing the same path to storage through the SAN. It's always best to spread out the application load over as many storage ports as you can. (This is called the *fan-in* ratio; 7:1 is about normal for each Gbps of speed, but it still always depends on the performance requirements of the applications.) Congestion can also happen when your servers are located on one switch, and the storage for those servers is located on another switch. If not enough ISLs (inter-switch links) are available to pass the data between switches, congestion can occur.

If you're using a SAN hub as your connection device for the SAN, then everything is connected with a loop. In a loop, all devices share the connection, and each device must take a turn using the loop. If you have a lot of high-performance applications all trying to get to their disks at the same time, congestion can occur.

The same holds true when running backup programs (copying all the data on disks to tape storage) over a SAN during normal business hours. Backup jobs are very read-intensive on disks. The backup server reads as much data at a time as it can, and then tries to write all that data to tape (or other backup medium) as fast as it can. Backing up is usually not advisable to do during normal business hours because it can really clog up the network.

One way to fix this problem is to use a separate Fibre Channel HBA in each server that's dedicated to backups. The idea is to separate your normal daily disk input and output (input = disk writes; output = disk reads) from backup jobs that require high data throughput. If you can do that, you can run your backup jobs during the day. Woo-hoo! Now no one needs to be around at night to run backup!

Over-subscription

In a SAN, multiple servers can share the same connection to a storage array. (See Figure 4-2.)

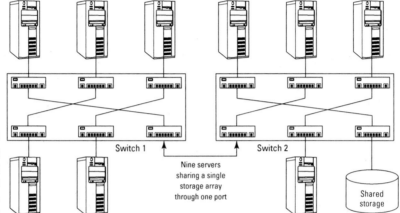

Figure 4-2:
Sharing
storage
ports.

Switch 1   Switch 2

Nine servers
sharing a single
storage array
through one port

Shared
storage

When too many servers share the same connection, another type of congestion can occur. This type of congestion is called *over-subscription*.

For SAN networks, my current best practice is to have no more than seven servers allocated per storage port (again, this is for each Gbps of bandwidth, but this is still a pretty good rule of thumb for even faster SAN components). Using this configuration allows those seven servers to share the connection and therefore the bandwidth of the storage port. This is commonly called the *fan-in ratio* of the storage port. The storage network provides connectivity to every storage port. You can limit how many servers have access to a particular port by zoning the SAN. (Zoning is a method of limiting connectivity in a SAN, covered in more detail in Chapter 5.)

The number of servers sharing a storage port can be moved up or down depending on the performance requirements of the applications running on the servers. Here are two contrasting examples:

✔ Database application servers always need high-performance capabilities because they have to move large amounts of data fast. One of two approaches will get that job done:

  • Use fewer servers per storage port.

  • Replace your SAN components with faster parts that have more bandwidth to share.

✔ File servers may not have as high a performance requirement. If yours don't, you can add more than seven servers per port.

You need to replace everything in the path to realize the benefits of moving to a faster Fibre Channel port. This means replacing the HBA in your server, the switch in the middle, and the storage array at the end. If even one component in the path does not support the higher Fibre Channel speed, then all the other components slow down to accommodate the slower parts.

Having too many servers per port also means each port has only so many I/O operations it can support at one time (the *maximum queue depth* of the port). Most current storage arrays support at least 256 queues per port (some support 512). So if you want each server to be able to queue up 32 I/O operations at one time (which is a good best practice), limit the number of servers to eight per port (256/32 = 8). Most HBA vendors configure the default queue depth for their HBA drivers at 32 anyway, so this is a good default fan-in ratio for server-to-storage port.

Using the Right Cables in the Right Way

The most important difference in SAN cables is the size of the glass core in the middle of the cable. (See Chapter 2 for more on core sizes, cable types, and uses.) Most SANs today use 50-micron multimode fiber-optic cables, the standard cable type for storage area networks in the United States. You'll probably find a lot of 62.5-micron multimode cable around, though, because 62.5-micron cable is the standard used for fiber-optic Ethernet-based computer networks. But look closely; even though these cables are the (ugh) same color as the 50-micron cables — bright orange — the diameter of the core is bigger, making it much more likely that the light going through the core will bounce around more, get absorbed into the cladding, and cause greater signal loss.

Many companies try to save money on the purchase of cables by re-using some of those 62.5-micron cables in a SAN, which is great, because they work fine. The 62.5-micron cables are limited in distance, however, to between 175 and 200 meters. Compare that to 50-micron cable lengths, which can reach 500 meters with 1 Gbps SAN components. Problems can arise with long cable runs inside a building — and one is the potential of a core size mismatch at connections. If someone used a patch panel to connect 62.5-micron cables to 50-micron cables, even more of the light signal would be lost.

A recent standard for mainframe-to-storage connections was to use 62.5-micron cables. When connected to a mainframe, these cables are called Enterprise Storage Connection (ESCON) cables. ESCON cables must be 62.5μ cables, so don't mix them up with the 50μ cables when connecting a mainframe to a SAN. The newer Mainframe FICON connection standard uses 9μ single mode cables.

Always use the right cables for the job. Stick with 50-micron cables for the storage network and 62.5-micron cables for the Ethernet network or ESCON mainframe connections. (Use 9μ cables for FICON mainframe connections, or best of all, refer to the switch manufactures recommendations for what you are connecting.)

Avoiding connection issues

Connection issues can arise anywhere in the network. We have seen backs of server cabinets that looked like orange spaghetti. All the cables were twisted and turned and bent into all kinds of knots. This is a *very* bad thing because fiber-optic cables use light to transmit data, and light wants to travel in a straight line. Cables that are wound too tight or are knotted can cause signal loss.

Avoid the following to prevent connection issues:

- ✔ **Don't wrap fiber-optic cables in a loop smaller than six inches in size.** Anything less than six inches is a *macro-bend* in the cable.

- ✔ **Never bend a fiber-optic cable more than 90 degrees.** Fiber-optic cables are made of glass, and glass (ahem) can fracture or break. You might never be able to *see* the break inside the cable, but it can cause all kinds of strange, intermittent problems to pop up.

- ✔ **Never use twist-tie wraps to bind fiber-optic cables together.** Use Velcro wraps instead; twist-tie wraps can cause crimps in the fiber-optic cable. A crimp in the cable will cause signal loss, making your life miserable.

Macro- and micro-bends, and the patch panel pain

Micro-bends occur when an optical cable is pinched and the light has difficulty getting through the cable. (See Figure 4-3.) The outer wrapping of a fiber-optic cable, called the cladding, prevents the escape of light from the glass core. When the cladding gets pinched tightly, the glass core can break — and then the cladding absorbs some of the light as it goes by. This can happen if tie wrap is tied too tightly around the cable, or the cable gets caught in a server cabinet's door.

Little things cause big problems

I know one fellow who tested his fiber-optic connections by running them over the computer room floor. He didn't notice that one of his buddies rolled a chair over the cable right after the testing was completed. After everything was neatly put in place, one of the connections would not come up. It took them days to discover the little crimp — a micro-bend — in the cable, caused by the chair.

You can sometimes feel a micro-bend in a cable if run your fingers gently along the length of the cable and feel for any indentations. If you don't find any and you're still getting signal loss, it may be time to call in a professional to use a light meter on the cable to see whether enough light is getting through.

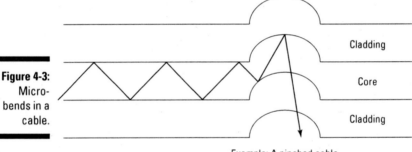

Figure 4-3:
Micro-
bends in a
cable.

Cladding

Core

Cladding

Example: A pinched cable

Macro-bends occur when an optical cable is bent or looped too tight. (See Figure 4-4.) When this happens, the light gets either dispersed or absorbed by the cladding around the glass core — and you get signal loss through the cable.

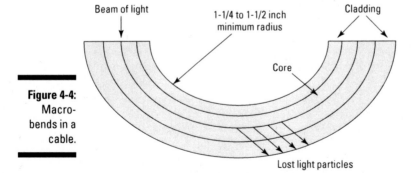

Beam of light

1-1/4 to 1-1/2 inch
minimum radius

Cladding

Core

Figure 4-4:
Macro-
bends in a
cable.

Lost light particles

You might have heard the term *wiring closet* used by network and telephone company service technicians; it's the actual room that contains the connection points for all the cables strung throughout a building. Those actual connection points form the *patch panel* (more about patch panels earlier in this chapter). When you connect two cable ends through a patch panel, some light is usually lost at the connection point. That's because those little glass cable cores are quite small; they're difficult to line up perfectly. Some light usually escapes at the connection point.

Try not to use more than two patch panels between your server and the storage in a SAN. Each patch-panel connection is a potential point of failure, and some signal loss occurs for every connection.

Cable labeling

One of the worst things that can happen to you when you get called to work in the middle of the night because something went wrong is to find out that things are not labeled properly.

When you're troubleshooting intermittent SAN problems, nothing is more of a timesaver than good documentation and labeling of cables. If you can't figure out which cables go where, you have to trace the cables from the servers, through the network, and down to the storage connection. If they're labeled, you're ahead of the game. But use a labeling scheme that makes sense. If two Fibre Channel cables are coming from a single server with two host bus adapters, make sure that you label the cables to show which cable goes to which adapter. If someone extends a server from its rack to perform maintenance on it, and the cables get yanked out, problems might occur if they are inserted back into the wrong adapters.

The same holds true for your switch and storage connections. Always make sure that your cables are labeled so you can remove a cable with confidence that you know where to plug it back in.

Choosing the right host bus adapter for your computer

Choosing the correct host bus adapter for your operating system is vital to the success of your SAN. As mentioned in Chapter 2, a host bus adapter (HBA) is the interface card that plugs into your server to connect it to the SAN. Try to stick with the HBA that's recommended by your server vendor.

If you're purchasing all your SAN components from a single vendor, the vendor should be able to recommend what's best. Most SAN vendors have very expensive *integration labs,* where they test all the different combinations of servers, storage, switches, and host bus adapters. After this exhaustive testing is done, they create a *certification matrix,* which is a listing of all the device combinations they have certified to work with their storage. Many vendors make you choose components from this certified list of products. We recommend using the host bus adapters that are listed in the matrix for that vendor.

The two dominant HBA vendors are

- ✔ **Emulex:** www.emulex.com
- ✔ **QLogic:** www.qlogic.com

Brocade (a major SAN switch vendor at www.brocade.com) has also entered the HBA market.

For iSCSI and Infiniband protocols, you can use Intel or Mellanox, in that order. (An Infiniband adapter is called an HCA, or Host Channel Adapter; an iSCSI network card is called a TOE adapter, or TCP/IP Offload Engine adapter.)

Each HBA vendor has strengths and weaknesses. Some of their products work better than others on a particular operating system and server platform. Your SAN vendor can advise you about which HBA to use with your particular operating system(s) and storage array. The HBA driver is the most important aspect of an HBA when it comes to the operating system. I have had great experiences with Emulex on the Windows platform, and Qlogic works great with the Unix and Linux platforms. Some of the storage vendors even repackage these HBAs as their own. For example, when you order an HBA using IBM part numbers for a host bus adapter, you get a re-branded Emulex HBA. When it comes to host bus adapters, standardization is a good thing; try to use the same HBA vendor across all your server platforms if possible.

Going with a single vendor

Standardize using a single vendor if possible. That way, if you have to upgrade the driver that the HBA uses to talk to the operating-system software, you can just get the latest version for your standard HBA from that vendor's Web site and upgrade all your servers to the newer version.

Using multiple HBA vendors means that you have to track any new driver versions from every vendor you use.

The server vendors who also sell SAN storage usually make you use their re-branded version of one of the main HBA manufacturer's products. This is because they like to enhance the products by adding functions and features to it. The SAN-only vendors add changes to the drivers to make sure that the HBA will work with their storage, although some just use the generic HBA and driver from the HBA vendor. This is why it's always best to use the HBA suggested by the vendor from whom you're getting your SAN.

From our experience, we have found that Emulex seems to have the most overall market share in the Microsoft Windows environment to date. Re-branded Emulex adapters are used by IBM and other companies in their SANs. We've found Emulex to be an easy HBA to use for booting into a SAN.

Sun tends to use QLogic HBAs, and Qlogic is a leading provider of Linux- and Unix-based HBAs and drivers, and is even competing with Infiniband in the extreme-performance market. QLogic is coming out with some very cool products, such as HBAs on a chip for use directly on the motherboards of servers. (This leaves a server slot open for other adapters in your server!)

Host bus adapters should be bought in sets of two for each server, and include load balancing functionality and/or path fail-over capabilities either using a driver that comes with the HBA, integrated with the operating system, or as a separate software option from your SAN vendor. This path failover software is also often called a "filter driver," in that it works like a driver and filters out all the available paths to a disk in the SAN to only one or two available paths at a time.

✔ **Load balancing** is the capability to use more than one HBA in the server to balance the input/output (I/O) load to your disks. (See Figure 4-5.) Load balancing makes I/O go much faster.

✔ **Path fail-over** is the capability of one HBA to take over the load of a bad HBA, so if you lose an HBA to a hardware failure, your server still stays up. (See Figure 4-6.)

Most SAN vendors have software that works with the HBAs they use, though usually you have to purchase this the software as a separate option. You can put as many as 32 HBAs in a single server using some of these programs that provide load balancing and path fail-over. Every vendor has its own name for its path fail-over software; some common names include Power Path, Secure Path, Dynamic Link Manager, MPIO, RDAC, and MPXIO.

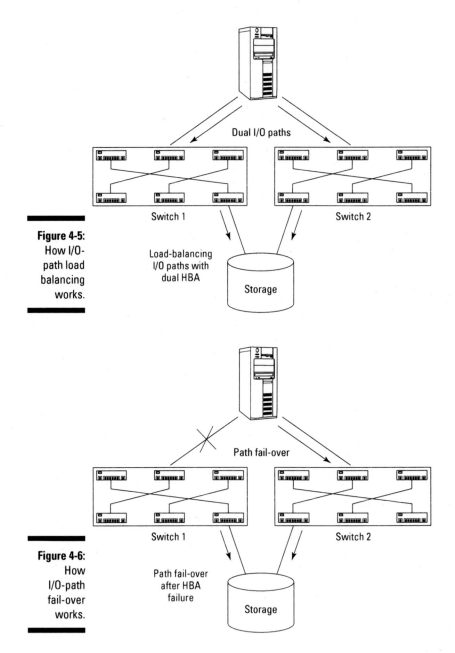

Figure 4-5:
How I/O-
path load
balancing
works.

Figure 4-6:
How
I/O-path
fail-over
works.

Mixing switch vendors

As noted previously, when you build a SAN, the switches are used to connect everything. The switches include most of the intelligence that makes the SAN function. Each switch vendor has functionality that sets its switch apart from the others. Your SAN will function just fine with switches from any of these vendors. Trying to use switches from different vendors within the same SAN fabric, though, gets real weird.

The major SAN switch vendors are

✔ **Brocade:** www.brocade.com

✔ **Qlogic:** www.qlogic.com

✔ **Cisco:** www.cisco.com

There are other SAN switch vendors, but the names are constantly changing as one vendor buys another and the industry consolidates. There are even specialized vendors who build niche components (such as Voltaire's super-fast Infiniband switches — for the scoop on Infiniband, see Chapter 15). Although standards are in place to make switches from different vendors "play nice" with each other, the standards tend to leave too much room for interpretation by different vendors. Take connecting two switches as an example. An *inter-switch link,* or ISL, is the link that ties two switches together in a SAN. QLogic calls it a *T-port*; Brocade calls it an *E-port.* Such terminology differences might cause confusion when managing the switches.

Brocade includes functionality on inter-switch links such as *trunking* — the capability to use multiple cable connections between switches, and define all those individual connections as a single link. Although you can do basic ISL between switch vendors, you can't trunk between switch vendors yet. Cisco even has a function called a V-SAN that enables multiple virtual SANs within a physical SAN. Also, each vendor has a different method of security within its switches.

All of this potential confusion means you'd better think hard before you connect two different vendors' switches. Then there's the potential conflict between vendors. One of the most compelling reasons *not* to combine switch vendors in a single fabric is to avoid the multivendor finger-pointing that will happen when a problem occurs. Interoperability testing shows multivendor switches *can* be connected, but it's generally not a good idea.

All switch vendors add proprietary functionality to make them stand out from the pack. The other consequence of proprietary functions is that they don't cross vendor boundaries, so they may cause trouble if you hook them up to other vendors' switches. If you find that one switch vendor has functions that are desirable to you, stick with that vendor.

For the sake of practicality (and sanity), standardize wherever possible. Stick with a single switch vendor, storage vendor, and HBA vendor. This will make connecting, managing, and troubleshooting SANs much easier in the long run.

Part I
SAN 101

"They can predict earthquakes and seizures, why <u>not</u> server failures?"

In this part . . .

The computer industry is funny. As soon as you get comfortable with the latest technology and become the resident expert, something new comes out, and the whole learning process starts all over again. Some people enjoy the challenge of learning about something new, and some think it just makes life more difficult. This first part of the book tries to make things easier by introducing you to storage area networks, or SANs. Just like in high school shop class, when you were introduced to the drill press, the table saw, and the first aid stations, we introduce you to the various tools that you use to build a SAN. We tell you what each tool does, why it's necessary, and how you can use it in your new SAN project.

Chapter 5

Designing the SAN

. . . .

. . . .

*I*n this chapter, you get a look at designing and creating a workable storage area network (SAN), according to tried-and-true basic principles of SAN design. After reading this chapter, you should be able to quickly pick out the best design for your needs. As you'll see, there are a lot of different ways to design a SAN. We start with a basic design that fits most requirements. We also show you how to scale up your SAN design, which will enable you to add more servers and storage as your needs require.

Basic SAN Designs: Understanding the Layers

As shown in Figure 5-1, SANs are built in three layers:

▮ **The host layer:** This is where all your servers reside. The servers run the high-performance applications that run your business, and those application servers need hard-drive storage space to store their data. Every server in the host layer uses a Host Bus Adapter (HBA) to connect it to the fabric layer. The HBA connects the server with a fiber-optic cable to the hubs or switches in the fabric layer.

✔ **The fabric layer:** This is the actual network part of the SAN. It's also known as the *SAN layer* because it's the basic plumbing of the storage area network. It's the central connection point between the servers in the host layer and the storage devices in the storage layer. The devices in the fabric layer house most of the intelligence that enables SAN communications to occur so your data can flow between the host layer and the storage layer.

✔ **The storage layer:** This is the layer where all the data storage takes place. It's where all the disk and tape drives hang out — the hardware that specifically handles storage.

You can read much more about the different layers of a SAN in Chapters 1 and 2.

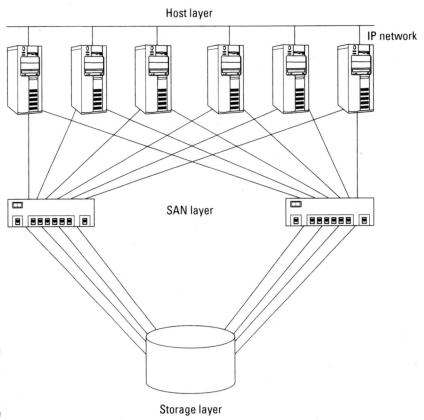

Figure 5-1:
Layers in a
SAN.

When you connect all these layers together, you create what is known as a SAN *topology* — the physical layout of how devices are connected. When switches are used in the fabric layer, all the interconnected switches are known as a *switched fabric.* The three basic SAN topologies for connecting servers to storage in a SAN are listed in Table 5-1. You can see these topologies in Figure 5-2.

Table 5-1	Basic SAN Topologies
Method	*Used for This*
Point-to-point	Direct-connect a server to storage
Arbitrated loop	Server-to-hub-to-storage
Switched fabric	Server-to-switch-to-storage

The different topologies present different challenges. Which one you choose can affect the performance and resiliency of your SAN. The most common SAN topology is the switched fabric because it is *nonblocking*, which means *any* device can talk to *any* other device at the same time (an arrangement defined as *any-to-any*). The loop and switched-fabric topologies actually have sub-topologies, because there are many ways to connect them together. The way you connect them determines how robust — and costly — your storage network becomes:

- **Point-to-point:** This topology doesn't require hubs or switches. It's the cheapest to implement but also the most limited in its capabilities. No surprise there; this network can only consist of two devices.

- **Loop:** This topology uses hubs, and is the next cheapest to build, but loops don't scale very well, so they're best used in small- to mid-size operations. In a loop, only one device can transmit at a time, so all the devices have to wait their turn. This limits the effective size of a single loop to only 127 devices.

- **Fabric:** This is the most common, most scalable — and most expensive — topology. If you move and store massive amounts of data, this topology is the way to go. A switched fabric can address millions of devices, so scalability is not an issue. Also, since the topology is considered nonblocking, any device can communicate with any other device at any time.

The topology that you choose should be based on your needs and your budget. The upcoming sections look at each of these major topologies.

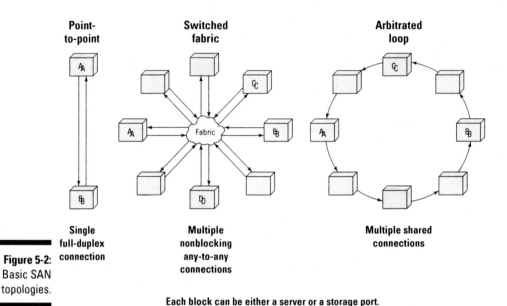

Point-to-point

Single full-duplex connection

Switched fabric

Multiple nonblocking any-to-any connections

Arbitrated loop

Multiple shared connections

Figure 5-2:
Basic SAN topologies.

Each block can be either a server or a storage port.

Point-to-Point Topology

Point-to-point connectivity, the simplest topology available, virtually eliminates the need for a fabric layer (which occupies the middle position in more complex SANs) because servers are directly connected to the storage they use. Strictly speaking, point-to-point topologies don't quite meet the criteria for the more complex storage area networks because there really *is* no network as such.

You're probably thinking, "Hey, isn't that what I'm doing now? All my disks are located inside my servers and they're directly attached." Well, sort of. All servers come with hard drives, but those disks are located *inside* the servers. See Figure 5-3 to see a direct attached storage (DAS) arrangement, which is the way most server hard drives are shipped from the server manufacturer.

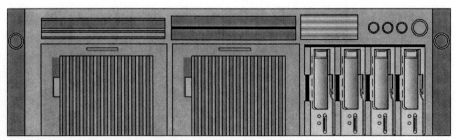

Figure 5-3:
Internal DAS storage.

Actually, a point-to-point topology is a way of using a fast, direct, optical Fibre Channel connection between the server to *external* storage, as shown in Figure 5-4. That keeps the server's hard drives separate from the server itself, so you can do things like upgrade the server without replacing the disks.

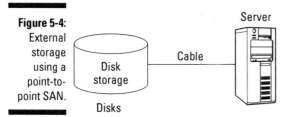

Figure 5-4:
External storage using a point-to-point SAN.

Using an external storage array connected via the point-to-point topology enables sharing that storage among more than one server. This is not possible with DAS (direct attached storage) because a server usually can't connect to the hard drives inside another server.

The number of servers you can connect to a storage array by using a point-to-point topology depends on the number of Fibre Channel ports your storage array has available.

The larger, more expensive storage arrays can come with dozens to hundreds of Fibre Channel ports. The smaller, more modular arrays usually come with between four and eight Fibre Channel ports.

 Point-to-point topology requires a dedicated port on the storage array for each server connected to it. For example, if you have a modular array with four ports, you can share that storage among four servers. But if you have one of the large arrays, you can share that array among 64 or more servers using a direct connection! This is all possible without buying a single hub or switch. All you need is a Fibre Channel HBA in each server and a cable from each server to the storage port on the array.

 Point-to-point is a good topology choice for people on a tight budget with only a few servers that use inexpensive storage, or for a system with a few very large servers (such as a mainframe) with one big, expensive storage array. You don't need any expensive switches or hubs to make this work, which saves on the up-front costs.

Of course, there is a downside to using point-to-point topologies. Because a single storage port can usually handle more than a single server, you end up wasting the bandwidth of the port. You get much more bang for your buck when you can share the expensive storage port with more servers. In order to share a storage port, you have to be able to get data to it from more than one server. This is where the other topologies come in.

Arbitrated Loop Topology

Fibre Channel loop SANs are the simplest SANs to create. A Fibre Channel loop is built by using Fibre Channel hub devices to connect servers to storage.

An *arbitrated loop,* which is based on SAN hubs, derives its name because all the devices connected to the loop of wire inside the hub need to arbitrate for access to the loop. The arbitration is accomplished by the set of rules provided by the FC-AL (Fibre Channel-Arbitrated Loop) protocol.

Back in the day, when we first started working with SANs (many years ago), hubs were the only Fibre Channel devices available. Those were the good old days, when things were simple. You see, hubs are fairly stupid devices. You connect the cable from your server to the hub, connect another cable from your storage to the hub, and badda-bing, badda-boom — you have a SAN. There's nothing left to do because everything just works auto-magically. A lot goes on under the hood, but you never see it. This is the least expensive and simplest method of creating a SAN. The design looks something like Figure 5-5.

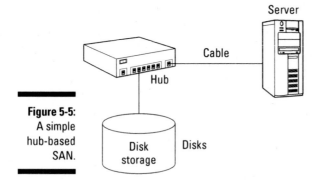

Figure 5-5:
A simple hub-based SAN.

Hubs come in various sizes and from various manufacturers. The connection points on a hub are *ports,* and the number of devices that you can connect to a hub is limited by the number of ports it has. Most hubs have from 6 to 24 ports. Hub devices make creating your first SAN easy; you can add more servers or more storage to the hub ports as your needs dictate. You can see in Figure 5-6 that expanding a hub SAN is simple. As new devices (servers, storage devices, whatever) are added, they're automatically assigned addresses by the FC-AL (Fibre Channel–Arbitrated Loop) protocol — and then they can arbitrate for access to the loop.

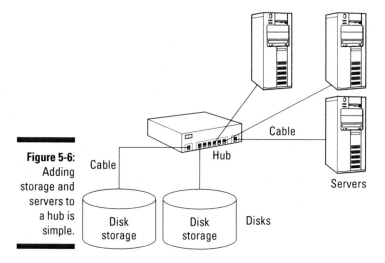

Figure 5-6: Adding storage and servers to a hub is simple.

Cascading hubs

If you run out of ports on the hub, just add another hub. Hooking hubs together to create an expanded loop is called *cascading hubs,* as shown in Figure 5-7. Fibre Channel loops can contain a maximum of 127 devices per loop; each port on the hub represents one device. (Note, however, that because the hub itself takes up one address, the real number of *active* devices is 126.) Thus you can connect hubs when you want to expand your loop to connect more servers and storage.

Although the limit is 127 devices per loop, when connecting other hubs, the manufacturers usually limit the total amount of cascaded hubs to three.

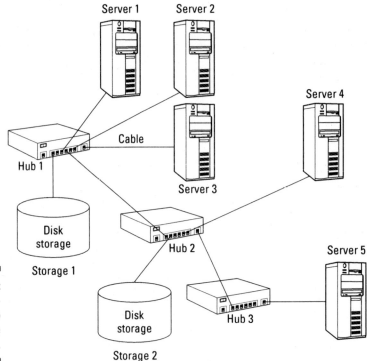

Figure 5-7:
Use cascad-
ing hubs to
add more
ports.

Fibre Channel loop devices have to share the bandwidth of the entire loop. Suppose that you have five servers connected to a single loop. Each server would have to wait its turn for access to the loop to get to its hard drives. The more servers you add, the more time each server has to wait. So adding servers to a single loop can slow things down when each server tries to use the loop.

Most hub vendors allow you to cascade your hubs at least twice, which can give you a total of three hubs connected to create a single loop. If you were using 12-port hubs, this would give you a loop with 36 connections. This is fewer than the maximum of 127 devices in a single loop, but for performance reasons (as mentioned earlier), this is probably all you would ever want to connect to a single loop.

Creating a cascaded loop with three hubs requires at least four of the loop ports to be dedicated to hub connections. The more hubs that you add, the more ports you need to dedicate for inter-hub connections.

Loop of hubs

Compare a cascaded hub solution (refer to Figure 5-7) with connecting your hubs to create a physical loop, as in Figure 5-8.

Creating a physical loop of hubs provides better redundancy for your connections. Redundancy is a good thing because if one of your hubs goes bad, the other devices on the loop might not be affected. (*Redundancy* means that more than one part or path can be used.) True, this topology uses more dedicated hub ports to connect the hubs, but it adds resiliency to the loop. If one of the cables connecting the hubs in a cascaded topology goes bad (as seen in Figure 5-9 in the next section), one or more servers would possibly not be able to connect to the storage.

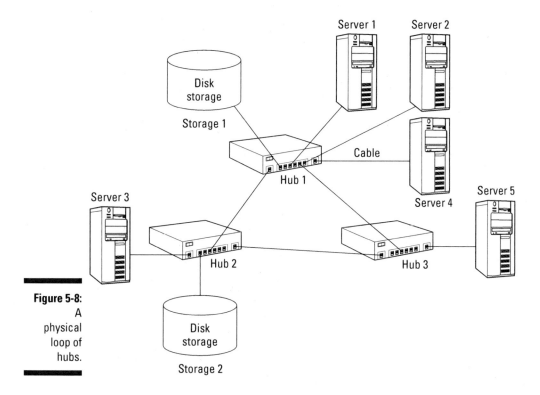

Figure 5-8: A physical loop of hubs.

Creating resilient hub networks

With resilient connections, you use dedicated hub ports solely for inter-hub connections. These connections cannot be used to connect servers or storage, so creating a more resilient network has trade-offs. You lose the use of a port or two for host connections.

Take a close look at Figure 5-9. If the cable connected between Hub 2 and Hub 3 goes bad, it will have no effect on any of the servers connecting to the storage devices on Hub 1 and Hub 2. Server 1 can still access any storage devices in the loop, as can any servers connected to either Hub 1 or Hub 2. However, Server 5 (connected to Hub 3) will lose connection to all the storage devices. This is not good, because Server 5 will go down when it loses its storage connection. To fix this problem, connect things as illustrated in Figure 5-10, which shows a more resilient topology.

Figure 5-10 shows a different kind of problem — a cable failure in a physical loop topology — with an inherent workaround. Resiliency!

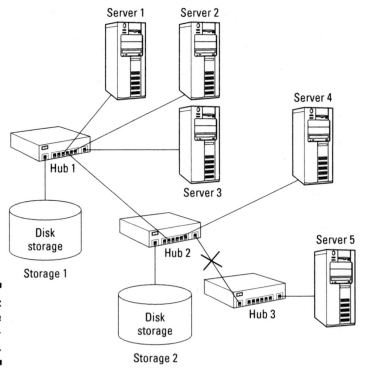

Figure 5-9:
Cable failure with cascaded hubs.

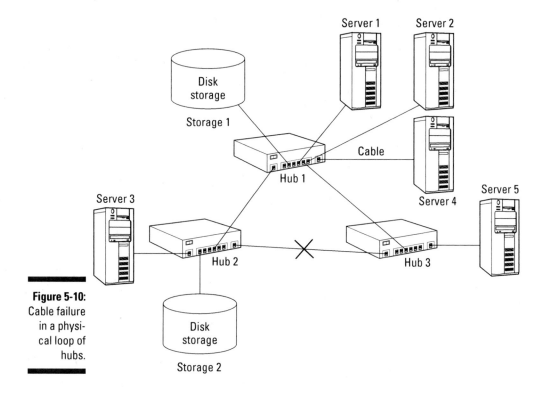

Figure 5-10:
Cable failure
in a physi-
cal loop of
hubs.

If the cable connected between Hub 2 and Hub 3 goes bad in this physical
loop topology, Server 5 still has access to any storage device by using the
alternate path through Hub 1. As you can see, just adding one more cable
between the hubs makes a great deal of difference in the resiliency of the
storage network.

Using resilient connections means using more dedicated ports that cannot
be used to connect servers or storage. In the example in Figure 5-10, however,
the trade-off is minimal, and the benefits outweigh the loss of two more ports.
The loop of hubs in Figure 5-10 requires a total of six dedicated hub ports:
two for each hub used for connecting the hubs. Assuming that you use hubs
that have 12 ports and that you need six ports for the resilient connections,
this would leave a total of 30 ports left over for servers and storage devices:

$(12 \times 3 = 36) - 6 = 30$ ports left over

Fault-tolerant loops

A *fault-tolerant* design, which is another method of adding resiliency to a SAN, uses two of everything in the fabric layer. This way, if any part in the fabric layer fails, another one just like it can take over the load. Most of the time, the fail-over to the redundant part happens transparently; that is, the failure doesn't disrupt normal operations. This design provides not only fault tolerance but also twice the speed to the hard drives if the both paths are active simultaneously. On the downside, creating two paths through two identical hub loops requires twice the amount of hubs, which doubles the cost of the solution.

Figure 5-11 shows a fault-tolerant hub design. With this design, you start configuring the SAN by using two separate hubs. You can then expand the hubs by creating two separate loops of hubs, as shown in Figure 5-12. The addition of more hubs allows more servers and storage to be added to the design. Each side is a mirror image of the other, and each server is connected using dual Host Bus Adapters in the server. This creates two separate paths to the storage. You can lose up to half of all your parts and data traffic can still flow.

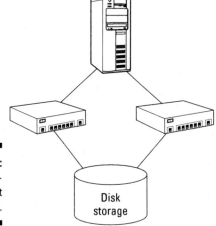

Figure 5-11:
Fault-
tolerant
hub design.

Disk
storage

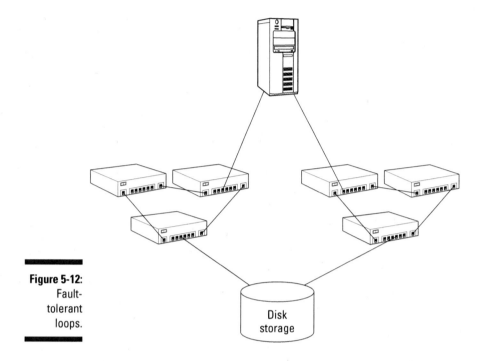

Figure 5-12:
Fault-
tolerant
loops.

Switched Fabric Topology

A *switched fabric* is a collection of switches tied together through inter-switch links to create a *fabric* of switches.

Switched fabrics are more expensive than hub-based loops because switches are a lot smarter than hubs. An average 8-port hub can cost a few thousand dollars, but a large 256-port director-class switch can cost upwards of a hundred thousand dollars. You do get what you pay for, though. Whereas a hub-based arbitrated loop topology can have a maximum of 127 devices per loop, a switched fabric can have up to 64 million devices in it. This is why switches usually come with high-availability features that make them very reliable.

For example, director-class switches have No Single Point of Failure (NSPOF) features: If one part breaks, a redundant part is ready to take over for the failed part. The good news is that electronics is one area where things get cheaper as they get faster! Soon, switch prices will have more intelligence and be cheaper than they are now.

High-availability features include dual power supplies and redundant smart cooling fans. If a power supply blows up in the switch, the other one takes over. If a fan goes dead, the other fans speed up to supply more cooling power. NSPOF features, defined by at least two of everything in the switch, are usually found in the more expensive director-class switches.

Before you attempt to connect two switches, see the section "Understanding Zoning," later in this chapter. Switches need to be set up properly before they're connected to create a switched fabric; otherwise, the switches won't be able to communicate with each other.

Types of SAN switches

Two classes of SAN switches are available: modular class and director class. The differences between the two classes of switches are the amount of available switch ports, the durability and maintainability of the switches, and the speed at which they work.

Older SAN switches run at 1 gigabit per second (or billion bits per second), which was the original Fibre Channel standard. One gigabit per second translates into a data rate of 100 megabytes per second. Newer switches run at 2 to 10 gigabits per second, which translates into a data rate of 200 to 1000 megabytes per second (1000MB is equal to a gigabyte). Thus, you can transfer over twice the amount of data in one second when using the newer 2-, 4-, 8- or 10-gigabit-per-second switches.

Modular switches (see Figure 5-13) are cheaper than director-class switches. They commonly come in 8-, 16-, or 32-port variants, although even higher density modular switches are becoming available. The original 1 gigabit switches used older and larger SC (subscriber connecter) type connectors, while the newer 2-, 4-, 8- and 10-gigabit-per-second switches have higher density LC (Lucent connector) ports, which allows them to have more ports than the older switches. Modular switches have good high-availability features such as redundant power supplies and smart fans. However, modular switches have a single controller component, which is a single point of failure. This is why multiple modular switches are needed to create a fault-tolerant SAN design. Modular switches are available from Brocade (who recently purchased McData), QLogic, Cisco, and other vendors.

Figure 5-13:
Modular-
class
switches.

16-port modular switch

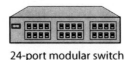
24-port modular switch

32-port modular switch

Director-class switches are expensive and have more ports than modular switches. Port counts usually start between 32 and 64 ports and go up from there. Director-class switches use *blades* of ports that can be swapped out in case of a failure. Directors also have redundant controller components, which are used to run the switch itself.

Each individual part can be maintained without having to bring down the entire switch. If one of the ports goes bad, you can simply remove and replace the blade that has the failed port on it. If one of the controllers goes bad, the surviving controller will automatically take over operation for the entire switch.

Director switches (see Figure 5-14) use fast electronics, are usually faster than modular switches, and can be configured with hundreds of ports. No wonder you can create a large fabric with a single large director switch — or use two of them as separate fabrics for a very efficient and fault-tolerant SAN. The major switch vendors such as Brocade, Cisco, and Qlogic all have director-class switch offerings. Cisco Systems, which is well known for Internet Protocol (IP) network switches, was late to the SAN party, but is beginning to get a lot of traction with their director-class switches.

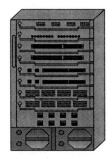

Figure 5-14: Director-class switches.

Choosing which switches to use

Two schools of thought exist when it comes to switched fabric SAN design. One approach is to start with the smaller modular switches and connect them as you grow the SAN. By its distributed nature, using this approach reduces the possibility of a single device failure bringing down the entire SAN. The other approach is to start by consolidating as much as possible onto the more expensive and reliable director-class components. Consolidating decreases the management effort and costs of maintaining many smaller components versus fewer larger ones.

Each approach has its advantages and disadvantages. You can even use combinations of the two approaches. Read on to discover these methods so that you can decide which is best for you.

Using the right bandwidth for the job

You can usually tell the difference in the speed (bandwidth) at which a switch runs by the size of the port connectors that it uses. The older 1 gigabit-per-second switches use the larger SC connectors, and the newer 2-, 4-, 8-, and 10-gigabit-per-second switches use the smaller LC connectors. By the way, the most popular switches as of 2008 are the 4 Gbit variety, since they currently provide the most bang for the buck, as they say.

Since the LC connectors are smaller than SC port connectors, the high-density ports on newer switches have an advantage because they use much less space. As of today, older 1- and 2-gigabit-per-second components are being phased out to make room for the faster 4-, 8-, and 10-Gbps parts. Using LC connectors allowed the switch manufacturers to create smaller, denser switches, which use less space for the same amount of ports.

So how do you determine what speed of switches to use? The answer is simple: Use the fastest switches you can afford to buy. This makes sense for two reasons. First, the older switches are getting hard to find because they're being phased out by the switch vendors. Second, the newer switches are smaller, are backward compatible to the older switches, and have better software running in them.

Although older, slower switches are cheaper — and will get the job done for 90 percent of the applications you run. The newer switches are more maintainable in the long run because parts are more readily available than are parts for the older switches. Also, the vendors will provide new software with the new switches, which might not be backward compatible with older switches. Fibre Channel switches are the core of your SAN fabric, and can account for quite a large investment in time and money. You don't want to go cheap with your switches, and find that in a short time they need to be replaced due to lack of vendor support, or they are not up to the task from a performance perspective.

Trunking and what it's used for

Some SAN switches also come with a technology called *trunking* — a method of using more than a single link between two individual switches, which makes those links behave like a single, bigger link. You can use multiple ports to connect the older switches, but they act like discrete links instead of one big link.

Suppose that you have two older switches hooked together with one cable to make an inter-switch link (ISL).When you connect the switches, a session is established between the switches. The switches use this path for all communication between the switches. If you then add another ISL, that path will be used only if something goes wrong with the first link or the first link is too busy to be used. Two devices communicating through the switches need to create another session across the second link. (See Figure 5-15.)

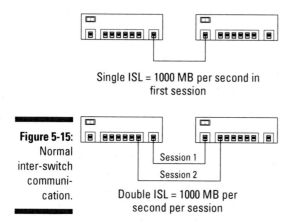

Single ISL = 1000 MB per second in
first session

Figure 5-15:
Normal
inter-switch
communi-
cation.

Session 1

Session 2

Double ISL = 1000 MB per
second per session

With the newer switches from some vendors (such as Brocade), you can create a trunk link that uses multiple ports to create a single ISL. A single trunk built using four individual 10 Gbit links will aggregate the bandwidth of those ports and allow you to pass all traffic among the switches at an astounding 4000 megabytes per second, which equals 4 billion bytes per second (4GB/s) — that's giga*bytes* per second, not giga*bits,* folks! (See Figure 5-16.)

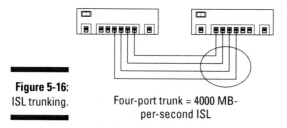

Figure 5-16:
ISL trunking.

Four-port trunk = 4000 MB-
per-second ISL

As you can see, using the newer switches with all this cool technology — which isn't available in older switches, mind you — makes a lot of sense in most cases. Using trunking between switches enables you to not worry so much about where you plug things into the fabric, since it will be harder to "oversubscribe" the ISL connections. (You can find out more on oversubscription and other things that can cause problems in Chapter 4.)

Basic Fabric Topologies

You can choose from a number of methods (topologies) of connecting switches to build a SAN fabric. Which one you use depends on how many servers you need to connect to the SAN, what type of switches you're using, and your budget.

As described earlier in this chapter, a *SAN fabric* is made up of one or more switched fabrics, and a *switched fabric* is a collection of one or more switches connected together through inter-switch link (ISL) ports. A SAN fabric can contain a single switched fabric or hundreds of switched fabrics.

Your first design goal should be to create a resilient SAN that seeks to eliminate single points of failure. Your other design goal is to provide an efficient path from your servers to the storage devices through the SAN. Here is a list of the basic fabric topologies:

- ✔ Dual switch
- ✔ Loop of switches
- ✔ Meshed fabric
- ✔ Star
- ✔ Core-edge

We cover each of these designs in more detail later in the chapter.

Dual switches, the SAN fabric building block

Most new SAN implementations today start small; people feel safer if they start out with only one or two of their critical servers connected to a newly implemented SAN. As they feel more comfortable with the SAN, they start adding servers to it. You can start out with one 8-port switch and add more switches as your SAN grows. This simple implementation is fine — except that if your single switch has a problem, your servers wind up with downtime.

The best way to implement a small SAN is to start with two 16- or 24-port switches. You'll probably outgrow 8-port switches very soon, so it doesn't make sense to use them. Use 8-port switches only if you will *never* need more than 16 total switch ports.

Using two modular switches is what we use as a basic SAN building block. We call this the *SAN cell*. Each switch acts as its own fabric. This means that your basic building block starts with two SAN fabrics, Fabric A and Fabric B, each consisting of a single modular switch. (See Figure 5-17.)

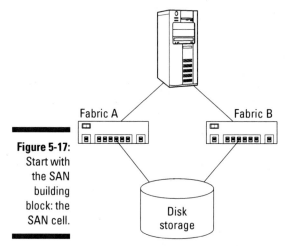

Figure 5-17:
Start with the SAN building block: the SAN cell.

The SAN cell shown in Figure 5-17 is very reliable because you have No Single Points of Failure (NSPOF) in the fabric layer. Using only two inexpensive 16-port switches for the SAN cell gives you a total of 32 available ports for servers and storage. The servers have two paths into the switches, from which there are also two paths from each storage device.

Using a single server and a single storage device requires four ports in the cell: two for the server and two for the storage. This creates a SAN cell that is fault tolerant. Using 16-port switches as the cell, you can have a total of 14 dual attached servers (two paths each) and a storage array with one path to each switch. Using larger 24- or 32-port modular switches will provide more ports as required.

Using two paths from the servers into two separate switched fabrics has many advantages. If one path fails, the other path automatically takes over for the failed path. You can also do normal maintenance to any part of the SAN without having to plan for downtime. Path fail-over requires software running on the host to detect the failure and transfer data to the surviving path. Most host-based path fail-over software can also load balance your data across both paths. Load balancing allows data to travel across whichever path is least in use at the moment.

Most paths fail because of a single component going bad in the path: A switch goes bad, a cable gets tripped over, or an HBA in the server goes bad. (See Chapter 4 for more on what makes failures occur.) Using path fail-over software on the host allows the data moving across that path to automatically be moved to the surviving path. When the path is fixed, the software automatically allows data across that path again. No intervention is required. Of course, this all requires two HBAs in your servers, as we describe next.

Using two HBAs

Connecting to two separate fabrics requires at least two HBAs in every server. Each HBA is connected to a separate switch. Most SAN vendors have software (called a *fail-over filter driver*) that you can buy (or even get for free in some cases) that enables you to place two or more HBAs in a server. Using two HBAs costs you more money when adding servers to the SAN, but the benefits outweigh the costs.

During routine maintenance of your storage network, you sometimes need to take down one of the devices in order to add functionality or fix problems. With only one path through the SAN to the storage array, this routine maintenance requires planned downtime.

Using two HBAs in every server can eliminate this planned downtime because you can work on one half of the SAN at a time. While you update the first half, all input/output (I/O) from the server to the storage is redirected to the remaining path through the fail-over filter driver. When you're done with the first path and bring the path back online, I/O resumes on that path. You can then work on the other path.

Using path-management software

Path-management software makes path fail-over transparent (no human intervention required) in a SAN. The most rudimentary path failover software only provides simple path failover functions as mentioned in the previous section. More advanced path-management software runs on the servers, and also provides more advanced functions like load balancing, which is a method of using all available paths to the storage to spread the I/O load from the server across all paths. If one of the paths fails, a surviving path handles all the I/O for the failed path. If you use two HBAs in a server connected to separate SAN devices, you can get twice the throughput to your hard drives. The more HBAs you put in a server, the more bandwidth you get to your hard drives. More bandwidth gets you higher data throughput, which means that your applications can run faster.

SAN vendors tend to use catchy marketing names for their path-management software. Table 5-2 lists some of the common path-management software vendors and names.

Table 5-2	Common Path-Management Software	
Vendor	*Path-Management Software*	*URL*
Hewlett-Packard	AutoPath, SecurePath	`www.hp.com`
Microsoft	MPIO	`www.microsoft.com`
Hitachi	Dynamic Link Manager	`www.hds.com`
EMC	PowerPath	`www.emc.com`
IBM	RDAC, MultiPath Driver	`www.ibm.com`
Sun	MPXIO	`www.sun.com`
VERITAS	Dynamic Multipathing (DMP)	`www.veritas.com`

Although the software is known by different names, it all provides the same basic functionality: path fail-over and load balancing.

Loop-of-switches topology

Another switch topology is the *loop of switches*. It's similar to the loop of hubs discussed earlier in (well, yeah) the "Loop of hubs" section. The basic technique is to create two separate fabrics of three switches each. (See Figure 5-18.)

The two switch loops are separate fabrics: Fabric A and Fabric B. Using only 16-port switches, this design provides for two fault-resistant fabrics of 48 ports each, for a total of 96 ports in the SAN. You can add more switches or use larger switches with more ports in each loop to *scale up* (make larger) this topology. By using this design, with two HBAs in every server, you can lose an entire fabric and still survive. If all the switches in Fabric A go down, you can still get to your disk storage through Fabric B.

The only problem with this design is how many switches you need to go through to get from the servers to the storage. As you add more switches, you add more hops to get to the storage. A *hop* is similar to hopping across stones in a stream to get to the other side. The wider the stream, the more stones you need to hop across. Unless you have *really* long legs, it takes time to hop across each stone.

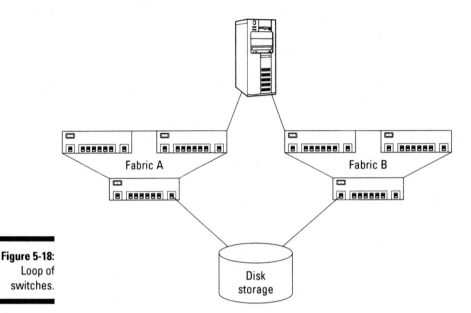

Figure 5-18:
Loop of
switches.

The same is true in a network. Each hop adds about a millisecond (ms) of latency to the data stream. *Latency* is the time required for the data to travel through the network. Each switch that needs to be traversed to get to storage adds one hop. The design goal is to minimize the number of hops from the servers to their storage. You can do this within the loop of switches topology by locating the storage closer to the servers. This will minimize the hop count, as shown in Figure 5-19.

In Figure 5-18, you can see that access to the storage through either fabric has to go through at least two switches (meaning two hops to storage), which will add about 2ms of latency to the data path. Figure 5-19 shows that data from Server 1 needs to travel through only one switch to get to Storage 1 but needs to travel across two switches to arrive at Storage 2. Access to Storage 1 has less latency and is faster than access to Storage 2. Storage and server placement can make a huge difference in performance in SAN fabric designs.

To minimize latency, minimize the amount of hardware and the distance that your data needs to traverse.

Meshed fabric topology

The next fabric design is the *meshed fabric topology*. Requiring a minimum of four switches per fabric, a meshed fabric always has an alternate path through the mesh to an available switch, making it a highly resilient design. (See Figure 5-20.)

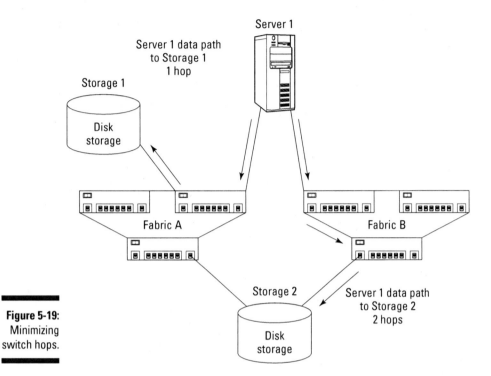

Figure 5-19:
Minimizing
switch hops.

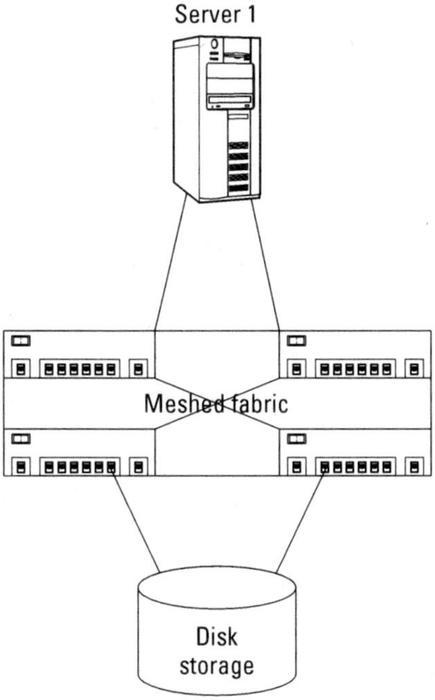

Figure 5-20:
Meshed
fabric
topology.

A single meshed fabric is resilient because every switch is connected to every other switch. If any path between the switches fails, data can be re-routed through an alternate path. Because a meshed fabric requires a minimum of four switches, using 16-port switches gives you a total of 64 ports in a single fabric. You can use dual meshed fabrics, as Fabric A and Fabric B, to add further redundancy. This would require eight 16-port switches, for a total of 128 ports in the SAN. (See Figure 5-21.)

Meshed fabrics are a great design for resiliency. As you can see by Figure 5-21, the meshed fabric can survive multiple cable and switch failures and still be active. The only problem with using meshed fabrics is the number of ISLs that are required.

An *ISL link* is the cable used between the switches to connect them. In a single meshed fabric, you need to set aside at least three ports from every switch as an ISL link. (Refer to Figure 5-20.) That's a total of 12 ports that cannot be used for connecting servers or storage to the SAN. Using dual meshed fabrics requires 24 SAN ports for the ISL links. If ISL trunking is used, even more ports are lost just to connect the switches together (although speed is improved between the switches). Hey, there's no such thing as a free lunch!

Take a look at Figure 5-22. As you add more switches to a meshed fabric, you get to a point where you need more ISL links for switch connections than you have left over to connect servers and storage.

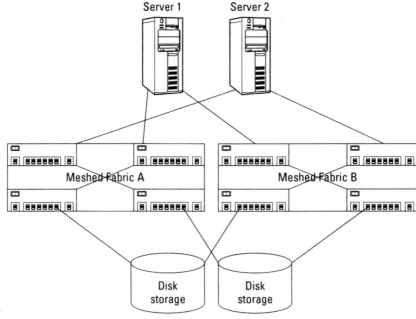

Figure 5-21:
Dual
meshed
fabric
topology.

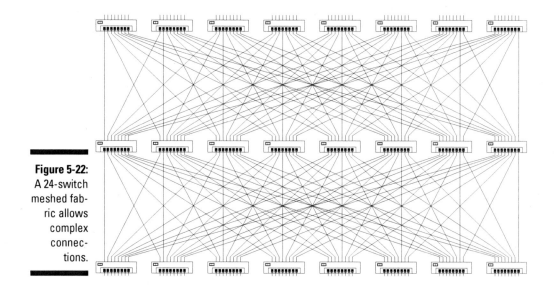

Figure 5-22:
A 24-switch meshed fabric allows complex connections.

Figure 5-22 shows a modified meshed fabric using 24 16-port switches. (Normally a meshed fabric must have every switch connected to every other switch.) This one is a pretty large fabric. (You can have a total of 239 switches connected in a single fabric, although I've never seen one that large yet.)

As you can see from the figure, every port on the switches in the middle is used to connect to the other switches. With a total of 384 switch ports in this fabric (24 × 16), you have only 128 ports left over from the 384 total to provide connectivity to servers and storage. This means that you lose a total of 256 ports to create a meshed fabric consisting of 24 16-port switches. (Kind of a waste of ports, don't you think?)

Star topology

Because meshed fabrics are a good design for resiliency but tend to waste ports when you add more switches to increase the available ports, someone came up with the idea of a star topology, which provides many more available host and storage ports in a single fabric. (See Figure 5-23.)

Note the lone 16-port switch in the center of this star fabric. Using the star topology requires one switch port for each switch at the edge of the star. The core switch in the star has all 16 ports used as ISL links to connect to the other switches at the edge. By using 16-port switches, the star topology yields 272 total switch ports per fabric. Of those 272 ports, 32 are designated as ISL links. This leaves a total of 240 ports that can be used to connect servers and storage.

Star Fabric Tolopogy

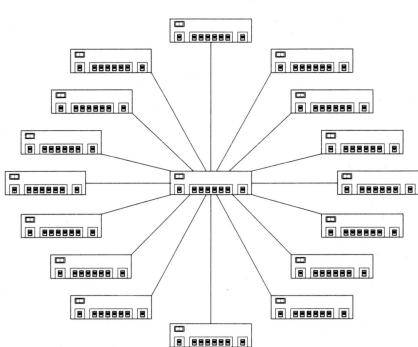

Figure 5-23:
Star fabric
topology.

The star topology allows for much more efficient use of switch ports than the mesh topology. The problem with this star topology is that you have a single point of failure in the center of the star. A single switch links all the rest of the switches together. And if that switch fails, the whole fabric goes down. You can alleviate this problem by creating a hybrid star called a *star ring* topology. (See Figure 5-24.)

To create this topology, you just need to connect all the edge switches in a ring. This requires only two more ports per switch, which is still more efficient than a mesh topology with this many switches. The problem with the star ring is that if the core switch fails, the only way for data traffic to travel is around the ring. This costs way too many hops and makes latency an issue. The fix for this is the core-edge design.

Star Ring Fabric Tolopogy

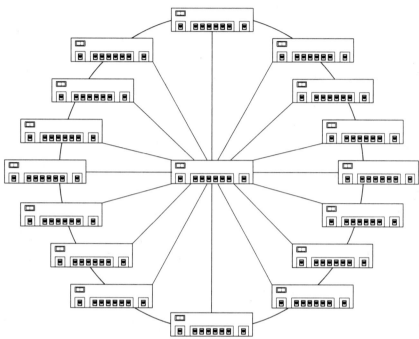

Figure 5-24:
Star ring
hybrid
topology.

Core-edge topology

The *core-edge* topology is a type of star topology but with two switches at the
core. The two core switches make a difference in the resiliency of the network. Every switch is connected to both core switches, which provide redundancy at the core. The two edge layers in this design are the host layer and
the storage layer. This design fits into the fabric layer approach, separating
each layer with its own switches. (See Figure 5-25.)

The core-edge topology is very scalable and provides great reliability. To
increase the size of the fabric — and therefore the available ports — you
simply add more core switches. You then have more core ports to add edge
switches to. The design in Figure 5-25 shows 12 16-port switches in a core-
edge topology. This design yields a total of 192 switch ports in the SAN. A
total of 40 ports in the fabric are dedicated as ISL links. This leaves a total of
152 ports available for server and storage connections. That's a pretty good
ratio of useful ports to dedicated ISL ports.

The core-edge design is by far the most popular large-scale fabric topology in use today.

You can also add more ports to the core-edge design by adding another complete core-edge as two complete fabrics. All your servers then get connected to both fabrics as Fabric A and Fabric B, just as in the loop-of-switches design. Server access to storage over two complete core-edge fabrics creates a very fault-tolerant SAN design . . . but it sure will be expensive.

You can use fewer switches in this topology, though. Instead of dedicating two 16-port switches as core switches, you can eliminate one half of the star. This leaves you a core-edge design in which the storage layer is connected to the core. (See Figure 5-26.)

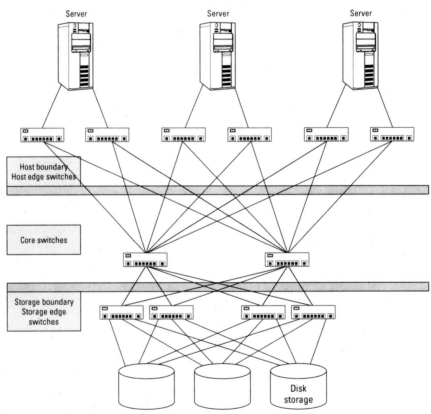

Figure 5-25:
Core-edge
topology.

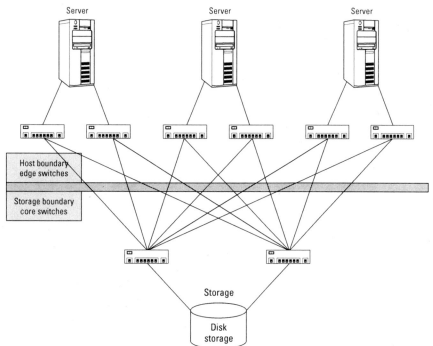

Figure 5-26:
Storage
core-edge
topology.

In Figure 5-26, you can see 8 16-port switches for a total of 128 ports available in this fabric. There are 24 dedicated ISL ports, leaving a total of 104 ports left over for servers and storage. You'll also notice from Figure 5-26 that only seven of the storage core ports are being used. Instead of connecting more storage to those switches, you can connect more switches to those ports.

If you leave available ports for more storage, 8 ports are left on each switch to add more switches: 2×8 switches at 16 ports each, minus the two required ISL links (this leaves 14 ports per switch), gives you another 224 ports for server connections. One more way to increase your port count in the core-edge design is to replace the core switches with larger, director-class switches. (See Figure 5-27.)

Using director-class switches at the core not only gives you many more ports available but also makes the core switches more robust. Director-class switches are usually more reliable and have many more ports available than modular switches. The director switches need to be more reliable because they have so many more ports. A failure of a director-class switch affects a lot more servers than does the failure of a single 16-port switch.

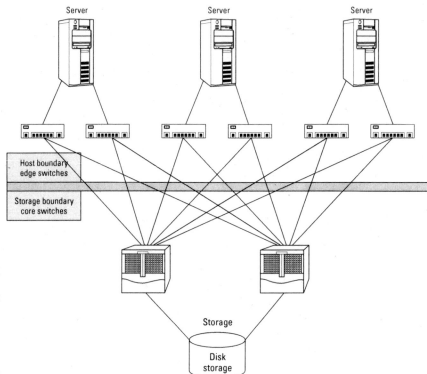

Figure 5-27:
Director-
class
core-edge.

Currently, director-class switches can be configured with multiple "port blades" or "port modules" and can have well over 300 ports. As time marches forward, and needs increase, versions will come out that will have many more ports than that, though. The switches shown in Figure 5-27 are the 64-port variety. Using those two switches at the core enables you to connect to 64 edge switches using two dedicated ISL links per edge (64 per core switch per side).

If the edge switches are the modular 16-port variety, that gives you 1,024 (64 × 16) switch ports for servers and storage. *Now* you're talking about a big fabric. By the way, you can expand this topology either by using director-class switches at the edge or another complete core-edge as a separate fabric; director-class switches can be configured with hundreds of ports.

Two core-edge fabrics of this type yield a total of 2,048 storage ports for the SAN. That's a lot of ports. You might never find a fabric *that* big because managing all those ports is very hard. Most large fabric designs end up being around 300–400 ports before another fabric is started. ***Hint:*** You can have a maximum of 239 switches in a single fabric today.

Understanding Zoning

Zoning, a method of SAN security, is used to segregate devices connected to a switched fabric. If you're familiar with IP networking, then you can relate a zone to a subnet — or even better, a virtual local area network (VLAN) in an IP network. Actually, that technology has been migrated in the storage arena by Cisco, who's director-class switches support the notion of a VSAN, or virtual SAN fabric, which provides error isolation and other benefits.

Zoning is available only in a switched fabric topology because hubs don't have the needed intelligence to perform zoning. Zoning can be done on an individual switch or across multiple switches in the same fabric. (See Figure 5-28.)

Zoning is typically used to prevent servers that are running different operating systems from seeing each other's storage in the SAN. This is important when multiple operating systems share the same switched fabric. For example, Windows is a greedy operating system. When you boot up a Windows server, one of its first actions is to try to locate all the storage devices that it can find. When it finds a hard drive, it writes a signature on that drive to mark ownership of it.

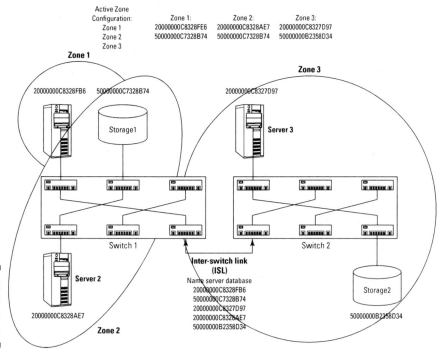

Figure 5-28:
Switched
fabric
zoning.

Writing a signature on the hard drive makes it unusable by Unix servers. If the hard drive originally belonged to a Unix server in the SAN, the Unix server won't be able to read the disk anymore, and the Unix server's data will be lost. This is one of the reasons you need to *zone out* (that is, block and keep separate) Windows server storage from Unix server storage in a SAN.

Zoning is also important because it can be used to keep test system storage separate from production systems, keep SAN traffic localized within each zone, and separate different vendor storage arrays in the same fabric. In other words, zoning can be used as a method of making the SAN more secure.

Imagine that you're running an application that uses Web servers to connect to a back-end database that uploads product information to people on the Internet. The Web servers must be on a network that has access to the Internet, and the database server is probably connected only to your internal corporate network — which is as it should be, from a security standpoint.

You need some sort of security on your internal database storage so no hackers can see it. Your Web server storage can be in one zone in the SAN (accessible to the Internet), and your database server storage can be in another zone (secure from access to the Internet). This allows you to share the same SAN and have good security at the same time.

Zoning can also be used to separate different management environments. If you have different people managing your Windows servers and Unix servers, you can place those servers and their storage in different zones. The two zones keep the two environments completely separate, even though they share the same switched fabric. This enables the Unix administrators to manage their environment, secure from anyone else messing with their hard drives.

Zoning also enables different ports on the same storage array to be included in different secure zones. Then two secure environments can share the same physical storage unit.

Using small zones consisting of just a single server and the storage ports that it needs can decrease the amount of management traffic in the SAN. Using small zones can also help performance by limiting the amount of servers that can share a single storage port. (See Figure 5-29.)

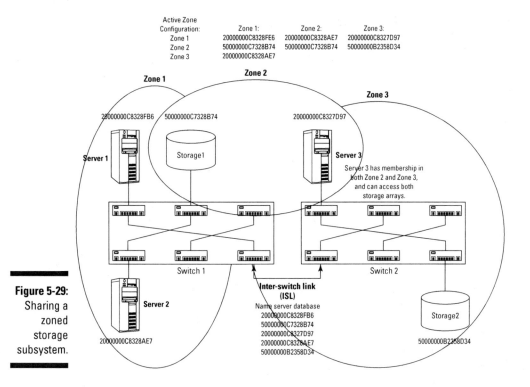

Active Zone
Configuration:
Zone 1
Zone 2
Zone 3

	Zone 1:	Zone 2:	Zone 3:
	20000000C8328FE6	20000000C8328AE7	20000000C8327D97
	50000000C7328B74	50000000C7328B74	50000000B2358D34
	20000000C8328AE7		

Figure 5-29:
Sharing a
zoned
storage
subsystem.

The parts of a zone

Zones are set up in a certain way, divided into two basic parts:

  ✓ **The zones themselves:** A *zone* is a specific list of switch ports or device addresses. You can have multiple active zones within an active zone configuration.

  ✓ **The zone configuration:** A *zone configuration* is the collection of multiple zones that becomes active when the configuration is saved. Only a single zone configuration can be active at any one time in a single fabric. A zone configuration is also referred to as a *zone set* because it consists of (what else?) a set of zones.

When you want to use zoning, you first group individual switch ports or fabric addresses (World Wide Names, or WWNs) into zones. You then group individual zones together into a zone configuration and, finally, activate a zone configuration.

You can create as many zones as you want in a fabric. You can group different zones into as many zone configurations as you want, but only one zone configuration can be active in the fabric at a time.

Types of zoning

Two types of zones are available in a SAN (detailed in the upcoming subsections):

- ✔ **Soft zoning:** Zones are identified by World Wide Name
- ✔ **Hard zoning:** Zones are identified by physical switch port

Soft zoning

Soft zoning is a method of grouping individual World Wide Names (WWNs) in the fabric into a zone set. *World Wide Names* are the 64-bit address assigned to every object connected to a switched fabric. (See Chapter 3 for more on WWNs.) Instead of using the physical-port information to create members of a zone set, you use the WWN address(es) of the device(s) connected to the port. (See Figure 5-30.)

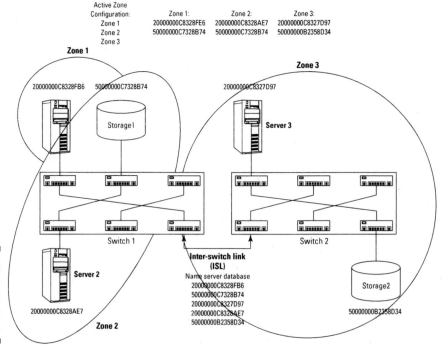

Figure 5-30:
Soft zoning, using World Wide Names.

WWN zoning (soft zoning) is more flexible than port zoning (hard zoning) because the zone information is based on the device's address instead of the port on the switch that it's connected to. If a switch port goes bad and you move the device connected to that port to a different port, you need to change the zone information to reflect the changed port before the device connected to the new port will work again in the fabric. By using WWN zoning, the address will have moved with the device, so no zone changes are needed.

Hard zoning

Hard zoning is a method of grouping individual physical switch ports in a switched fabric together into a *zone* that only allows communication between physical ports on the switches. (See Figure 5-31.) Only the physical ports in the zone can communicate with each other. No other ports in the fabric can communicate with those ports, and members of that zone set cannot communicate with any other ports in the fabric.

Zone members can communicate only with other members of their zone. A zone set can accommodate multiple zones; switch ports can be members of multiple zone sets. If a switch port is made a member of multiple zone sets, it can communicate with the ports of all the zone sets that it has membership with. The same holds true for soft zone members (see the preceding section).

Hard zoning at the level of physical ports is the most secure method of zoning.

You can mix domain and port names along with WWNs in the same zone, but after you do, all the ports revert to soft zoning. (See Figure 5-32.)

Zone alias names

An *alias* is a custom name that you can assign to switch ports and WWN addresses in a zone. You use an alias to rename the port names of the switch and the WWNs of the HBAs connected to the switches with something that makes more sense to a human. Trying to figure out what has access to what by using port IDs and/or WWN addresses is hard. Using more human-understandable naming makes better practical sense.

As an example, suppose you have four servers and one storage array in your SAN, as in Figure 5-33. This is your production SAN. Two of the servers run an Oracle database under Unix, and the other two run your mail system under Windows NT. The servers each have two HBAs apiece, connected to the storage array through two different switches. As you can see from the figure, the switch ports assume the address of the HBA of the server that's plugged into it.

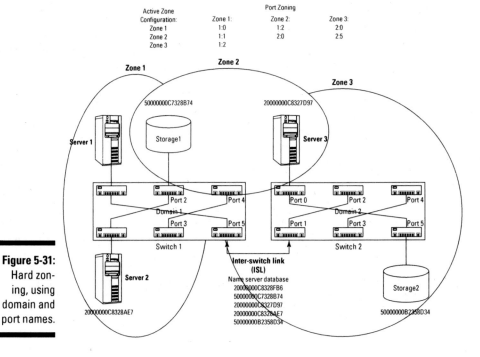

Figure 5-31:
Hard zoning, using domain and port names.

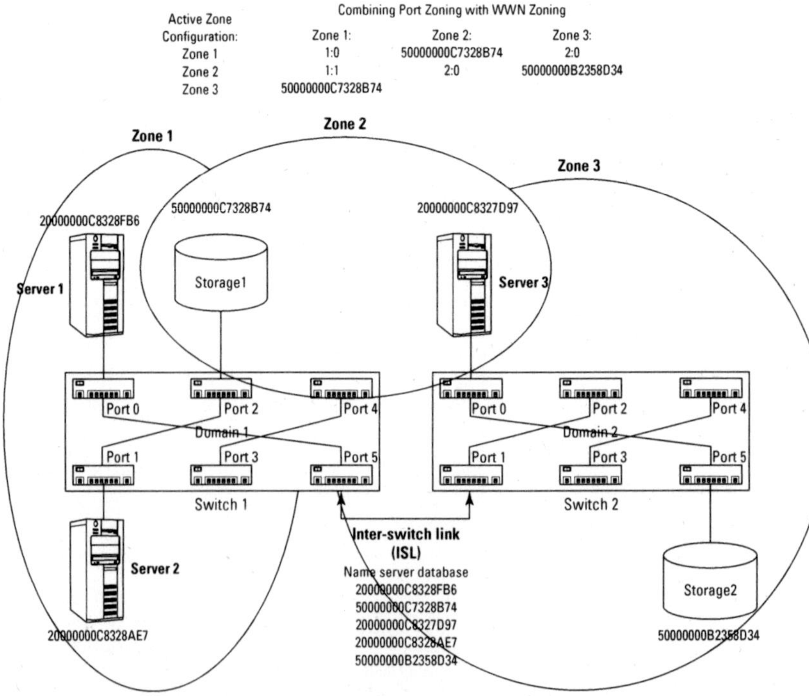

Figure 5-32:
Combining port names and World Wide Names in a zone.

With an alias, you can rename the addresses of each server HBA to something that makes more sense to you — and do the same to the storage ports they're assigned to in the switch. Instead of using the WWNs of the HBAs for `mail server 1` in the zones, you can actually call it `Mail_1A`. The other HBA can be called `Mail_1B`. The different zones can be called `Oracle` and `Mail`. (Feel the headaches receding already? Good.)

The Brocade switch commands used to create the zone information in Figure 5-33 would be as follows:

```
admin> cfgCreate "Production", "Mail_Zone; Oracle_Zone"
admin> zoneCreate "Mail_Zone", "Mail1A; Mail2A; Mail1B;
          Mail2B; Mail_disk"

admin> zoneCreate "Oracle_Zone", "Oracle1A; Oracle2A;
          Oracle1B; Oracle2B; Oracle_Disk"
```

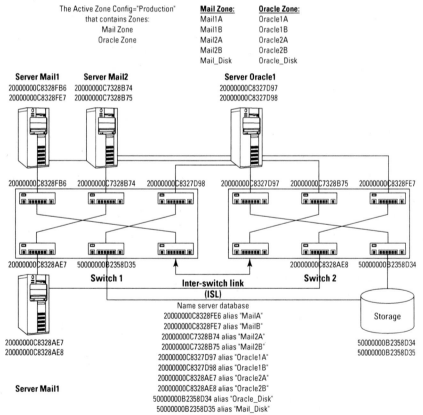

Figure 5-33: Sample zone alias naming.

```
admin> aliCreate «Mail1A», «20:00:00:00:C8:32:8F:E6"
admin> aliCreate «Mail1B», «20:00:00:00:C8:32:8F:E7"
admin> aliCreate «Mail2A», «20:00:00:00:C7:32:8B:74"
admin> aliCreate «Mail2B», «20:00:00:00:C7:32:8B:75"
admin> aliCreate "Oracle1A", "20:00:00:00:C8:32:7D:97"
admin> aliCreate "Oracle1B", "20:00:00:00:C8:32:7D:98"
admin> aliCreate "Oracle2A", "20:00:00:00:C8:32:8A:E7"
admin> aliCreate "Oracle2B", "20:00:00:00:C8:32:8A:E8"
admin> aliCreate "Mail_Disk", "50:00:00:00:B2:35:8D:35"
admin> aliCreate "Oracle_Disk", "50:00:00:00:B2:35:8D:34"

admin> cfgEnable "Production"
zone config "Production" is in effect
```

To create the zones and make them active, run through the Initial Switch
Setup section that follows and then come back here and enter these commands before exiting your session with the switch. You need not enter this
information into any more than one switch in a fabric; that's because the
zone information is shared among all connected switches.

Initial Switch Setup

When you connect switches together with a cable, that connection is an *inter-
switch link* (ISL). When switches are connected together by an ISL, they share
information. The list of device addresses connected to each switch is shared
among the switches so that the devices can communicate with each other.
All zone information is combined among the switches. Accordingly, when you
name things in each switch (alias names, for example), those names must
remain unique when you connect the switches together.

Every switch is the master of its own universe before it's connected to
another switch. The switch's kingdom is called its *domain*. Every switch
domain has a domain ID associated with it. Switch-domain IDs default to
domain ID 0 (zero). Therefore, before you connect switches together, make
sure that you set each switch's domain ID to a unique number. When you
connect two or more switches together, the domain ID can be used to figure
out who's who.

The switches use their domain ID, along with the WWN address of the
devices connected to them, to route information among the devices connected to different switches. The first step when setting up your switches is
to connect to each switch and make sure that the domain IDs are unique.

In the next section, we discuss how to do the initial setup of a modular Brocade
switch. We chose Brocade switches because they're the most prevalent in the
current installed base of SAN fabrics today. There is not enough room in this

book to go through every vendor's switch setup, so we will focus on a single vendor for now. If you purchase a Cisco switch, and you currently know how to work with the Cisco IOS software on their network switches, it's fairly straightforward. Qlogic switches are also very easy to install and configure.

For more information on setting up a Cisco switch, point your Web browser to www.cisco.com, and do a search on *Cisco MDS SAN-OS Configuration Guides.* For Qlogic switches, go to www.qlogic.com, click the support tab on the top of the Qlogic home page, and search for *SANbox configuration guide.*

All the major switch vendors have their installation and configuration guides available for download. After all, they want you to buy their products! If you don't feel comfortable hacking away at the user interface of your brand new SAN fabric switch, then by all means, buy installation services through your vendor. You'll be happy you did — and you can always look over the vendor's shoulder while he configures everything to make sure he does it right (and learn how it works as it happens).

Setting up a Brocade switch

The first step is to unpack your switches and power them on. Follow the user's manual that came with your switch to make sure that you have the correct power requirements and all that other good stuff so that you don't blow the switch up when you power it on.

Every switch comes with a network connection so that you can manage the switch from a remote terminal. The default IP address that comes with each switch can usually be found on a label on the top of the switch. Have your IP network administrator use that address to install the switches so that you can see it from your network.

From any computer on your network, open a communication session to the switch.

- ✔ From an NT server, start the communication session by choosing Start⬦ Run and entering **CMD** in the Run dialog box that opens. A new screen will open. Connect to the switch by typing **telnet *<IP address of switch>*** at the command prompt. This will open up a *Telnet session,* which is geek-speak for a communication session with the switch.

- ✔ From a Unix server, open a new command window and then connect to the switch by typing **telnet *<IP address of switch>*** at the command prompt. This will open up a Telnet session.

To connect to the switch, you need to type in a username and password. (Hey, security is a good thing!) When your Telnet session tries to connect to the switch, a screen pops up and asks you for the username and password.

The default username is `admin`, and the default password is `password` (all lowercase). After you're connected to the switch, you can always change the username and password to something else. Just issue the `passwd` command at the switch's command prompt:

```
switchName:userName> passwd
```

Step 1: Name the switch

The first step is to name the switch. Note that Brocade switch commands are case sensitive. Type the commands exactly as shown. You can use any name that you want for your switches, but make sure that each switch uses a different name. To name the switch in this example to switch1, type **switchName "switch1"** at the `switch:admin>` prompt on the screen, and then press Enter.

Note the use of double quotation marks around the switch name. You must enter those quotation marks to specify `switch1`.

You will see a message reading `Updating flash`. This means that the switch is recording the new name into the switch's memory. The `switch:admin>` prompt reappears when it's finished.

```
switch:admin> switchName "switch1"
Updating flash...
```

Step 2: Set the domain ID

To set the domain ID of the switch, the switch has to be disabled first. Disabling the switch takes it offline so no SAN traffic can move through it.

To disable the switch, type **switchDisable** at the `switch:admin>` prompt, as in the following:

```
switch:admin> switchDisable
```

Switch commands are case sensitive.

After you type the command and press Enter, you'll see all the port lights on the switch go from solid green to a flashing amber color. The `switch:admin>` prompt will return when the switch is disabled. Now you can run the `configure` command. At the `switch:admin>` prompt, type **configure** and then press Enter. The following will appear:

```
switch:admin> configure
Configure...
Fabric parameters (yes, y, no, n): [no] yes
```

```
Virtual Channel parameters (yes, y, no, n): [no]
Arbitrated Loop parameters (yes, y, no, n): [no]
System services (yes, y, no, n): [no]
```

When you run the `configure` command, you will be asked a number of questions about which parameters of the switch you want to configure. Type **yes** to fabric parameters (line 3) and then press Enter to take the default no answer for each of the remaining parameters.

You'll then be asked questions about fabric parameters settings and prompted for a response to each question. The only thing that you're concerned with is the switch's domain ID. Because this is the first switch in your SAN, set the domain ID to 1.

To change the domain ID of the switch, type **1** when prompted for the domain ID (line 4). Press Enter to accept the default parameters for everything else.

```
switch:admin> configure
Configure...
Fabric parameters (yes, y, no, n): [no] yes
Domain: (1..239) [1]
BB credit: (1..16) [16]
R_A_TOV: (4000..120000) [10000]
E_D_TOV: (1000..5000) [2000]
Data field size: (256..2112) [2112]
Non-SCSI Tachyon Mode: (0..1) [0]
Disable Device Probing: (0..1) [0]
Unicast-only Operation: (0..1) [0]
VC Encoded Address Mode: (0..1) [1]
Per-frame Route Priority: (0..1) [0]
Virtual Channel parameters (yes, y, no, n): [no] yes
VC Link Control: (0..1) [0]
VC Class 2: (2..5) [2]
VC Class 3: (2..5) [3]
VC Multicast: (6..7) [7]
VC Priority 2: (2..3) [2]
VC Priority 3: (2..3) [2]
VC Priority 4: (2..3) [2]
VC Priority 5: (2..3) [2]
VC Priority 6: (2..3) [3]
VC Priority 7: (2..3) [3]
Arbitrated Loop parameters (yes, y, no, n): [no] yes
Send FAN frames?: (0..1) [1]
System services (yes, y, no, n): [no] yes
rstatd (on, off): [off] on
rusersd (on, off): [off] on
Disable Translative Mode: (0..1) [1]
```

When you're finished, the `switch:admin>` prompt will return.

Step 3: Enable the switch with its new ID

To enable the switch again, enter the `switchEnable` command at the `switch:admin>` prompt and then press Enter. The following will appear:

```
switch:admin> switchEnable
value = 0 = 0x0
10 9 8 7 6 5 4 3 2 1
fabric: Principal switch
fabric: Domain 1
```

After you type the `switchEnable` command, the switch will reboot itself. The switch will run all kinds of diagnostics as it reboots, and you'll see all kinds of stuff flash by on your screen. When the switch finishes rebooting, it returns with the `switch:admin>` prompt.

At this point, all you have to do is log off from the switch to close your session. The switch is now configured, ready to participate in a SAN.

To log off from the switch, enter the `logout` command at the `switch:admin>` prompt. Press Enter, and you'll be logged out of the switch. You can now close the Telnet session window by clicking the X on the top-right corner of the window.

```
switch:admin> logout
Connection closed.
```

This finishes your session with this switch. Now you just do the same thing with the other switch.

Use a different switch name for the other switch, such as `switch2`, and use a different domain ID for the switch, such as domain ID 2.

We recommend keeping the domain ID number the same as the number in the switch name. As an example, switch name `switch12` should use domain ID 12.

That's it! You're ready to rock and roll! Just plug in the cables and go. Well, maybe *almost* ready to go. You still need to set up the storage array, create LUNS, set up zoning, implement LUN security . . . you know, the usual. The other chapters in this book will help you accomplish those tasks. It's still usually best to have your vendor set everything up for you first, and have them document everything. Once everything is up and running, you can simply hop on the switch and play with the commands to learn more. Simply save the configuration first before you play with the `configUpload` command as follows:

```
switch:admin> configUpload
Protocol (scp or ftp) [ftp]: ftp
Server Name or IP Address [host]: 192.1.2.3
User Name [user]: b
File Name [config.txt]: /pub/configurations/config.txt
Password: xxxxx

configUpload complete: All config parameters are uploaded.
switch:admin>
```

Setting up an original McData (Brocade) director switch

Director-class switches are a bit more complex than plain-vanilla, 16-port modular switches. The McData director comes with EFC Manager software, which is used to set up and maintain the switch. Setting up a director-class switch improperly can really screw up your storage network. Our advice here is to ask your SAN vendor to help you set up the director switch.

The instruction manual can be ordered directly from Brocade at www. brocade.com.

Best Practices — Tips from the Trenches

You can see that you have a lot of choices when designing a SAN. So how do you figure out what's right for you? We've been designing SANs for quite some time now, and we've found that there is really no clear answer that works equally well for everyone. A one-size-fits-all solution just doesn't exist. From our experience, though, we have found certain designs that work really well. We call these the *best practices* for SAN design.

Keep in mind that your SAN design is usually done by your storage-array vendor, so you really shouldn't have to worry about it that much. Each storage vendor knows what design works best for its products.

But what if the person from your vendor doing your design just wants to rip you off by selling you something that's really overkill for your company? Or what if that person was out partying all night before doing your design? You need to do your homework to make sure that the design and topology being recommended to you are actually good for your business — and to keep your vendors honest.

When to choose a director-class switch

Choosing whether to use a director-class switch or a modular switch is a fairly easy proposition. The answer to this question is easy: It depends on your budget. Sixteen-port switches, for example, are cheaper than switches that offer hundreds of ports.

Always use a director-class switch if you can afford it, because they have more available ports, are more reliable, and enable you to connect a lot of servers and storage devices without having to manage tons of individual switches. As your needs grow and you require more ports, you can always attach modular switches to the director switch and build yourself a core-edge topology.

Director-class switches make great core switches. They are faster than modular switches and usually come with better tools for switch management.

Standardize on a single vendor's switches

The standards for connecting different vendor switches together are still quite new, and vendors still tend to implement these standards differently. The best approach is to have all your switches from the same vendor. This isn't as important for hubs, because the arbitrated loop protocol has been around longer. Hubs from different vendors don't seem to have intermix problems.

Standardize your firmware versions

Because all your switches should be from the same vendor (see the previous section), make sure that the firmware that makes those switches run all use the same version. *Firmware,* the intelligent code that resides inside a chip inside the different hardware components within the SAN, allows those components to operate. We have seen weird things happen when two switches in the same fabric have different levels of firmware. This is not as important when you connect modular and director-class switches from the same vendor. Director-class switches usually use a different firmware version than the modular switches do anyway, even though they're from the same switch vendor.

Standardize your HBA drivers

Try to use the same version HBA driver for all the HBAs that come from the same vendor. You should also make sure that you use the latest drivers available, because the vendors fix bugs in the drivers and add new functionality that you might be able to take advantage of. (For more about HBAs and their drivers, see Chapters 1 and 2.)

Use unique zone alias names

If you're setting up a SAN with two fabrics, such as Fabric A and Fabric B, make sure that all your zone information is unique between the two fabrics. We mention this because if you ever have to connect the two fabrics together for some reason, you'll have problems if the non-unique information is contained in both fabrics.

Take the domain ID of the switches, for example. Because you have two fabrics, you can use the same IDs in both fabrics. You might have two ID 1s, two ID 2s, and so on. If you try to connect the fabrics together under those circumstances, the switches will reject the connection if they find the same domain ID in both fabrics.

Using storage from multiple vendors

When using storage arrays from multiple storage vendors in the same fabric, use zoning to put them into separate zones. This keeps them as separate management entities; also, if one vendor's array has some weirdness going on with it, it won't affect the other storage. If you also use *single-server zones* that include only a storage port and a single server, it will keep your SAN running smoothly when devices are added or removed from the fabric.

Always use two fabrics

When you use two SAN fabrics instead of one, your SAN can withstand failures of any device in a single path. You can lose a cable, HBA, switch, or storage port and still have your applications available. Using two fabrics also enables you to do normal maintenance to the SAN without any planned downtime, because you can maintain one fabric at a time. Using two fabrics does require twice as many HBAs (two in each server, plus fail-over software) and twice as many switches — but these are worth it in the long run. This is especially true if downtime is costly to your business.

Chapter 6

SANs and Disaster Recovery

*P*eople don't like to think about really bad things such as disasters, but disasters do occur, and businesses need to be prepared for them. Being prepared for disasters is one of the main reasons why companies are investing in storage area networks, because consolidating data into an intelligent SAN makes replicating data much simpler than using noncentralized approaches.

Let's face it: Having a disaster-recovery plan for your business is an absolute necessity in today's world. Lots of things can go wrong and lead to data loss: fires, floods, building power loss, sprinkler systems going off, malicious employee actions, data corruption, equipment failure, natural disasters, acts of terrorism, viruses, political unrest, police action, and criminal mischief. If any of these events occurred, what would happen to your business? How would you restore your critical data, and how long would it take? How would you keep your business going in the meantime? Is everybody safe? Where would they go and what procedures should they follow if communications are down? Implementing a good disaster-recovery plan can pay for itself in hours if you have a real disaster.

Someone in your company needs to be on top of two related areas: a disaster-recovery (DR) plan and a business continuity plan (BCP). Whereas the DR plan focuses on getting things back to normal after a major disruption, the BCP keeps your business operations running in the meantime. The disaster-recovery plan makes sure that your data is safe; the business continuity plan makes sure that you can keep your business running during the disaster.

Covering all the details of developing disaster plans is well beyond the scope of this book, but I want to give you a feel for some basic disaster-recovery considerations, and why a SAN should be a major part of that plan.

How Much Downtime Can You Afford?

Downtime is the actual amount of time your computers are not operational because of any type of planned or unplanned outage. Most companies' computers need to run 24 hours a day, seven days a week (24×7) to keep up with the new global economy. What would happen if your company had a catastrophic failure but your competitor was still operational?

Consider what the cost of downtime would be for your organization. If your server went down for an hour, how much business would be lost? If your mission-critical application servers went down for the whole day — or even worse, your building caught fire and you lost everything, including all your data — how much business would be lost and how long would it take you to bring everything back up again? (You need to make sure you have your priorities straight, and ensure everyone is safe first!)

Take a look at Figure 6-1 for an indication of what one hour of downtime costs by industry. This dollar amount should determine how much your company should spend on a disaster-recovery (DR) solution.

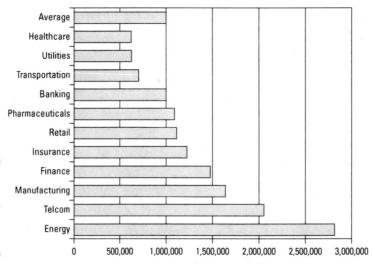

Figure 6-1: Cost of one hour of downtime per industry.

When you calculate what downtime will cost your business, you also need to factor in these two considerations:

- ✔ **Recovery Time Objective (RTO):** This factor is the amount of time that it takes to get your systems back online. If you have a disaster, how long would it take you to get all your applications up and running again at another site? In most cases today, that answer is *way too long.* Most businesses back up their data to tapes and ship the tapes to an off-site location. Recovering the data from tapes back onto disks takes too long. This is why companies are consolidating their critical data into a SAN with the capability to replicate in real time to a recovery site. By using a SAN to replicate blocks of data to a remote site for disaster recovery, your data is already on disk at the DR site and ready to use if your primary site goes away.

- ✔ **Recovery Point Objective (RPO):** This is the last consistent data transaction before the disaster. If you had a disaster, how much data would be lost? In most cases today, that answer is *way too much.* Most companies today can't afford to lose any data. What if the data they lost was the record of your last mortgage payment or that huge stock purchase you made just before the stock went into the stratosphere? You wouldn't like that very much, I'm sure. That is why using real-time data copy with an intelligent SAN makes sense for many companies. Using SAN technology as a basis for disaster recovery allows you to recover *more* data *faster.*

Gathering the data for a disaster-recovery plan

Creating the building blocks of a disaster-recovery solution using a SAN requires some thought on your part. In a nutshell, the questions to address are the following:

- ✔ **Data capacity and change rate: How much data do I need to copy?** You should have to copy *all* your data to your disaster site only once. After the bulk of the data is there, you need to copy only the data that changes from day to day. This means that you are concerned about only the data that you *write* on a daily basis, not the data you *read.* You need to determine what percentage of your data changes every day, not the total amount of data you have.

You can determine your daily total write rate by finding out the size of your daily incremental backups. Incremental backups deal with only the data that was changed between backups.

✔ **Distance and latency: How far does the data have to go?** Some companies now have to comply with new government regulations (SEC rule 17-a4) that require greater distances between production and recovery data centers. A few hundred miles should be sufficient to be safe from most disasters.

✔ **Analysis of critical records: What can I afford to lose?** In most cases, you can't afford to lose *any* data. But to be realistic, some data will be lost in a disaster (such as the in-flight transactions between the sites at the time of the disaster). Your goal should be to lose as little data as possible. To meet this goal, the recovery solution you choose should be able to copy data transactions in real time to your disaster site without affecting the performance of your applications. If you can afford to lose some data, you can simply ship backup tapes to your disaster site or do bulk copy transactions at the end of each day.

✔ **Bandwidth requirements: How fat are the pipes to the other side?** The speed of your remote links determines how much data can be copied in what time period. This is pure physics. The faster the link, the more data that can be copied in a given time frame. (See Chapter 8 for more information.)

✔ **Application dependencies: What's required to bring the application(s) up at the other side, and in what order?** Many of today's mission-critical applications depend on data feeds from other applications or are dependent on other applications' tiers. (For example, applications such as SAP depend on a database tier, application logic tier, and a web tier.) You need to be sure the solution you choose can group related data so it can be recovered consistently on the other side. This is known as a *consistency group.*

✔ **Hardware requirements: How many servers are involved?** Disaster recovery gets expensive if you have to build a mirror copy of your production site to recover from a disaster. In many cases, it just doesn't make financial sense to have duplicate sites, unless those sites are both active and contributing to the bottom line of the organization. Disaster recovery is where server consolidation and virtualization make a lot of financial sense. Storage consolidation and virtualization also make sense for disaster recovery.

When the data from many servers must be replicated for disaster recovery, host-based software replication makes less and less sense. It can be more expensive to buy a software license for each server you want to use for host-based replication software than it is to buy a SAN solution with *inherent* replication capabilities in hardware or software. It is also much simpler to create consistency groups for application dependencies when all the data from those servers is consolidated into the SAN.

You need to understand the details of each of these questions because each will affect your plan's feasibility and required budget. You also need to understand how recent technical innovations can contribute to reducing the costs of data recovery — in particular, continuous data protection (CDP), data de-duplication, sub-block-level storage differencing (data micro-scanning), and fabric-based continuous data replication (CDR) . (You can find out more about these topics in Chapter 10 and Part V.) As an example, the budget required to lease enough network bandwidth to copy 200TB of data is much greater than the network lease expenses for enough bandwidth to copy only 200GB of data. You should know the going rates for leasing network lines and which type of network would suit your needs best.

When implementing a disaster-recovery solution, the intersite network connections used to copy data between sites are usually the most expensive part of the solution. To be sure of this, just call up your local telephone company and say that you want to lease a dedicated fibre link between two cities. Make sure you're sitting down, though, before you ask for a price.

When sourcing a DR solution for your company, test each vendor's solution and the technology they bring to the table to assure you choose the *simplest and most efficient solution* available.

Create a detailed plan that meets your requirements

When drafting your requirements for disaster recovery, these are the details that need to be considered:

- **Budget:** Determine what you can afford to spend, based on how much time you can afford to be down. (Refer to Figure 6-1.) As a general rule, at least 1 percent of gross income is a good place to start.

- **Remote site:** Determine how far away the remote site should be. The farther the better, to protect against things such as hurricanes and floods. At a minimum, the site should be on a separate power grid from the production site. If your company already owns another facility in another location, determine that location's feasibility for use as a recovery site. If that location isn't practical, you may have to lease floor space from a hosting facility. (See more on this in the section "Choosing the Recovery Site," later in this chapter.)

- **Replication method:** This is how you get your data to the recovery site. The method depends on your budget, the distance between locations, the amount of data that needs to be copied, and the number of servers involved. Your choices are host-based software for data replication (including application-level solutions such as Oracle Data Guard or Sybase Replication Server), replication "appliances" that connect to the storage fabric, or replication using the intelligence embedded in advanced SAN storage arrays. In the past, it usually made sense to consolidate all data into a SAN and use hardware-based replication, but recent advances in host-based and appliance-based solutions are beginning to make traditional storage array-based solutions look clumsy. (More on replication methods later in this chapter.)

✔ **Replication costs:** The cost of replication varies according to your network expenses, hardware and software expenses, and the services needed to implement the solution.

✔ **Client access of the data in a disaster:** You need to consider all your application dependencies and how your servers interact. Do your Web servers depend on the availability of a database server? Will the IP addresses of the servers change in a disaster? What about computer names? Does the remote site have a network to connect to the new servers? All the things you need to have in place at your production site also have to be in place at your disaster site for your business to operate. All of this should part of your business continuity planning.

✔ **Critical applications:** To reduce the costs of your recovery solution, you need to determine which applications you can live without for a while. Not every server in your company is mission critical. If you can be without some of your applications for a few days or weeks without affecting the business to any great extent, think about excluding these applications from the plan. Doing so reduces not only the amount of data that must be recovered but also the number of servers required at the recovery site.

✔ **Number of servers needed to recover critical applications:** You may have to buy a duplicate server for every critical application — servers that do nothing but sit there waiting for a disaster to occur. A better idea is to run half of your production at each site and have each site function as a backup for the other. This plan at least lets you utilize your recovery servers during normal production operations, have the network connections in place and verified that they support production work, and have the staff in place to recover in case either site becomes unavailable. You can then run in degraded mode during a disaster by doubling up on the application load at the surviving site.

✔ **Staff preparation:** What are the steps needed to bring each server back online? Are experienced staff available for either site? Where is the recovery plan documentation; will it be lost if the primary site is lost? Consider having a way for your staff to access step-by-step procedures to recover all your applications after a disaster happens. A good way to always have your recovery plan accessible is to keep the recovery documentation available via a Web portal application. The portal can be hosted by an outsourcing vendor or can be as simple as a standalone Web server located at each site, used as a documentation server.

Recognizing the Importance of Distance, Bandwidth, and Latency

All parts of life have trade-offs. People who marry for money don't usually end up with the most attractive spouse in the world. In SAN-based disaster recovery, the farther your recovery site from your primary site, the safer your data will be, but the more it will cost to get the data there.

Distance

The distance to your recovery site is important. Natural disasters have a tendency to affect a wide area. Blackouts can affect entire cities or even entire regions of a country. Local disasters such as tornadoes and fires might affect only the building you're in. The greater the distance between locations, the lower the probability that both sites will be affected during a disaster.

Bandwidth and latency are two factors that limit how far your recovery site can be from your primary location.

Bandwidth

Bandwidth is the total amount of information that can be sent through a communications link. All communication equipment has the capability to transmit and receive information. The amount of information that can be pushed through that link is its bandwidth. Table 6-1 lists the most common communication links and their bandwidth.

Table 6-1	Common North American Communication Network Types and Bandwidths (Speeds)
Type	*Bandwidth (Speed)*
Modem links	
Standard modem	14.4 Kbps to 96 Kbps
Cable modem	512 Kbps to 52 Mbps
Copper Telco links	
T1/DS1	1.544 Mbps
T2	6.312 Mbps
T3/DS3	44.736 Mbps

(continued)

Table 6-1 *(continued)*

Type	Bandwidth (Speed)
Optical Telco links	
OC-1	51.84 Mbps
OC-3	155.52 Mbps
OC-12	622.08 Mbps
OC-24	1.244 Gbps
OC-482.488 Gbps	
OC-192	9.6 Gbps
Fibre Channel	1 Gbps–2 Gbps
Ethernet links	
10Base-T	10 Mbps
100Base-T	100 Mbps
Gigabit Ethernet	1 Gbps

The prices to lease these lines range anywhere from what it costs you to use your modem over a standard phone (Plain Old Telephone Service, or *POTS*) line to thousands of dollars per month for the faster optical communication links. One of the most expensive pieces of putting together a disaster-recovery solution is the cost of the leased lines between the sites.

The speed of the connection that you'll need is largely determined by the amount of data to be copied every day and the time it will take to get it there. (See Chapter 8 for more on the time it takes to copy data over Telco links.)

When speaking about transmission links, speed is usually expressed in bits per second, or bps. (A *byte* is 8 bits.) A standard T-1 link runs at about 1.544 megabits per second (Mbps).

When talking about storage, speed is expressed in bytes per second. Each megabyte (MB) of data is 2 to the 20th power, or 1,048,576 bytes. If each byte contains 8 bits, and you're trying to push a million bytes across a link in one second, then you need a link that can handle around 8 million bits per second, or 8 Mbps.

Understandably, overhead costs are associated with moving data across a link. For overhead, figure about 20 percent of the cost of the link speed. Thus, for every megabyte of data that you need to transfer per second, you need at least a 10-megabit link. This is equal to standard Ethernet speeds.

You can use a simple formula when trying to design a data-replication solution that transfers data in real time:

10 megabits of network capacity are required for every megabyte of data that has to be transferred in one second.

The formula is a good guideline when figuring out what kind of link you need between your primary and recovery data centers when data is in native format and not compressed or de-duplicated. For satisfactory performance in the real world, do a study on how much data changes over a given period of time, and then use the formula to calculate the bandwidth requirements. Then look at compression and de-duplication technologies to see whether they can help reduce the bandwidth requirements.

Latency

Latency is the time it takes to access or transmit data. The time that it takes for a single bit of information to get through a communications link from point A to point B is its *latency.* The longer the distance between sites, the greater the latency. Latency is important when designing a remote copy solution. If your recovery site is very far away from your production data center, the latency of the inter-site links might affect the performance of your production applications.

I have found that the latency of a SAN connection between sites using Fibre Channel cabling is approximately 1ms (one millisecond) for every 25 miles of distance. Each write over a Fibre Channel cable requires four round trips, due to the protocol. (I haven't figured out a way to speed up light yet, so the physics of the speed of light still apply.)

How latency can determine your recovery solution

Latency is especially important when determining which remote copy method to use: Data can be sent over a telecommunications link either synchronously or asynchronously.

Synchronous data transmission means that each data bit is sent in order over the wire serially and in lock step with the receiver at the other end. Synchronous data transmission guarantees that the data is written in the same sequence at both locations. Synchronous data transmission is a good method for ensuring database transactional consistency during remote copy operations.

Asynchronous data transmission means that the bits can be sent out of order and not serially or in lock step with the receiver. Asynchronous transmission is commonly used in modems and during the transmission of data characters. Because asynchronous transmission does not by itself guarantee that each bit will be written in the same sequence at both locations, a method to guarantee transactional consistency is needed during data replication.

Synchronous remote copy solutions tell the application that a write operation is completed only after the write is written across the link to the remote facility. This ensures that your data is consistent up to the last write. The problem is that this happens for every darn write to a disk. If you have a ton of latency across your remote links because you have a lot of distance between the sites, your applications will start performing poorly.

Asynchronous remote copy solutions tell the application that a write operation is complete immediately. This allows asynchronous remote copy solutions to be unlimited as far as distance is concerned because there is no impact to the application as the distance increases.

When creating a long-distance SAN-based disaster-recovery solution, make sure that your storage vendor supports true asynchronous remote copy. Under asynchronous copy, the application receives an "I/O complete" message as soon as the data is written into the cache of the local storage array. This process eliminates the application performance penalty for copying data over long distances. Make sure that the vendor also supports some sort of time stamping or sequencing of those writes, so that the data can be reordered and written to disk in the same sequence that was used at the primary site. This sequencing of data is important for database applications to assure write order fidelity and transactional consistency.

Both synchronous and asynchronous solutions require enough network bandwidth for the amount of data you are writing to disk at the primary location to be copied to the remote site in real time. Not having enough network bandwidth causes the remote copy links to fill up and fail.

A new type of replication, which uses intelligent appliances attached to the SAN switches, is called continuous data replication (CDR) with continuous data journaling and protection (CDP). (For more information, see Chapter 14.) This approach to replication differs a bit from traditional storage-array-based sync and async solutions; it tends to be more dynamic in how it handles replication and can work across the boundaries of any vendor's storage solutions.

Choosing the Recovery Site

Choosing your recovery site is one of your most important decisions. You need to make sure that the site has all the amenities needed to make it right for use as a recovery facility.

If your company already has a facility that can be used as a disaster-recovery site, you're in luck. You can probably save a lot of money by making use of that site during a disaster. If not, you will have to outsource your recovery site to a hosting facility or a company that specializes in disaster recovery, which may actually be cheaper than building a facility just for DR.

Existing facility

If you can make use of an existing facility, doing so may save you tons of money. For you to use *any* facility for disaster recovery, that facility must cover all the requirements of a good DR site:

- ✔ **How much space is available for your equipment?** Will all your servers and storage fit into the available space? Some hosting facilities lease small cages to keep your hardware secure. Make sure that they have one that is sized to fit your needs.

- ✔ **When is the space available?** In the event of a disaster, is this first-come, first-served floor space?

- ✔ **Is there enough parking for employees?** It would be a pain if your employees kept getting parking tickets during a disaster.

- ✔ **Does the parking lot have lights?** Some hosting facilities are located in industrial areas. Make sure your employees will feel safe.

- ✔ **How many entrances are there, and are they secure?** Again, safety is foremost. You also want to be able to get out fast in case of fire or an earthquake.

- ✔ **Is there security-card access into the building?** What would you do if, during a disaster, you found out that you paid all that money for a recovery site that no one could get into?

- ✔ **What is the process to get employees security access in an emergency?** It would be horrible if the employees who *did* have access were lost in the disaster. You need a plan to address that possibility.

- ✔ **How many hours per year do the tenants experience electrical outages in this building?** Make sure that the building has clean power and good cooling. They may have most servers turned off all the time but power them up in a disaster. It can get hot real fast.

- ✔ **Is the building connected to a fast network so your data can get there?** You may want to know the type of network equipment used in the facility and make sure that it's similar to what you're using now. You need enough bandwidth for all your needs.

If your company already has another data center (where the majority of your computers are located) in a remote location, remember that staying up in a disaster requires distance. If the other data center is down the block and you're in the middle of a local blackout or a hurricane, it won't be of much help.

Consider having your remote data center far enough away to be at least within a separate power grid. Even better would be to have it in a different state, away from the coast — and not on top of a fault line, for heaven's sake.

Co-location facility

If you don't already own a property that can be designated as your recovery site, you have several options. Many telephone company providers (Telcos) from which you lease communication lines also have facilities that can be used as recovery sites. Other companies specialize in providing secure locations expressly for outsourcing DR.

These recovery sites, called *co-location facilities,* are data centers built for use in disaster recovery, managed information technology, and outsourcing. They get their name because they house equipment from different companies. Each company's equipment is located in secure cages — next to other companies' equipment (also in secure cages). The facility can help provide you with the necessary network and server equipment to help you run your business. Its staff can even manage everything for you, at a cost. Some co-location facilities even let you outsource all your computing requirements to them. This can let you concentrate on your business rather than having to worry about all this darn computer stuff.

To find a co-location facility near you, just look in your local Yellow Pages under *Computers*. Another way to find a co-location facility is to use an Internet search engine. You'll be surprised by how many are out there. The cost of these facilities varies, but you are usually charged per square foot of floor space, or per gigabyte of data stored, or both. The charges also vary depending on whether you or the facility will be providing management of the remote recovery solution. The total cost will most likely be a bit more expensive than what you are currently paying today for per-foot charges in your own facility.

Getting your data to the *COLO* (industry-speak for co-location facility) is only the first step. You also need to recover, so you may need the facility to provide servers in case of disaster. For security, I also recommend data encryption. Try to leverage server consolidation and virtualization wherever you can to reduce costs. (For more on virtualization, see Chapter 15.)

Choosing Where to Run the Data Replication Process

Disaster recovery can get pretty confusing very fast, as there is a lot to know and understand. Some people make a living consulting with companies about disaster recovery, and you can even get industry certification to become a true business-continuity professional! To make it simple for you, though, I list the basic ways you can accomplish the most important aspect, which is choosing the data-replication method, and how to determine which method makes sense for your situation. There are four methods to replicate data: Host-based replication, appliance-based replication, array-based replication, and shipping tapes.

Host-based data replication solutions

In a host-based solution, you use software running on your servers. This type of solution generally requires another server (the target server) running at the remote site as a target for the replicated data. The target server at the remote site takes the place of the primary server during an outage. Some host-based software solutions can replicate to a target appliance; this method consolidates data changes and eliminates the need for a recovery server running all the time. A few host-based solutions can even de-duplicate data at the host to reduce the bandwidth requirements for replication to the DR site. Most database applications, such as Oracle and Sybase, have built-in replication known as log shipping, which can also minimize bandwidth requirements, be a cost-effective solution in a pinch, and integrate with the application directly. However, log shipping cannot protect against data corruption or deletion. Options in the operating system itself can now provide basic data protection and replication, such as Microsoft Data Protection Manager (DPM) or newer file system–based solutions in Solaris known as ZFS, QFS, and SAMfs.

The advantages of a host-based solution follow:

- ✔ Can be cost-effective for small organizations with minimal servers to protect and no SAN in place.
- ✔ Most host-based solutions can also protect the internal storage (such as the C:\ drives on Windows-based servers).
- ✔ Some host-based solutions can also provide a solution known as bare metal recovery, where the entire server can be swiftly rebuilt from the replicated internal drives if a similar server is used as the replacement.
- ✔ Replication usually uses the existing IP network.
- ✔ Simple to implement.

The disadvantages of a host-based solution follow:

✔ Depending on the solution, you may need duplicate servers always running and sucking up power at the DR site.

✔ Multiple points of management.

✔ Takes up CPU cycles on the host. This is especially true for host-based solutions which also use the CPU in the host to de-duplicate the data prior to replication.

✔ Can be complex when you have many servers to protect.

✔ Cannot create consistency groups across servers for data dependencies.

✔ If network quality of service or network throttling is not included with the solution, host-based replication can suck up all the IP bandwidth between sites, leaving no network resources available for production or client access.

✔ Most solutions do not provide a mechanism to encrypt data in flight to reduce security risks.

Choose a host-based solution when . . .

✔ You have just a few servers, a limited budget, and a server that can be up all the time at the DR site.

✔ You have many small remote offices, you need to consolidate data protection at the DR site but have no IT staff at the remote sites, and you don't want to use and ship tapes.

✔ The solution provides client-side (host-based) data versioning or data de-duplication to reduce WAN bandwidth.

✔ The solution can replicate many-to-one to a NAS share or appliance at the DR site to minimize server requirements at the DR site.

✔ The solution integrates with virtual servers to reduce infrastructure costs for DR (virtual server-to-virtual server replication).

✔ When the proposed solution is more cost-effective than array-based or appliance-based solutions and still solves the problem at hand.

Appliance-based data replication solutions

Special-purpose appliances are used with an application-based solution. Data replication appliances are fairly new in the storage industry and have become a thorn in the side of many traditional storage vendors who ship storage array-based solutions. Many companies adopt special-purpose appliances for data replication because they are usually implemented at the switched fabric layer, which is above the storage layer in the SAN. Operating at a layer above the storage eliminates the need to have the same vendor's storage at the remote location, which with few exceptions is a requirement for array-based replication solutions.

By moving the replication intelligence away from the storage itself and into the fabric layer of the SAN, you don't need to buy array-based licenses for data replication and data can be replicated between any storage arrays. Fabric-level replication appliances may also include other functionality, such as data de-duplication or continuous data replication and protection. Continuous replication is usually dynamic, and therefore self-healing, so no manual procedure is required to recover the replication process when the network link goes down. If continuous protection journaling or snapshots or both are supported, recovery points and recover times can be greatly optimized. If data de-duplication is supported, the WAN bandwidth and storage costs can be reduced. Appliance-based solutions are available from FalconStor, EMC, NetApp, Data Domain, and others.

The advantages of an appliance-based solution follow:

- ✔ Appliances work at the fabric level and eliminate the need for host-based or array-based replication licenses such as EMC SRDF, IBM PPRC, or HDS UR. (Now there's a bunch of acronyms for you to get rid of!)

- ✔ Appliances used for data replication often include other nice features such as data de-duplication, self-healing, encryption, or CDP.

- ✔ Virtual tape library appliances can be used with or as a replacement for physical tape, and when data de-duplication with replication is included, the solution can be a cost-effective alternative to shipping tapes offsite.

- ✔ Using appliances enables you to use the same replication solution across all storage in a heterogeneous SAN with storage from multiple vendors.

- ✔ Some appliances also integrate with the applications for recovery.

- ✔ Simple to implement, and can be used to create consistency groups across entire multitier applications and storage arrays.

The disadvantages of an appliance-based solution follow:

- ✔ If high availability features are unavailable, the appliance can be a single point of failure.

- ✔ Some solutions may have performance issues or become a bottleneck. Make sure the solution you choose can scale to cover your current and future needs.

✔ If the appliances are not certified to work with your SAN, the vendors may point fingers when the data-replication process breaks.

✔ Possibility of data corruption if the solution does not adhere to strict write order fidelity and transactional consistency.

Choose an appliance-based solution when . . .

✔ You can use it with a host-based solution as the target for data replication from multiple remote sites.

✔ You have SAN storage from multiple vendors and are looking to use the same solution across the entire data center.

✔ The solution also provides other advanced functionality such as data de-duplication to reduce WAN bandwidth or CDP or snapshots to improve recovery time and recovery-point objectives.

✔ You want to replicate data over an existing IP network and without SAN-to-SAN extenders or Fibre Channel extension equipment.

✔ The proposed solution is cheaper than either host-based or array-based replication.

Array-based data replication solution

In an array-based solution, you use intelligence in the storage array to replicate data directly to another storage array. Storage array-based data replication is the most mature of all the technologies listed, and will work with almost any server platform or operating system, including legacy platforms such as mainframes, Tandem servers, IBM AS400 servers, Unisys servers, VMS systems, and other proprietary server platforms. Array-based data replication, along with SAN-based backup, was one of the driving forces for adoption of a SAN in many corporate environments. Array-based replication is the standard bearer; even though it's now considered a traditional approach, it's still a great solution to get data from point A to point B when it absolutely needs to be there — and when cost is not an issue. Storage array-based data replication solutions usually cost a bit more than the other methods, so you often find them in banking environments where stodgy, tried-and-true methods are preferred. (Also, most banks also use mainframes, and array-based data replication is the most common method of replication for mainframe data.)

The advantages of an array-based solution follow:

✔ It's a mature technology.

✔ It can be fast and can handle hundreds of servers at a time.

✔ It's great solution for synchronous data replication over Fibre Channel for short distances, where no data can be lost.

✔ It's great for legacy servers and mainframes.

✔ It offers some arrays (HDS Tagmastore) that can virtualize cheaper storage to be used as target storage for the DR site, which helps minimize costs for mainframe DR.

✔ It includes specialized functionality for mainframe environments.

✔ It can connect to FICON and ESCON equipment (mainframe stuff).

The disadvantages of an array-based solution follow:

✔ It usually requires the same hardware at both locations from the same vendor.

✔ It can be very complex and expensive to implement and manage.

✔ It has very high bandwidth requirements.

✔ It usually cannot create consistency groups across storage arrays.

✔ It's expensive to buy and maintain.

✔ It offers only limited application integration.

Choose an array-based solution when . . .

✔ You need to replicate mainframe or legacy data.

✔ You have deep pockets and want what the banks use.

✔ You expect to be standardizing on a single array vendor anyway.

✔ You need to replicate only a short distance, have plenty of bandwidth, and want to use synchronous replication to avoid the chance of data loss.

✔ The proposed solution is cheaper than either host-based or appliance-based replication.

Shipping tapes as a solution

The last method is to back up to tape and then ship the tapes offsite for recovery. Companies without a SAN have shipped tapes to companies such as Iron Mountain and SunGard for years. Shipping tapes can be cost-effective to implement but does not provide the enhanced recovery time or recovery-point objectives gained from SAN-based data replication.

The advantages of shipping tapes follow:

✔ It's usually cheaper than SAN-based replication.

✔ It doesn't require a wide area network (WAN).

The disadvantages of shipping tapes follow:

✔ It has only a very poor recovery-time objective and recovery-point objective; in some cases, the data is difficult (if not impossible) to recover.

✔ It still incurs costs, along with the need to manage and store tapes.

✔ It's a very manual process.

Choose a shipping tapes solution when . . .

✔ No other solution is available.

✔ Your recovery-time objective is not very stringent.

✔ The thought of losing all the data from the last backup does not especially threaten your business or bother you.

The Importance of Testing

No planned recovery solution is valid unless you test it. Testing the actual recovery process and plan should be carried out at least a few times each year. Over time, applications are added and new servers are brought online. People come and go. You should test your recovery plan — and the actual recovery process — several times a year. Sometimes a little unforeseen change can be the thing that bites you if you ever have a real disaster.

Make sure that your recovery plan is always up to date. Make the plan easily available so that anyone who needs it will know where to find it at 3 a.m. on a Sunday. Keep in mind that if you have a disaster, your building may be gone. Keep copies of your recovery plan available in every location, in both hard-copy and soft-copy formats.

Chapter 7

Putting It All Together

*I*n this chapter, I walk you through creating a storage area network (SAN) from scratch. Nowadays there are both legacy Fibre Channel–based SANs and newer iSCSI SANs, which run over common Ethernet networks. I tackle each one independently to avoid confusion between the two.

Since "age before beauty" may hold true with technology, our iSCSI SAN implementation will have to wait until I finish tackling the more established, slightly more involved, Fibre Channel–based SAN. If you prefer to go with the new stuff first, skip down to "iSCSI, You SCSI, We All SCSI." (Wow, what a cheesy section name.)

Read along to discover the steps of designing and building a fully functioning, redundant Fibre Channel–based SAN fabric. Then you see some of the ways to move your data from an existing server to your new storage area network. If you don't want to do all this yourself, check out the bonus chapter "Outsourcing SANs Solutions" (available for downloading from dummies.com/go/sansfd2e) for details on outsourcing your installations. Otherwise, roll up your sleeves and read on.

Building a SAN by Hand

For all the setup in this pretend SAN, you'll do everything manually without the help of any fancy SAN management framework (see Chapter 11) or graphical user interface (GUI). I want you to get your hands a little dirty to help familiarize you with the underlying steps when setting up a SAN. After you understand these concepts, troubleshooting any problem in the future will be much easier. (See Chapter 12 for the skinny on troubleshooting.)

All the example command lines are mock-ups of real commands that you would normally have to type. Because so many different storage, switch, and HBA vendors are on the market, showing you an example of each would be time consuming and, ultimately, confusing. The generic commands that I show here highlight the important information and functionality that needs to be performed for that step. To put it simply, all the vendors have similar commands that basically do the same thing, with minor cosmetic variations. Check with your HBA, switch, and storage vendors for the appropriate procedures to accomplish each of the following tasks that you'll be performing in this make-believe SAN deployment:

- ✔ HBA installation and configuration
- ✔ Switch configuration and zoning steps
- ✔ Storage array RAID configuration and LUN (Logical Unit Number) assignment
- ✔ Storage array LUN security assignment
- ✔ Server operating system's disk subsystem configuration

Making a drawing of your intended SAN is the best way to see whether you forgot anything. Plus it makes the SAN easier to explain to others in your group (much easier than reading your mind). Figure 7-1 shows the intended design for your SAN. The drawing shows your basic SAN components of a storage array at the top, containing your disk drives, and the array's ports connected to a set of Fibre Channel switches. The switches, in turn, are connected to your servers, the foot bone connected to the leg bone, and so on. It might look confusing at first, but hang with me as I take the diagram apart section by section to show how each step brings this design to life.

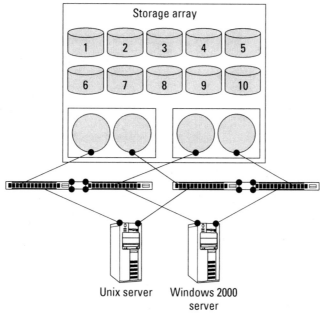

Figure 7-1:
Planning the
SAN.

Storage array

Unix server | Windows 2000 server

The SAN Plan

The SAN Plan

This chapter exercises everything that I discuss in earlier chapters. Here's where you insert Tab A into Slot B . . . and implement a real SAN. (Well, not a *real* SAN, but a make-believe one. I wouldn't put any real production applications on it, yet, — not until you get your imaginary backup solution up and running.)

In your make-believe SAN, you want to build something that is multiplatform, redundant, and has good performance. Start with the following components (see Chapter 2 for more details about these components):

- ✔ **Two servers,** one Unix based and the other Windows based (for the most common server platforms, Unix and NT, respectively).
- ✔ **One high-performance storage array** with hardware-based Redundant Array of Inexpensive (or Independent) Disks (RAID).
- ✔ **Four SAN fabric switches** to make two redundant fabrics.
- ✔ **Four host bus adapters (HBAs) for your servers.** Each server will get two for redundancy and performance.
- ✔ **Fiber-optic cables to hook everything up.**

Your SAN plan will also use fabric zoning and LUN security to ensure that the two different operating systems are isolated and don't interfere with each other's performance or data integrity. (Our user community is overly cautious about its data.)

Fabric Zoning 101

Zones, zone sets, aliases . . . what are all these things? A *zone* is a bunch of ports or World Wide Name (WWN) addresses that are isolated together into a group. Only members within the group can see each other and communicate among themselves. Think of it like a phone conversation: If you want to talk to Aunt Betsy on the phone, you dial the number (her phone number is like a World Wide Name), and the phone company puts your phone and Aunt Betsy's into a zone. When you're connected, nobody else can communicate with your phone or Aunt Betsy's, but your two phones can communicate with each other. If you want to bring Aunt Polly into the conversation, you can have a three-party call by adding Aunt Polly's number into this zone, and then the three of you can all chat with each other. (For more on World Wide Names, review Chapter 3.)

Because the phone company obviously deals with more users than just you and your two favorite aunts, millions of these zones are in use simultaneously — making up a zone set. A *zone set* is a given group of zones that, when activated, becomes the current configuration that a particular switch or fabric uses to enforce the rules of who can talk to whom.

You can have only one zone set active. All the others are on standby, waiting in the wings to be activated if need be.

Members of zones have names such as *Domain 4, Port 16*, or *6a:0f:5c:ae:81:9c:a8:4f*. Because these names aren't easy to understand, someone came up with a way to give them nicknames, or *aliases*. A *zone alias* is just a friendly name used to refer to a real WWN or port address within a SAN fabric.

For example, you can give your HBAs' WWNs aliases of `UNIXBOX-1` and `UNIXBOX-2`, give your storage array's ports aliases of `ARRAY1-A`, and so on. Then, when you want the HBAs to see the array's ports, you create a zone called `UNIXBOX` with members `UNIXBOX-1`, `UNIXBOX-2`, and `ARRAY1-A`. Add this new zone to the active zone set and activate it. Now both HBAs on your `UNIXBOX` server can see and communicate with the storage array port `ARRAY1-A` through the switch fabric of your SAN.

This type of zoning is *soft zoning* because you're using the WWN address in the zone (even though it's an alias in this case, that doesn't make a difference). The beauty of soft zoning is that no matter what port you plug the cable into within the fabric, the WWN is the same — therefore, the zone still works. Some people didn't like that idea, and they wanted to control which physical port has access to what physical port, so they came up with another kind of zone: the hard zone.

Hard zoning occurs when you refer to the physical port on the switches within the fabric instead of the WWN of the device connecting to the fabric. This essentially makes a virtual pipeline, and any connections plugging into this set of ports can communicate with any others that are also plugged into them. To define ports on multiple switches, each switch within a fabric has a domain ID. If three switches are connected together into a fabric, each has its own domain ID — for example, 1, 2, and 3. To refer to port 6 on the third switch, you call it 3, 6 — as in *domain 3, port 6.*

And because you can combine soft and hard zoning in the same zone, you can have a zone with plain old WWNs, soft-zoning zone aliases, and hard-zoning *domain, port* information in it at the same time. For example, you can have a zone like this:

```
Zone1 = [6a:0f:5c:ae:81:9c:a8:4f;Larry1;4,13]
```

In your make-believe SAN, the Unix server uses hard zoning by restricting communication through the SAN to specific switch ports. The Windows server, on the other hand, employs soft zoning by using the WWN of the HBAs and the WWNs of the storage array's fiber-optic ports. Actually, in this running example, I have you create a zone alias for each WWN to make things easy to understand within the zone configuration. Then I show you how to use both technologies on the same SAN to show the differences, benefits, and pitfalls of each in a practical example.

The zoning methods to be used in this example SAN plan are

- **Unix server:** Hard zoning (via physical port address)
- **Windows:** Soft zoning (via WWN aliases)

LUN security

To make sure that neither server will see the other's disk devices by accident, use LUN security from the storage array to lock down which WWN (HBA) can see which LUN on the array.

LUN security is a storage array function that might or might not be supported on your storage array. For this example, it *is* a feature on the one used in your make-believe SAN plan. The way that it works is simple: For each LUN that you assign to a port on the storage array, you also associate all the WWNs of the HBA cards that need to use that LUN. If an HBA card connects to that port through the SAN and its WWN isn't listed for that LUN, it can't see it at all. This allows multiple WWNs to share the same storage array ports but address only the LUNs that they need to see without stepping on the other server's LUNs.

Setting Up the SAN

Set the stage in your mind: You've signed the lease on your make-believe computer room and flipped on the lights. Now it's time to install your hardware. To begin, the servers, switches, and storage arrays should be relatively close to each other so that all the cables can reach. (See Chapter 11 for a discussion of proper cabling layout and labeling practices.) Don't plug anything in just yet, though: You need to perform some configurations first to prepare each component in your SAN to do its required function.

Keeping good notes

No matter how many servers you put in your SAN, the basic steps are always the same. However, the process does contain a lot of numbers to remember, so always keep a notepad handy and write things down to simplify the process. I like to create a simple table that lists all the basic information, filling in the blanks while I go through each step. At the end of the process of hooking things up, configuring settings, and finally seeing storage on our server, I have all the details documented in case I need it later. Having that diagram (refer to Figure 7-1) is a big help too, because you can use it to double-check your cabling and configuration settings if you run into trouble.

Throughout this chapter, I make a point to tell you what you need to jot down for future reference — and when. Start with four tables of information: one for the SAN switches, one for the server HBAs, another for the storage array connections, and a fourth for the fabric-zoning information. Use these tables to keep track of everything neatly, and you'll know what I'm talking about when I refer to each of them throughout the chapter.

Setting up the switches

The four switches that you'll be using each have 16 ports. Plan on having two separate fabrics, using four switches — two in Fabric-A and two in Fabric-B. (See an illustration of these two fabrics in Figure 7-2.) This means that the two fabrics are isolated from each other and contain their own unique fabric configurations. This is a good practice because this configuration eliminates the possibility of a problem of one fabric affecting the other and, therefore, disconnecting your servers from their storage . . . ouch!

Figure 7-2:
The SAN plan: Begin with a pair of two-switch fabrics.

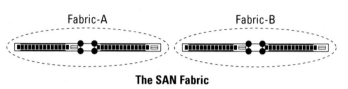

Fabric-A   Fabric-B

The SAN Fabric

Figure 7-2 shows the switch-only view of your SAN plan. Notice how each set of two switches is interconnected with fiber-optic cables. The connections are called *inter-switch links* (ISLs). This allows the switch to transfer data from one to the other, effectively making them look like one larger switch that's made up of two (or more) smaller switches. Because they're connected, they make up a fabric that shares zoning information among the connected switches.

After you plug in the switches to the AC outlets, you need to configure them with the following:

✔ A **TCP/IP address** so that you can manage the switch remotely.

✔ A **domain ID** to give the switch a unique address within its fabric.

✔ A **name** so that you know which switch is which. (Say *that* five times fast!)

And before you can configure them, you need to know what the TCP/IP addresses, domain IDs, and switch names will be. Here's where you get your planning documents out and make sure that you keep track of this stuff. (If you think the diagram in Figure 7-1 is complicated, wait until you start filling in all these little details around the ports, cables, and components! Actually, I'm just joking; the more detail that you add to your diagram, the clearer it becomes because you eliminate guesswork and assumptions.)

Open your notepad and create a table like the one in Table 7-1, showing the fabrics, domain IDs, switch names, and TCP/IP addresses of your SAN switches.

Table 7-1		Fabric Switch Configuration Information		
Fabric	*Switch #*	*Domain ID*	*Name*	*IP Address*
A	1	1	Switch-A1	192.168.0.1
A	2	2	Switch-A2	192.168.0.2
B	1	3	Switch-B1	192.168.0.3
B	2	4	Switch-B2	192.168.0.4

Notice the naming convention that I use. The switch's name is `Switch-x`, where *x* is replaced with the fabric that it belongs to, followed by its switch number within the fabric (1, 2, 3, and so on). Note that the IP address just so happens to follow the domain ID. This isn't part of any naming convention; it just worked out this way for this example. The domain ID needs to be a number between 1 and 255. If you set it to 0 (zero) on most switches, it will automatically be set to something unique if it joins another fabric (gets plugged into another switch). But for your first-time SAN, just set it yourself.

I made all domain IDs unique even though they're in different fabrics because if you decide in the future to connect this SAN fabric with the other one and expand with more switches, the two fabrics will be easier to merge with each other if they have unique domain IDs between them. (But that's a whole other story . . . perhaps *Advanced SANs For Dummies* . . . hmmm.)

Configuring the switches

Most switch vendors give you a way to set the TCP/IP address through the front display on the switch. You press the appropriate buttons to navigate though the menu until you find the IP address settings and cycle through the numbers. It's just like setting the clock on your VCR. Can't do that either, eh? Well, if that doesn't work or the switch doesn't have a display on the front, here's another way.

A default IP address is usually assigned to the switch from the factory — something that no one else uses, such as 1.1.1.1 or something similar. To communicate with the switch and change settings, you need to take a laptop or PC and set its IP address to 1.1.1.2 or something close so that it can talk IP to the switch. Connect a network cable between the laptop and the switch, either directly via an Ethernet crossover cable or through a hub. Use the `telnet` program from the computer to the switch, and you'll be able to log in to the switch's interface to make the necessary changes. Figure 7-3 shows the connection to the switch from a PC or laptop using a `telnet` command.

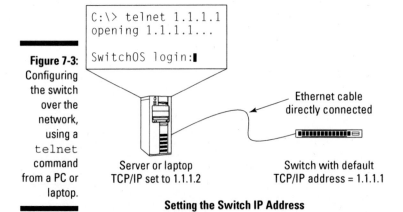

Figure 7-3: Configuring the switch over the network, using a `telnet` command from a PC or laptop.

Setting the Switch IP Address

If you get the response back from the switch to log in, you got connected to it over the little network that you created between the laptop and the switch. Log in to the switch by using the user ID and password used for the administrative account that the vendor uses by default. (Make a note to change this password later!)

After you're into the switch's operating system, you can make the changes that you want. For the first switch in Fabric-A (refer to Figure 7-2), use the following commands to name the switch and set up its TCP/IP information.

These are our generic commands — in this case, switchname — so consult your switch vendor's documentation for the appropriate commands for your switch model.

The commands that you enter are in bold:

```
'unnamed switch':> switchname "Switch-A1"
Name of switch changed successfully.
Switch-A1:>
```

One down; two to go. The next task is to set the domain ID and the IP address so that you can talk to this switch via your regular corporate Ethernet local area network (LAN). *Note:* The TCP/IP netmask and gateway (router) parameters need to be set as well, and those depend on your network's configuration. Consult with your network-management group to get valid IP addresses and the correct netmask and gateway addresses for them.

Here are the commands you enter, again in bold, to set the domain ID (line 1) and IP address information (lines 3–5) on your switch. Also, you use the command showconfig (line 6) to verify your settings after you make them.

```
Switch-A1:> set domainID = 1
Domain ID changed successfully. (Not in effect until
          reboot).
Switch-A1:> set IPaddress = 192.168.0.1
Switch-A1:> set IPnetmask = 255.255.255.0
Switch-A1:> set IPgateway = 192.168.0.254
Switch-A1:> showconfig
Switch Configuration:
Switch Name: Switch-A1
Fabric Domain ID: 1
Network IP Address: 192.168.0.1
Network IP Netmask: 255.255.255.0
Network IP Gateway: 192.168.0.254
 .
 .
 .
(other configuration information will be listed here as
          well)
```

When you've finished with changing the setting, enter the following command (in bold) to reboot the switch and put the changes into effect:

```
Switch-A1:> reboot
```

The switch now reboots, does its self-test, and reloads all its settings along with the ones that you changed. Because the IP address is now different, you won't be able to connect to it via the laptop anymore. To circumvent this problem, either change the laptop's IP address or connect the switch to the regular computer room network.

Perform these steps for each switch, referring to the configuration information listed previously in Table 7-1.

Verify connectivity

To make sure that you can now manage the switches via your corporate network, plug each of them into the corporate LAN and try to `telnet` to each one, using the new IP address. You should be able to get to each one this way just as before, except from a PC or server on the regular corporate LAN. If not, check your IP addresses and make sure that the network cables used to plug your switches into your corporate LAN are active and on the right network for the IP addresses that you assigned to them.

Creating fabrics

You're now ready to tie the individual switches in each fabric together with ISL links. This configuration technically now has four fabrics because each switch is independent and forms its own fabric. To create only two fabrics, connect Switch-A1 with Switch-A2 and then connect Switch-B1 with Switch-B2. This is easy to do (just plug cables in between), but you should do one fabric at a time to make sure that Fabric-A is connected correctly before you attempt it with Fabric-B. Following this tack keeps things methodical and focuses your concentration on one task at a time.

Begin with a `telnet` into Switch-A1. Watch the switch for information messages that pop up when the two switches connect to each other and exchange fabric information:

```
C:\> telnet 192.168.0.1  or telnet Switch-A1 if you added
           into your DNS tables.
SwitchOS login: admin
Password: ******

Switch-A1:>
```

Now grab one of those fiber-optic cables, preferably one that isn't a mile long, because you have to go only from a port on Switch-A1 to a port on Switch-A2. Plug the cable into the *last* port on Switch-A1 (to keep it out of the way of the 1-2-3 ports where you'll plug in your hosts). Plug the other end into Switch-A2's last port (16) and watch your telnet session on the console for update messages from the switch:

```
Switch-A1:>
11/17/02-15:24:00 [FABRIC EVENT] - Domain:1 (Switch-A1) E-Port Connect Port:16
11/17/02-15:24:02 [FABRIC EVENT] - Domain:2 (Switch-A2) Discovered Port:16
Checking Fabric Compatibility...Done
Merging Fabrics...
11/17/02-15:25:12 [FABRIC EVENT] - Fabric Merge (Domain:1 <-- Domain:2)
11/17/02-15:25:15 [FABRIC EVENT] - Merge Completed - 0 Errors, 0 Warnings
Switch-A1:>
```

What you see here is Switch-A2 connecting to Switch-A1 (via the cable on port 16). As soon as a switch connects to something — anything — it asks the device what it is and what it wants to do. In this case, the two switches said "Hello" to each other, realized that they were two fabric switches, and decided to join forces. Two SAN switches connect via a special port: an Extended Port (E_Port). It gets its name because the fabric is extended outside this switch to another switch.

When two E_Ports are created, a SAN fabric merge takes place in which the zoning information unique to both switches is compared. If no errors, duplications, or other problems are found, the switches copy their configurations to each other and make one big combined copy of the zones that they use.

A fabric merge is like introducing two groups of friends to each other, only some of them might have the same name. If, for instance, you have two friends named Bill, you can introduce Bill from work as Bill A and Bill your college buddy as Bill B to use their last names as qualifiers. Unique names help everyone keep track of who you're talking about. The same goes for SAN fabrics: If you have two zones named Zone1 (one on each switch), but they have different entries, the fabrics would fail to merge. You need to change the name of one of them to Zone2 or something unique to fix the duplication. But for the example merge here, no zones have been defined, so the two blank zone configurations combine into one big empty list.

From now on, any zone configuration change made to either switch will *propagate* (be copied) from one switch to the other (or to any other switches that are connected and have merged into the same fabric.)

As mentioned earlier in this chapter, the connection between the two switches is an ISL. If any data from a host goes into Switch-A1 and is destined for a port on Switch-A2, the data is sent across the ISL to the other switch to its destination. Figure 7-4 shows the path that the data takes between ports in a fabric over the ISL to its destination.

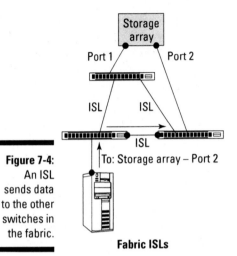

Figure 7-4:
An ISL
sends data
to the other
switches in
the fabric.

Fabric ISLs

Now you need to hook up a second ISL connection between Switch-A1 and A2.
This gives you two paths to send data between the switches. The reason for
two connections is twofold:

- ✔ **Plan for growth:** The number of switch-to-storage connections between
  your switches might be only one-to-one today, but that number could
  grow. (You can see a more complicated inter-switch configuration in
  Figure 7-5.) Under certain conditions, such as a cable or port failure on
  the array, you might direct all traffic that was going through the two
  switches to go through only one switch. A lone ISL will become a bottleneck in the SAN traffic, so planning for it is a good idea. Having multiple
  ISLs means that you can "trunk" them together into a larger pipe that
  allows many ISLs to act like one higher-speed connection between
  switches. This is typically done automatically by the two interconnected
  switches. (Chapter 5 details ISL trunking.)

- ✔ **Plan for redundancy:** Having a redundant link between the switches
  ensures that you won't be in jeopardy of a second cable or port failure if
  you have to start using it as the only path between storage and HBAs.

You can probably already figure out that you need to enable the same ISL
connectivity between Switch-B1 and Switch-B2 to create the B fabric. After
you do that, you have two fabrics (A and B) consisting of two switches each,
instead of the four independent ones with one switch each.

So far, your make-believe SAN should look like Figure 7-6.

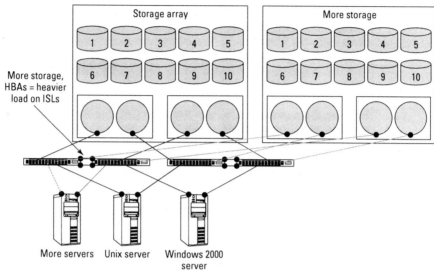

Figure 7-5:
Use ISLs to handle the potential load of failures and future expansion.

The SAN Plan: ISLs provide redundancy and bandwidth

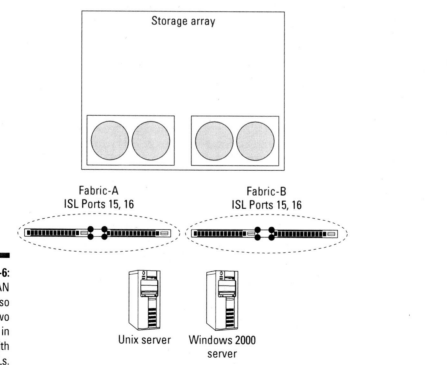

Figure 7-6:
The SAN project so far, with two fabrics in place with ISLs.

The SAN so far, with switches and fabrics set up

You have one last thing to do with the two fabrics: Create empty zone set configurations to populate later with zones. By default, a switch that has no zones behaves like a hub: It lets every port see every other port. This is not good because you don't want your servers to see your storage before you're ready to assign the right zones and LUN security. For now, create a zone set within each fabric, but leave it blank.

To make the new zone sets, use the ConfigCreate command. (A zone set is also known as a *configuration*.) Do this for both fabrics. Here I show you only Fabric-A's commands:

```
Switch-A1:> ConfigCreate "Fabric-A"
Configuration Fabric-A created. (Zoning will be enforced!)
Switch-A1:> ConfigEnable "Fabric-A"
Configuration Fabric-A is now in operation.
```

The ConfigEnable command puts the defined zone set into operation as the current configuration of the fabric. This allows you to predefine many zone sets so you can switch quickly from one to another by enabling the one you want as the current setup. Now your fabrics are zone enforced. And because no zones are defined yet, don't worry about any accidents happening when you start plugging things in randomly later on.

Time to move on to the servers and get them ready to connect to the switches.

Preparing the Servers

After you have the middle of your SAN ready to go — that is, after you have defined the switches and fabrics — you can drop down to the servers themselves and prepare them to get hooked up to the SAN. This is where you set and customize host bus adapters (HBAs).

Host bus adapters are the cards that plug into the slots in your server. These cards allow your server (host) to connect and communicate (adapt) by using its own processing backplane (bus) to the SAN. The card connects with the fiber-optic cabling and communicates with the operating system (OS) via a driver file. The driver makes the OS think that the device at the end of the fiber-optic is a standard Small Computer System Interface (SCSI) storage device, like a physical disk inside the actual server. In reality, however, the LUN that your OS sees is more likely a collection of blocks of data that the storage array creates out of multiple disk drives in multiple RAID sets and presents as this pseudodevice. As far as the server is concerned, the LUN is a physical disk of a determinate size.

Loading the driver

The *driver* is the little program that connects the physical hardware of the card itself with the OS software. The process of loading the driver depends on the OS you use.

In Windows, the automatic hardware detection finds the new HBA in the server and asks you for the location of the driver. Load the CD or floppy disk that came with the HBA card and direct the installer program to look there for it. If you downloaded the driver from the Internet, point the installer to the directory where you downloaded the files. (First, however, make sure that you decompress the driver files with WinZip, if necessary.)

Customizing the HBA card's configuration

Every HBA card has several settings. Some settings are never changed because they control generic parameters such as fiber-optic timing values, which are pretty standard. Some settings depend on what kind of SAN you're building, what kind of storage arrays are going to talk to it, and what kind of server and OS you're putting the HBA card in.

Because many HBAs can be used in many different hosts and OS combinations, you need to know the proper driver version and its settings for your particular server, OS, SAN configuration, and storage array. This might seem daunting, but it isn't. Your HBA will come with a plain-vanilla configuration file that's 99.9-percent complete and will probably work right out of the box with that file. Even so, you want to make sure that your SAN vendor hasn't tweaked anything to make things work better on *its* platform. The vendor will let you know what to change in the driver or configuration file to make it work perfectly with *all* the components in your SAN. Usually your storage-array vendor will have these parameters in its documentation on how to connect your servers to its disk arrays.

Planning the HBA connections

Now is a good time to plan the connectivity to the SAN using your newly installed HBAs. If this were a real SAN implementation, you'd be getting out your notepad and jotting down the information contained in Table 7-2. Use one line in your table for each server and each HBA that you connect. Record the server's name, the HBA instance number, and the WWN of the

HBA card. (In Table 7-2, I show only the last 4 digits, but you should put in all 16 hexadecimal digits because you need to know the entire number.) Next is the fabric that you'll connect it to (remember to always alternate fabrics for redundancy); then comes the switch name within the fabric (again, rotate if you can so that you distribute the load among switches); next, the switch port on the switch; and finally, the zoning alias you'll use to call this WWN/HBA combination within the fabric.

Table 7-2			Server HBA Connectivity Information			
Server	**HBA #**	**WWN (Last 4)**	**Fabric**	**Switch Name**	**Switch Port**	**Zoning Alias**
UNIX	1	43:21	A			UNIX01-1
UNIX	2	12:34	B			UNIX02-2
WIN2K	1	56:78	A			WIN2K-1
WIN2K	2	87:65	B			WIN2K-2

Right now (as you can see from the blank columns in Table 7-2), you don't know for sure which switch and port number you should connect to. Assume that you don't know what ports are open on any of the switches, which could be the case if this SAN has been in operation for a while and has other servers already connected. In the upcoming section "Plugging Things In," I walk you through filling in the rest of the table.

Configuring the Array

After you have the fabric set up and the server ready to participate in the SAN, go to the other side of the SAN plan to take care of the storage array. The storage array you'll be using is managed through a command-line interface (CLI) via your TCP/IP network. Imagine that the array is hooked up to the network, and that its IP address has an alias: Larry. (Sorry, it was the closest name that sounds like *array*, so cut me some slack.) You'll be using that name in your commands to refer to the array. The generic command for talking to Larry-the-array is arraycfg (for *array configure*).

The hardware

The make-believe storage array, Larry (you'll get used to it), consists of ten physical hard drives, which can be put into any RAID hardware configuration. (Review Chapter 2 for information on the different types of RAID and how it works.) Groups of these disk drives will be combined into redundant sets; each set can tolerate one of its disks failing.

Larry also has two storage *controllers* — cards that handle communication between a LUN on a RAID group and the ports that connect to the SAN (and therefore to your servers). Each controller, called A and B, has two ports called 1 and 2 (how novel). Thus you have a total of four ports: A1, A2, B1, and B2.

Use the arraycfg command to get the storage array's port information:

```
C:\> arraycfg array=larry GetPortConfig

[Acme Array Company - Array Configurator 1.0]
List of 4 Port elements:
    An instance of Port
       portID=1
       topology=Point-to-Point
       lunSecurityEnabled=true
       controllerID=A
       WorldWidePortName=50.06.0E.80.00.00.20.A1
    An instance of Port
       portID=2

       topology=Point-to-Point
       lunSecurityEnabled=true
       controllerID=A
       WorldWidePortName=50.06.0E.80.00.00.20.A2
    An instance of Port
       portID=1
       topology=Point-to-Point
       lunSecurityEnabled=true
       controllerID=B
       WorldWidePortName=50.06.0E.80.00.00.20.B1
    An instance of Port
       portID=2
       topology=Point-to-Point
       lunSecurityEnabled=true
       controllerID=B
       WorldWidePortName=50.06.0E.80.00.00.20.B2
```

Presto! Here's the port information for your array. You have four ports: Controller A, Port 1; Controller A, Port 2; and so on. You also now have the WWNs for each port. Write those down; you'll need them later.

This storage array is designed to be highly available; the two controllers back each other up in case of a failure. If Controller A fails, then Larry's brain, which controls all the components in the array, moves all the RAID groups and LUNs on Controller A over to Controller B so they have some way to communicate with the SAN. Doing so means the servers on the SAN stay connected to their disks, and the applications running on them aren't affected.

The configuration of your pretend SAN has two hosts: a Unix server and a Windows server. Each has an application needing one LUN or disk. Although you could put hundreds of LUNs out to these servers in the same way, I'm keeping things simple for this chapter.

RAID setup

The Unix server requires a LUN that comes from a RAID 10 array. Because of the application's need for very fast and random write input/output (I/O), RAID 10 fits the bill. The Windows server, on the other hand, does simple file sharing, that is, lots of reads and not much write activity. Put that LUN on a RAID 5 set; doing so wastes less space on reliability. (RAID 10 uses 50 percent of the physical space for its data protection; RAID 5 loses only the space of one physical disk in the set.) Figure 7-7 shows the proposed disk layout for Larry-the-storage-array.

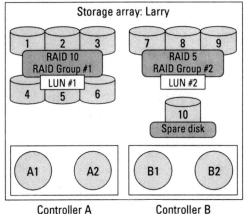

Figure 7-7:
Array con-
figuration:
How to
carve up the
pretend disk
drives.

Now create some RAID sets. Make two RAID sets, like those in Figure 7-7 — one RAID 10 with six disks (three data and three mirrors) and one RAID 5 set of three disks (two data and one parity drive). Use the addraidgroup parameter to accomplish this as an additional parameter to arraycfg. It looks like this:

```
C:\> arraycfg addraidgroup raid=RAID 10 disks=1,2,3,4,5,6
[Acme Array Company - Array Configurator 1.0]
New Array Created:[#1]:Devices = 1,2,3,4,5,6 [RAID
        10(3D+3P)]

C:\> arraycfg addraidgroup raid=RAID 5 disks=7,8,9
[Acme Array Company - Array Configurator 1.0]
New Array Created:[#2]:Devices = 7,8,9 [RAID 5(2D+1P)]

C:\> arraycfg addsparedrive disks=10
[Acme Array Company - Array Configurator 1.0]
New Spare Allocated: Devices = 10
```

In the preceding code, you created your two RAID sets, one with six drives and the other with three. Note the RAID group IDs (#1 and #2; see lines 3 and 7); you need those to create the LUNs for your servers. The third command creates a spare drive out of the last disk in the array, disk #10. You need more than one disk to create a RAID array, so the last drive is perfect to set as a spare drive that can take over in case any disk in the other RAID groups fails.

Now create the LUNs for your Unix server from the RAID 10 set (RAID group #1). This is easy to do; another great parameter to the fictional `arraycfg` program does the trick: Use `AddLogicalUnit` on a RAID group to create a LUN on that set of disks:

```
C:\> arraycfg AddLogicalUnit raidgroup=1 size=10000000
        defcntl=A
  [Acme Array Company - Array Configurator 1.0]
Controller A - New LUN: LUN 1 = 10,000,000 KB (10GB)
```

This command creates a 10,000,000KB (that is, 10GB) LUN and gives it to Controller A to manage. Only one controller has control of a LUN at any time, so you need to pass control of the LUN to a default controller to start with. If that controller fails, the array will pass control to the remaining, surviving controller.

Because you now have the WWNs of both server's HBAs from Table 7-2, you have all the information you need to assign the proper LUN security to the proper HBA WWNs. This is also known as assigning a *path* to a LUN because it resembles tracing a line from the HBA through the SAN to the LUN via the port that the LUN is allowed to talk to. The paths from the Unix server's LUN on the array through the array's ports to the HBAs are shown in Figure 7-8.

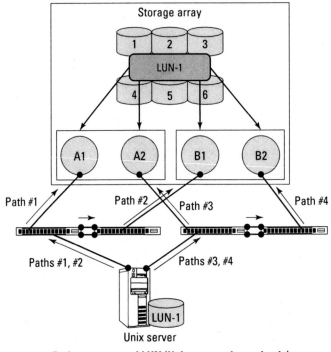

Figure 7-8:
Paths to a
port and
LUN (Unix
system
only).

Paths to a port and LUN (Unix server pictured only)

Following is the command line for your storage array to set the LUN security information for our two ports on Controller A. The parameter is securelun, and you pass to the command the controller, LUN number, and the WWN of the HBA you want to assign to that port and LUN:

```
C:\> arraycfg securelun lun=1
         wwns="10:00:00:00:00:00:43:21" cntl=A port=1
C:\> arraycfg securelun lun=1
         wwns="10:00:00:00:00:00:12:34" cntl=A port=2
```

Now LUN security is set for this LUN on this controller. But what if something fails with this controller, and the LUN moves to Controller B? Because no LUN security for this set of HBAs is defined there, the LUN can't be accessed! Therefore do the same for Controller B as well:

```
C:\> arraycfg securelun lun=1
         wwns="10:00:00:00:00:00:43:21" cntl=B port=1
C:\> arraycfg securelun lun=1
         wwns="10:00:00:00:00:00:12:34" cntl=B port=2
```

Good. Now you're protected from controller failures and not having the right permissions for the server's HBAs on the other controller. If you're wondering how I knew *which* WWNs to give permissions to, refer to Table 7-2: The HBA with the WWN ending in 43:21 goes to Fabric-A. I know that the ports on Controllers A and B numbered Port 1 will connect to the two switches in Fabric-A. Port 2 on both controllers will go to Fabric-B. This makes things redundant, which will become evident later when you cable things together. Trust me. (And if you don't trust me, keep reading anyway.)

Plugging Things In

At this point, your servers are ready to participate in the SAN, the fabric switches are ready to go, your storage array is carved up, and storage is assigned to your HBA's WWN, using LUN security. Now you can start cabling things — but first, plan how everything is to be connected.

To have redundancy from controller, switch, and HBA failures, crisscross the connections of your switches and controllers and HBAs. Table 7-3 lists the controller ports, as well as which fabric and switch they're connected to. Note how Controller A's ports are connected to either fabric and to two different switches. The same goes for Controller B. Multiple paths like these keep you from getting into a jam when something goes wrong with hardware. Redundancy in the design *eliminates a single point of failure* — one of the major reasons to go to a storage area network in the first place.

Table 7-3			Array Connectivity Information			
Controller	*Port #*	*WWN (Last 4)*	*Fabric*	*Switch Name*	*Switch Port*	*Zoning Alias*
A	1	20:A1	A	Switch-A1	14	LARRY-A1
A	2	20:A2	B	Switch-B1	14	LARRY-A2
B	1	20:B1	A	Switch-A2	14	LARRY-B1
B	2	20:B2	B	Switch-B2	14	LARRY-B2

Now that you know where Larry's controllers will be connected, fill in the information about which HBA will plug into what switch. Using Table 7-2 from earlier, fill in the empty columns Switch Name and Switch Port to create a newly updated table: Table 7-4.

Table 7-4		Server HBA Connectivity Information (Completed)				
Server	*HBA #*	*WWN (Last 4)*	*Fabric*	*Switch Name*	*Switch Port*	*Zoning Alias*
UNIX	1	43:21	A	Switch-A1	1	UNIX01-1
UNIX	2	12:34	B	Switch-B1	1	UNIX02-2
WIN2K	1	56:78	A	Switch-A2	1	WIN2K-1
WIN2K	2	87:65	B	Switch-B2	1	WIN2K-2

Congratulations! You know how everything will be connected to your SAN. Now update your initial SAN plan diagram with all this information. Figure 7-9 shows the updated diagram.

Follow your tables and diagram to properly connect the fiber-optic cables to each HBA, storage array port, and switch. I'll wait till you're finished (hmm, hmmmm, hmm).

Confirm that everything logged in to the fabric correctly, and that everything is plugged in where it should be. Run a telnet to each switch in each fabric and also use the SwitchShow command to show the ports and what is connected to them. Here's how that looks for Switch-A1:

```
C:\> telnet switch-a1
trying "switch-a1" ... connected

FabricOS login: admin
Password: ******

Switch-A1:> SwitchShow
Port 1:   [F] 10:00:00:00-00:00:43:21

Port 2:   [G] No Light
Port 3:   [G] No Light
Port 4:   [G] No Light
Port 5:   [G] No Light
Port 6:   [G] No Light
Port 7:   [G] No Light
Port 8:   [G] No Light
Port 9:   [G] No Light
Port 10:  [G] No Light
Port 11:  [G] No Light
Port 12:  [G] No Light
Port 13:  [G] No Light
Port 14:  [F] 50:06:0E:80-00:00:20:A1
Port 15:  [E] 60:00:00:00-ed:fa:31:a5 - ISL/Domain:2
Port 16:  [E] 60:00:00:00-ed:fa:31:a6 - ISL/Domain:2
```

This display shows Switch-A1's port listing. Note that Port 1 has a Fabric Login (denoted by [F]), with the WWN 10:00:00:00:00:00:43:21. The ports showing [G] and No Light mean that the port is still in General mode and nothing is plugged into the port. The [E] ports are Extension ports, extending the fabric to another switch via an ISL link.

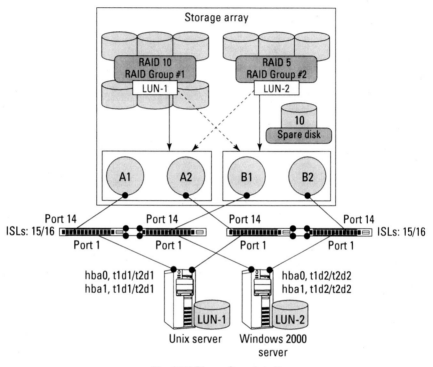

Figure 7-9:
Your SAN so far, with all the cabling connected.

The SAN Plan – Completed!

Look at your table of server HBA connections (Table 7-4), and you can see the WWN of your Unix box, right where it should be on Port 1. Port 14 has a WWN ending in 20:A1, which, going by your table of storage array connections (Table 7-3), is Larry-the-storage-array's Controller A, Port 1.

See those connections on Ports 15 and 16? Remember your ISLs connecting Switch-A1 with Switch-A2? There they are, showing up as [E] ports going to Domain ID 2 (Switch-A2 is Domain 2; see Table 7-1).

If you go through the rest of the switches, you should see similar information, with all your HBAs and storage ports connected as well. This is another way to find out the WWNs of the connections to your SAN components, such as the HBAs and the storage arrays. But if you use this method to get the addresses, you risk assuming that you hooked up everything correctly. I recommend getting the WWN — as well as the HBA's driver — directly from the storage array's vendor or configuration tool; use those WWNs in your tables when planning your SAN. Then you'll have everything set up the way you want it instead of having to work around how it wound up being connected. Just be sure to copy the numbers correctly; finding a typo in a 16-digit hexadecimal number can be difficult. Believe me, I know.

Configuring the Zones

As discussed earlier, *zoning* is what allows each of your connections into the SAN fabric to see what it has to see . . . and not see what it doesn't. (Is that a double negative?) When you start, no zones are defined; you have just a blank zone set with no members (if you followed my tip when creating the fabrics). This keeps all the connected ports from seeing anything at all.

After a SAN fabric is established and being used, you'll be making new zones and adding them to the existing active *zone set*. The active zone sets you created for your two SAN fabrics are `Fabric-A` and `Fabric-B`, respectively. Makes sense to me. You make new zones for your HBA to storage array port connections through the fabric and plop them into the active zone sets.

Mapping the zones first

The guideline to making zones is usually one HBA per zone as well as all the storage ports that it should be able to see within that fabric. In your make-believe SAN, because each server has two HBAs (one to each fabric), you'll have one zone for that HBA within the fabric that it attaches to. For example, with your Unix box (because it has two HBAs), make one zone for the first HBA in Fabric-A and one zone in Fabric-B for the other HBA. Included in these two zones are the respective storage ports *within that fabric* that you want the HBA to use storage from.

I like to differentiate the names of zones with `z-` at the beginning so I know I'm dealing with a zone and not with a zone set or a zone alias.

Table 7-5 shows the zones that you need to create within each fabric. I explain why I chose the particular aliases from Tables 7-3 and 7-4 after you read through our choices.

Table 7-5		Fabric Zoning Information	
Fabric	*Zone Set*	*Zone*	*Zone Members*
A	Fabric-A	Z-UNIX	1,1; 1,14; 2,14
A	Fabric-A	Z-WIN2K	WIN2K-1; LARRY-A1; LARRY-B1
B	Fabric-B	Z-UNIX	4,1; 3,14; 4,14
B	Fabric-B	Z-WIN2K	WIN2K-2; LARRY-A2; LARRY-B2

Confused yet? Are you curious about why there are four storage ports on the array but only two show up within each fabric's zone definitions? Same thing with the HBAs: Only two of the four total HBAs are in each fabric's zone set. Again, because the storage array ports and HBAs connect directly to Fabric-A *or* B — not A *and* B — why make a zone that will never show up within that fabric? Besides, because the two fabrics are completely isolated, Fabric-A doesn't even *have* a definition for, say, LARRY-B2. That alias and the WWN for that alias exist only on Fabric-B. You couldn't make that zone if you tried. (Actually you can make a zone *alias* for a WWN that doesn't exist, but that just causes confusion; I don't recommend it.)

In Table 7-5, you can see a zone in Fabric-A for the Unix server called Z-UNIX, with members 1,1; 1,14; and 2,14. Huh? What are these weird numbers? Remember the SAN plan: The Unix server was going to use hard zoning, so you'll be using the actual domain ID and port numbers for the zoning information.

In Tables 7-1, 7-3, and 7-4, you have all the information you need to map out how your SAN is configured. You have the fabric definitions, the switches, the ports, the HBAs and their WWNs, and the storage ports (as well as their connection details). All your info is contained in three neat, cross-referenced tables; if you follow along with them, you can easily create the proper zones for your SAN without having to worry about making errors (provided you filled in the tables correctly). Besides, tables might look pretty, but these aliases are still just your own way of labeling the connections; only the zone aliases that you enter into the fabrics will make them available to use in reality (even in your pretend SAN).

I'm zoning out . . .

Remember connecting to the switches with the telnet command? Use that to get to Switch-A1. I'll use Switch-A1 to populate the zoning for Fabric-A first, and then use Switch-B1 for Fabric-B. The commands to use are

AliasCreate, ZoneCreate, ConfigAdd, and ConfigEnable. The first creates zone aliases, the next creates new zones, and the next one adds your zones to a zone set (called a *config*). Last, ConfigEnable turns your changes on so they'll become the current configuration of the fabric.

```
C:\> telnet switch-a1
trying "switch-a1" ... connected

FabricOS login: admin
Password: ******

Switch-A1:> AliasCreate "WIN2K-
         1","10:00:00:00:00:00:56:78"
Switch-A1:> AliasCreate "LARRY-
         A1","50:06:0E:80:00:00:20:A1"
Switch-A1:> AliasCreate "LARRY-
         B1","50:06:0E:80:00:00:20:B1"
Switch-A1:> ZoneCreate "Z-WIN2K","WIN2K-1;LARRY-
         A1;LARRY-B1"
Switch-A1:> ZoneCreate "Z-UNIX","1,1;1,14;2,14"
Switch-A1:> ConfigAdd "Fabric-A","Z-WIN2K;Z-UNIX"
Configuration Fabric-A updated.
Switch-A1:> ConfigEnable "Fabric-A"
Configuration Fabric-A is now in operation.
```

The preceding code completes the zoning for Fabric-A. Yes, six simple commands. Review them so that you understand what they do. Using the first command, AliasCreate, three times creates three new aliases: WIN2K-1, LARRY-A1, and LARRY-B1. How do you know which WWN numbers to use? Refer to Table 7-4 for the WWNs of the HBAs and to Table 7-3 for the storage array's port WWNs. You want only the entries that exist on Fabric-A. When you log into Fabric-B using Switch-B1, you add all the aliases and zones for Fabric-B there.

Using the next command (ZoneCreate) twice, you create the zones Z-WIN2K and Z-UNIX. The Z-WIN2K zone contains the aliases for the Windows server's HBA (WIN2K-1) and the two storage ports on array Larry that plug into Fabric-A (LARRY-A1 and LARRY-B1; note Table 7-3 for those aliases listed for Fabric-A). Now, the zone for Z-UNIX looks different because you aren't using soft zoning with zone aliases. You're using hard zoning, or directly using the ports themselves. Here, 2,14 means domain ID 2, Port 14. According to Table 7-1, Domain 2 is Switch-A2. And according to Table 7-3, Port 14 of Switch-A2 is Larry-the-array's Controller B, Port 1. Likewise, 1,1 is Domain 1, Port 1 — so that's Switch-A1, and is connected to Unix HBA #1 (see Table 7-4).

Using tables is a great aid when tracking what's connected to what.

The last set of commands — ConfigAdd and ConfigEnable — puts the new zones into the active zone set Fabric-A and makes them take effect. Without running ConfigEnable, the zone is defined but the switches won't enforce the use of the zone. Zone sets that are not the currently active zone set (set with ConfigEnable) are in standby mode, waiting to be enabled when you need them.

Now double-check your work by listing the new configuration, using the zoneshow command on Fabric-A (via Switch-A1):

```
Switch-A1:> zoneshow

Fabric Zoning Configuration:
Active Zone Set: Fabric-A
1 Zone Sets defined
Zone Set: Fabric-A = {Z-UNIX; Z-WIN2K}

2 Zones defined
Zone: Z-UNIX =   {1,1; 1,14; 2,14}
Zone: Z-WIN2K = {WIN2K-1; LARRY-A1; LARRY-B1}

3 Zone Aliases defined
Alias: WIN2K-1 =   {10:00:00:00:00:00:56:78}
Alias: LARRY-A1 =  {50:06:0E:80:00:00:20:A1}
Alias: LARRY-B1 =  {50:06:0E:80:00:00:20:B1}
```

Looks good. You have your zone set that now contains the two zones for the Unix and Windows servers. The zones have the right information in them, too.

Do the same with Fabric-B for its required zones, and you'll be able to access the storage array from your servers.

Back to the Servers: Did It Work?

The vision for your SAN plan, which began with a virtually empty computer room, is now alive with switches, storage, hosts, and fiber-optic cable buzzing with, er, light? (Does light buzz? Make that *flicker*.) Fiber-optic cable flickering with activity. (Whew.)

The next step is to see whether everything you did works. Going back to your servers, you need to check whether the OS now recognizes the disk devices that you assigned. Each OS is different; some allow you to add storage devices online (without rebooting) and some don't. Just to be certain that the new disk devices don't mess anything up, add the storage during off-hours.

Here's a big assumption that I now must face: To have multiple HBAs see the same LUNs and load balance and fail-over, you need a software or OS feature that allows this functionality. Using multiple paths from your server to the LUN is called (well, yeah) *multipathing;* I'm assuming that your servers have multipathing software installed or built into the operating system. That way, if the same LUN appears across two different HBAs, the OS will know it's looking at the same LUN. Operating systems are dumb, and they don't usually expect to see the same disk on two different host adapters.

Just keep pretending that your OS will handle multipathing for you and not allow you to see four LUNs when you have only one with four paths.

Unix servers

Log in to the Unix system first. In this pretend Unix system, the OS is Solaris and it contains a few key files that you need to be aware of before you expect to see any disk devices appear.

Persistence pays off

First, make sure that the HBA's configuration file has the proper entries. A few paragraphs from here is a segment of a typical configuration file called `/etc/hba.conf`. I removed all the mumbo-jumbo entries for timeouts and the like; they're standard, and your SAN vendor will tell you what you specifically need to put in for them.

The important line is the one starting with `hba-bind-WWNN`. That line controls *persistent binding,* which is used to make sure that when a server reboots and scans its HBAs for disk devices, it always finds the same LUNs that it used before in the same place. You see, computers are funny — when they start up and go out initializing their devices (such as HBAs), they don't always remember where things were the last time they were used. If you don't use persistent bindings, the LUNs that you had on HBA card #1 might suddenly show up on HBA card #2 the next time around. This is not good because your applications expect to find your files on a specific device, and if they aren't there, the applications will fail to run.

When multiple HBAs are in a server, the same driver for each HBA loads multiple times: each one called an *instance.* An instance name typically starts with a shortened name or abbreviation for the HBA card manufacturer (here it's the generic `hba`) and then a number, usually starting with zero and incrementing with each physical HBA card found in the server. With this section of the configuration file, you can associate each instance of the HBA driver to a specific port on the storage array. Use the World Wide Port Name (WWPN — same as the WWN of the storage port) to bind each instance to a specific card and SCSI target # ID. This will make all the devices appear in the same place every time upon a server reboot.

For example, the WWN ending in 20:a1 (Larry-the-storage-array's Controller A, Port 1; refer to Table 7-3) is to be linked with HBA instance `hba0`, and that path to the disks will be called _SCSI target 1_ (abbreviated as _t1_). You do this with each port on the array to create four paths to your one LUN because there are four ports on the SAN presenting the LUN, potentially. I know this is confusing, but think about it: You want each HBA card to be able to see its given LUNs through any port on the array that is presenting those LUNs. Your Unix box needs to know by what HBA instance (and which SCSI target) that path is going to be called, every time. You're just helping it remember by telling it that it should look for port `WWN  .  .  .20:a1` via card instance `hba0` and should use `SCSI target 1` for those LUNs.

The HBA instance names, targets, and LUN numbers are then reused in the `/kernel/drv/sd.conf` file later to match with specific device files that Unix uses to create your file systems.

Here is an example of `file /etc/hba.conf`:

```
# Acme HBA Company - HBA Configuration File
#

#persistent binding section

hba-bind-WWPN="50060e80000020a1:hba0t1",
              "50060e80000020a2:hba1t1",
              "50060e80000020b1:hba0t2",
              "50060e80000020b2:hba1t2";

#queue depth section
lun-queue-depth=32;
tgt-queue-depth=512;

#SAN topology settings
# Settings: 1=Loop, 2=Point-to-Point
topology=2;
```

The next file you need to modify is the `/kernel/drv/sd.conf` file, which tells the Solaris OS which SCSI devices your server should look for. Although SAN devices are connected via fiber-optic cable, they're still treated as standard SCSI disks. Each entry that you add is for a LUN that might exist on the `hba` driver instance (`hba=?`) and SCSI target (`target=?`).

Here is an example of the `/kernel/drv/sd.conf` file:

```
# /kernel/drv/sd.conf for SAN Plan UNIX server
#
# internal disk entries are up here
#
# Beginning of SAN entries
#
# Entry for HBA "0", and target "1" in hba.conf
```

```
name="sd" parent="hba" target=1 lun=1 hba="hba0";
#
# Entry for HBA "1", and target "1" in hba.conf
name="sd" parent="hba" target=1 lun=1 hba="hba1";

# Entry for HBA "0", and target "2" in hba.conf
name="sd" parent="hba" target=2 lun=1 hba="hba0";
#
# Entry for HBA "1", and target "2" in hba.conf
name="sd" parent="hba" target=2 lun=1 hba="hba1";
```

In this example, you tell the server to look on the first HBA card tagged as hba0 for SCSI targets 1, LUN 1. Then it looks for target 1, LUN 1 on the second card, hba1. I do the same thing with target 2 (the Controller B ports) in the same way. Now if the LUN fails over to the other controller, Solaris Unix will know what this device is — and will continue to use it.

Load balancing and path fail-over software

When Unix finds a LUN, it creates a special file under the /dev/rdsk directory that is unique to that particular instance of the LUN. In English, if you find a LUN as the HBA scans the fiber-optic cable connected to it, it makes a special file. If it finds the same LUN connected to another HBA card, it makes *another* special file. Unix doesn't know that they are the same disk.

Software on your server that's provided by either the OS or your SAN vendor (usually the storage array vendor) can manage all these multiple instances of the same disk device for you. This multipathing software usually gives you one single device name to use instead of all the others. The multipathing software handles the interpretation of which disk is which behind the scenes, leaving you with only one special file to create your file systems on, masking the complexity of the multiple paths to the real disk device through the SAN. (How nice of them.)

The moment of truth

You're ready to see whether your server sees storage. You need to recycle the server's OS to allow it to reload the HBA's drivers and configuration files and then rescan for new devices. To do this, reboot with the -r parameter to rebuild the device files in Unix. If it sees the new LUNs that you created, they will have their own c#t#d# files in Unix's device file area under the /dev/rdsk directory:

```
# reboot -- -r
```

After you reboot, watch the console for messages such as New device found or Device acquired.

Run the Unix `format` command to view what devices are available to be used:

```
# format
Searching for disks...done


AVAILABLE DISK SELECTIONS:
       0. c0t0d0 <ST320011A cyl 38790 alt 2 hd 16 sec 63>
          /pci@1f,0/ide@d/dad@0,0
       1. c3t1d1 <ACME-DISK cyl 10014 alt 2 hd 15 sec 96>
          /pci@1f,4000/hba@1/sd@1,1
       2. c4t1d1 <ACME-DISK cyl 10014 alt 2 hd 15 sec 96>
          /pci@1f,4000/hba@2/sd@1,1

Specify disk (enter its number):
```

Congratulations! You can see disks 1 and 2 off two controllers, c3 and c4 (c#t1d1), called `ACME-DISK`, which is the pseudomanufacturer of the storage array `Larry`. That's SCSI target 1, LUN 1 on both cards. You now have two ways to talk to this disk device, which your load-balancing software will auto-detect and handle for you.

Now, just as you would with any new disk device, put a label on it and make your file systems.

Windows system

Windows is much easier to use with disk storage than the previous Unix system. You don't have to set up persistent binding files or edit `/kernel/drv/sd.conf`. Windows automatically detects new devices and tells you to reboot the server so that it can rescan its SCSI bus and add the device's parameters to its registry. Then it makes you write a *signature,* which is a special sequence of data, to tag the new disk. That's how it knows which LUN is which the next time that you reboot.

To force Windows to find your new disk device, reboot the server and let Windows do its thing with the Add Hardware Wizard, which finds the new hard disk and adds it to the registry.

Then make your partitions and file systems the usual way by choosing Start⇨Settings⇨Control Panel⇨Administrative Tools⇨Computer Management⇨Storage⇨Disk Management (local).

You'll also find load balancing and path fail-over software for the Windows server platform. Check with your storage array vendor on how to go about configuring it, because it differs depending on the vendor.

When dealing with multiple paths on Windows, I usually recommend that you create your file system on only the first instance of your new disk in Disk Administrator. The rest of the copies are just the second instance, third instance, and so on of the first — so you don't want to do things twice, three times, or as many times as there are copies.

iSCSI, You SCSI, We All SCSI

The iSCSI protocol runs on top of standard Ethernet TCP/IP networks, so you may already have all the cables and network switches you need to use it for your SAN. You might even have 10 gigabit-per-second LAN links, which are even faster than today's 8 gigabit-per-second limit for Fibre Channel.

Because iSCSI uses traditional Ethernet networks to communicate, it is quickly becoming a more prevalent way to connect storage arrays with servers. Although not everyone has Fibre Channel cabling in their datacenter, just about everyone has an Ethernet network. Using what you already have is always quicker, cheaper and easier. However, many users who implement larger iSCSI solutions prefer to build a dedicated network for the storage traffic, just to keep it more secure and easier to troubleshoot. For the purpose of explanation, I'll put iSCSI on its own network to show you everything from the ground up. That doesn't mean you can't put it on an existing Ethernet network. It's up to you and your network folks to decide whether you have the room to add that traffic on top of your existing LAN traffic.

Before you start plugging in new stuff, you should make sure you understand the basic iSCSI terminology.

Initiators and targets

In iSCSI, it is important not to confuse an initiator and a target. An *initiator* is the device that initiates the conversation between your host computer and a storage device. (Instead of using specialized Fibre Channel HBAs, your host initiates a conversation between one of its regular Ethernet LAN ports and another device on the same network.) A *target* is an Ethernet LAN port on the network which is on the iSCSI storage array. (Target ports are where LUNs from the storage array will be assigned to initiators.)

One more concept to understand is the *session* — the two-way traffic between specific initiator and target pairs. Each session is unique to help ensure that data coming and going across your network ends up in the right place.

When a session is established between the initiator and target, you have an open communication link to get information back and forth, just like an open phone connection between you and grandma.

IQN: iSCSI qualified name

Remember the concept of World Wide Names? Each port on a Fibre Channel SAN, whether it was an HBA or a storage port, has a unique number. iSCSI also requires unique names, but it uses a less cryptic and more descriptive way to keep things straight. This is the concept of an iSCSI Qualified Name, or IQN.

The software that manages the iSCSI initiator automatically creates an IQN for you. You can change it to something else if you want to micromanage your iSCSI SAN. However, if you rename your host, the IQN probably will change as well. This could affect any drive mappings made previous to the host name change.

Each storage target on the iSCSI network also has a unique IQN, which usually has the vendor and serial number of the storage array embedded in it. The idea is to make sure each one is always unique.

SCSI Name Service

So you have all these IQNs now. How do you keep them organized and use them wisely? The answer is a SCSI Name Service server. This server is a computer on your network that all the iSCSI devices say "hello" to when they start up. The "hello" message is a registration of the IQN into a master list that you can use to match up your initiators and targets.

Microsoft uses a service for their users called iSNS. It allows initiators and targets to register and be managed centrally. Most other operating systems, such as Unix, Linux, and Mac OSs, have similar ways to manage iSCSI names.

The best thing about SNS servers is that now you have a central way to see and control your iSCSI initiators, which otherwise would be randomly looking around the network for targets to talk to. This is where the concept of a data domain comes in handy.

Data domains

In a basic iSCSI SAN, a storage array advertises its SCSI LUNs to the network (the targets), and clients run an iSCSI driver (the initiators) that looks for those LUNs. In a larger setup with, say, fifty or more clients or storage devices or both, you probably don't want every client to see every storage device. It makes sense to block off what each host can see and which storage devices they have the potential of using. This is accomplished by registering the names of the initiators and targets in a central location, and then pairing them into groups. A logical grouping, called a *data domain,* partitions the registered initiators and targets into more manageable groups.

Every iSCSI initiator and iSCSI target is either in the default DD (Default Data Domain) or in a specific DD that you create. For example, the accounting servers can belong to the Accounting DD and the storage devices they need to talk to are also set up to belong to that same DD. When scanning the network for storage, the accounting servers will see only iSCSI target ports in the same data domain.

You're probably asking, what if the same server needs storage from two different data domains? Well, you can add an initiator or target to multiple domains, so it's just like having the same HBA in multiple Fibre Channel zones.

Getting started with iSCSI

It's easy to set up iSCSI SANs. Almost too easy.

These are the very basic steps you need to follow:

1. **Install iSCSI initiator software client on the host computer.**
2. **Install iSCSI storage device on your Ethernet LAN.**
3. **Configure the iSCSI storage to present LUNs to particular clients.**
4. **Set iSCSI clients to attach to particular iSCSI targets.**

Microsoft is a major supporter of iSCSI. It has both an iSCSI initiator client for its operating systems and an iSNS server for handling initiator and target registration, domain grouping, and overall iSCSI-management tasks.

You can download the client and server, plus documentation, for free from Microsoft's Web site (www.microsoft.com/). Search for *iSCSI* and you should be able to find what you need to give iSCSI a try.

Check with your LAN admins before you begin putting storage traffic out on an Ethernet LAN. Some networks are already bogged down with data traffic — the extra storage communication will bring things down to a crawl if you're not careful.

Getting serious with iSCSI

Although iSCSI is easy to get started with, using it heavily will bog down your server's CPU cycles with all that Ethernet talk. Because the SCSI commands that usually go back and forth to a disk drive are now being converted into TCP packets that go out on the LAN, all those SCSI-to-Ethernet and Ethernet-to-SCSI translations take processor horsepower. A dedicated Ethernet card called a *TCP off-load engine*, or *TOE card*, takes the translation burden off your server's CPU. If you put a TOE card in your server to do all the CPU-intensive work of translating SCSI to Ethernet and back, you free up your CPUs to do calculations, perform database searches, serve Web pages, or calculate pi, depending on your applications.

Data Migration

You've done it! Starting with an empty computer room, you've designed and put together an entire multiplatform SAN that is fully redundant and ready to host applications. But that was just pretend.

In your *real* data center, you probably have a bunch of servers with applications running on internal disks. Suppose you really built this SAN and had it ready to use. How would you get your applications from the internal disks to the SAN disks without completely reinstalling them?

Here are the most common ways to migrate the data over to the SAN:

- ✔ Connect servers to the SAN and use the OS to copy volume to volume
- ✔ Back up to tape and restore to SAN disks
- ✔ Use the network to copy from the existing server to a SAN-based server

The next sections look at these solutions, eliminate the ones that don't always work well, and concentrate on the most effective.

Network migration

Using your existing LAN to copy your application data via File Transfer Protocol (FTP) or to file-share to your SAN disk is a viable option. However, copying is painstakingly slow; the process could take days or even weeks to complete, depending on how much data you have. You'd have to stop your applications for that amount of time to get a copy that hasn't changed from the start of the copy to the end. If you're a small shop (or you just want to do some small-scale testing of your SAN), this might be a cheap way to get data over to your new SAN. But don't hold your breath.

Backup/restore migration

Ah, the classic tape solution. This is the back-pocket solution for any data migration operation: Back up your application data to tape and restore it somewhere else (to the SAN-attached server). Again, as with the network-based migration, this method takes time. It might be neither fast enough nor foolproof enough to get all the data moved before the application has to be up and available to users. A clean backup can only be done with all the files closed, so the application can't be running while the backup-and-restore process is happening. However, it should be faster than going through your average network, depending on how robust your backup system is.

Disk-to-SAN migration

The fastest and most logical method is to take your existing application server and drop an HBA into it. Then you put *this* server on the SAN. After you have a SAN disk assigned to your application server, use the OS to copy the server's internal volume to the volume on the SAN. Then just run your application from the SAN-based disk instead of from the internal disk drives. You don't have to reinstall anything, and you don't need a second server standing by to catch the data, as you do in the other two solutions.

Part II
Designing and Building a SAN

"We take network security here very seriously."

In this part . . .

*I*f this were a book about home audio, Part I is about what a CD player does and how an amplifier works. This part covers how you get music out of these components by linking them together. We explain how to use hubs, switches, HBAs, fibre cables, and associated software to design a functioning storage area network.

This part also goes into detail about how to prepare for the worst. Although the subject is bleak, disaster recovery planning is very important and can save you a lot of time and money, keeping your business running if something bad happens.

After we cover how all the different pieces of a SAN work together and how to protect it, we take you through an actual soup-to-nuts SAN-building example to show you a complete step-by-step implementation.

Chapter 8

Networking SANs

. . . .

In This Chapter

▶ Defining a SAN island

▶ Connecting SAN islands

▶ Creating a SWAN

▶ Looking at connection protocols

▶ Understanding the new iSCSI protocol

▶ Choosing and using SAN extenders

▶ Choosing the correct link for the job

▶ Using compression to save money

▶ Getting a handle on virtualization and storage pooling

. . . .

*I*magine you've grown to love this storage area network (SAN) stuff so much that it's reproducing like rabbits throughout your company! Things are starting to get out of hand again. You have little islands of SANs in multiple buildings, and it's hard to manage all those separate SAN environments.

SAN management provides an exciting capability: You can access and control a company's storage resources from a centralized administrative desk — using a single management console — and replicate data between locations for disaster recovery. One reason all this is possible: You can connect SANs across a distance.

Having SANs in multiple places is a good thing, because you connect them and use a remote location as a backup or recovery site for your company. You can actually make the gloom-and-doom disaster-recovery guys happy.

This chapter covers methods of connecting SANs. It also covers the fundamentals of choosing the correct links between SAN islands to do the job right. This chapter also touches a bit more on the iSCSI protocol, some virtualization techniques, and virtual storage pooling. (For more on virtualization and storage pooling, see Chapter 15.)

Defining a SAN Island

A *SAN island* is a storage area network that is physically isolated in a single location and managed as a separate physical entity, as shown in Figure 8-1.

Departmental SAN island

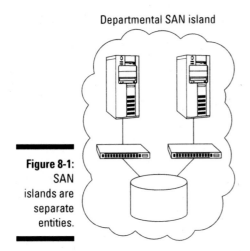

Figure 8-1:
SAN
islands are
separate
entities.

Similar to a local area network (LAN), a SAN island consists of all servers, switches, and storage arrays that are physically connected in one location.

The difference between a SAN island and a *storage wide area network* (SWAN) is the same as the difference between a TCP/IP–based local area network and a wide area network (WAN): geography. When any two separate local area networks are connected, they become a wide area network. The same is true with SANs; tie two of them together, and they become a SWAN.

Some SAN islands can be quite large — for example, when a SAN is isolated in one building but some of its components are located on different floors in different departments. Multiple small SAN islands can be used in the same physical location but for different applications (or perhaps by separate business units) within a company. Figure 8-2 shows such a configuration.

For example, a mainframe computer might be hooked up to its own dedicated SAN storage network, while another small SAN might be connected only to Unix and NT servers. Many companies that rely on IBM mainframes have two separate Information Technology (IT) organizations — one for the mainframe people and the other for Unix and Windows server people.

Corporate Data Center Building 1

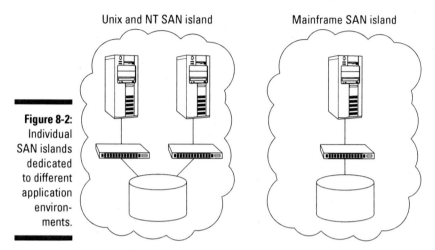

Unix and NT SAN island   Mainframe SAN island

Figure 8-2:
Individual
SAN islands
dedicated
to different
application
environ-
ments.

Traditionally, many large companies have multiple lines of business or business units, and without the proper guidance from upper management, each business unit can be in charge of its own independent IT department. Often these smaller departments of the same company act independently of one another, similar to small independently governed countries. Each business unit has its own technology budget, with each one doing its own thing.

The problems for companies using multiple independent IT departments become apparent during downturns in the economy. Companies often find that having separate IT departments causes duplication of personnel and equipment, and hampers the company's ability to leverage the consolidated buying power of all business units. This wastes a lot of money. Consolidation is the fix, and companies are now consolidating and centralizing their IT infrastructures so they can combine the buying power of their individual business units. In the process, these companies find that a SAN lets them consolidate their storage environments, which enables them to create a disaster-tolerant infrastructure for the company.

If you've been around the computing industry for a while, I'm sure you've heard the terms *server consolidation, data consolidation,* and *restructuring.* These all mean about the same thing: Do more with less.

This chapter will help you do just that. I show you how to connect SAN environments in your company together over an IP network for centralizing management and control — and how to extend SAN fabrics to enable the copying of data between SAN islands for data sharing and disaster recovery.

Connecting SAN Islands

Individual smaller SANs are connected to form a larger SAN to share and copy data:

- ✔ **Disk/data sharing:** The need to share disks among servers in different SANs is brought about by applications such as e-mail, application clustering, and access to information in large databases. (Read more about clustering in the following section.) Data sharing can be accomplished by enabling access from multiple servers to the same physical disks, or by enabling access to the files located on those physical disks. Sharing physical disks has to be done through a SAN; sharing files can be done over a LAN.

- ✔ **Data copying:** The need to keep data safe and recoverable in the event of a disaster is one of the main driving forces behind a company implementing a SAN (see Chapter 6 for more on disaster recovery). The data at one location can be easily copied to a second physical location over the storage network. Backing up your data to a remote location enables you to get access to that data in the event of a disaster at the primary location.

Disk/data sharing

Sometimes different departments in the same company are somewhat autonomous — with different budgets and buying habits — and no storage-vendor standards in place. One of the disadvantages of letting folks do their own thing is this lack of standards. For example, a company could have a number of small SAN islands in place, each consisting of different types of servers and storage from many vendors.

The servers might be connected to a low-cost departmental storage array in a small SAN in one department, and an expensive high-end array in another department with a larger budget. This business would run a lot more efficiently if it could share storage arrays and allow data access from all the departments by connecting those departments into a larger consolidated SAN.

Take a college campus as an example. Servers connected to separate SAN islands in different buildings on campus might need access to the same data for sharing research information. You need a way to connect those buildings so all servers in every building can see the same storage. Connecting everything creates a pool of storage resources, accessible by any server connected to the pool.

The need for disk sharing can also be driven by the need to create server clusters. A *server cluster* is a method of tying together two or more individual physical servers to look like a single logical server. If one of the servers has a problem, another one takes over for the failed server. To create a hardware cluster, each server needs access to the same physical disks. The members of a server cluster can be located in different buildings by using a SAN to connect to disks over long distances.

Data copying

People need copies of their data for multiple reasons. Maybe you need a copy of a production database to use for testing live data for a new version of an application. You might have developers located in another country who need a recent copy of data for testing. You might also want to keep a recent copy of your critical data on disk to recover corrupted files.

The main reason for keeping copies of data is for recoverability. Many companies back up their data to tape and ship it off-site for this reason. The downside to using tapes is the need to restore data back to disk before it can be used again. Recovering data from tapes takes time, and time is not a luxury that many companies have these days.

This is where SAN data replication comes in. All the critical data housed in SAN storage can be copied in real time from a main production facility to a remote storage array located in another building, state, or country. Having the ability to copy critical data to a remote disk in real time — versus recovery from a tape backup — means that you can recover from a disaster in minutes instead of hours or days. If your company also invests in data de-duplication technologies, you can even save money by sending and storing the copies as efficiently as is technically possible. (For more about continuous data protection and data de-duplication, see Part V of this book.)

The Storage WAN, MAN, and SWAN

You can connect SAN islands in multiple ways, using many different devices and for different reasons. Whether the distance that needs to be covered is over a single metropolitan area, across the country, or across the globe will determine the kind of network connections you'll need.

Let's plow through a few acronyms first:

- **MAN:** A *MAN,* short for a *metropolitan area network,* covers a single metropolitan area, such as a city or multiple buildings within a college campus. The limited distance requirements of a MAN normally allow you to extend the Fibre Channel connections between SANs using optical Fibre Channel extenders.

- **WAN:** A *WAN,* or *wide area network,* can cover the globe. Because Fibre Channel networks are limited in distance, creating a storage network that spans the globe would require IP-based Fibre Channel extenders.

- **SWAN:** When two or more SAN fabrics are connected over a wide area, the larger storage network is known as a *SWAN,* or *storage wide area network.*

The distances involved and the types of available connections will determine what kind of network and the type of equipment you need, as well as the capabilities you have after you're finished.

Using the network only for storage management

Ironically, most SAN devices are managed using an IP connection. Connecting just the management ports by using only the IP network can help centralize management of all the SAN islands spread out in your organization. The SAN islands are connected for management purposes only. Your SANs remain separate, but you can now manage them all from a single console at a central location.

SAN-management software allows you to allocate storage to any server connected to any SAN island attached to your network. The SANs are not really connected, so you cannot share access to disks between the islands. However, because the management of your SANs becomes centralized, you can use fewer people to manage your storage. (See Figure 8-3, in which *FC* stands for Fibre Channel.) Having the tools to allow you to be more productive is a good thing.

Figure 8-3 shows just the network ports of each device in the independent SAN islands connected to the college campus IP network. The IP connection enables the SAN-management station to connect to and manage each device as if it were local. This remote management capability allows the storage administrator to manage devices from anywhere on campus.

Every SAN device comes with at least one IP network connection for management of the device. Your SAN hardware vendor can help you set up the required software and connectivity to manage its equipment.

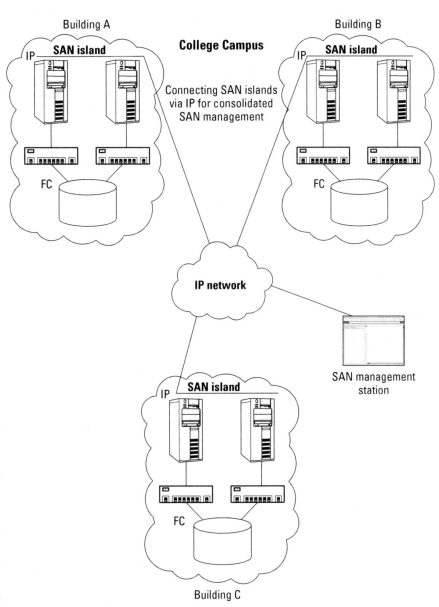

Figure 8-3:
Centralized
SAN
management uses
IP for
connectivity.

The storage SWAN

Creating a storage network that spans multiple buildings or locations is similar to creating a wide area IP network (WAN). If the area covered is limited in distance to a single metropolitan area, the network is a metropolitan area network (MAN). If the geographic distance covered is over a wide area, the network is a storage wide area network (SWAN). A WAN connects many smaller local area networks (LANs) running the Transmission Control Protocol/Internet Protocol (TCP/IP) by using either privately owned network links or leased lines from a Telco provider. (The *Telco* is usually your local phone company or a company that specializes in providing leased network links.)

To solve the issue of sharing disks between individual SAN islands, use a SWAN, which is created by linking two or more SAN islands at the switched fabric level. The network can be either an IP network that carries Fibre Channel frames over IP or an extended Fibre Channel network that uses Fibre Channel extenders or long-wave Fibre Channel cables to connect the sites.

I show you the different methods of extending a SAN when I cover how to stretch a SAN in the upcoming sections "Stretching the SAN (The Rubber-Band Approach)" and "Using Connected SAN Islands (The Two-Rubber-Bands Approach)."

Choosing and Using SAN Extenders

SAN extenders are the devices that connect SAN islands to one another. The SAN extenders that you choose will depend on how you want to connect your SAN. If you simply want to manage a bunch of SAN islands as a single entity, you don't even need SAN extenders. Just buy a SAN-management software suite that lets you manage everything through a Web browser (refer to Figure 8-3 for an illustration of using a software-management tool) and connect your storage to your IP network. I don't have room to mention here all the products that accomplish Web-based SAN management. Just contact your storage vendor and ask for a recommendation.

If you want to create one big SAN fabric so you can copy data between sites through the SAN, you can use an FCIP-based extender using IP (FCIP stands for Fibre Channel over Internet Protocol), or long-wave cables between switches using fiber-optic cable, or a Dense Wave Division Multiplexing (DWDM) solution. Keep in mind that using fiber-optic cable to connect SAN islands has distance limitations of around 100 km. The FCIP-based solution over IP can connect SAN islands at almost any distance.

FCIP solutions are available from

- ✔ **Brocade:** www.brocade.com
- ✔ **Cisco:** www.cisco.com
- ✔ **Qlogic:** www.qlogic.com

DWDM solutions are available from

- ✔ **Alcatel-Lucent:** www.alcatel-lucent.com
- ✔ **Ciena:** www.ciena.com
- ✔ **Cisco:** www.cisco.com
- ✔ **Nortel Networks:** www.nortelnetworks.com

Long-wave dark fiber solutions are usually leased from a network provider in your area, although some companies are lucky enough to have their own dark-fiber runs between buildings or locations (there's more about dark fiber in the upcoming "Dark fiber" section).

If you want to keep your fabrics separate yet retain the capability to copy data between sites, you can use either an iFCP-based (Internet Fibre Channel Protocol) extender or an iSCSI (Internet SCSI) solution that uses standard IP connections. Nishan developed iFCP and brought it to the storage industry as a standard. Even though iFCP and FCIP sound similar, they are fairly different in how they work. In simple terms, FCIP works by tunneling Fibre Channel frames within an IP connection and creating one big SAN. iFCP works by using the iFCP nodes as the session controllers and keeping the SAN fabrics logically isolated while allowing multiple FCP sessions across the IP link to the other fabrics.

During the recent consolidation in the storage industry, McData bought Nishan, and then Brocade bought McData. So if you want iFCP, you should contact Brocade. The iFCP protocol lets you scale up to connect as many sites as you want because you don't hit the limits of the maximum size of a single SAN fabric.

iSCSI is a protocol that uses a standard IP connection to transfer SCSI commands between devices. In fact, with iSCSI, you don't even need a Fibre Channel HBA to communicate. Most of the more progressive operating systems offer native iSCSI connection capabilities for free. Also, many switch vendors also support native iSCSI connectivity in their SAN switches. You don't need a dedicated host bus adapter to use iSCSI, and it's cost effective because the same IP network can be used as the communication network between iSCSI devices. iSCSI simply turns your current IP network into a storage network, so make sure your network has enough bandwidth to accommodate any iSCSI communication.

iSCSI solutions are available from almost every SAN vendor, including but not limited to

- ✔ **Alacritech:** www.alacritech.com
- ✔ **Cisco:** www.cisco.com
- ✔ **Dell:** www.dell.com
- ✔ **EMC:** www.emc.com
- ✔ **FalconStor:** www.falconstor.com
- ✔ **HDS:** www.hds.com
- ✔ **HP:** www.hp.com
- ✔ **IBM:** www.ibm.com
- ✔ **Intel:** www.intel.com
- ✔ **Microsoft:** www.microsoft.com

Some of these vendors manufacture network adapters that include the capability to run the Ethernet and iSCSI protocols in hardware. These network adapters are called TCP/IP offload engines (TOE). A TOE works similarly to a SAN HBA, in that it offloads the protocol overhead from the CPU in the server to increase performance for the iSCSI protocol. You can use a TOE in conjunction with the free software-based iSCSI drivers provided by your operating system vendor to increase iSCSI performance.

You can get iSCSI solutions and other advanced network hardware and software (like Infiniband (IB) and Fibre Channel over Ethernet (FCOE) solutions) from many other companies. For a list of almost everyone who has something to do with the storage industry, go to the Storage Networking Industry (SNIA) Web site at www.snia.org. SNIA monitors a lot of the standards being developed regarding the storage industry. When you get to their Web site, click the About SNIA tab and then click the Member Directory link for company listings and their Web sites.

Choosing the Correct Link for the Job

The link that you choose to connect one SAN island to another is probably going to be the most expensive part of tying two SAN islands together. If you're in a large corporation that has a large IT budget, you might already have a private dedicated link between your data centers and remote offices.

If you're like the rest of us, you probably have to lease a line from your local Telco provider, which is probably your local telephone company or a company in your area that specializes in data communications.

You can choose from a number of connection types; the cost of each connection type is usually associated with the speed of the connection. If you happen to live in an area with limited network connectivity services, you might still be using a modem in your personal computer over a dial-up connection for access to the Internet. Dial-up connections use standard telephone lines in your home to connect to the Internet. The technical term for this older connection type is a *POTS line,* which stands for Plain Old Telephone Service line.

The telephone connection sends data over the line as audible pulses or tones of sound. These pulses are routed through your phone network to the modem in the server at your Internet service provider's location, which then converts them into digital signals. The nice thing about POTS connections is that although the bandwidth may be limited, you're charged only for the time that the connection is made. When you hang up or log off from your computer, the connection is closed and the charges stop.

This connection is fine for sporadic Web surfing, but to connect SAN islands, you need more bandwidth than a standard POTS line. Those that can afford it usually connect to the internet today using either their cable provider or a phone company–provided digital subscriber line (DSL) at much higher speed than a POTS connection for a flat monthly fee.

The link type that you choose depends on what is available in your area, the distance between your sites, and the amount of money you have to spend. The faster the link, the more expensive it becomes.

IP connections

Internet Protocol (IP) connections are the most common types of links that can be leased from your local telephone company for your business. IP connections are used when you need to send data long distances. By combining an IP connection and an FCIP or iFCP SAN extender, you can send data between almost any two locations in the world.

Most SAN extender vendors recommend at least a T-3 link or greater for connecting two distant SAN islands. The link speed required is determined by the bandwidth needed for your specific environment. You can see the type required per bandwidth in Table 8-1.

Table 8-1	IP Network Link Type and Bandwidth
Link Type	*Bandwidth*
POTS modem	14.4 Kbps–56 Kbps
T-1	1.544 Mbps
T-2	6.312 Mbps
10BaseT	10 Mbps
T-3	44.736 Mbps
Digital Subscriber Line (DSL)	512 Kbps–8 Mbps
Cable modem	512 Kbps–52 Mbps

OC-type connections

OC (optical carrier) connections are the most common optical fiber connections that can be leased from a network provider. These connections are very expensive and might not even be available from your local Telco. You might have to get in touch with a dedicated network provider to lease one of these connections; or, if the locations that you're trying to connect aren't far from each other, you can get out your shovel and dig a trench to lay your own cables.

Optical fiber connections are used between sites that are located up to 100 km apart. Any further than that and you're hitting the upper limits for the transmission of light over optical cables. See Table 8-2 for fiber connection types and their bandwidth.

Table 8-2	Fiber Connections and Bandwidth
Type	*Bandwidth*
OC-1	51.84 Mbps
FDDI	100 Mbps
OC-3	155.52 Mbps
OC-12	622.08 Mbps
OC-48	2.488 Gbps

Two more types of links that can be used to connect SAN islands are Dense Wave Division Multiplexing (DWDM) and dark fiber. These are both optical fiber connections but usually aren't available for lease in most locations. Instead, these connections are usually reserved for those with very deep pockets who can afford to lay their own cables between locations.

Dense Wave Division Multiplexing

DWDM is used when you want to enhance the bandwidth of a single fiber-optic cable and when you want to extend the distance between sites up to 100 km. The DWDM equipment splits light waves into multiple frequencies, and each new frequency can carry data at 100 megabytes per second. By using a single fiber cable, you can split the light into 32 separate links.

Dark fiber

Dark fiber is the nickname for 9µm long-wave single mode fiber connections. It's called dark fiber because the light that travels through the cables is invisible to the naked eye. One really cool advancement in data transmission technology is the ability to split up the light waves traveling in a single mode dark fiber connection into multiple frequencies using something known as a DWDM.

I know it sounds like something out of a *Star Wars* movie, but DWDM stands for Dense Wave Division Multiplexing. A DWDM can actually make a single optical cable carry multiple data transmissions at the same time, and all the transmissions can even run at the same speed! A DWDM in effect can make the single cable carry the workload of 32 cables! The large network providers use dark fiber and DWDM to facilitate multiple simultaneous client subscribers, each sharing the bandwidth of a single cable to save money. Multiplexed dark fiber is the actual backbone of the Internet, and is used to carry most of the data transmissions under the oceans.

No matter which link type you choose, you need to make sure that it has enough bandwidth to move the amount of data that you want to copy between your sites. Table 8-3 lists the different connection types as well as how long it takes to copy a terabyte (TB) of data across the link. (A *terabyte* is equal to 1000 gigabytes.)

Table 8-3	Connection Types and Copying Speeds for Data Transfer				
Line Type	Industry Standard Bandwidth in Megabits per Second	Bandwidth in Megabits per Second after Network Overhead	Bandwidth in Megabytes per Second	Number of GB Transferred in 1 Hour	Time to Copy 1TB of Data
E1	2.048	1.8	0.225	0.81GB	>9 weeks
T1	1.544	1.3	0.1625	0.585GB	>10 weeks

(continued)

Table 8-3 *(continued)*

Line Type	Industry Standard Bandwidth in Megabits per Second	Bandwidth in Megabits per Second after Network Overhead	Bandwidth in Megabytes per Second	Number of GB Transferred in 1 Hour	Time to Copy 1TB of Data
E3	34.368	30	3.75	13.5GB	74.07407 hours
T3	44.736	40	5	18GB	55.55555 hours
OC3	155	130	16.25	58.5GB	17.09401 hours
100 Base-T	100	70	8.75	31.5GB	31.74603 hours
1000 Base-T (Gigabit) Ethernet)	1000	300	37.5	135GB	7.407407 hours

Reducing Costs with Compression, Data De-duplication and WAN Tuners

Since ordering up high speed connections from a network provider can cost a lot of money, you need to make sure you are managing the data that is moved over those connections as efficiently as possible so you can purchase the minimum bandwidth you need. In order to be as efficient as possible, you can use software or hardware compression and de-duplication solutions to limit the amount of data that needs to be moved. A data compression, data de-duplication, or WAN tuning solution that reduces the network link requirements you have to lease can pay for itself very quickly.

Compression

Compressing data before transmitting it over an IP connection allows you to use less bandwidth to transmit the same amount of data. Suppose that you want to use your connection to link a SAN in New York to a SAN in Boston, which is your disaster recovery site. You want to use the link to transmit data in real time from New York to Boston for online backup of your mail servers. You can't afford to buy a large tape library for both locations, so only the Boston location has been outfitted with the expensive tape library. You what to know what kind of link you need to lease between those locations so that your remote backup solution works.

To figure this out, you need to know how much data is changed in the e-mail sever on a daily basis at the New York site. Because only *write* data (data that's written to disk) needs to be copied across the link, you don't need to worry about data that is only read from your disks.

 If you use the rule that every megabyte of write data written per second would require a 10-megabit-per-second network link to copy the data across, you can easily calculate the bandwidth requirement for your remote backup solution. Suppose that on a daily basis, all the e-mail users in New York change between 56GB and 58GB of data per day. These changes occur at about the same rate during a normal eight-hour workday. This would mean that you need a network link that can handle a peak rate of 2 megabytes per second, which, using the rule above, would equal a 20 Mbps link, which is about half a T-3 link.

Here how to calculate this:

2 megabytes per second × 60 seconds = 120 megabytes per minute

120 megabytes per minute × 60 minutes = 7.2 gigabytes per hour

7.2 gigabytes per hour × an 8-hour day = 57.6 gigabytes per day

You can determine that you need at least half a T-3 link to accommodate your requirements. T-3s can be expensive when leased on a monthly basis. *Psst —* wanna save your company some monthly expenses by using a cheaper leased line? You could either put limits on everyone's e-mail to make sure that they can store only half the amount of data, or use a SAN extender device that provides compression. If your extender could use two-to-one compression (2:1), the size of the transmitted data would be halved. This means that instead of leasing half a T-3 link, you could get away with a standard 10BaseT Ethernet link.

20/2 = 10-megabit link

Compressing your data before transmitting it over the network is a great way to save money in leased line expenses. When you choose your SAN extension device, make sure the vendor supports data compression in the device.

De-duplication

Since data de-duplication is covered in much more depth in Chapter 13, here I only touch on the topic as it pertains to saving bandwidth for tying SANs together for data replication. De-duplication, like compression, is a method you can use to reduce costs and bandwidth requirements for data replication between two SAN fabrics. Where compression can typically achieve a savings ratio between 2:1 to 5:1, a good data de-duplication solution can show results between 20:1 to 30:1. De-duplication works very differently than compression, but you can use the two together to get even better results. Trying to figure out how much bandwidth savings a data de-duplication solution will bring can be difficult, because your results will vary depending on the data types and the de-duplication solution used. With data de-duplication, a typical reduction ratio is about 10:1, meaning ten times less data will need to travel over the network.

Some data de-duplication solutions work like compression solutions, where the data is not really de-duplicated per se; the solution simply monitors the data streams at a very low level (byte level) and sends only changed bytes over the network. Since many operating systems are inefficient at natively reducing the white space (unchanged bytes between changed bytes) during network transmission, the inclusion of these more intelligent monitoring solutions can save more than 80 percent of the bandwidth required to move a specific dataset.

To put this into perspective, look at these data de-duplication ratios:

2:1 = 50% less data
5:1 = 80% less data
10:1 = 90% less data
20:1 = 95% less data
30:1 = 97% less data

Your goal should be to get at least a 10:1 de-duplication ratio because it provides the most bang for the buck. From the preceding table, you can see the diminishing point of return after 10:1. There is a 10 percent difference between 5:1 and 10:1, and only a 5 percent difference between 10:1 and 20:1. Although some vendors claim to get fantastic results, it doesn't make that much difference after 10:1. If you are using a de-duplication solution during data transmission, using 80 percent, or a 5:1 de-duplication ratio, is a conservative estimate for bandwidth requirements.

Note that some data de-duplication solutions (see Chapter 13) work only with backup software, so you need to do your homework.

WAN tuners

WAN tuners can be used over IP networks to either cache data between sites to reduce the effects of slow or low bandwidth links, or replace or enhance the TCP/IP protocol to minimize issues of low-bandwidth and high-latency IP links during data transmission. (High latency means it takes a lot of time to transmit data, which nobody wants.) Companies such as Riverbed, FalconStor, Cisco, and NetEx provide WAN tuning solutions to provide efficient data movement between SANs over IP connections.

SAN Connection Protocols

FCIP and iFCP are the two protocols involved with linking Fibre Channel SANs. *FCIP* is a tunneling protocol that allows two separate SAN fabrics to be combined into one large fabric, connected over IP. *iFCP* is a bridging, or *gateway,* protocol, that allows two SAN fabrics to be connected but the local Fibre Channel traffic within each SAN island to stay separate. The FCIP and iFCP protocols have been approved by the Internet Engineering Task Force (IETF) standards body as methods for inter-SAN communication.

The motivation behind using the FCIP or iFCP protocols to connect SAN islands is to allow for remote disk access, remote tape backup, and live mirroring of data between the sites.

FCIP: The SAN tunnel

The *Fibre Channel over IP (FCIP)* protocol describes the methods that allow the interconnection of Fibre Channel SAN fabrics over IP networks to form a single, unified Fibre Channel fabric.

The FCIP protocol connects two Fibre Channel SAN fabrics into one big fabric, using IP as the network connection between the physical locations. A device called an *FC extender* (Fibre Channel extender) is used at the edge of both fabrics to connect them. The extender uses the FCIP protocol to create a communication link between the fabrics by creating a logical tunnel within the IP protocol. The extenders are linked by the tunnel, and the tunnel transparently passes all Fibre Channel traffic between locations (see Figure 8-4).

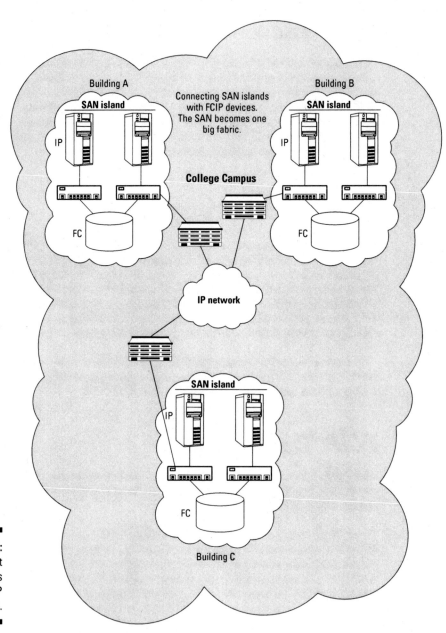

Using FCIP to connect SAN islands makes each island part of a larger, cohesive SAN. All Fibre Channel traffic is seen by every node in the larger fabric. As long as enough buffers (called *buffer credits*) are available within the extenders, no real distance limitations exist as to how far each SAN island can be from each other. Buffer credits are a whole other story, and the details can get technical. Just be aware that the more you have, the farther you can go and the better off you will be.

The Fibre Channel protocol is "tunneled" within the IP protocol. All Fibre Channel transmissions can be seen across the link on both sides. A single communication session is created between the extenders, and all traffic on one side is seen on the other side of the connection. Using FCIP to link two SAN fabrics creates, in effect, one big SAN fabric. This is the *rubber-band* approach: You stretch the fabric between locations.

FCIP extenders are best used for connecting SANs for intermediate distances (say, from New York to Boston), data replication, data management, and those who want to create one big fabric. Using FCIP makes the switches at either side think they're connected with a local inter-switch link (ISL). In other words, the IP network is transparent to the SAN, and the switch simply think the switch on the other side is connected by a local E_Port. (See Chapter 2 for more on E_Ports and Chapter 3 for more on ISLs.)

iFCP: The SAN gateway

The Internet Fibre Channel Protocol (iFCP) enables Fibre Channel device-to-device communication over an IP network. Instead of creating a tunnel the way FCIP does, iFCP extenders actually map the Fibre Channel frames into TCP/IP packets and send them over the IP network as TCP/IP packets. Anything you can do with TCP/IP, you can do with Fibre Channel Frames.

All local Fibre Channel traffic stays inside each connected SAN island. Only traffic destined for devices in other locations is passed across the link. iFCP lets you connect SAN islands but still keep the islands separate unto themselves, as you can see in Figure 8-5.

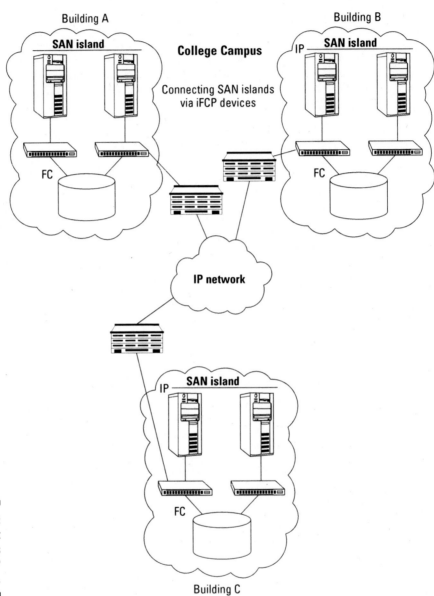

Figure 8-5:
Connect
SAN islands
with iFCP
gateways.

The FCIP protocol shown in Figure 8-4 shows the SAN extended across all locations, which is why a big cloud covers all the little clouds that represent the original SAN islands. In Figure 8-5, the big cloud is gone because, although the SANs are connected and devices in each location can communicate, the actual fabrics remain separate (no cloud). The iFCP protocol doesn't use E_Port connectivity between the switches in the fabrics, so the fabrics stay separate. (See Chapter 2 for more on E_Ports.) The major difference between iFCP and FCIP connections is that FCIP expands a fabric to make the connection, whereas iFCP keeps the fabrics separate.

Multiple communication sessions can be created over the link between the gateway devices, using the iFCP protocol. All Fibre Channel traffic destined for devices in each local fabric is isolated to that fabric. Any traffic that has the destination address for a device located on the other side of the link is sent to the other location. When a device on one side needs to communicate with a device on the other side, a new communication session is established between the devices over the link. Using iFCP to link two SAN fabrics is like tying together two rubber bands. Each rubber band is still separate, but there is a connection at the knot.

iFCP is a gateway approach, whereas FCIP is a tunnel approach. A gateway is more intelligent than a tunnel; it provides implementation-specific naming services, addressing, and flow control. A tunnel just connects the two sides together, and passes everything (including errors) from one side to the other.

A gateway helps when a less reliable network connection is used between the devices that connect the SAN islands. I suggest using iFCP devices for data-replication connections between SAN islands when the connections go over long distances. The iFCP extenders do not use E_Port *buffer credits* (that's the technical stuff that has to happen between switches connected over a distance), so it's simpler to implement — and it works great for long-distance communication when you're trying to move a lot of data.

The FCIP and iFCP devices cost about the same, except iFCP devices don't require a connection to a switch (no E_Port needed), so they might be a bit less expensive to implement.

Nishan Systems invented the iFCP protocol — now a standard — but some switch vendors implement only the FCIP protocol. Brocade is the only major vendor currently selling iFCP-based SAN extenders. (McData corporation bought Nishan, and then Brocade bought McData.)

Stretching the SAN (The Rubber-Band Approach)

The result of using the stretched-rubber-band approach is the creation of one single SAN fabric from two connected SAN islands. The link that joins the SANs becomes a stretched E_Port between the switches at the different physical locations. (See Chapter 2 for more about SAN ports.) Connecting fabrics by creating an extended E_Port effectively stretches the fabric across both physical locations. This is similar to stretching a rubber band within its physical limits to accept more paper. However, you need to be careful that you don't break the rubber band while you stretch it.

You can extend a SAN fabric into one large fabric in several ways:

- ✔ **Long-wave fiber connections between switches:** If you use 9μm Fibre Channel cables with long-wave single-mode lasers between switch ports, the distance between switches in a single fabric can be up to 10 km. You can run 9μm single-mode Fibre Channel cables directly between the switches to each location, as shown in Figure 8-6. Because you need a higher-powered laser to connect over a long distance, long-wave Gigabit Interface Converters (GBIC) are used in the ports that connect the switches. Better bring your wallet, though; those long-wave GBICS and 9μm cables can be fairly expensive!

- ✔ **Dense Wave Division Multiplexing (DWDM):** *DWDM* equipment boosts the light signal between switch connections so distances between switch ports can be longer. DWDM gear also splits a single wavelength of light into multiple frequencies. Each new frequency can be used as another connection. Using DWDM enables a single fiber-optic cable to carry huge amounts of data over long distances. If DWDM equipment is used between SAN locations, the amplifiers and high-powered lasers enable a single SAN fabric to extend beyond 100 km, as in Figure 8-7.

- ✔ **FCIP-based Fibre Channel extenders:** You can use FCIP-based extenders (such as the CNT Edge device) to extend a single SAN fabric over normal TCP/IP network connections. FCIP allows almost unlimited distances between switches in the same fabric. You can connect SAN islands using a private network connection or a leased line from a Telco. (Refer to Figure 8-5.)

Using IP-based Fibre Channel extenders is the most common method of extending SANs for remote data copying and disaster recovery when long distances are required. The stretched-rubber-band approach can connect SAN islands, meshing individual fabrics at each location into one large fabric.

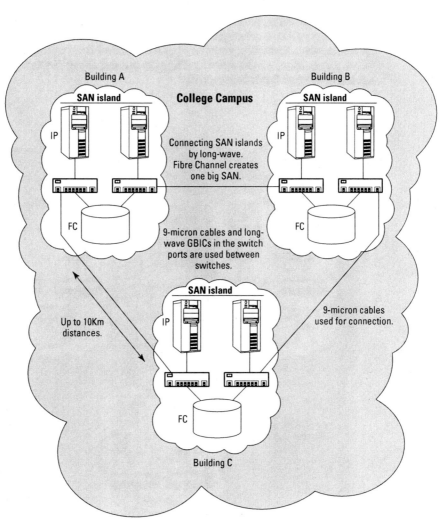

Building A

SAN island

IP

College Campus

Connecting SAN islands
by long-wave.
Fibre Channel creates
one big SAN.

FC

9-micron cables and long-
wave GBICs in the switch
ports are used between
switches.

Building B

SAN island

IP

FC

Up to 10Km
distances.

SAN island

IP

9-micron cables
used for connection.

FC

Building C

Figure 8-6:
Using long-
wave
cables to
connect
SAN
islands.

Before you opt for this approach, however, consider how it uses switches.
Within a single SAN fabric, when the switches are first powered on (or added
to the fabric), an election process elects a single switch as the principal switch
for the fabric. The principal switch is used as a master switch and holds all the
address information about all the devices connected to the fabric. A principal
switch is also elected when a switch failure in the fabric or the loss of E_Port
communication occurs. In large fabrics, problems can happen during the election process. The election process takes longer as the SAN gets larger because

during this process, no application data can traverse the SAN. This means you need to be cautious when creating large fabrics by extending the SAN fabric between sites. Basically, your link between sites drops out when the election takes place. Also, all the error traffic gets passed along the link, which can eat up some of your link's bandwidth.

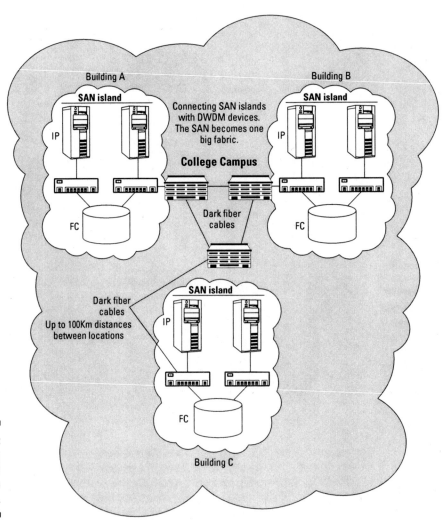

Figure 8-7:
Connecting
SAN
islands with
DWDM.

Although a single SAN fabric can theoretically be huge, the physical size of a SAN has limits. The largest tested single Fibre Channel fabric had a maximum of 239 switches connected together. Each switch must be configured with its own unique identifier from 0 to 239, which is the switch's *domain ID*. (Okay, that's really 240 numbers, but who's counting?) When you connect two SAN islands by using an extender that uses the FCIP protocol, you need to make sure that everything on both sides has a unique name (including alias names in your switch zones) and domain ID.

Using Connected SAN Islands (The Two-Rubber-Bands Approach)

Using an IP network to connect SAN fabrics into one large fabric, FCIP allows the extension of a Fibre Channel fabric over distances. The FCIP connection is invisible to the Fibre Channel switches and works seamlessly with existing SAN devices. Because FCIP extends an existing Fibre Channel fabric, it doesn't change or improve the scalability or interoperability limits of Fibre Channel fabrics.

An iFCP gateway actively participates in switching and routing traffic between Fibre Channel fabrics and Fibre Channel devices. It does this by mapping Fibre Channel addresses to IP addresses and then routing them to the other fabric by using standard IP routing protocols. Using iFCP connections, you can create a storage network as scalable as any other IP network. Because each fabric connected via an iFCP gateway remains a separate entity, the 239-switch limit per fabric is harder to reach. Also, the election process within a fabric isn't extended to the other fabrics connected via iFCP, which makes the entire solution more scalable and stable. Using iFCP devices connected through your TCP/IP network, you can create a SAN that spans not only cities but the entire county or even the globe, as shown in Figure 8-8.

Using iFCP works like tying two rubber bands together: Each rubber band has its own limits as to how far you can stretch it before it breaks, but tying the two allows you to make the separate rubber bands into a single larger one. iFCP products use TCP/IP functions — which (in effect) makes them a more intelligent network router rather than a simple tunnel device like the FCIP products. Each SAN island connected through iFCP acts autonomously and is isolated even though Fibre Channel traffic can still flow between islands. Re-election processes are contained within a SAN and are not propagated. Communication failures between the iFCP links will not lead to the switch re-election process in the separate SAN islands.

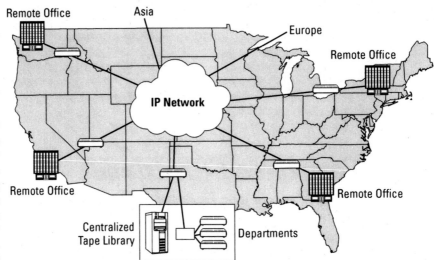

Figure 8-8:
Use iFCP devices to connect SAN islands across the country or the globe.

Because they act like an IP router, the iFCP devices can send Fibre Channel traffic to more than one location over the Internet. You can use this functionality to transfer data from one SAN location to many SAN locations at the same time. You can also transmit data from many remote locations to a single consolidated site for remote backup. You can even replace your SAN switches with iFCP devices. You can also connect your storage and servers to the iFCP equipment, and then connect the iFCP equipment together to connect your SAN islands using IP. (See Figure 8-9.)

Using a SAN as Network Attached Storage

You can use your SAN disk storage like a big Network Attached Storage (NAS) device. *NAS* uses the TCP/IP protocol to connect to servers that need to share files over the network. Storage locations using NAS are shared via the TCP/IP network, and server clients connect to the shared files in the NAS server by using standard network adapters.

NAS is a method of using IP networks to share data; it uses the Network File Services (NFS, created by Sun Microsystems) protocol over IP networks to create file-based access to Unix servers. NAS uses the Common Internet File Services (CIFS) protocol for creating file access to Windows servers over IP. (CIFS was created by Microsoft.) The NFS and CIFS protocols provide a

method of locking files so only one client can update a shared file at one time.
NAS is commonly used for creating locations for network users to store their
files in a central location so they can be backed up. NAS also provides shared
access to files that Web application servers need.

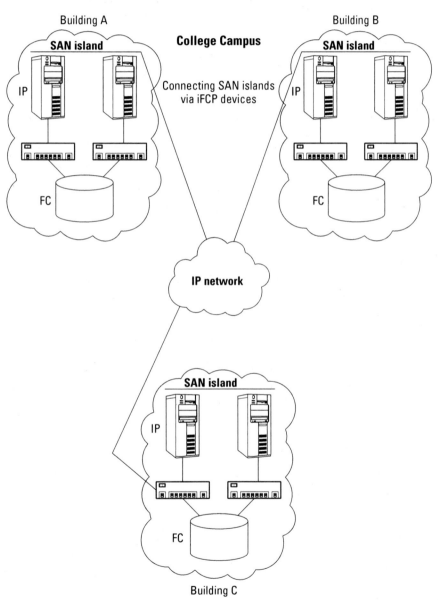

Figure 8-9:
Using iFCP
devices
to replace
Fibre
Channel
switches.

To use the SAN storage as a NAS device, you could easily create a file share on one of the servers connected to the SAN. The SAN is used to store the data, and the network file share is the connection point to that data from remote servers connected to the corporate network. Servers not connected to the SAN get access to the disk storage in the SAN through the file share by using the corporate IP network.

Using very fast SAN storage with a dedicated Windows or Unix server acting as a NAS head makes for a very fast network attached storage solution. It not only lets you reuse your SAN storage for another purpose, but also allows you to manage both types of storage from a single location. You can also stretch access to your SAN by using an IP network as the method of connection (as illustrated in Figure 8-10).

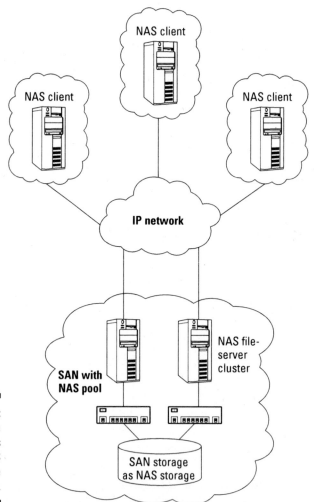

Figure 8-10:
Using the SAN as a NAS storage device.

iSCSI: An Alternative Method

The *Internet Small Computer Storage Interface* (*iSCSI*) protocol is a completely different approach to storage networking. iSCSI is a protocol developed with the Storage Networking Industry Association (SNIA) as a method of connecting servers to storage devices using a standard TCP/IP network adapter. iSCSI encapsulates standard SCSI storage blocks into the IP protocol, which allows you to transmit block-based SCSI data destined for a disk drive using a standard IP network.

iSCSI is getting so much attention these days because you can use it without having to install an expensive Fibre Channel network. The servers are connected to storage through a standard network interface card and a software iSCSI agent — or a specialized network card that includes an iSCSI agent in the hardware. (An *agent* is a small piece of intelligent, application-specific software code that runs on a server; see Chapter 11 for more on agents.) If you want faster performance with iSCSI, you can also use a specialized TCP/IP Offload Engine (TOE) network adapter card. These specialized cards also place the TCP/IP protocol stack in hardware to keep the CPU utilization needed to move data through the TCP/IP stack to a minimum.

You can use iSCSI to connect to storage today in two ways: Buy a storage array that supports iSCSI connections natively, or use a bridge device to connect iSCSI coming in over the network to a Fibre Channel storage array. Many storage arrays on the market support native iSCSI, but the gateway approach is the one used most often to make existing Fibre Channel storage arrays iSCSI-capable (see Figure 8-11).

Figure 8-11 shows IP network–connected servers accessing a remote Fibre Channel storage array over the corporate network. No SAN is needed at the remote locations; the corporate network works as the storage network.

The idea behind iSCSI is to eliminate the need to keep people on staff who are experienced with Fibre Channel SANs and to leverage the experience people have with standard IP networking. When more iSCSI-capable devices begin to appear in the market, you'll start to see iSCSI taking over the low end of storage networking. iSCSI will be easy to deploy, will leverage existing knowledge of IP networking, and will probably be cheaper than installing a Fibre Channel SAN. iSCSI is well suited for connecting remote servers to a central storage array for data access. A robust network connection would be needed between sites for the best performance. (I suggest at least a 10Base-T Ethernet network or greater, depending on performance requirements.)

iSCSI can also be used in place of a SAN, but you'd better be running Gigabit Ethernet on your network to get good performance. New iSCSI solutions and vendors are coming to the market, and iSCSI will make major inroads in the storage industry as more companies look to reduce costs.

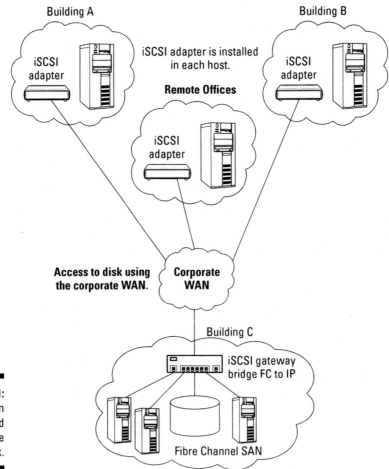

Figure 8-11:
Building an
iSCSI-based
storage
network.

Chapter 9

SAN-Based Backup

*F*ace it: Stuff happens. Servers crash, things go bump in the night, and people trip over power cords. An assortment of things can cause you to lose important data. Backing up is one of your most important tasks to do to keep data safe and secure. In this chapter, I cover the things that you need to consider when implementing a backup solution in a storage area network (SAN) environment. I show you how a SAN backup can make your life easier, can make backing up a lot faster, and can help keep your information safe.

Understanding Backup

Backup is the process of saving your data so it can be restored in case of problems such as system failure or data corruption. A backup is a copy of data, and you should store it apart from your production copy. The time it takes to copy your data is known as the backup *process,* and the time allocated for the backup process to run is known as the *backup window.*

Backups should be done as often as possible to keep data loss to a minimum. Most companies back up most or all of their critical data assets every night. A SAN comes in real handy in this situation due to the data movement bandwidth it provides. Some companies, due to government regulations, must keep backups of specific customer data or e-mail messages for more than seven years or, in some cases, forever! The process of backing up data and storing it for a long time is known as *data archiving.*

The most prevalent method for backing up and archiving data is to move the data from disk drives to tape drives. As media go, tape is cheap — and can store large amounts of data. Another method is to use optical media such as CDs or DVDs, because of the adoption of highly reliable RAID types such as RAID 6 (see Chapter 2 for more on RAID) and because disks are becoming cheap enough (in relation to tape) to use for long-term archives, especially when the data is de-duplicated to take up less space. (Find out more on de-duplication in Chapter 13.)

Using disks for backup and archives has a distinct advantage over tape in the speed department. Tape drives work by moving tape over a stationary head, which reads and writes data to the tape. A *sequential* medium requires data to be written and read in sequence, and the tape has to be physically moved over the stationary tape head to the next file to be written or read.

Disk drives are *random-access* media, meaning the disk heads are movable and can seek to any point on the disk at any time to read any data. The disk rotates below the heads at very high speeds. The access time to read a file from a disk is in milliseconds; a tape read can take many seconds.

In this chapter, I cover the advantages and disadvantages of both disk-based and tape-based media for backup and archiving.

Here are some questions to consider when deciding on a backup solution:

- ✔ What backup methods are available?
- ✔ What is the best backup method to use for your type of company?
- ✔ How do you back up data without bringing down the applications?
- ✔ How do you back up your data in the allotted time?
- ✔ What's the best hardware to use?
- ✔ What software should you use?
- ✔ How often should you back up data?
- ✔ How long will it take to back up?
- ✔ If you have a problem, how long will it take to restore the data?
- ✔ How much will the backup solution cost?

I touch on each of these concerns as I cover the different backup methods. You can compare how well they resolve these concerns.

Understanding SAN Backup

A SAN centralizes all your data externally from the server, and makes moving data between two points very fast. Using the SAN to back up the centrally stored data moves the backup data stream away from your corporate network and onto the storage network where it belongs. Using a SAN for backup also opens up a whole new world of methods that can be used to protect your data.

The backup window

A *backup window* — the total amount of time that you have available to back up all your data — is a window in time when your production applications are allowed to be taken down (or taken offline to user input) so all the files that need to be backed up can be closed.

To back up data without a SAN, you can choose two methods:

✔ Use a locally attached tape drive on the server to back itself up.

✔ Use backup software agents on the server to back up the data over a local area network (LAN) to a backup server.

Either method is fine if (a) you have enough money to buy a tape drive for every server or (b) your LAN is robust enough to handle all the backup traffic along with your normal production applications. Because neither scenario is normally the case, backup usually occurs at night after the users go home so the files can be closed and the applications taken down during backup.

The backup window has been shrinking dramatically for most businesses. Today, business never stops. Corporations must operate in global markets to be competitive; when your customers and employees on the east coast of the United States are asleep, customers and employees in Asia are awake, happily pounding away on keyboards and using the applications on your corporate network. This leaves little or no time to take down your applications, back up your data, and restart he applications.

If your company has hundreds of gigabytes or multiple terabytes of data to be backed up, you need a solution that can move that amount of data really fast. If you have a large budget, you might be able to buy a separate LAN to use just for backup. Using a dedicated LAN for backup traffic removes all that traffic from the production LAN, allowing you to schedule backup for some of your applications during the day. Figure 9-1 shows an example of a separate backup LAN.

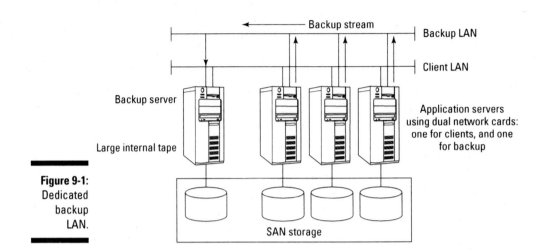

Figure 9-1:
Dedicated
backup
LAN.

The main goal in using a SAN in your backup design is to eliminate the backup window altogether. By using some of the capabilities of a SAN, you can minimize the time your applications need to be taken down for backup. You can also run your backup over the much faster SAN, rather than a slower LAN, and speed up the time that it takes to back up your data. (Because SAN networks are block-based, they can move large amounts of data faster and more efficiently than file-based Ethernet LAN networks.)

Tape drives

Using high-capacity tape drives is the most common method to back up data and provides one of the most cost-effective means for long-term data archives. Tape is not going away anytime soon. Tape is removable, so it can be taken offsite. And once a tape is full and removed from the drive, it requires no power, so it's green. Even if you use disks, snapshots, or CDP (Continuous Data Protection) for fast backup and recovery, tapes are still the king for long-term retention at low cost. (See Chapters 10 and 14 for more on snapshots and CDP.) Getting the data to those tapes quickly is part of what this chapter is all about.

Tape drives vary in cost depending on their capacity and whether they are stand-alone drives or consolidated into a library of drives.

Table 9-1 lists the types of tape drives available today, along with their capacity and speed.

Table 9-1	Common Tape-Drive Capacities and Speeds	
Type	_Native Capacity_	_Transfer Rate_
DAT	1.3–80GB	0.5–6.9 MBps
DLT	40–800GB	6–60 MBps
SDLT	110–300GB	11–36 MBps
AIT	50–400GB	6–24 MBps
LTO1-5	100GB–1.6TB	15–180 MBps

As you can see from Table 9-1, the type of drive you use will affect how many drives you need for storing your data, as well as how fast that data can be stored. Using individual drives is fine if every server can fit all its data on one tape. If not, you need some method of changing the tapes in the drive so your backup can continue. This is the realm of tape operators, who spend all night drinking coffee trying to stay awake so they can swap tapes for all the servers. A cheaper method in the long run is to purchase a tape library that includes robotics that change the tapes automatically.

Tape libraries

A _tape library_ is a mechanical device that automates the old manual tape operation process by stacking tape drives inside the library and using a robotic arm to insert and remove tapes from the drives. Libraries are available in sizes that range from a single tape drive with a few tapes to those that hold tens of drives and thousands of tapes. The cost varies by the size of the library. A large tape library can cost more than a million dollars.

Tape libraries are common in large corporations. Although they can be costly, they alleviate the need for several tape operators since the robotics in the library automate backup. Too many tape libraries are on the market to list here, but I can give you an idea of how they vary in size and capacity. HP has a small library that fits on a shelf, has one DLT (Digital Linear Tape) tape drive, and holds up to ten DLT tapes. IBM, Sun/StorageTek, ADIC, and SpectraLogic have libraries that can scale to thousands of tapes and hundreds of drives, with total storage capacities in the multiple-petabyte (PB) range. (A _petabyte_ is equal to 1000 terabytes.)

Backup policy

A number of backup policies are available. Overall, you can back up all your data all the time or back up only what changed since your last backup. The policy that you choose affects how long the backup takes and how many tapes you need. Here are the most common backup policies:

- **Full backup:** The *full backup* policy backs up all your data every time, even if the information has not changed since the last backup. You select a disk to be backed up, and the backup software backs up everything on that disk to tape. If your tape media can fit the contents of the entire disk onto tape, a full backup provides for fast recovery because all the information is stored on just one tape. To restore your data, you select the tape that has the backup job on it and restore it to disk.

- **Incremental backup:** An *incremental backup* backs up the files that have changed since the last time you ran the last backup job. Because you back up the data every day, only a small percentage of data usually changes between backups, shortening backup times.

Because an incremental backup copies only files that have changed since the last incremental backup, you cannot use a single incremental backup tape to restore your data. You first have to restore your last full backup and then restore each incremental backup in the order that it was taken on top of the full backup to bring everything up to date. Using an incremental backup reduces the time that it takes to back up your data, but it increases the restore time as well as the amount of tapes needed to restore everything.

- **Differential backup:** A *differential backup* copies all data that changed since the last full backup. A differential backup is cumulative; every time you run the backup, it updates the backup tape to include all the files that changed since the last full backup. When restoring from a differential backup, you first restore the latest full backup and then the latest differential backup on top of it. A differential backup is used with full backups to reduce your backup time. It also reduces restore time because you need only the last full backup and the last differential backup to get everything up to date.

Choosing a Backup Solution

Although using tape drives to store information is the most common method of backing up data, you can choose a different solution when creating a data-backup design. Which solution is right for you depends on how many servers you have, how much data needs to be backed up, how much time is available to back up the data, and your budget. Another major aspect of choosing a backup solution is restoring data and recovering applications (discussed in more detail in Chapters 6, 10, and 14).

You can choose from the following designs for backing up the servers that run your business. Each of these is described in more depth in this section:

- ✔ **Integrated tape drive in each server:** In this design, each server has an individual tape drive with enough capacity to store all the data to which the server has access. This solution is a great low-cost method if you have just a few servers to manage and not a lot of data. Also, you can overwrite the tape each time.

- ✔ **Backup over the corporate network to a tape drive connected to a dedicated backup server:** This policy allows the backup server to back up the data on the application server's behalf. By using this policy, you can use a single high-capacity tape device rather than include a tape drive in every server. This is a great method, but it requires someone to change the tapes when one becomes full.

- ✔ **Backup over the corporate network to a robotic tape library connected to a dedicated backup server:** This is the most common backup policy for larger corporations. It allows data to travel across the network to the backup server, which is connected to a large tape library. The library includes robotics to change out tapes when they become full.

- ✔ **LAN-less (LAN-free) backup to a shared tape library over SAN:** Using the SAN as the data path for backup eliminates the need for the backup stream to use the corporate LAN. Using the SAN also removes the time constraints that backup imposes on production applications. You can back up anytime without affecting the performance of the production LAN.

- ✔ **Serverless backup to a shared tape library through SAN:** You need a SAN to accomplish serverless backup. One method of serverless backup uses a SAN backup protocol called E-Copy to move data directly from disk drives to tape libraries, which removes the servers from the data path.

- ✔ **Disk-to-disk backup:** Because disks are becoming less expensive every day, some companies are foregoing tape drives altogether and backing up data from the primary disk subsystem to a less expensive array of disks or to an off-site disk array in a remote location. Disk-to-disk backup enables very fast restoration of data from disk. If the backup is done to a remote disk array, the solution can also be used for disaster recovery. Virtual Tape Libraries (VTL) fool the backup software into believing it has access to high-speed tape drives by making high-speed random-access disks look like tapes.

- ✔ **Image copies and snapshot copies in the SAN:** SAN-based image copy is a method of using intelligent storage arrays to create duplicates of your data on another disk inside or outside the array. Full image copies, known in the industry by their marketing term *business continuance volumes* or *BCV*, are full copies of all the data. You can also use a more space-efficient technology known as *snapshots,* or *Point-in-Time (PiT)* copies to create an instant recovery point in time. (Chapter 10 has more on snapshots and BCV copies.) The BCV copy can be used to recover your data in case of primary disk failure or data corruption; array-based snapshots are a fast and space efficient way to protect data from corruption or deletion, but not disk failure, since snapshots still depend on the original production disks for read operations.

Image copies can also be used as the source for backups. Instead of using the original production disk, you shut down the application only long enough to create the image. Many applications now have the ability to keep running while a BCV copy or snapshot copy occurs. This ability to keep running is known as *hot backup* mode.

The application works in conjunction with the solution and uses internal methods to pause or "quiese" I/O operations for a short amount of time to take a BCV or snapshot copy. The BCV or snapshot image is then used as the source for backing up to tape or disk through the SAN. Since snapshot creation and BCV copies do not have to move data, it happens extremely fast, so it pretty much eliminates the backup window. (See the earlier section, "The backup window.")

✔ **Continuous backup:** Continuous Data Protection (CDP) continuously protects every write the application makes, so the application is always backed up. Instead of a backup process, there is continuous data protection. CDP has an advantage over traditional backup: Because every write is protected, every write can be recovered to any point in time. Whereas traditional backup is a periodic process, CDP is a continuous process. CDP has no backup window; backing up is simply based on policy and on the service level needed for recovery of the application. (See Chapter 14 for more on CDP.)

✔ **SAN-based data replication/remote backup:** Another backup method, commonly used as part of a disaster recovery solution, is to replicate data from one site to another through an extended SAN or over the LAN. This keeps data safe at a remote contingency site in case of fire or other disasters. You can use BCV copies, snapshots, or tape backup at the remote site to eliminate backup operations from the primary data center.

Integrated tape drive in each server

In the first backup method, you place a tape drive in every application server (see Figure 9-2). The sever uses operating system software or add-on third-party backup software to back itself up to the tape drive in the server. This approach is commonly used by smaller businesses with only a few servers.

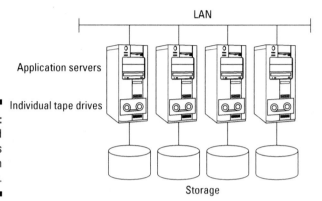

Figure 9-2:
Integrated
tape drives
in each
server.

LAN

Application servers

Individual tape drives

Storage

Using internal tape drives is one of the simplest methods to use. It can be inexpensive if you don't have much data to back up; you can simply use the backup software that comes with the server's operating system to do the job.

The problem with using internal tape drives in every server emerges when you have many servers to back up: You need a tape drive for every server, and have to manage the backup for all those servers independently. This could easily turn into a nightmare if your tape drives don't have enough capacity to back up the entire server on a single tape; you would need someone to swap the tapes when the first one becomes full. If you use third-party backup software from companies such as Legato, Symantec, CommVault, IBM, Hewlett-Packard, or Computer Associates, you also need a software license *for each server.* That can get expensive if a lot of servers are involved.

Backup over a corporate LAN to a tape drive connected to an independent backup server

A common design for smaller offices or remote offices of larger corporations is a dedicated server that runs software to back up all the other servers in the office. This backup server, which uses an internal large-capacity tape drive, is connected to the corporate network, through which it pulls the data to be backed up from the other servers in the office. Agents in the application servers allow the backup server to pull the data from the disks connected to the application servers (see Figure 9-3).

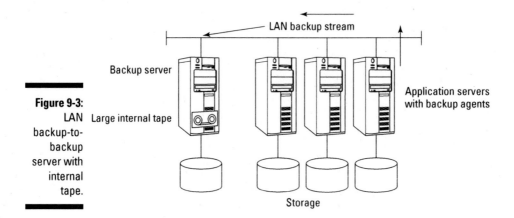

Figure 9-3:
LAN backup-to-backup server with internal tape.

Backup over corporate network to robotic tape library connected to an independent backup server

The most common backup method in large company data centers is a dedicated backup server connected to a large, external robotic tape library (see Figure 9-4). As the amount of data in the company grows, larger libraries with more tapes are hooked up to the backup server. Backups can be automated because the library can hold many tapes, and the robotics can swap them in and out as needed.

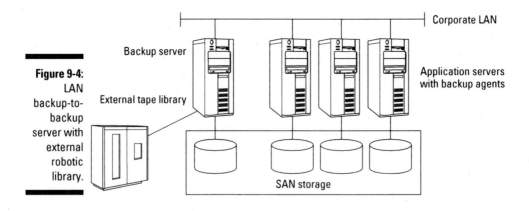

Figure 9-4:
LAN backup-to-backup server with external robotic library.

LAN-less backup to shared tape library over SAN

LAN-less backup lets you move the backup data stream off the corporate LAN and redirect it through the SAN. LAN-less backup improves backup performance dramatically because LAN communication has a lot of overhead. A typical 10 megabits per second (Mbps) LAN can move backup data at around 1 Mbps. A typical 100 Mbps LAN can move data at 10 Mbps. An 8-Gbit SAN can move data at 800 Mbps. (Note that a separate 10-Gbit Ethernet, which has a bandwidth of approximately 1 gigabyte per second, can also be used for backup over a LAN!)

LANs are also typically used for communication traffic for normal production applications; running a backup at the same time over the LAN affects the performance of those applications. Because most companies cannot afford to bring down production applications during the day, LAN-based backup operations are usually relegated to the folks on night shift. These underappreciated people make sure that all critical data is backed up and secure.

Using the LAN-less backup method solves the data-movement problem because all backup traffic goes over the faster SAN instead of the LAN. You can even save money by reusing older SCSI-attached tape libraries by going through a Fibre Channel to SCSI router. (See Figure 9-5.)

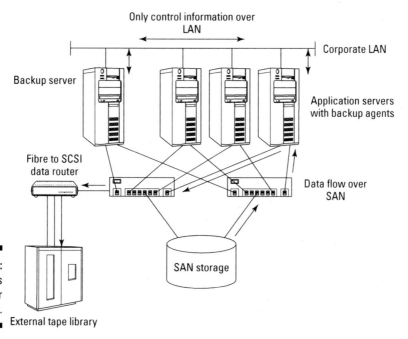

Only control information over
LAN

Corporate LAN

Backup server

Application servers
with backup agents

Fibre to SCSI
data router

Data flow over
SAN

Figure 9-5:
LAN-less
backup over
a SAN.

SAN storage

External tape library

To accomplish LAN-less backup, you need SAN-aware backup software. Most major backup software vendors have options to let you do LAN-less backup. (For example, Symantec NetBackup uses a solution called SSO, or shared storage option.) The backup client software is loaded on every server attached to the SAN. One of those servers is set as the primary backup server, which acts like a traffic cop for access to the shared SAN-connected tape library. The primary backup server directs each SAN-connected server to take turns using the shared library. If the library has more than one tape drive, multiple servers can back up to the library at the same time.

Because the servers can pull data off their drives through the SAN and out to tape at hundreds of Mbps, the bottleneck in SAN backup is no longer the network but the speed at which the tape drives can write to tape. You should see backup speeds around 20GB per hour, per tape drive, if you use DLT35/70 or DLT40/80 tape drives in a library. More expensive tape libraries using tape drives such as LTO-1 through LTO-5 can accommodate hundreds of megabytes per second when streaming data to tape. For more on tape-drive speeds, see Table 9-1.

You can use Table 9-1 for figuring out how many tape drives you need to back up all your data in a given amount of time. Suppose you have an application server with 100GB of data that needs to be backed up every day, but you can bring the application down for only an hour to back it up. To back up that much data in one hour, your tape drive must have at least a 100GB capacity and a speed rating of at least 28MB per second, so for this server, you should select a DLT, SDLT, or LTO tape drive. (For more on how to figure out how long a backup will take, jump to the "Determining How Long a Backup Will Take" section.)

Of course, your backup speed will vary depending on the size of the files, how many files you're backing up, and the compression ratio of the files (if your backup software or tape drive can also compress data). Fewer, larger files can be backed up faster than many smaller files. A two-to-one (2:1) data compression ratio means you can back up the same amount of data in half the time or twice the amount of data in the same time. Using tapes for backups, you can assume that restore times will usually be one-and-a-half to two times as long as the backup times.

Serverless backup to shared tape library through SAN

Serverless backup is just that. The backup data stream doesn't have to travel through the server to get to the tape drives. You can achieve serverless backup by using snapshots or BCV copies of the data as the backup source (see Chapter 10), or by using a protocol for backup called *E-Copy,* which is an extension to the Small Computer System Interface (SCSI) command set that provides for device-to-device communication. E-Copy is sometimes called *third-party copy* or *extended copy*. The commands are implemented in the devices in the SAN by the switches, bridges, tape libraries, or storage arrays themselves.

If you want to use E-Copy, the backup server's backup software must be E-Copy aware. The backup software communicates with the device with the E-Copy command set on board, telling it to copy the data from device A to device B through the SAN. After the command is given, the data stream goes directly between the devices themselves (see Figure 9-6).

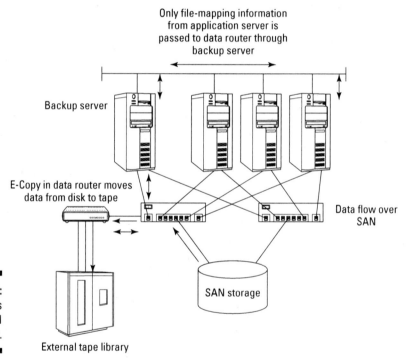

Only file-mapping information from application server is passed to data router through backup server

Backup server

E-Copy in data router moves data from disk to tape

Data flow over SAN

Figure 9-6: Serverless SAN backup.

SAN storage

External tape library

Notice in Figure 9-6 that only control information is issued by the backup server. The data flow is directly from the disk drives to the tape drives in the attached SAN tape library.

Disk-to-disk backup

Disk-to-disk backup eliminates tape drives altogether, and uses low-cost, high-capacity disk drives to store backup data on disk. The disk-to-disk backup method is used by companies that require very fast restore times. To use the disk-to-disk backup method, the backup software uses disks as a destination device for backup. A virtual tape library is a good example of a disk-to-disk backup solution. A VTL uses fast disks instead of tapes as the backup medium. Since disks are faster than tapes, the disk-to-disk method trades the lower cost of tapes for the higher speed of disks. You simply substitute an array of disks for the tape drives (see Figure 9-7).

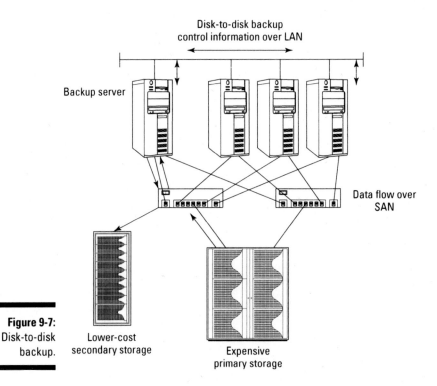

Figure 9-7:
Disk-to-disk
backup.

With the disk-to-disk backup method, you can also substitute the disk drives used for the backup target with optical media such as CD or DVD. Optical media can be removed from the drives, so you can store the data off-site to prevent data loss if a disaster occurs. Optical media can also be used as WORM (Write Once Read Many) storage for data that must be kept in an immutable state for long-term retention for regulatory compliance.

Using disks with tapes can speed up backups. You can create a tiered backup design by configuring classes of storage in the backup software. Disk classes are used for very fast disk-to-disk backup from your primary disks to the secondary disk class. You then use the secondary disks as the source drives for backing up the data to tape-class devices (see Figure 9-8).

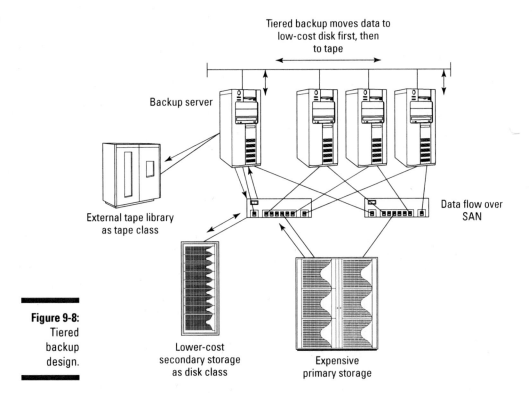

Tiered backup moves data to low-cost disk first, then to tape

Backup server

External tape library as tape class

Data flow over SAN

Figure 9-8:
Tiered backup design.

Lower-cost secondary storage as disk class

Expensive primary storage

The data flow in a tiered design moves from the primary disks on the application servers through the backup server to the secondary tier of disks. The data then flows from the secondary disk, back through the backup server, and out to the tape devices. This is a two-stage backup. The first stage backs up to fast disks and is offloaded to tape at a later time for archive storage. After the data is on tape, the information on the disks can be erased and the process can be repeated.

Using a tiered backup design is a good way to utilize older disks arrays that you might have lying around. Use those less-expensive arrays for disk-class storage. You may also be able to reuse these older disks as storage for a virtual tape library. Check with your VTL vendor to see whether its solution allows you to make use of existing storage so you can save money.

Image copy and snapshots in the SAN

SAN-based image copies and snapshot copies are part of the advanced functionality that the SAN offers.

Image copies

Image copies are exact full-copy duplicates of your production disks. After creation, you can use them as a source for backup for your production data. This allows your production applications to keep humming along while you're backing up from the image copy.

Snapshots are point-in-time copies of production data, and can be taken almost instantly, since only pointers to the production data are stored. Snapshots are also sometimes referred to as *metadata* copies, since no real data actually resides in the snapshot. (More on snapshots in Chapter 10.)

The intelligent firmware of your storage array can create image copies by mirroring the data on the production disks to another disk inside the array (see Figure 9-9). The firmware of the array is smart enough to do the copy. Not all storage arrays have this capability. Check with your storage vendor to see whether it offers this functionality. The image copy can be made available for use by the backup server or any other server in the SAN.

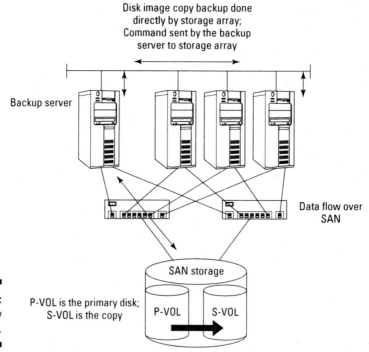

Figure 9-9:
Image copy
backup.

In Figure 9-9, the storage array mirrors the production LUN to another LUN inside the array, and just breaks off the mirror when an image copy is needed.

Snapshot copies

You can also use the array to take a snapshot copy of the data. Hardware-based snapshots use the firmware in the array and some extra disk space called a *snapshot pool* to hold any changes to the original data and the snapshot metadata itself.

A *snapshot copy* just copies the metadata of the disk. (The *metadata* are the pointers to where the data resides on the disk.) Think of metadata as the table of contents for the disk. When an application must read data from a snapshot, the application is redirected through the metadata to the disk, which contains the actual data (see Figure 9-10).

Application needs to read block 7 from snapshot drive G.
Both drives E and G point to the same logical block 7.

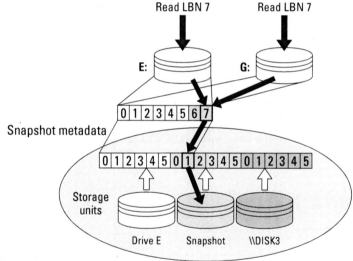

Figure 9-10:
Software-based snapshot copies.

Snapshot copies don't take up much space, and can be taken very quickly, so they're a very efficient way to protect your applications from the corruption and deletion of data. Snapshots take up less space and are easy to create — and you can usually have up to 255 snapshot copies of any LUN, so you can set a schedule to take a snapshot (say) every hour for a week if you need to. Snapshots reduce recovery-time and recovery-point objectives.

The drawback of snapshots is they use a technology called *copy on write*, which means the original data must be copied to the snapshot pool before any new writes can occur, which may slow down performance. But the trade-off is usually worth it. Think of it — you can have 255 snapshot copies, using just a little space to hold the new data, or split off a single image copy using twice as much space.

SAN data replication/remote backup

One of the main reasons people back up data is to have it available in case of a disaster. They back up to tape in the local office and take those tapes off-site so the data will be safe if their building burns or some other disaster occurs. This procedure can be automated through the use of data replication or remote backup. *Data replication* is the real-time or periodic copying of your data over a network to another disk-storage array at another location. *Remote backup* is the process of backing up your data over a network to a tape device at another location. Both solutions let you copy your data off-site in real time so it can be available in case of a disaster. The only difference between the two techniques is the storage medium used at the remote site.

- ✔ **Data replication:** This technique moves the data to disks at the remote site. Using this method, you don't have to restore the data from tape; it's available immediately to servers at the remote site. Data replication is the fastest available way to get your business back up in a disaster.

- ✔ **Remote backup:** This technique uses your backup software to do real-time online backup to a tape drive located at your remote site. The tapes are already off-site in case of disaster; you still have to restore the data from tape back to disk if you do have a disaster. You can do the remote backup in real time, or, if your network can't handle the load, you can back up to a remote tape drive across the network in the same way you do daily backups — at night, when the network isn't being used for anything else. Either way, your data is located off-site immediately.

Determining How Long a Backup Will Take

Before you can implement any backup solution, you need to determine how long it will take to back up and restore your data. The time that it takes to back up is affected by the policy that you choose (full, incremental, differential), the backup method (LAN, SAN, and so on), and the type of drives to use (tape, disk, optical). The fastest method available is to back up to disk using image copies in the SAN. Because you want to keep your data off-site in case of disaster, backing up to tape is still a requirement. How long it takes to get your data from your production disks onto tape is a simple matter of mathematics.

You need to determine the factors that limit the speed of your backup — and eliminate them if possible. If you back up over a LAN, the network might become the factor that determines how long backup will take. If you use only one tape drive to back up 20 servers, the tape drive will probably be the determining factor. If you're backing up very slow disks on your servers, how fast your drives can be read (*feed speed*) might be the determining factor.

Figure 9-11 shows a typical backup solution with the application server on the left backing up to the tape drive over the LAN, through the backup server, to the tape drive on the right. Backup speed is limited by the feed speed of the disk drives that are being backed up. The disk drive, which can be read at a maximum rate of only 5 megabytes per second, is the slowest link in the backup process. The way to fix this problem is to use a faster disk subsystem.

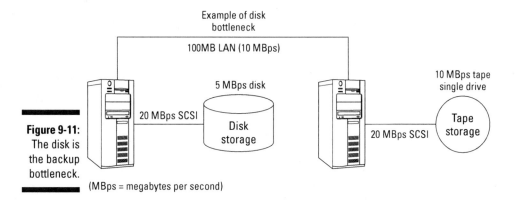

Figure 9-11: The disk is the backup bottleneck.

In Figure 9-12, on the other hand, the 10MB LAN (which can move data at only 1 MBps) is the factor that limits backup speed. The only way to fix this problem is to upgrade the LAN to a faster speed.

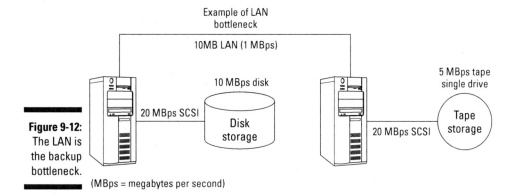

Figure 9-12: The LAN is the backup bottleneck.

As you can see by these examples, you have to balance the speed of all the components in the backup solution so no single component becomes a bottleneck. If you have a LAN that transfers data at only 1 megabyte per second, it makes no sense to go out and buy fast tape drives, because the LAN is the limiting factor. The same holds true for the backup server itself. Make sure that your backup server can handle the load of backing up all the servers in your environment.

Always use a server with lots of memory and very fast disks as your backup server. The more memory a backup server has, the more data can be cached on its way to the tape drive. The faster the disk your backup server uses, the faster it can write and read the data it compresses (using its disk as temporary storage) before sending it off to tape.

Determining backup speeds

If you back up over a LAN, you should always try to schedule backup during off-hours when the LAN is not being used for production work. The same can hold true for a SAN as well.

In SAN-backup solutions, it's preferable to use a separate SAN connection for backup. If your servers have two host bus adapters (HBAs) connected to the SAN for disk access, you can dedicate a third adapter to backup. Then you can run backup jobs across the SAN during normal business hours because the backup data stream won't affect production. Using two HBAs is fine as well, so long as you dedicate only one of them to backing up data to a shared SAN-attached tape library. You can zone the SAN to force this to happen. (See Chapter 5 for more on zoning.)

Table 9-2 lists common network types, the maximum theoretical throughput, and the typical throughput during backup if the network is dedicated for that purpose. Keep in mind that if you're also running other applications over a LAN while you're backing up, your backup speeds will decrease because of congestion on the LAN. Notice that the typical throughput of a 1GB SAN is much faster than the typical throughput of a 1GB 1000Base-T LAN. Both networks run at the same speed, but the vastly faster Fibre Channel protocol allows for a huge difference in backup speed over an Ethernet network.

Table 9-2	Typical Backup Speeds	
Network Type	*Max Throughput*	*Typical Throughput*
10Base-T	3.6GB per hour	2GB per hour
100Base-T	36GB per hour	15–20GB per hour
1000Base-T	360GB per hour	160–200GB per hour
2-Gbit Fibre Channel SAN	720GB per hour	540GB per hour
4-Gbit Fibre Channel SAN	1440GB per hour	1080GB per hour

This is a good time to talk about *compression,* which is a method of passing data through mathematical algorithms to compress the data to a size smaller than normal. The *compression ratio* is the difference in size that the algorithm achieves during the compression process. Backup programs can compress data in two ways: The software can use an agent to compress the data on the server whose data is being backed up, or the software can compress the data in the backup server itself before writing the data to disk.

Both methods allow you to store more data on the tape than its normal capacity, but the software agent method also lets you pull twice the amount of data across your network. Because the data has been compressed before it goes over the network, you can use a smaller-size network to handle the same amount of data as a network twice its capacity. (Compression ratios are normally at least 2:1.)

Compression is why tape drives are always associated with two numbers. The DLT 7000 tape drives are also known as 35/70 drives because the tapes have a normal capacity of 35GB and a compressed capacity of 70GB. Backup speeds are also determined by the compression ratio achieved by the backup software. If the software can compress data at a ratio of 2:1, your backups should run twice as fast.

The formula for backup

A standard DLT 7000 (35/70) tape device has a native maximum transfer rate of 5 megabytes per second. You'll normally see typical transfer speeds of between 18GB and 30GB per hour, per drive, depending on your compression ratio over a SAN. You can use these typical speeds to figure out how many tape drives you need to back up your data. I know these are older tape drives, but thousands of them are still out there chugging away because they're inexpensive. The formulas work with the new faster drives as well.

Suppose you have 200GB of data to back up and you want to be able to back everything up in three hours. You know that between your backup hardware and software, you usually get a 2:1 compression ratio. You will be buying more DLT 7000 (35/70) drives to stay compatible with your current tapes. Now do the math:

How many tapes will you need? Each tape holds a maximum of 70GB at 2:1 compression.

> 200GB / 70GB = 2.8GB

> At least three tapes will be needed.

How many drives do you need to back up 200GB in three hours? If each drive can back up 30GB per hour at 2:1 compression, divide 200GB by 30GB to figure out how many drives will be needed to fit within the three-hour backup window.

200GB / 30GB per hour = 6.6 hours

One drive can back up 200GB in 6.6 hours. To fit within the three-hour window, you need three drives (6.6 hours / 3 hours = 2.2 hours).

You can use this formula to figure out how many drives you need for any speed drive that you want to purchase. Just change the GB-per-hour number for the speed of the drives you're using. If you buy drives that go twice as fast as DLT 7000s, you need only two (1.5 rounded up to 2) to back up the same amount of data in the preceding example.

If you're using tape libraries that can replace tapes automatically when they become full, factor in about a 7-percent reduction in backup speed: the time it takes to replace the tapes in the drives in the library when the tapes are full. Also, each drive can back up only a single server at a time. The more drives you have, the faster you can back up all your servers.

Restore times will be about twice as long as backup time. During restore, the data is read sequentially from the tapes, which is slower than reading the data from disks during backup.

By the way, many tape drives are rated not in gigabytes per hour (GB/hr) but rather in megabytes per second (MB/s). Some are listed as megabytes per minute (MB/min). To determine different data rates, you can use these formulas:

Conversion	*Formula*
Convert MB/s to GB/hr	Multiply by 3.6
Convert GB/hr to MB/min	Multiply by 16.66
Convert MB/min to MB/s	Divide by 60

You can use these formulas to calculate the differences between how the tape drives are rated by the manufacturer to the throughput you will get in GB per hour to determine how many drives you need to get back up all your data in the required time.

For more information on using snapshots or other Point-in-Time solutions for backup, see Chapter 10. For more information on newer backup methods such as CDP, see Chapter 14.

Chapter 10

Mirror, Mirror:
Point-in-Time Copies

A *Point-in-Time (PiT) copy* is exactly what its name says: a copy of your data at a particular point in time. To best understand what this means, look at yourself in the mirror and make some funny faces; everything that you do is reflected back instantly as a perfect copy. Well, maybe not *perfect*, but. . . .

Now get a digital camera ready, make a face, and snap a picture of the mirror. Print the picture and tape it to the mirror over your reflected image. The picture is of you at the exact moment you snapped the picture, but your face has continued to change expressions (such as the frustrated look of trying to find the lost end to the roll of tape). The printed image is a Point-in-Time copy of the real thing . . . possibly your good side, too.

Translating this concept into computer-speak, you can make a perfect copy of your application's data, frozen in time. Now what do you do with this copy?

This chapter guides you through the basics of Point-in-Time copy technology, which allows you to use your SAN (storage area network) to create duplicate copies of your data — which can then be used for alternate purposes, such as backup, recovery from application corruption, testing, or migrating applications from server to server. The reasons for the copies are endless, and the SAN's flexible connectivity allows you to give the required storage to or take the storage from whatever server needs it.

Figure 10-1 shows the basics of Point-in-Time copy technology, in which you create a mirror image of a volume, split it off (described later), and give that copy to another server on the SAN.

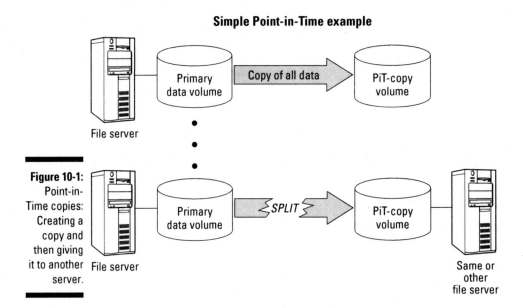

Simple Point-in-Time example

File server · Primary data volume — Copy of all data → PiT-copy volume

Figure 10-1: Point-in-Time copies: Creating a copy and then giving it to another server.

File server · Primary data volume — ⟩SPLIT⟨ → PiT-copy volume · Same or other file server

The Uses of Point-in-Time Technology

One of the major benefits of a storage area network is the flexibility you get by not having to physically dedicate storage to a particular server. You can move storage resources around without having to shut down, power off, open a server case, put disks in or take them out, re-cable, and interrupt what the server is doing. Not interrupting a server's processing is important, especially if you're in a 24/7 business that can't tolerate interruptions.

Make backups

A common interruption in processing is when you have to take an application offline for its daily or weekly backup — which means users and applications temporarily can't access files and change information. Backups must be done this way because backing up is a *linear* (progressive) operation: It starts at a given time, runs through all the files on the disk, and then ends sometime later. What your data looked like at the beginning of the backup might not be what it looked like at the end of the backup if users or applications made changes while that tape was being created. Figure 10-2 shows what data looks like at the beginning of your backup, the fact that it can change during the process, and how it looks on tape after the backup is completed.

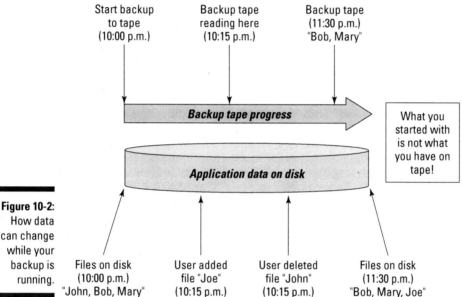

Missing data updates during a backup routine

Start backup to tape (10:00 p.m.) Backup tape reading here (10:15 p.m.) Backup tape (11:30 p.m.) "Bob, Mary"

Backup tape progress

What you started with is not what you have on tape!

Application data on disk

Files on disk (10:00 p.m.) "John, Bob, Mary" User added file "Joe" (10:15 p.m.) User deleted file "John" (10:15 p.m.) Files on disk (11:30 p.m.) "Bob, Mary, Joe"

Figure 10-2: How data can change while your backup is running.

Enter the Point-in-Time (PiT) copy to save the day. When you take a PiT snapshot of your data and back up that copy, the data won't change while it's being written to tape. Also, you don't have to take the application offline to keep the data static while a backup dumps it all to tape, so your users aren't inconvenienced.

Also, when your backup software is reading from a separate set of disks to do the backup, you aren't slowing the production disks that your application is running from. This both increases the speed of the backup process and lessens the effect of the backup on your application's response time to the user community. In fact, if your PiT copy is being backed up by a separate server (other than your application server), there is *no* effect on the application.

Make corruption-recovery images

Imagine being able to make a copy of yourself at 6 a.m. every day. You're probably in bed, asleep, dreaming about your new SAN. You get up, go to work, and while crossing the street, you get hit by a bus. Bummer. There goes that new SAN implementation you were hoping to complete.

But what if you could resurrect yourself as you were at 6 a.m. this morning and start the day over? (Ahem . . . and look both ways this time.) Now, apply this to computer technology. Here's a classic scenario that happens all the time in IT Land. . . .

If you make a copy of the high-profile XYZ application every morning at 6 a.m. before the users start tinkering with it, you have a fallback to go to if something goes awry at, say, 1 p.m. You're probably asking, "Isn't this what backups are for?" Well, yes and no. Your backup tape is typically in one of two places at 1 p.m. when the XYZ application crashes because of data corruption: at your off-site tape archive location (which takes three hours to retrieve the tape from) or still in the tape drive (but the backup job failed last night!). Assuming that you still have the tape *and* it was a good backup, how long does it take you to restore the XYZ app? And is that soon enough to get that big report up to the CEO?

If you had that 6 a.m. copy from this morning, you could restore from that image and be up and running in a matter of minutes (or seconds, even). And be a hero to the users of the XYZ app.

Business-critical applications must have a way to recover from human or application errors that cause corruption. Many operations can use PiT copy technology to keep a rotating set of copies that are only a few hours or even minutes old and can be used to fall back on in an emergency.

Now take this success story a step further. Imagine making a PiT copy at 6 a.m. and then another separate one at 9 a.m. At noon, you overwrite the 6 a.m. copy and, at 3 p.m., you overwrite the 9 a.m. copy. This rotation keeps your data at most only three hours old, and prevents you from accidentally destroying your old copy *while* you make the new copy. (Argh! Imagine someone reporting that XYZ is corrupt *while* you're overwriting the only good copy of it!) When you rotate PiT areas, the *secondary volumes* that you copy your data to are sometimes called *business continuance volumes* (BCVs); if something happens to your primary volumes (such as accidental corruption, hardware failure, or a stray cup of coffee), you can continue your business by using the data located on the secondary volume. Figure 10-3 shows how this works.

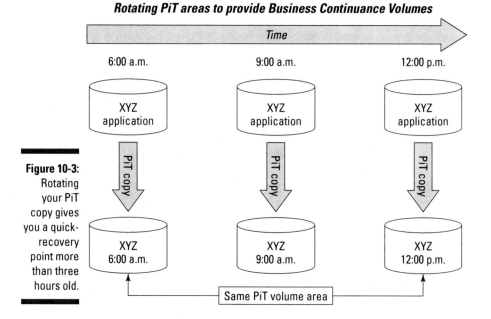

Rotating PiT areas to provide Business Continuance Volumes

Figure 10-3:
Rotating
your PiT
copy gives
you a quick-
recovery
point more
than three
hours old.

Most backup software packages are SAN-aware, so they can communicate with the SAN hardware to make these copies automatically and do the rotation for you. However, even if your software isn't up to speed on SANs yet, all backup software supports some type of scripting that can be used to do the commands to create and mount the PiT copies to where they can be backed up. You're covered when it comes to integrating PiT into your current backup schedules.

Creating a PiT copy offers an enormous advantage over standard tape backup processes. When tape is too slow to restore from, an on-site PiT of your critical apps saves you from a lot of headaches. And because disk is much faster, easier to access, and more flexible than tape recovery, it provides a great tool for IT departments to keep in their toolbox for critical applications.

Save space

Running a SAN with PiT copies doesn't force you to use a lot more disk space than before. With a SAN, you don't have to dedicate disk-copy areas on a one-to-one relationship with your application data. Because you can move disks around from server to server, you can move the PiT areas as well. You can share the disks needed to make the PiT copies.

For example, if you have three servers each with 10GB of storage, you can designate one 10GB area for making PiT copies (see Figure 10-4). One by one, you snap a copy of each server to the PiT area and back it up. When the backup is completed, you snap the next server in line to the PiT area and back up that disk again; this time, it's the next server's data. Rotate through all three servers like this and you use only 10GB more space than the 50GB total among the three servers. Compare this to the 100GB you would have used if each server had another 10GB of PiT space dedicated to it exclusively.

Sharing PiT volumes with multiple servers

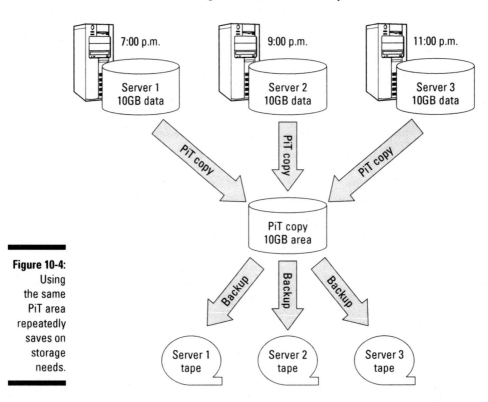

Figure 10-4:
Using the same PiT area repeatedly saves on storage needs.

The possibilities are endless

Tricks to make regular backups faster and more reliable aren't the only reason why PiT copies were invented. Some people have to make a copy of their data because other systems must use it, too. This process was born in the days of old mainframe data centers, where time on the system was expensive and processing vast amounts of data took a long time. Systems that could have branched off and continued processing with a portion of the dataset were left waiting for the entire process to complete to be able to use their chunk of it. With a PiT copy taken at the right juncture in the long batch process, the other processes could grab their subset of data and complete more processing while the main system continued to crunch and massage the original data.

Another great use for PiT technology is to make separate copies of data to test and develop applications. After your developers write enough code to make the application operate, they need real-life data to test whether the code works. You can hand over a PiT copy of your real data to the developers' server, and then they can run it against the latest version of an application. The developers can test the new code as much as they want without worrying about corrupting the real production environment. And here's the best part: If they *do* corrupt it, they can quickly do a resync to go back to the drawing board and tweak their code to correct the problem. All this happens without stopping the real production application or putting your data in harm's way (see Figure 10-5).

Give developers a separate, up-to-date version of data to test new applications.

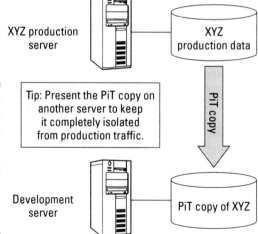

Figure 10-5: Developers can have their own up-to-date copies of data to test applications.

Complete versus Metadata Copies

The data in a PiT copy is created in one of two distinct ways. The first is a complete bit-for-bit copy of the source disk to the destination disk. This is an *image* copy, or *complete* copy, meaning that each data bit is read from one disk and written to another disk. The data exists in two places. The other type of copy is a *metadata* copy, which doesn't copy any bits until something changes. It is (pardon the pun) a *bit* different.

The term *metadata* comes from *meta-* (changed) and *data* (information); it's essentially a changed-data copy. Metadata is not a one-for-one copy but a copy of only the data that has *changed* since the PiT snap took place. To understand this, go back to making faces in the mirror.

Staring at yourself in the mirror, you already have a perfect copy of your face in the mirror. As long as you don't move, the reflection is frozen in time. Consider that your personal PiT copy. However, if you blink, your reflection will mirror that, and your PiT is ruined. Here's where the changed part of metadata comes into play. Before you blink (and you *know* you will blink), snap a picture of just your eyes and then tape the picture to the mirror over the reflected image of just your eyes. Now when you blink, the image in the mirror (your PiT copy) doesn't change: It's *still* frozen in time. Next, make a big frown and take a picture of just your mouth and then tape that over the reflection of your mouth in the mirror. Your original big smile still exists because the PiT copy (the mirror) doesn't change.

Metadata copies work on this same simple principle: You take a specific snapshot of the original data and copy it to the PiT area *before* it updates the original. All metadata copies work with a specifically sized chunk of data that defines how much information should be copied when a change is made. This makes managing the map of what is and isn't changed easier for the PiT management software to, uh, manage. This chunk size is usually one or more physical disk tracks. To keep track (pardon another pun) of these tracks, a bitmap or table is kept by the software or hardware managing the PiT copies. Figure 10-6 shows how a snapshot of a to-be-changed track is moved over to the PiT area before it is updated. The table or bitmap of tracks is updated to show that the current location of the original data (Track 5 in Figure 10-6) is now on the PiT disk. The copy of Track 5 is like the photo of your eyes, which is saved as the image of your face before it is changed by blinking. For more about the primary and secondary volumes mentioned in Figure 10-6, see the upcoming section "Pair up your volumes."

The software or hardware maintaining the PiT uses a set of pointers to mark what data is the original and what is now the PiT copy version of it. (Read a comparison of software-based versus hardware-based PiT copies in the upcoming section "Creating a PiT Copy.") By making a copy of the change and using the track pointer to point to the new area, you use only the minimum amount of space. When a metadata PiT is read from later, it uses these pointers to keep track of whether the data is still on the original primary data volume or has been copied over to the PiT area because it has been altered. You can see an illustration of this in Figure 10-7. (For more on bitmaps, skip down to the section "Doing a resync: Refresh and restore.")

Figure 10-6:
How metadata PiT copies save the original chunk of data before it is changed.

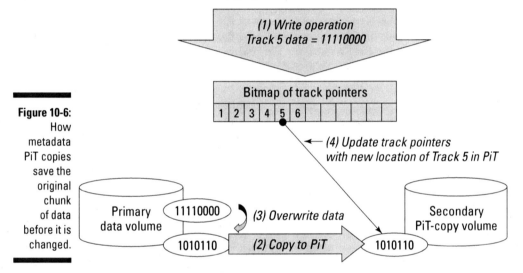

Changing data on a metadata volume

(1) Write operation
Track 5 data = 11110000

Bitmap of track pointers
| 1 | 2 | 3 | 4 | 5 | 6 | | | | | |

(4) Update track pointers with new location of Track 5 in PiT

Primary data volume — 11110000

(3) Overwrite data

Secondary PiT-copy volume

1010110 — *(2) Copy to PiT* — 1010110

Figure 10-7:
Metadata PiT copies use the track pointers to find the correct chunk of data.

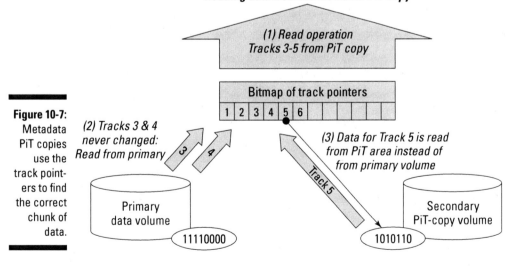

Reading data from the metadata PiT copy

(1) Read operation
Tracks 3-5 from PiT copy

Bitmap of track pointers
| 1 | 2 | 3 | 4 | 5 | 6 | | | | | |

(2) Tracks 3 & 4 never changed: Read from primary

3 *4*

(3) Data for Track 5 is read from PiT area instead of from primary volume

Track 5

Primary data volume — 11110000

Secondary PiT-copy volume — 1010110

The neat thing about metadata copies is that you don't have to make a complete bit-for-bit initial copy. A metadata PiT copy is instantaneous because you don't have to read and write the original to another area to make a second copy of it. You just make all the PiT pointers point to the original blocks of data.

The other benefit of metadata copies is that they use only as much disk space as is required by the amount of data that changes in the original. Different implementations of metadata PiT exist, so check with your vendor on how this feature is implemented. Some vendors require that you pre-allocate the same amount of space as the disks you want to copy, just in case you change all the source data. Some vendors use a reserved area of disk to dynamically size the area for the changed data to be written to. As long as you don't run out of reserved space, you can keep making as many copies as you want.

Okay, now remove those photographs of your eyes and mouth from the mirror; otherwise people will think you're weird.

Which PiT Type Should You Use?

The decision to use a complete copy or a metadata copy for PiT snapshots of your data depends on a few things. Basically, ask yourself what the PiT copy will be used for and whether you can tolerate any performance impact on your source production disk drives.

Here are some guidelines to follow. Use a complete data PiT copy when

- ✔ The second copy of your data must be 100-percent reliable.
- ✔ The initial copy time is not an issue.
- ✔ You can bear the expense of an additional 100 percent of the original disk space for the second copy.
- ✔ The use of the copy cannot affect the original source's performance.

Use a metadata PiT copy when

- ✔ The copy must be available immediately after it is snapped.
- ✔ You can't spare the space for a complete duplicate copy.
- ✔ The performance impact on the original data is not important.

Creating a PiT Copy

You use one of two methods when creating a Point-in-Time copy. The first is to use the disk storage array itself, where the source and destination disks are in the same physical box, and the storage array handles all the copying and managing of data. This method is termed *hardware-based* because the storage hardware does all the work. The other method uses software on the server to make and manage the copies. Called *software-based* or *host-based,* the software on the host does all the work. See the comparison in Figure 10-8.

Hardware PiT copy uses storage array's hardware to create copies.

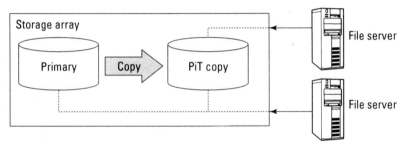

Software PiT copy uses the server's operating system to make copies.

Figure 10-8:
Hardware-
based
versus
software- or
host-based
PiT copy
technology.

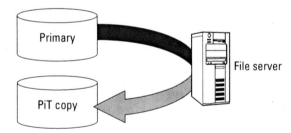

Each method has its pros and cons. The best ways to measure the differences are to compare speed, flexibility, and price, as follows (see Table 10-1 for a quick comparison):

For hardware-based PiT copy technology:

✔ Copies are performed by the physical storage array, thus bypassing the servers.

✔ Because hardware-based PiT copies are direct disk-to-disk, this way is much faster than making software-based copies.

✔ This technology is typically more expensive than software-based because it's faster.

✔ Administration is easier because you centrally manage it from the storage array instead of separately from each and every server.

For software-based PiT copy technology:

✔ Copies are performed by third-party software running on the server's operating system.

✔ Because the host does all the work, the CPU of the host is busy moving data when it could be working on other tasks.

✔ The underlying storage doesn't matter, so you can use any combination of storage arrays and even in some cases an internal disk to make copies.

✔ With metadata-based software PiT copies, only the host that made the copy can access the copy image because only that host holds the pointers to what data is original and what is the copy. This *host isolation* lowers your flexibility, such as being able to use the copy on a different server for backup or development and testing.

✔ Software-based PiT copies are typically slower because they read and write through the SAN infrastructure instead of directly disk-to-disk as with hardware-based PiT copies.

✔ This technology is cheaper than hardware-based because it's slower, simpler, and less flexible.

✔ Because software-based PiT copies are administered on a server-by-server basis, managing tens or hundreds of copy operations is more difficult.

Table 10-1		Comparison of PiT Copy Technology	
Technology	*Speed*	*Flexibility*	*Price*
Hardware-based	Faster	More flexible; better administration; doesn't use servers	More expensive
Software-based	Slower	Less flexible; more difficult administration; uses host	Cheaper

Managing Your Point-in-Time Copies

You manage your PiT copies using a graphic user interface (GUI) or a command-line interface (CLI). Either interface does the same thing; the GUI looks prettier and the CLI requires some typing. Some GUIs can be run from anywhere on the network; others must be run on the specific host that sees the source and destination disks for the copy. This is especially true with software-based copies. (Read more on software-based and hardware-based copies in the preceding section.) Regardless of which interface you use, the steps involved in creating, using, and managing them are similar.

Pair up your volumes

Whether you use a GUI or a CLI, you'll usually see a list of all the disks that are available to be copied *from*. These disks are typically referred to as *primary volumes,* which are disks that already have a file system and your application's data laid out on them.

Be careful when selecting volumes! You don't want to accidentally overwrite a primary volume because it contains your production data.

This grouping of primary and secondary disks is called a *pair*, which defines the two partners in the relationship you just created.

Here's another thing that differentiates software-based PiT solutions from hardware-based ones: With a hardware-based solution, neither the primary nor secondary volumes have to be visible to any host's operating system (OS) to be paired. If you're using a software-based PiT solution, the host on which you're running the management interface has to be able to "see" and access both the primary and secondary disk volumes that you plan to pair. Because the application software is doing the work of copying, it must be able to use the disks the way a normal application would.

You must make sure that the secondary volume is the same size or larger than the primary volume. However, properly written software won't allow you to make the mistake of exceeding the space available. On the other hand, you should also be careful not to waste space on an oversize secondary volume. Sometimes you can't get that space back if it contains a PiT copy. The rest of the space is lost because it's not separately addressable by the SAN — and therefore, by your hosts. When the two disks are closer in size, you end up with less wasted (that is, overhanging and unusable) space.

When dealing with metadata copies, you don't always have to pre-allocate a landing area (secondary volume) for your data. Most metadata copy solutions use a special reserved disk area to hold the copied blocks of changes from the primary volumes. Each vendor's solution varies, but when dealing with pure metadata PiT solutions, you typically choose your primary volume, give the new copy a name, and say "Go." The software handles the rest behind the scenes.

Create the pairs

When you choose your primary and secondary volumes, you create a relationship between the two areas of disk storage. You haven't copied any data yet. To make the secondary copy usable, you must copy the primary volume over to the secondary volume. When you want the PiT copy to happen, you tell the interface to create the pair. This causes the array (if it's a hardware-based solution) or the host (if it's a software-based solution) to start copying data from the source to the target.

If you're working from a metadata copy, the PiT is available to be used immediately because you don't have to wait for the initial copy to complete. If you're working with a complete copy, first you have to do a bit-for-bit copy from the primary volume to the secondary volume.

Creating the pair does a few things. First, the secondary volume is put in read-only mode. This is a precautionary step so that nothing on the secondary copy can be altered while the primary is being copied to it. You don't want anyone changing the data on the secondary without doing it on the primary first. If the secondary disk were still in read-write mode, another host or application could really screw things up behind the scenes while you thought you had a perfect copy in the works. The initial copy phase in a complete-copy implementation can take a while, depending on the speed of the disks, how the vendor implements the copy process, and how much data you copy. The most important thing to recognize here is that an initial copy captures *everything* on the physical volume, whether used or free space. A logical device that's 10GB, with a 5GB file system that is 50 percent full (2.5GB of files) copies all 10GB — unused space and all — when the copy is made. That behavior is explained next.

Although operating systems have a concept of free and used space, PiT copies deal at a much lower level and use cylinders, tracks, and blocks of the disks. If the primary volume is 10GB but only 2.5GB is used by files, the initial copy will still move all 10GB-worth of bits — it doesn't know whether a 1 or a 0 is part of a file or just unused disk space, so it copies everything. Naturally, there are exceptions to this rule, depending on your storage vendor. Some arrays actually know which bits are real data and which are blank space. Check with your storage vendors to find out on how this copy process works with their gear.

The initial copy, done at a very low level (literally down to the actual tracks on the disk), is faster than copying file by file. File systems reside at a high level that only the host OS understands. Asking the OS about each little bit of data while it's copied takes too much time and ties up the server too much to do other tasks. Also, trying to be compatible with every version of OS is too difficult. When you stick to the basics across all different operating systems, SAN vendors don't have to worry about what is and what isn't compatible. And if you copy everything at a low level, the copy will be perfect on the other side. You want this process to be as transparent to the users as possible. Also, each OS has it's own way of dealing with a copy of an existing volume. Some may get confused if they see a second instance of a volume (they look identical). I strongly recommended that you consult with your operating-system vendor on how to activate and use a second copy of a volume.

Splitting the mirror, snapping a copy

After you complete the initial copy, the primary and secondary volumes are now *synchronized*. The secondary volume reflects the primary in every way, and all further changes to the primary are reflected to the secondary copy immediately because they are kept in sync. This reflection is called *mirroring*. (And you thought that making faces in the mirror was a stupid analogy.) The two disks will stay paired in this mirrored state until you want to begin using the secondary copy as a unique entity.

When you're ready to start using the copy independently, you must perform an operation to split the mirror into the two discrete disk volumes that they started out as. If you're uneasy about calling it *breaking the mirror*, you can call it a *split* and avoid the seven years' bad luck. Or, because you can have multiple copies of a primary, you can also call it *snapping* a copy off the primary. After a copy is snapped, the synchronization between it and the primary stops, and this secondary copy takes on its own personality and can be accessed the same as any other disk.

Seriously, here are a few other reasons why it's not good practice to call this process *breaking the mirror*. For one, the original term for a mirrored disk described a way of accessing your data if something happened to the original media it was on or that media was defective. Another reason for the distinction between mirrors and snaps is that when you use metadata copies, the primary and secondary disk areas are not true mirrors. The secondary copy in Metadata Land is a combination of the original unchanged primary data plus any changes that happened since the snap occurred. If you took away the primary disk medium, the secondary would be incomplete and unusable. Therefore calling it a mirror is wrong because the secondary copy isn't a complete reflection of the primary, but only of the differences. Remember the photos of your blinking eye and frown? Without the original reflection behind it, it's just pieces of a face.

Doing a resync: Refresh and restore

A PiT copy of your data gives you a parachute to use in case something goes wrong with your original disk image. Apart from outright failure of a physical disk, which is usually covered by Redundant Array of Inexpensive Disks (RAID) and mirroring technologies, data corruption or other types of human error can happen easily and quickly. Errors can come about, for example, through programming errors in an application or by typing a wrong command that erases the entire payroll system (yikes!). The PiT copy that you made this morning can save the day. You're probably asking, "But don't you have to copy all that data back to the original disks to use it?" The answer: Not really.

One of the neat things about PiT is that most vendors (check with the ones you're working with) have a way to keep track of the changes that occurred between the original disks and the copy you snapped. Their method, commonly called a *bitmap table* or *track change table*, marks what sections of the original data have been altered since the last snap. When a bit is changed on the original disk, that section's representative bit is flagged as changed in the bitmap table. Now, the storage array knows that if it needs to recreate the data in that section, it should copy *just that section* of the data back from the PiT copy (assuming that nobody changed the copy either, of course). These bitmap tables are similar to how the metadata copies are handled, described previously in the "Complete versus Metadata Copies" section of this chapter.

The bitmap table is usually kept for both copies of the data: the original source disks and the copy itself. This table allows you to *resync* the copy, based on only what changed. The cool thing is that because two maps of what changed exist, you can go either from source to destination *or* from destination back to source. Thus you can *refresh* the PiT to be current (bringing it up to date) or *restore* the source data from the PiT image, bringing back only the changes. Either process is much faster than a full copy, depending on how much has changed. Figure 10-9 shows a PiT pair, each with a bitmap table showing what tracks have been altered since they were snapped apart. You can resynchronize either copy by sending only the changes that have happened since the snap, instead of the complete volume.

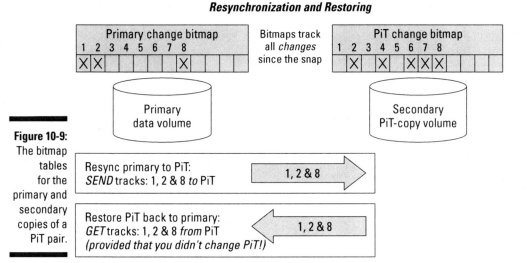

Figure 10-9:
The bitmap tables for the primary and secondary copies of a PiT pair.

The most common reason for doing a resync of your PiT copy is to reduce the time required to make a new copy. The amount of data to be moved from the source disk to the destination disk is much less when you copy only what changed since the last time they were synchronized. So, for example, if you do a snapshot every night for a backup routine, why copy 100 percent of your data to the PiT copy when you can move maybe just the 10 percent that changed since the previous copy you made last night?

I need my data now!

Suppose that you don't have time to do a resync in either direction. You know you have a good copy of your data on your PiT copy and you want to make that your real production disk *now*. This is called a *swap* (or *quick restore*) of your original source disk and your destination PiT disk. While the process starts copying your PiT data back to the original volume, it simultaneously allows you to *use* the PiT as if it were the original source without your having to do anything fancy on your server. Many software and hardware solutions allow you to swap the identities of your source and destination disk so that you can immediately restart your application and bring yourself back to the point in time (there's that name in action!) when the data was good. Check out Figure 10-10 to see a quick restore in action. It shows how the PiT copy is now used for access while the primary volume is refreshed with a known good copy of data from the PiT copy. Eventually, the primary will be fixed with the data from the PiT.

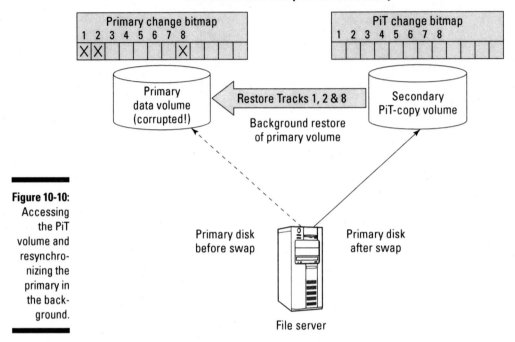

Quick Restore or Swap of PiT and Primary

Figure 10-10:
Accessing
the PiT
volume and
resynchro-
nizing the
primary in
the back-
ground.

Using a PiT copy

Using a PiT copy of your primary disk is easy because it works just like a regular disk in your servers and operating systems. Thus, depending on your operating system, you mount the PiT copy and access the file system on it just as you would any other disk. Yes, it *is* that simple.

The Finer Points of PiT

If you've already read the previous parts of this chapter, you know about the great benefits of using PiT copy technologies. If you're wondering about any potential downsides, stick with us here to discover the pros, cons, and tricks of using PiT copies. I also discuss some guidelines to follow to help steer you clear of those "wow, I never thought about that" issues that come up when using PiT copy technologies.

Also, I want to preface these guidelines with the word *typically*. In *typical* environments, certain things are always true: PiT copies are created and snapped off and hardly ever used, except for reading them for backup to tape or by developers for testing. They sit there as backup copies of your data volumes, dormant until something bad happens, and *then* they're put into action. So what I'm saying is that *typically,* PiT copies don't require high-performance Fibre Channel or SAS hard drives. *Typically,* PiT copies reside on relatively inexpensive Serial ATA drives. However, if I say that this is the hard-and-fast rule, you'll call me crazy and throw this book in the garbage. None of us wants that. You know your environment — and the needs of your user community — better than anyone. These tips are a guide to simple things that people *typically* don't think about at the start and end up having to fix later on.

Guideline #1: Understand when to snap a copy

The most popular use of PiT copies is for backups. Why make a copy of data that's already good, right? For one thing, having a copy of your data that's frozen in time keeps the backup tape consistent across the entire length of the backup. Because applications and users are always changing data — and lots of that data is interrelated — restoring data that changed halfway though a backup session might be as good as wiping mud across your disks. The data restored from tape might be just as (un-)useful.

The data-is-constantly-changing realization comes into play with PiT technology. Remember that even the most widely used applications and databases don't know anything about PiT copy technology (not yet, but SAN technology is getting more and more intelligent by the hour). Applications know only about server memory (where they exist), processors (where they are executed), and storage (where they read and write data to). Because applications use a server's local memory to do lots of the work and hold information close to the vest, the most current data isn't necessarily on the disk drives themselves. So what does that mean to PiT copies? You have to get your application to quiet down before you make a copy to the disk that the application's data lives on.

By *quiet down,* I don't mean stopping the application and kicking users off the system. Rather, you have to get the application to organize its data and write out the data in the server's memory to the disk so the physical storage contains the most current information. This quieting-down process, called *quiescing,* is invoked in different ways with different applications. Some applications don't have a way to do this directly, and some have a command that does the same thing but with a different name. Most database programs have a backup mode that flushes all their memory-based information to disk and holds off any other writes to disk until they are taken out of this backup mode. In this case, the copy of your application on disk is in a *consistent state,* meaning that if you have to restore this copy from a tape, the application won't complain. Talk to your application vendor about how you could quiesce its application to take a consistent PiT copy of it.

As you can see in Figure 10-11, the database running on the server has its data disks paired to a secondary PiT disk. To get a good snap of the database files, we must tell the database to flush all its work in the server's memory to disk (and therefore to the PiT disk as well) using the quiescing process. In this case, a special backup mode that the database understands is used to flush all the data in memory to the primary disks. When that's done, in the second step in the figure, you can safely snap the PiT copy off its primary. The last step in Figure 10-11 shows the snap taking place. As soon as the snap is completed, you can turn off the backup mode on the database and it will resume writing to the primary disk.

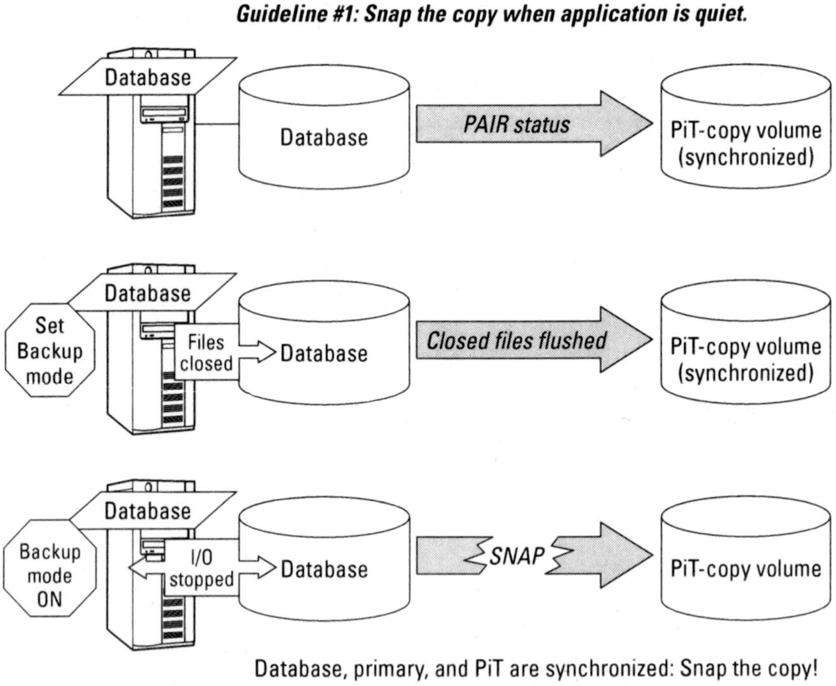

Guideline #1: Snap the copy when application is quiet.

Figure 10-11:
Quiescing
a database
using its
data-
flushing
backup
mode to
get a good
copy.

Database, primary, and PiT are synchronized: Snap the copy!

Guideline #2: Keep your PiT pairs separated

One reason for making a second or third copy of your original data is so you can use your copy separately from the original. You also want to keep the original and the copy performing at their best, both during the copying process and after the copy is finished being created. A key to making this happen is knowing on which disks your original and copy are located in the SAN or storage array. Most storage arrays use multiple RAID groups to make up all the volumes you can assign to your servers. Some of these RAID groups are on separate controllers in the array. Spreading out the primary and PiT volumes from each other allows you to keep the read and write operations from fighting against each other when it comes time to copy the data back and forth between the disks. Also, the more disks in use behind a RAID group, the faster the copy usually goes. (See Chapter 2 to review RAID groups.) The key is to keep the physical mechanical heads that read from and write to disk from thrashing, or jumping back and forth like crazy to read and write tracks when the copy process takes place. This slows down the drive from doing other I/O, which can slow down your applications.

In a SAN environment, from one server you can access volumes from multiple disk arrays. Use a primary volume from one set of RAID disks and a PiT disk from a different set of RAID disks to keep the disk heads from thrashing. If you use software-based PiT copies, you can pair up a volume on one array subsystem with a PiT disk on a different array subsystem. This spreads the load across the two arrays as well as the SAN cabling to balance the workload and make things faster. Separating the volumes is especially crucial when you use Serial ATA disks. Serial ATA disks, unlike Fibre Channel disks, are not designed to do many simultaneous I/O streams. If you place many secondary volumes on the same RAID set of Serial ATA drives and try to create or resync those copies at the same time, you'll choke the Serial ATA interfaces. Try to keep everything spread out as much as you can.

As Figure 10-12 shows, the primary and secondary disk areas are on separate sets of physical disks. This keeps the disk heads from jumping back and forth when they have to copy data between the pairs during an initial copy or resynchronization process, as would happen if they were on the same physical disk drives.

Guideline #2: Keep primary and PiT volumes separated.

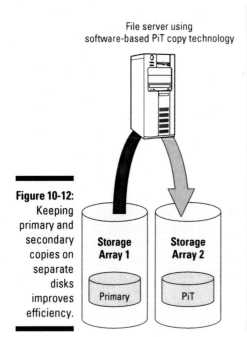

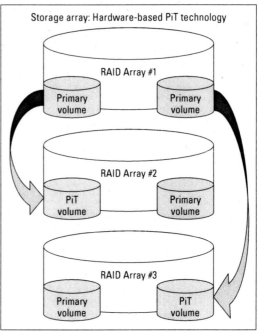

Figure 10-12:
Keeping
primary and
secondary
copies on
separate
disks
improves
efficiency.

Guideline #3: Use the right disk storage for PiT copies

You're probably not going to use a PiT copy 24 hours a day. Depending on the reason for using it, make sure that it's not taking up expensive real estate (high-performance disk drives) if it doesn't have to. That is, try to use cheaper disks or slower disks or both in the SAN for copies that don't require high speed or high reliability. If the PiT copy is used for another production application to do secondary processing, maybe it requires the same class — or possibly *better* — disk resources.

The key to this rule is that even though a SAN gives you flexibility — and therefore seemingly abundant resources to work with — you should still be conservative and plan things with some logic so you don't paint yourself into a corner technologically. Using an array, a disk, or a device on the SAN that costs less both in terms of dollars and performance leaves prime real estate open and available to the applications that need them. If you have some slower performing disks that you don't use for your regular applications, maybe they're a good place to throw PiT copies that don't need high performance . . . just a place to stay temporarily. Disk drives that perform at 7,200 RPM, on slower disk technology such as Serial ATA (SATA), are perfect for secondary volumes that (with any luck) won't be needed. High-speed Fibre Channel drives in the 15,000 RPM range perform better — and are therefore more expensive. These should be used for secondary copies that will be *actively used* after they're snapped off.

In Figure 10-13, the left side shows that the software-based PiT solution uses a cheaper Serial ATA disk array for all the secondary PiT copies. In this particular case, we can get by with having them on that class of disk. Your environment may be different. With the hardware-based PiT, such as on the right side of Figure 10-13, the PiT copies are placed on lower-performing disk spindles, which are usually cheaper. Also, some PiT copies are on fast disks (such as 15,000 RPM Fibre Channel disks) because they must be used in further parallel processing in the data center. This balances the use of higher-performing disks for critical production applications and lower-performing disks for BCVs or backup processes.

Guideline #3: Use the right storage type, depending on PiT usage.

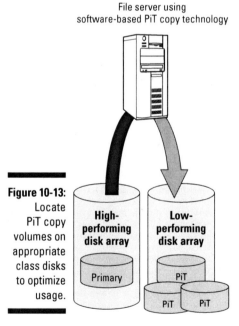

Figure 10-13: Locate PiT copy volumes on appropriate class disks to optimize usage.

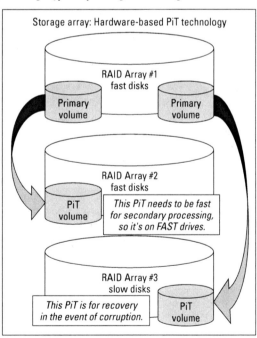

Questions to ask your SAN vendors

PiT copies aren't an industry standard, and the many different vendors implement them in different ways. Some ways are good, some are bad, and some are so-so. Following are some good questions to ask prospective storage vendors:

- How many copies can I make of a source volume? (Think about how many you really need.)

- Can I resync and restore from any of the copies back to the source?

- Is the copy read-write during the copy or read-only?

- Are the copies write-enabled after the snap, and can I force the PiT copy to be read-only?

- For software-based metadata copies, is the changed data stored in the servers' memory or on a disk?

- Must I have 100 percent of the source space reserved on disk for the metadata copy?

- Can I resync and restore instantly (usually done as a metadata copy)?

- Can I snap a copy instantly like a metadata PiT so that the secondary volume will become a complete copy in the background?

- Are there restrictions on where the source and destination copy reside (different RAID types, disk sizes, and so on)?

- Does the vendor's solution interface into many popular applications to make the application PiT snapshot-aware, such as backup software?

Part III
Using Advanced SAN Features

"Remember, I want the bleeding file server surrounded by flaming workstations with the word, 'Motherboard' scrolling underneath."

In this part . . .

Don't let the word *advanced* scare you. In previous chapters, we cover the parts, reasons, and steps that go toward building a SAN. But up to now, the concepts have been pretty basic; after all, what's a brand-new home stereo system without some music cranking through it? You didn't get this far to stare at a bunch of boxes connected with wires. You want to see what advantages this new technology offers you.

This part of the book dives into how you can use your SAN-based storage in a different, more flexible manner than you're used to with the internal disk drives in servers. We go into the new possibilities that SANs offer you, such as more efficient data backup solutions, using snapshots, and using the SAN to make multiple copies of your data (giving you more options for using that data for different purposes simultaneously). And these topics are just the tip of the iceberg when it comes to what a SAN can do for you.

Chapter 11

Approaches to SAN Management

*M*anagement refers to control. Whether the control is of people or things, management serves as a monitor and a focal point for subordinates. (And you thought your boss was around just to give you a hard time.) To make the analogy with your managers at work, their job is to make sure that you're doing something constructive instead of standing around the water cooler flapping your gums about last night's ball game. Also, managers look to see that the work you're doing is correct (at least, they're supposed to) and that the work going on is consistent with the goals of *their* managers.

Managers also devise new things for you to do. New projects and tasks come down the line, and your task is to get those projects and tasks accomplished. At the end of the day, your boss notes what you've accomplished for further review down the road. To manage effectively, a manager must understand what's going on within the organization — what's good and bad, what works, what needs improving, and where the wasted energy is.

SAN management covers many aspects, from physical-asset inventory to daily configuration changes to long-term historical reporting. Figure 11-1 shows an example of how delivering a SAN to your customers relates to the idea that you are using a layer of abstraction between the customers' needs and the physical components that deliver them, making both your job and your customers' jobs easier to accomplish.

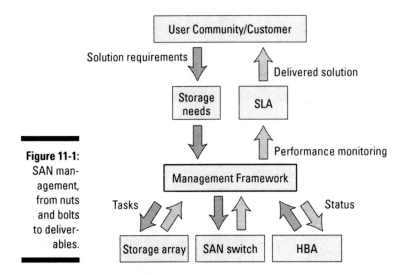

Figure 11-1:
SAN man-
agement,
from nuts
and bolts
to deliver-
ables.

Management: From Simple Networking to SANs

In the old days, room-size computers ran your business. Inside these enormous boxes were processors, memory chips, and some type of storage. If the
application that was running on one of these computers suddenly stopped
working or ran slowly or incorrectly, you knew that the problem lay somewhere within the box. It had to. Gremlins couldn't get in. Technically, bugs
(critters, that is) could, but that's a different story.

Enter the age of networking and hardware interconnectivity. Every server has
some little wire that comes out the back, plugs into the wall, and goes who
knows where. All these components and variables present a bigger debug-
ging problem: Is the application problem in the server or out on the network?
And how do you know?

In the past, you needed to call the networking group, which used network
management tools to determine whether the devices on the corporate network were still functioning (or functioning optimally) and whether anything
had changed recently that affected the application server's ability to deliver
services to your users — increasingly angry users, at this point. The networking group used its tools to debunk any issues you were having and tell you
whether the problem was with its components or (as they always seemed to
say) with *your* server. (According to them, the problem was *never* the network.) The group always had those neat reports and graphs to prove that it
wasn't their problem.

Wouldn't it be great to have your own sets of reports and graphs to help you decide that everything is hunky-dory with your equipment? Now you can!

Have I sold you on SAN management yet? If not, here are a few more been-there-done-that reasons.

SAN Management from the Ground Up

Defining and building a SAN involves more than just connecting components willy-nilly. You need to start small and above all, document, document, document. Oh, and don't forget to document. (You can thank me later.)

Start small; think big

Your SAN probably will start in a test environment as one or two servers, a switch, and some storage. You'll have some of that neat bright-orange fiber-optic cable coming out of the backs of your components, connecting every-thing. The system will be a mess, but who cares? The test SAN exists for you and your work compadres to gather information from, to train others on, and to test the functionality of the new SAN-centric hardware and software.

The real production SAN probably will start small as well, comprising maybe two or four switches and some key application servers, but it will grow as people realize the benefits of a SAN (with luck, from reading this book). After things really start moving with the SAN, more and more servers will be attached, and you'll undoubtedly be able to migrate some large, high-profile applications to it. Welcome to the 21st century!

Documentation is key

From Day 1 of your SAN, if you aren't keeping track of what's hooked up to what, which host bus adapter (HBA) is in what server, and how many giga-flops are flowing into the whoseamawhatsit, you're going to be in big trouble if something goes wrong. You can't call the networking group this time: Keeping track of this stuff is up to *you*. Even if you use management tools that tell you when something's wrong, you still need to know how to ferret out problems so that you can solve them. It is impossible to memorize where all that bright-orange cable running out the back of your servers and under the floor goes, so you need to keep things written down somewhere.

Effective SAN management starts with having a really good grip on the components of your SAN, how they're connected, and their functioning status. And to know what you're working with and how it all fits together, you have to document what you have, including hardware, connections, and software configurations.

You need to treat your SAN components just the way you do your servers and networking equipment. The SAN is an integral part of your computing infrastructure, so whatever practices and procedures you use to document and track changes with servers and network components, you should apply to the SAN as well.

To drive the point home, I can draw a parallel from (arguably) the largest network that exists: the telephone system. Imagine that a telephone company didn't have a way to measure what its equipment was doing all over the world. If a failure happened in a call-routing-switching-box (that's the official term), and no management platform were in place, the phone company would never be able to figure out what had happened or how to fix it — or even know that a problem existed at all! Some box somewhere just smoked. Oh, well, better luck next time. Now Aunt Sally from Albuquerque can't call to say "Hello" anymore. (Whether that's good news or bad is up to you.)

As far as SANs go, if components in your infrastructure aren't working properly or have failed for some reason, and your XYZ application is suddenly running at 1 percent of its usual speed, you're going to want to know about it pronto. (*Pronto,* for those who don't know, is Spanish for *before your boss finds out.*) Complete and up-to-date documentation makes the problem discovery and resolution process possible. With documentation in hand, you can manage components (hardware), management frameworks (software), and connectivity (cabling).

Cable Management: Spaghetti, Anyone?

Cable management treats the cables and wires running between your SAN components with the same importance as it does the components themselves.

Before I start discussing managing your servers, switches, and storage, make sure that you don't start tripping over your tangled interconnecting wiring. Fiber-optic cable is expensive, and after snapping a strand under a chair or around a corner, you'll be scratching your head about why things aren't working . . . and paying for it when you need to replace the cable.

Take a look under your desk, and find the power strip where your computer, monitor, printer, scanner, fax machine, coffee machine, and desk lamp are all plugged in. Spaghetti, right? A twisted knot of fiber-optic cabling can be dangerous: It's an invitation for someone to trip. But cables can easily be damaged if they're strewn all over the floor.

Seemingly, nobody really has time to run or label cables in an orderly fashion. They just plug 'em in and string 'em to equipment. If you follow this approach to cable management (um, if you don't do any cable management), you can't expect to figure out quickly which cable is which. If you have to unplug your fax machine while running something really important on your PC, would you feel comfortable pulling that plug? If cables are labeled, you can be much more confident that the change you're about to make is correct.

Cable management involves both physical and logical levels. The combination of the two levels makes it very easy to understand how your SAN communicates and where everything goes. I discuss the best ways to put cabling in, then how to mark them so you know what each cable is for.

Physical cable management

The *physical* level of cable management covers the actual cabling itself. Using physical cable management systems ensures that you keep your cables in a safe, neat layout.

Because fiber-optic cabling is brittle, the glass fibers within the cables can bend only so far. If they get twisted into a knot or around a tight corner, they snap like . . . um . . . glass. Broken fiber-optic cable is hard to identify, because sometimes the light still gets through just enough to work. Think of a garden hose with a kink: Some water still gets through, but in spurts versus a steady flow of water. When a fiber-optic cable sometimes lets light through and sometimes doesn't, you end up with a flaky connection that can cause all kinds of issues out on your SAN. With orderly cable placement, if a cable does get broken somehow, it's easier to replace it if you don't have to fight with that giant day-glow orange spaghetti under the floor.

A good cable management system usually comes in the form of a rack or some type of 19" rackmount panels that securely hold the cabling. The rack or panels have tracks where the cables run next to or inside your equipment racks so that they can easily yet safely flow between one component and another.

Some of these systems come with *patch panels,* which have rows of fiber-optic ports on the front that allow you to connect the cables that come out of components or other patch panels. Patch panels give you a prelabeled system you can use to interconnect your components without having to run new cabling every time you want to add or change something in your SAN layout. With patch panels, you hook up all the connections on each of your components to the ports on the panels. You run the fiber-optic cables from your servers' HBAs to a patch panel as well. All cabling is run en masse to the backs of these centrally located panels. When you want to connect components to your servers, you use short fiber-optic cables *(patches)*, usually less than 3 meters long (about 10 feet), to patch the ports from your arrays to the ports of your switches to the ports for your HBAs.

Figure 11-2 shows how a typical patch-panel solution connects your SAN components without requiring you to lift a floor tile or roll a spool of cable across the floor. Another benefit of using a patch panel is that running fiber-optic cable on a one-by-one basis can be very expensive. In larger data centers, the wiring is typically done by electricians — who, as we all know, cost money. The fewer times electricians have to come in to put in more cables, the better. Running a group of cables in one shot from the very beginning is much cheaper and faster than doing it one by one later.

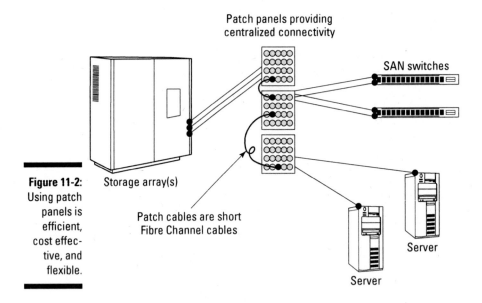

Figure 11-2: Using patch panels is efficient, cost effective, and flexible.

Patch-panel systems also make things very flexible. Now that you have all the endpoints of your SAN components in one place, you can easily control what talks to what by using the short, easy-to-manage patch cables.

Logical cable management

When I say logical cable management, I'm talking about managing which components your cabling system is connecting together. Every cable has two ends; each one is supposed to be connected to a component in the SAN. You need to keep track of every endpoint. The idea is simple but critical, and it all revolves around proper labels on your cables.

Labeling Your Cables

After you've run all your cables around the data center, keep track of what they're used for. (Remember my harping about documentation?) Where does this cable plug in, where does it go, and where does it come out at the other end? Looking at things simply, going from end to end (as in Figure 11-3), you plug a cable into a component such as a storage array and then plug the other end into a SAN switch or hub. Then another cable goes from the SAN switch to one of your server's HBAs.

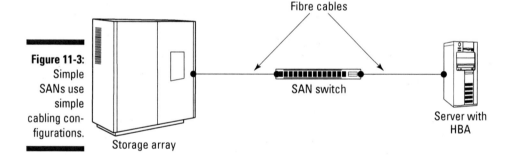

Figure 11-3:
Simple SANs use simple cabling configurations.

Fibre cables

SAN switch

Server with HBA

Storage array

Figure 11-3 shows straightforward, component-to-component cabling. In small to medium SANs, this way of cabling things together works fine. The storage arrays typically are in one area of the computer room; the switches are in a rack or stacked together on a table; and your hosts are in racks or on shelves. As long as things don't get too out of hand, following the flow of the cables is pretty easy.

Don't get complacent, however. As your SAN grows, it can quickly get out of hand.

The key to making your cabling setup work is labeling the cable ends so that you know where one end is supposed to be plugged in — and, more important, where the other end goes. I stress knowing where the *other end* goes. When you deal with cables that start on one side of the computer room and disappear under the floor, you'd better know where the other end (pardon the pun) ends up. Without a tag that tells you its destination, every cable in your data center could be the other end of the cable that you're holding. When you're dealing with this kind of problem, the old "tug one end and see what other end moves" procedure doesn't work. Fiber-optic cabling can run for hundreds of meters, and a spool of it is probably hidden under a floor tile.

Also, abandon all hope of tracing cables under the floor. You must find a better way.

The two standard ways to map out where the endpoints of cables go are

- ✔ The data center coordinate system
- ✔ The standard naming convention

I discuss both methods in the following sections.

Data center coordinate system

In a data center of any size, you can develop a system of coordinates to pinpoint the location of every rack, server, and piece of hardware in the room. When you use these coordinates, you can locate anything. You create these coordinates by using a top-down view of your data center. Just superimpose a see-through grid on the blueprint of the room and mark the room's coordinates on the grid.

Marking the coordinates on a grid

To mark the coordinates, start with one wall, marking off set distances with letters, like columns in a spreadsheet. Then mark off the second wall (the perpendicular one to the left) with numerals, like rows in a spreadsheet. The top-left corner of the grid is named A1.

You can get broad or specific and make the grid large or small. Many data centers have raised floors that use a standard floor tile size of about 2' x 2'. A grid this size is easy to count off when you walk through the data center, staring at your feet. Make sure that the grid is on a scale that makes items easy to locate — within a specific rack, for example — but that isn't so granular that you have coordinates ranging from A1 to ZZZ8,832.

Looking at the data center grid in Figure 11-4, you see storage arrays at B3 and B5, SAN switches in a rack at B1 and B7, and servers in racks in rows E and F. (You sank my battleship!)

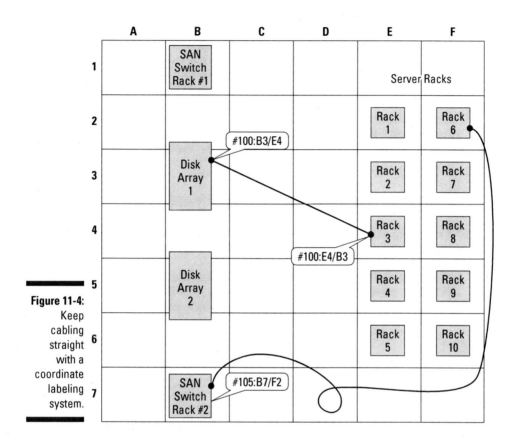

Figure 11-4:
Keep
cabling
straight
with a
coordinate
labeling
system.

Numbering cables

When you use the data center coordinate system, you can mark individual cables as well. In Figure 11-4, for example, the simplest label for a cable from a server in Rack 6 to a switch in SAN Rack 2 is F2 to B7, or F2/B7 for short.

You should assign a unique number to each cable. You'll undoubtedly have multiple cables running between locations, so using this system enables you to see which cable is which by checking the labels at both ends. In Figure 11-4, Cable 105 at location F2 is Cable 105 at location B7.

Never use the same cable number twice. Keeping numbers unique is important, because you may reuse a cable that once went from F2 to B7 but now runs from A1 to F7. If you have two cables labeled 105 between the same two locations (which end up with the same tags at both ends), you're up a creek trying to figure out which one is which. Keep a running total of each and every cable so that you never get a duplicate. (That pesky documentation pops up again and again.)

You can go further by addressing what each endpoint is, such as with the following description: F2:Emailserver1/HBA-Slot#4 – B7:Switch#5/Port#7. If you take this tack, however, you have to relabel cables whenever your environment changes. Also, that's a lot of info to write on a little label. (All this labeling is a manual process that you must do every time you make a change.)

The best practice is to keep a simple label that has the unique cable number (the same at both ends) and the coordinate from/to designation, like this: #100:B3/E4, like the one in Figure 11-4 between Disk Array 1 and Rack 3.

Standard naming convention

The other system of cable labeling is the standard naming convention system, which uses a unique short name for every component in the SAN.

In Figure 11-5, the switches are called SW## and the arrays are called SA##. *SW* means a switch, *SA* means a storage array, and the ## symbols are variables to indicate the number. Each cable is labeled with a unique number and then the components connect.

Standard naming convention + labeled cables = Happy SAN

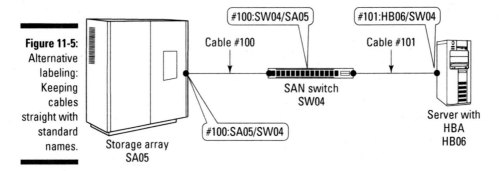

Figure 11-5:
Alternative labeling: Keeping cables straight with standard names.

If your organization already has an asset tracking system, in which every piece of equipment is assigned a unique ID number, this system is a great way to exploit those numbers. Use the SA and SW codes to identify what kind of component the cable plugs into; then use the asset tag number as your unique number. Ideally, you plop asset tag stickers on your components, so the trouble of labeling the physical box is already done for you.

This system is good for components that don't necessarily stay in the same place, such as when you move your test environment from the lab into a production rack but want to keep the components cabled the same way. Even though you move a server to a different rack, the HBA's asset tag stays the same.

Documenting the cable arrangements

After you have the cables in place, with the endpoints noted and the cables numbered, you have enough information to track where the ends of those cables get plugged into. A logical cable map can be as simple as a spreadsheet or as complicated as a database. Some SAN management systems have a cable management add-on that helps keep track of your cables along with your SAN components. Treating your fiber-optic cables with the same level of importance as your switches and storage arrays is crucial to simplified support and maintenance of your SAN.

In your spreadsheet or database, you have a list of all your cables, numbered uniquely. Also, each endpoint has an entry showing what that cable is plugged into. You can use this information to create a complete map of every interconnection in your SAN. You should update this spreadsheet *every time* you add, change, or remove a cable.

Using a SAN Management Framework

A *SAN management framework* consists of various pieces of software that run on a server in your data center. In the simplest definition, its job is to discover, report on, and control all the components that make up your SAN.

A storage area network isn't a single object, of course; it's a collection of components such as hubs, switches, cables, host adapters, servers, storage, and tape drives. Because a SAN technically is a network, the various components all communicate with one another and rely on one another to provide a path so that information gets from your application running on your server to the disk device containing its data, and vice versa.

Keeping track of what all these components are and what they're doing, and making sure that they're working properly and aren't overloaded, is the basis of SAN management. A few more tasks build on this foundation. I discuss all these topics in this section.

Working with SAN management software

Of the many software packages that do SAN management (and more are being developed every day), some are better than others. A program that allows you to view the status of (but not modify) the storage arrays themselves may be weak at handling the rest of the SAN, such as the hubs and switches. Another program may be great for controlling the hardware but poor for checking the status of the components or the level of detail in reports. If you're lucky, you may be able to see how much of your fibre channel bandwidth is being used by the traffic going between hosts and storage arrays.

Most SAN management applications alert you to critical events by paging you, sending an e-mail, or actually calling your home phone and (using a voice synthesizer) telling you what the event was. Pretty cool stuff — but creepy to your grandmother if she happens to answer the phone.

One more thing a SAN management package can do is perform an action based on an event, such as running a script that allocates more fiber-optic links to a disk if utilization goes above 90 percent on the current links. The possibilities are endless, and everything depends on how you need the SAN to be automated. (See "Automating Your System: 'SAN? Do You Read Me, SAN?'" later in this chapter for more information on automation.)

Most frameworks consist of some type of database that stores all the information about your SAN. Having a single repository for collecting, monitoring, and controlling your SAN is vital to seamless management. These dedicated repositories make it simple to keep track of what makes up your SAN. Also, a central repository gives other vendors a chance to integrate their particular expert niche of SAN management into the framework, resulting in true best-of-breed solutions.

A good SAN management framework isn't necessarily a one-vendor solution. In fact, the more, the merrier. As long as vendors coordinate their efforts by being the best at what they do and then using a common language to monitor and control components, a seamless cross-vendor SAN is quite easy to manage.

Communicating in a common language

If you're wondering how to foster world peace — or at least how to get vendor X's software to talk to vendor Y's switch — the answer is easier than you may think. You create a common language (call it Z) and teach it to both vendors' hardware and software. Now, because the components speak the same language, they can communicate, and the same framework software can manage them.

The Storage Networking Industry Association (SNIA) standards group (www. snia.org) is tasked with promoting efficient, interoperable, and robust solutions in emerging SAN technologies. Several of the big storage companies are members of SNIA, giving it a lot of clout.

SNIA is pushing the Storage Management Initiative (SMI) code-named *Bluefin,* which is designed to bring to market a storage management platform (or platforms, take your pick) that can powerfully yet efficiently manage heterogeneous storage platforms simultaneously. At the core of Bluefin is a common interface that all storage vendors — array, HBA, or switch vendors — will use to manage their products.

This common interface doesn't stop with SAN components. Initiatives are under way to expand this standard way of intercommunicating to other types of components — such as server hardware, operating systems, and networking devices — so that frameworks specializing in each class of component can intercommunicate and share information. This way, all management can be rolled up into one global framework that you can view and use to control any piece of hardware that you decide to use in your computing infrastructure.

Speaking the language yourself

To accomplish all its intercommunication tasks, the computer industry created a few new abbreviations:

- **CIM:** The *Common Information Model* is another way of saying something like this: "We all agree to call a thing with four legs that you sit on a *chair.* Anyone who sits on your dog will not be allowed to participate in the SAN." A CIM is a way of setting the ground rules of a language. You point to an object and call it a chair, for example, and everyone else in the group understands that if they want to talk about that object, they'd better call it a chair. Otherwise, nobody will understand them.

- **SOAP:** The *Standard Object Access Protocol* isn't for washing your hands. It's an established set of rules that different entities use to communicate. If CIM covers the language to speak, SOAP covers how to put together sentences in the language.

- **WBEM:** *Web Based Enterprise Management* is a language that uses Internet browser–based technology to communicate with and control SAN components. All it takes to run a WBEM (pronounced *web-em,* although it looks more like *double-you-beem* to me) application is any old Web browser.

    CIM/WBEM management tools will be little Web applications. When you point your browser to one of these tools, it will build the user interface on your screen by using Web-friendly languages such as Java, Python, Perl, Hypertext Markup Language (HTML), and eXtensible Markup Language (XML).

Putting everything together

Figure 11-6 shows a block diagram of how these components sandwich together to make everything translate efficiently.

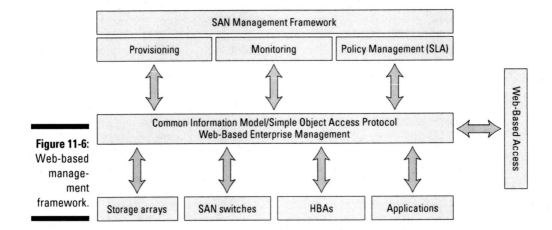

Figure 11-6: Web-based management framework.

The really cool thing about using a Web-based management framework is that you can get to it through any Web browser, so you don't have to install an elaborate console to manage your infrastructure. In addition, because the framework is Web based, it really doesn't have a single entity to which you need to funnel all the information. The framework knows whether you should be getting information from a central server for something like alerts or whether you need to communicate (via the same Web interface) directly to the Web address of a storage array to carve up some volumes. It handles the redirection of your commands for you instead of making you launch five separate consoles to look at your five different storage platforms.

You view changes via the Web page for the task being performed, all handled dynamically by the little embedded Web server application on each SAN component. When a new feature is added to a SAN component or a new component is added to the SAN, the Web apps communicate and figure out how to play together.

What SAN Management Gives You

SAN management gives you peace of mind. Seriously. Why do you get an alarm for your car? Because you know that if someone tries to steal your car, the alarm makes noise to scare away the would-be thief (not to mention annoy your neighbors at 3 a.m.).

Management platforms usually come with some sort of basic health monitoring. You can check each component of the SAN — switch, HBA, or storage device — to see whether it's okay. This type of monitoring is the most basic level, because a component is declared either alive or dead to the management software. (I discuss more specific monitoring levels in the "Health monitoring" section, later in this chapter.)

Apart from warnings about problems, SAN management is designed to give a storage area network administrator (hey, neat four-word title; just add *technical* before *administrator,* and you're SANTA!) the tools to view the SAN in many ways.

A bird's-eye view of your network

A SAN management platform gives you a view of your entire SAN infrastructure, as well as tools that allow you to make additions and changes to the SAN components from one console. This central point of control and monitoring makes a SAN management framework successful.

Ultimately, a SAN management framework ties all the components and views of their status and operation together into one, all-encompassing window that you use to see what's happening in your SAN at a high level. From there, you can drill down into more and more detailed views until you get to the most rudimentary component or task that can be accomplished. It's like a satellite view of planet Earth: You see how everything connects at a very high level, but you can zoom into a particular continent, country, state, city, or neighborhood, and eventually down to someone's house.

As an analogy, you could highlight a house (server) in Cairo, Egypt, and a house (storage array) in Nome, Alaska. The framework would show you the path to take to get from one place to the other (via fiber cables), showing all the bridges and tunnels that you'd cross (switches), current traffic conditions (use of the path), and information on any construction projects along the way (historical status of the components along the path). I know, I know — you can't drive directly from Nome to Cairo. But you get the idea. This type of mapping is just one of the many quick-and-dirty tasks that would take you hours or days to complete on your own without a tool such as this . . . if it were even possible to do manually.

Figure 11-7 shows a typical SAN management screen shot. Most frameworks have similar information panels, showing a tree view of SAN components, a drawing of the SAN infrastructure, and a list of events that have occurred recently.

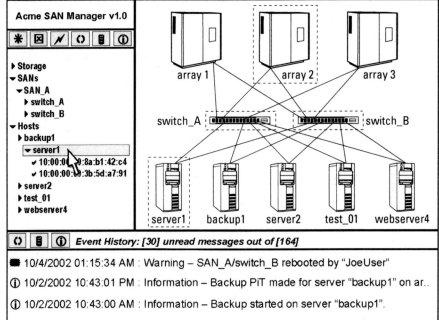

Agent-based management

To funnel the status of all your SAN components into one easy-to-understand view, you need some way for each component to communicate its status to the SAN management framework. This task is usually accomplished by little software programs called *agents,* which are small pieces of code that run on a server, switch, or storage array; monitor the status of the component; and report back to your SAN management framework.

This agent technology exists because different vendor components aren't universal (interchangeable), just as Chevy parts don't fit on a Ford. Competition causes vendors to make things unique to their products because that gives them an advantage in the industry. These advantages are ultimately disadvantages, however, when it comes to trying to get these products to work together. To circumvent the lack of compatibility, someone writes an agent that knows how to translate from one component's language to the other's so that the component can be monitored and controlled.

Health monitoring

Health monitoring works in conjunction with the agents that I mention in the preceding section. Because the agent talks to the components, the hub, switch, HBA, or storage array can give the agent an update on what it's doing, how it's performing, and whether anything is going on that the administrator needs to be warned about. Then the agent forwards this update to the management framework so that it can be logged and presented to the SAN administrator. Any changes in the status of any component on the SAN can be displayed on the SAN administrator's console immediately, and then the administrator can take action.

Levels of monitoring

Health monitoring involves various levels of detail:

- ✔ At the simplest level, you're notified whether a component is up or down (in other words, on or off).

- ✔ The next level gives some information on whether the status of the component is good or bad.

  A SAN switch, for example, can report that all its internal components are working properly and that the status is good. If one of its dual power supplies burns out but the switch is still operating, it reports that things are bad but that it's still functioning.

- ✔ The lowest level of monitoring reports details about a component — in the case of a switch power supply, for example, the actual voltage level coming in from the outlet.

All these health-monitoring levels allow you to capture the status of everything in your SAN without having to run around the computer room checking the status lights on all your components. Your SAN management framework takes all these messages and converts them to events or icons on the administrator's screen to show you what's going on.

In-band and out-of-band management

You have two ways to communicate with your components to read their status or tell them to do something:

- ✔ In-band management
- ✔ Out-of-band management

Figure 11-8 shows the two ways that your management server can communicate with your SAN components.

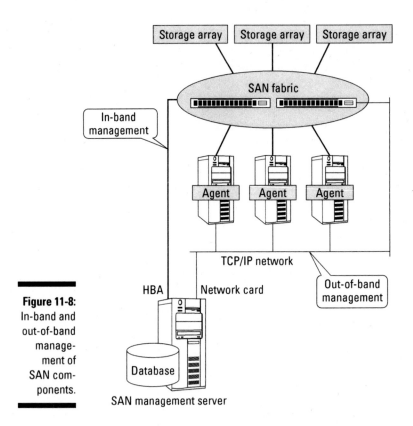

Figure 11-8:
In-band and out-of-band management of SAN components.

In-band management means that the communication from your management server and components travels along the same media that you use for making the SAN: the fiber-optic cabling. All the communication happens out of the management servers' HBAs via regular storage protocols — except that you aren't doing regular reads and writes of data to and from disk, but only passing messages between devices. A server with an HBA can talk to a storage array by using a special Logical Unit Number (LUN) called a *gatekeeper* or *command device* (see your storage vendor for the name it uses). Messages are passed back and forth from a SAN management application via this device, directly to the storage array.

Out-of-band management uses an external method to communicate — usually via Transmission Control Protocol/Internet Protocol (TCP/IP) over your network. In this case, any component that requires out-of-band functionality needs to have an Ethernet port and an Internet Protocol (IP) address assigned to it. Most SAN switches have a management port that's a basic 10/100 or even gigabit Ethernet port, which they can use to communicate with management software over the local area network.

Records of events

Instantaneous views of the SAN are nice, but what happens at 3 a.m. when the operations team is on coffee break or on the phone, or someone looks away from the screen for a minute? As everyone knows, computers are fast, and a problem can be less than a split second long; you have to be in the room to notice whether the lights flicker. By recording every little hiccup that happens in any component in the SAN, you can be sure that you'll know what's going on, no matter what time it is. Attach this recording ability to an alert system, and you can be paged or e-mailed whenever something goes bump in the night.

Keeping a record of things that go wrong is important, but so is keeping records of what goes *right*. When you have a system that comprises many components such as a SAN, someone could make a change in one place that affects something seemingly unrelated, yet possibly dangerous, to the rest of the SAN. This situation is where change management comes into play.

Change management

Change management, in the traditional sense, is the process of documenting and informing the environment of a potential change in configuration *before* it's made. This notice allows the staff of a data center to review the potential change and determine whether it would hurt anything in the production environment.

In addition to keeping random changes out of the production environment, change management greatly assists in documenting the environment. If everything you add or change or delete in a system is written down, you can re-create the entire system by following the changes from beginning to end.

Finally, proper recording of changes ensures that if something does go wrong, you can infer (barring an outright failure of something) that the last change or changes may be responsible, and you'll know exactly how to undo them because they were written down and reviewed.

How does change management tie in with SANs? During the course of using a SAN, you create volumes, assigning them to servers and applications; you also create zones on the switches and apply security so that only the right server sees the storage. All these operations count as a change to the environment. Furthermore, these changes occur across many components: storage array, switch, server, operating system, and HBAs. If your SAN management framework keeps track of these changes for you, you won't have to document them yourself and possibly do it incorrectly. If you have a record of every single change in hand, you can use that information to see how your SAN is progressing and where it may be going.

Predictions of problems

A SAN management package not only warns you of current problems, but also warns you of potential problems. When you stay a step ahead of your users, you're in proactive versus reactive mode. By viewing the historical information on your SAN, you can establish a trend for your SAN.

Take this hypothetical scenario: On Day 1 of your SAN, you have two servers, a storage array with 500GB of storage, and two switches in between. Two months later, you have 30 servers, 5 terabytes (TB) of storage, and four switches. How did you get to this point? Do you remember all the incremental changes along the way? Was the growth linear or exponential? You must have had a busy two months — and some salesperson is very happy with your SAN implementation (because he sold more storage and components)!

The trending information that you can glean from a SAN management framework is very important. This feature gives you crystal-ball insights into what should happen next — info such as how much storage to buy during the next budget cycle and how many servers, HBAs, and switches you need. Trends are the best way to justify your budget to your executives and financing people.

Streamlining SAN Administration

To see the benefit of controlling your SAN via a management framework, consider the following scenario:

You've just installed a new server, and you want to put 10GB of fast-access SAN-based RAID-5 storage on it. You put in two brand-new HBAs and plug them into the switches that are connected to your storage arrays.

Step-by-step administration

To take this SAN-attached server and add storage to it, you need to complete four completely isolated operations (all of which are covered in detail in Chapter 7):

1. To provide the fast-access requirement, find a storage array with 10GB of RAID-5 that's not currently on a RAID group that's busy. Oh, and also create that 10GB LUN, if you haven't already done so.

2. Assign LUN Security to the new LUN for the server's HBA World Wide Names (WWNs).

3. Create zones on the switches so that the storage array and the server's HBAs can communicate.

4. Tell the server's operating system to rescan devices to locate the new storage volume.

5. Oh, yeah — you really have to complete five operations. The last is to document what you did on each component so that you can undo it if it breaks something.

Without a centralized framework and console to make all these changes, you'd have to log in to each component separately, perform the given task, record that you did it (remember change management?), and then move on to the next component in the path . . . all the while hoping that you typed everything correctly and that nobody called or stopped by your cube while you were waiting for the next console to load or for an operational step to finish.

Doing this step by step is possible, but it takes a long time and is very prone to error. Also, if you want to back out of this process, you need to go back and undo your changes one by one. This process reminds me of crossing a brook by hopping from rock to rock . . . but you don't know what other rocks you can jump to until you get to the next rock. Further, your boss may be yelling at you to "just *jump*, already!" Yipes.

You don't want to fall in (especially in front of your boss!). Wouldn't it be nice to have a plan for when you get to the edge of the brook and then just hop across, knowing that you won't even get the bottoms of your shoes wet ('cause you picked the best nonslippery rocks ahead of time)?

Using a framework

Switch this mundane task to using the centralized SAN management framework. The framework communicates with the storage arrays, switches, host operating systems, and HBAs via various agents. You tell the SAN management software that you want 10GB of fast RAID-5 and that you want it assigned to such-and-such server. The framework takes over and communicates among the components in the SAN as follows:

✔ It determines the best storage array and RAID array group to get the 10GB from, carves out 10GB of RAID-5, and gives it a LUN number.

✔ It finds the most efficient port on the array to present the LUN to the SAN, making the zones on the switches between HBA and array.

✔ Next, it secures the new LUN to the HBA by its WWN address so that only this server is allowed to use it.

✔ Last, it determines the right LUN number to use on the server and forces a device rescan by the server's operating system (OS) so that the server sees the 10GB disk volume.

The framework makes all these changes automatically, complete with a record of all the changes that can be undone with one click of the mouse. Well, okay, maybe you have to click a Confirm Undo button or something, but you see the difference from before. Simple, isn't it?

When you perform this same operation of adding storage to your new server with the framework, you provide a service called *provisioning*, which is the act or process of providing.

When you provision storage, your SAN management framework acts as an all-knowing provider of storage, like some type of storage guru. You request the physical disk resource, but your SAN management framework is the real brain behind the scenes doing the work. This situation leaves you free to carry out your other responsibilities: plan for the future of the SAN and surf the Internet (not necessarily in that order).

Automating Your System: "SAN? Do You Read Me, SAN?"

In the 1968 Stanley Kubrick movie *2001: A Space Odyssey,* a computer named HAL is in charge of all aspects of a spaceship's functions. (If you're in the computer field and never saw *2001,* where have you been?) HAL flies the ship, keeps the crew members alive and fed, reminds them to exercise, entertains them with chess games (which he always wins), and critiques their artwork during the long trip from Earth to Jupiter. The ship's system is completely autonomous, not needing any input from the crew whatsoever. If something goes wrong or needs attention, HAL can take care of it himself (or, *itself,* I suppose). HAL was programmed with the proper way to respond to certain situations.

Much like HAL, your SAN (apart from also having a three-letter name) can be programmed to respond to situations. Programming something to respond automatically to events is *automation,* and it makes your job much easier.

Automating your SAN is quite simple in theory. Planning automation starts with answering three simple questions:

✔ What do I need to measure?

✔ What event or circumstance triggers an action?

✔ What does the action accomplish?

Because a SAN is a collection of multiple components that interact, a change in one component's behavior can cause or require another component to make a corresponding change in its behavior. To make automation work, you need to understand what you're trying to accomplish with the automated task and what components will be affected by the changes.

As a simple example, consider that ubiquitous application: backup.

Backing up

Suppose that your backup server does its backup by reading a Point-in-Time (PiT) copy (see Chapter 10 for the lowdown on PiT copies) of the XYZ application's data and writing it to a locally attached tape drive. The PiT copy isn't assigned to your backup server all the time — only when the backup is taking place. So you must do whatever it takes for it to see the PiT volume and read it as though it were any other regular disk on the SAN (because it is, basically).

By using some automated scripts within the backup process, you can make your SAN do the following:

1. At 10 p.m., a script runs and communicates with the storage array to create a PiT copy of XYZ's data volume and assign it to port B on the back of the array.

2. The next part of the script tells the SAN switches to create a communication path (using zoning; see Chapter 7) between the storage array's port B where the PiT copy is and the HBA on your backup server.

   At this point, the automation script has created a frozen PiT copy of your application's data disk and assigned it to your backup server for use.

3. Your backup software backs up this volume to tape, as it would any other volume.

4. Upon completion of the backup, the automation script unmounts and disconnects the PiT copy from your backup server, and removes the virtual connection through the SAN between storage array and backup server.

5. Finally, the script deletes the PiT volume so that it can be used for another app somewhere else on the SAN.

All this magic happens at 10 p.m. while you're off dreaming of your next cool automation script, knowing that your SAN is operating flawlessly, as usual. (If things aren't working flawlessly, make sure to read Chapter 12 for information on how to troubleshoot.)

Managing database storage

Another example — much more complicated but still completely autonomous — proves that people are completely useless after a SAN is put in operation. (HAL, did you say that, or did I?)

Suppose that your database (XYZ) is getting larger and larger, and it begins to run out of space one night. At the 99 percent capacity level, automation can step in, allocate more disk space to your database server, and then tell the database software to expand to the new storage area. This function keeps your database administrators (DBAs) from getting paged at 3 a.m. and shows how flexible your new SAN environment really is. This example is a bit more involved than the backup example in the preceding section, requiring coordination with your DBAs to developing the scripts, but it can be done.

Oh, by the way, the SAN framework also makes sure to send you an e-mail to tell you (when you get in at 10:30 the next morning) that the XYZ database grabbed a few more gigabytes of space last night . . . and you're welcome.

As you see, the possibilities can be relatively simple or get quite complicated, depending on what you need to anticipate and how you go about delivering the fix for the problem. Compare these two examples with what you'd have to do today without a SAN in place. Order a disk? Wait for your vendor to install it and configure it? With a SAN that's automated, your problem is solved in about five minutes at 3 a.m. without waking anyone up.

Providing a Service Level Agreement

A *Service Level Agreement* (SLA) is a contract between your end users and you. It quantifies a level of performance, reliability, and support that you promise your users, in essence making them your customers.

With an SLA, you define a set of parameters that you must meet to keep your customers from yelling at you. As long as the computing environment that you promised doesn't go outside the bounds of the SLA that your customers agreed on, you won't have to worry about getting a phone call that something is wrong.

What happens if an SLA is breached? Usually, someone gets angry and starts calling people to find out what's going on. Sometimes a monetary penalty is assessed. Usually, the customer doesn't have to pay for service during the outage, just like when your cable television service goes out.

Simple versus complex SLAs

The simplest SLAs usually revolve around *uptime* — that is, the hours of the day when your computing environment will be available to the customer. Most SLAs read something like this: "The XYZ application will be available for use from 9 a.m. to 5 p.m. Monday through Friday. System maintenance can be performed off-hours, and backups will be done nightly at 10." This simple paragraph tells the customers (the users of the XYZ app) that you promise to make sure that XYZ is up and running for their use during regular business hours; you will take it down for server upgrades and maintenance only outside those hours. You also state when application backups will be done.

Some SLAs are much more involved. Complicated SLAs cover every possible piece of equipment that an application uses; they also describe the performance and recoverability of an application if a problem occurs somewhere along the process flow. These SLAs usually aren't made just between the user community and the server administrator. They also deal with the networking group; the server group; the in-house application developers; and in some cases, third-party outside vendors who have a stake in making the application work.

You can incorporate an SLA into your SAN management platform by defining different levels of service and matching the right level to each application that uses the SAN for its data storage.

Managing an SLA with software

Service Level Agreements started out as regular paper documents. The only way to know whether you were meeting your SLA requirements was to translate the wording in the paper document to what was really going on with the application. What was the response time of the application? Does the uptime match? When was the application last backed up? Can I recover it to the point that the SLA requires?

This process used to involve manual measurement and comparison. With the advent of software that measures these parameters against programmed SLA levels, however, you have a way to compare things automatically and generate reports to your customers (and alerts to your operations staff if something falls outside the threshold of the SLA).

Setting service levels

SLA levels for SAN-attached applications can have virtually any parameters. To make things simple, here are a few basic service levels that you can define to match your application's requirements. Each level has a specific cost that you would try to sell to your customers, depending on the level of service that they feel is required for their application's data.

- ✔ **Level 1 — High availability, high performance, disaster recovery (DR):** This level offers dual HBA connections to your SAN with no single point of failure between the storage array and your application's server. The uptime on this level is in the 99.999 percent range (<5 minutes of unavailability per year). Also, the data at the primary site is replicated to a secondary remote site so that it can be used for recovery in the event of a disaster at the primary site (see Chapter 6 for more on disaster recovery).

  This level is the most expensive but most resilient level of service for a SAN. If the business can justify the cost, this service is well worth the peace of mind.

- ✔ **Level 2 — High availability, high performance, no DR site:** This level offers the same high availability as Level 1 but without the remote mirroring to another site for disaster recovery. Perhaps a second copy of data (see Chapter 10 for the scoop on PiT copies) is stored locally so that you can recover the data in case of application corruption.

- ✔ **Level 3 — Low availability/no DR:** This level offers single HBA connectivity, so single points of failure do exist between the server and the storage. Uptime is in the 99.99 percent or lower range (about one hour of downtime per year). No DR is provided with this level.

  This is a low-cost option that allows the server to be on the SAN but not benefit from its redundancy capabilities.

You want to make sure that the level of service covers the expectations of your users without going overboard and making them pay for something that they don't really need.

Building a Storage Management Team

The people who take care of your SAN have many responsibilities covering physical as well as administrative tasks, and each role is closely tied to all the others. Finding the right people to throw at your SAN is important in making it successful. SANs are relatively new technology to most IT folks, and with any new technology comes a learning curve. The basics behind a SAN are quite simple; it's the combination of tasks that makes it seem overwhelming. It isn't. Focusing the right people on the right chunk of it will make a SAN a breeze to design, build, and run.

Much like any good team, as in baseball, football, or golf (scratch that last one), people are given specific tasks or positions on the team. They focus on that task, yet what they do is productive for the whole team. Aligning a person's skill set with his or her job role is the best way to succeed and to keep your employees happy. Key skills need to be focused when your organization is being altered to support a SAN environment.

The SAN management group is a team of people interacting to accomplish the following tasks:

✔ Design the SAN architecture

✔ Build the SAN infrastructure

✔ Monitor the SAN infrastructure

✔ Ensure that the SAN is meeting or exceeding application SLAs

✔ Monitor daily provisioning of storage to new and existing applications

✔ Plan upgrades and modifications of SAN hardware, software, and procedures to meet growing requirements and new SLAs

Depending on the size of your IT organization, several people can be assigned to one of these jobs, or only one person (lucky you) may be responsible for all of them.

SAN architects

SAN architects are responsible for coming up with the initial and future designs of the SAN: what kind of storage, switches, and HBAs to use. Architects are similar to members of the networking group, who decide what vendors to use and how to put all the components together.

Here's how to break it down:

1. First, define your SAN's requirements.

   Remember that SAN is a storage area *network*. Networks have been around for a long time, and most people in the IT industry understand this concept. The core of a good SAN design may not be obvious on Day 1, because you could be starting with only one or two switches. An architecture this simple doesn't have much chance of error; just plug in your storage and your servers, and poof! You have a SAN.

   Things start getting hairy when you have many existing storage devices, servers, and differing needs. Being in tune with the initial requirements of your SAN is important to building it right from the start.

2. Get someone who understands your entire computing environment.

   If nobody like that exists, at least grab the heads of each department and lock them in a conference room for a few hours. They need to understand what one another's issues are and what kind of applications they need to support on the SAN.

3. After you have a good idea of how many servers and how much storage you need — as well as how much information passes back and forth between the servers and disk — you can design your SAN.

SAN engineers

SAN engineers, who actually build the SAN, should be skilled with hardware and cabling. (These guys carry screwdrivers with them all the time.) When you're building your SAN, the engineers follow the established labeling scheme according to your naming conventions (refer to "Labeling Your Cables," earlier in this chapter).You could also have your SAN vendor do the installation, so finding engineers may not be an issue, depending on what vendor you go with. (See Chapter 13 for some info on outsourcing and having an outside vendor install your SAN.)

If you decide to put your SAN together yourself, someone who has a networking background may be of help here. People with networking skills are used to being around many boxes and wires, interconnecting them and making things organized. (Well, not *always*, but sometimes.)

The infrastructure of a SAN usually stops at the HBA, which may be handled by the server group itself or by a server vendor who is responsible for installing and loading the drivers for any cards put into its boxes, depending on the skill level of your server administrators and/or the warranty stipulations of the server vendors. Many companies have service contracts that don't allow you to open and tinker with the hardware; they have their service technicians make all modifications.

Also, most external SAN vendors — such as the switch and storage array vendors — can't touch the customers' servers because of the liability concerns of breaking something. Again, let the legally responsible party do its appropriate tasks to keep from getting into trouble. The SAN group will still take on the responsibility of configuring the HBA's driver files, because those folks know the exact settings for it and its drivers . . . or at least will communicate closely with those who are responsible for installing the cards.

Monitoring team

The *SAN monitoring team* comprises those people who keep an eye on your SAN. This team is important to your SAN's ongoing health. Perhaps you already have an operations staff to watch the servers and applications, such as a Network Operations Center (NOC). You can educate this staff on using the SAN monitoring software to keep an eye on the SAN components too. Then the NOC can follow its standard procedures for alerting the right people about any issues that arise, just as it does with the servers, networking hardware, and applications that it monitors.

SAN hardware can be integrated with most large Simple Network Management Protocol (SNMP)–based monitoring packages, so you can get your switches and storage arrays to send alerts to the same system that the NOC staff already knows how to use and have them take action as they already know how to do.

The worst thing that can happen in your SAN is that something breaks and nobody knows about it until it's too late; then you'll have your boss's boss's boss looking for someone to yell at. The task of being in lockstep with your SAN's health level is very important when you're justifying its inception and promoting its ongoing use. Nobody wants to be in charge of a runaway train.

Having staff to monitor your SAN is all well and good, but the key is educating these folks about what to do when they get an alert or see something that isn't the norm. A good idea is to sit down with your monitoring staff and your SAN management platform vendor to go over what alerts and messages will be presented, and discuss what each one means and what the right action to take is. This meeting can help make the alerts more useful and eliminate confusion and wrong assumptions about what to do about them.

SLA and performance specialists

Making sure that your users are happy is the goal of any IT environment. The SLA (see "Providing a Service Level Agreement," earlier in this chapter) is designed to define the level of service that the application servers — and, therefore, your users — expect to get.

The key is knowing how to keep the SLA from being violated in terms of response time, capacity, uptime, and so on.

The *performance specialist* — someone who understands storage and I/Os and how they work with applications — plays a key role by tracking performance metrics of the SAN components and figuring out, if anything, what is changing over time. This person can also identify issues that cause SLA violations — or, more importantly, catch them before they occur.

If your SLA promises a given response time to your users, and the SAN has gradually been growing and becoming more busy, performance will generally begin to slow, assuming that you've done nothing to increase overall speed and capacity. A slowdown could be the result of the number of fiber-optic cables between storage and server, what type of RAID level the storage uses, or even how much work the storage array itself is trying to juggle.

This role usually is a combination of performance trend watching and deep analysis of the current utilization of the SAN over the course of time (lots of looking at graphs and charts, but with a future-facing look on things). Performance specialists interface with the SAN design and monitoring folks to make sure that those alerts don't start going off in the middle of the night — keeping the user community (customers) happy.

Provisioning staff

The whole point of having a SAN is to make it easy to carve out your storage for the applications that need it. The *provisioning staff* comprises the people who go through the steps to make your SAN deliver storage and services to your application servers. These folks are the ones with their hands on the console.

This role needs input from your application and server folks on how much and what kind of storage is needed, as well as where it needs to show up. These people interface with the application developers to understand how to best deliver disk storage to a given system. When they have this information, they push all the buttons that make the storage appear to the servers.

Planning for the future

After you have a SAN up and running, you want to stay a step ahead of it. The tasks covered by the monitoring and SLA compliance roles are pretty good at making sure that your SAN doesn't run into any problems or run out of gas, but you want to keep your eye on the horizon, too. Starting small with a SAN is fine, but if it really takes off, you need to make sure that you have the infrastructure in place to support it before you actually need it.

Being able to roll out a new 100TB data warehouse (which your CEO promised last night in a CNBC interview) without breaking a sweat is the ultimate goal of your SAN environment. Your team should already know the plan of attack before the CEO drops a two-week deadline down the chain of command. (If you think I'm kidding, you're wrong.) Standard practices and working knowledge of what works and what doesn't are the linchpins of running a tight ship in any organization.

Because new technologies are always emerging, you should always be looking for the next best thing to make your application servers and users even happier than they already are. An upgrade doesn't have to be expensive, because many SAN hardware vendors are fully aware that technology gets old quickly. Many vendors offer leasing programs so that you can trade your clunky 3-year-old, 16-port switch in for a nice, shiny new 128-port director.

Common responsibilities

All the virtual teams of people working on your new SAN need to get up to speed on new hardware, software, processes, and procedures. The learning curve can be steep, especially because they probably already have lots of other work to do. Getting them trained in their new tasks quickly and thoroughly is the key to getting the SAN off the ground successfully.

Your SAN component vendors are great resources for education and help; they know their products best — and know how to get the most out of them. Many vendors offer training classes. The more input you have from vendors, the less guesswork and frustration you and your staff have to deal with. Work closely with your vendors so that their expertise can rub off on your staff and turn them into the resident SAN experts.

Figure 11-9 shows the interactivity and information flow among the major roles in a SAN management group. Note that outside SAN vendors and your user community are also involved in the flow of information and feedback.

SAN Management Team-Process Flow

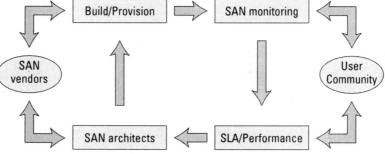

Figure 11-9: How the roles and responsibilities of the SAN management team interrelate.

Chapter 12

Troubleshooting SANs

Nothing is particularly hard if you divide it into small jobs.

— Henry Ford

*T*roubleshooting is a series of steps that focuses on and eliminates possibilities within a larger, unknown problem. I could write a whole book
on troubleshooting, but in this chapter, I try to cover everything you need
to know about how to locate and resolve common problems in your storage
area network (SAN) environment. Read this chapter for every kind of problem,
from the initial "Now why doesn't this work?" to the sudden "Whoa, what the
heck just happened?" to my personal favorite: "Hey, do you smell smoke?"

Murphy's Law states that anything that can go wrong *will* go wrong, so being
prepared and understanding what can happen and how to fix it will go a long
way toward keeping your SAN healthy and operational — and you employed
and sane.

Troubleshooting is basic problem solving. First, you have to know what the
right setup looks like. When you have that knowledge under your belt, recog-
nizing what's wrong is easy.

The Best Method: Prevention

The key to avoiding having to troubleshoot, of course, is doing things right the first time. Unfortunately, to err is human. Mistakes happen. Don't let screaming users and deadlines rush you when you're making changes in your SAN. Because many things are tied together in the system, you can affect one application over there when you pull a cable over here. Be careful.

Understand what you're about to do before you do it, and keep your documentation up to date. The scenarios described at the end of this chapter are accompanied by diagrams that show how things were supposed to be connected. These diagrams are luxuries, though, and aren't always available when you're scratching your head at 3 a.m. over a problem. Take a deep breath, follow the data path methodically, and confirm that everything looks right before you peel back the things that work from the things that don't. Then the cause of the problem will stare you right in the face. Good luck!

Troubleshooting Methodology

Most SAN management frameworks (read Chapter 11 for more) allow you to monitor many of the components of your SAN. These frameworks can catch and alert you to many problems. But not all problems — such as accidentally unassigning disks from a production server or assigning the same disks to two different servers — are obvious to a management platform. This is where human troubleshooting comes into play. Because humans cause more problems than computers do (didn't you know that?), humans are responsible for solving the problems.

The first thing you have to understand about troubleshooting is that no matter how simple a problem seems to be, it can get very complicated if the seemingly simple fix doesn't do the trick. Assumptions are your enemy when it comes to troubleshooting. Your misperception of what's happening and how things are currently set up can turn you around, leading you on a wild goose chase. Before you know it, your so-called simple problem turns into a huge mess, a bunch of wasted time, and an angry user community.

You can prepare yourself for the unwanted task of finding a gremlin in your SAN a number of ways. The next few sections give you the details.

Go with what you know

The first thing to do when you run into a problem is get in your Wayback Machine and go back in time to when you read the manual. Seriously. If you learn everything there is to know about how your SAN components are supposed to work, and you understand what "normal" is, you'll be able to spot something wrong immediately and fix it before it becomes a bigger problem. (Also see "Didn't read the manual, did you?" later in this chapter.)

You also should make sure that you have these key things in hand before you go flipping switches, changing configuration files, or pulling cables:

✔ **Documentation:** Don't go by memory; stick with known, documented facts. If you keep your documentation up to date (which I hope you do), you can compare the current settings of a particular component with the settings that worked when it was first configured. Chapter 7 covers a pretend SAN installation; the tables defined there are a very good model for proper documentation of your switches and disk assignments.

To solve a post-installation problem, it's much better to use the documentation you created for your particular SAN setup than to use the vendor's documentation. Vendors typically have either/or settings that depend on what the user is trying to accomplish. When you're wading through this material in search of a solution to a problem, you need to make those same either/or decisions — but you may not know the answers and may lead yourself on a wild goose chase, creating more problems by making incorrect assumptions. The documentation that *you* make from your working setup has the answers to those questions already in place.

✔ **Tech support:** If you're paying a vendor for any amount of support, use it. Get the vendor involved early, because that vendor has probably seen this issue before and may already have a fix in its bag of tricks.

✔ **Patience:** If an issue comes up but it doesn't critically affect your business, try to track down what the problem is and figure out how to fix it during off hours, when you have the opportunity and the safety net of time. You don't want to change things hurriedly and possibly end up making them worse.

Elementary, my dear Watson

Most issues that arise are elementary. Remember that even an extremely complicated system such as the space shuttle is put together with No. 10 machine screws. One loose screw can avalanche into a catastrophic problem if you don't know where to look.

For another example, take an automobile (figuratively, I mean; I'm not promoting grand theft). It has wheels, windows, an engine, doors . . . fuzzy dice (optional). All these components make up a car. But what if one of the subcomponents of the engine, such as the battery, is dead? A dead battery keeps the spark plugs from firing, keeps the engine from starting, and keeps you stranded. If you've ever watched an auto mechanic diagnose a problem with a car, you've seen how he follows the logical paths to the obvious problem. If the engine doesn't turn over, he doesn't check the tire pressure. Because he knows how a car works, he knows what should happen when you turn the key, so he follows the process along until he finds the thing that is wrong, broken, or failing.

Following a logical path

When you follow the logical path of what should work, you can always find the problem. (Sherlock Holmes used a similar approach: He eliminated all the possibilities, and the one that was left, no matter how improbable, was the solution to the riddle.) Figure 12-1 shows a logical path through a SAN's components.

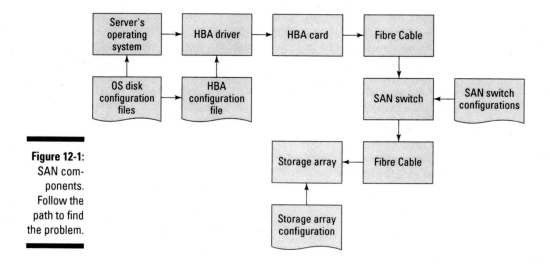

Figure 12-1:
SAN com-
ponents.
Follow the
path to find
the problem.

The key to locating a problem is isolating and testing each suspect component individually. Because everything in a SAN works together to make a disk drive show up on a server, a problem with a disk not showing up could lie with any or all of the components in between. Follow the paths in Figure 12-1 to highlight every possible point where a problem could arise. Check each point in the chain carefully, making sure that nothing is wrong; then move to the next one in the chain. The source of the problem that you're experiencing is somewhere along this path.

You can plan ahead for problems by reviewing some of the diagnostic procedures that many SAN component companies build into their products. These are usually status lights on the front or back of a component, a command you can run to query a component for status, or a simple GUI screen that tells you something is wrong. Monitoring and understanding these dashboard lights to know what looks healthy and correct can help you when things aren't going so well.

Being proactive versus reactive

Most SAN components come with at least basic monitoring software that can run a quick health check on your SAN components. Checking this software on a regular interval — say, once a week — may be a good way to keep tabs on your SAN before something serious happens that causes your pager to go off. This process is called being proactive instead of reactive. *Reactive* is hopping out of bed at 3 a.m. to fix something. *Proactive* is scheduling an upgrade to make sure that your SAN doesn't run out of steam during the next month-end processing cycle.

Didn't read the manual, did you?

We've all used enough table lamps to know that the plug goes in the wall, the bulb screws in the socket, and the switch turns on the light. But whenever we encounter something completely new, we think that it's a good idea to read that little booklet in the bottom of the box to gain some "Hmm . . . I didn't know *that*" knowledge.

One thing that separates the people-who-know from the people-who-think-they-know all about a product are those little factoids in product manuals that most people skip — things like "Note: This component supports only five devices even though it has ten plugs." Weird facts like this are commonly referred to as the *fine print*, because product-marketing folks don't like to make the limitations of their stuff obvious.

You should always be up to speed on what your SAN components can and can't do, what they do, and how they do it. Maybe you don't need to know everything, but at least know the basics that must be in operation for things to works smoothly, what `config` files a certain host bus adapter (HBA) uses, and what settings are mandatory for your configuration.

 Make a cheat sheet with a standard `config` file for your setup, and keep it handy to reference when you're double-checking a suspect one. Print the screen shot of your switch's `config` settings for reference, and so on. If you add all this material to your documentation, you'll never be struggling when you're asking yourself, "Does this look right?"

Build a golden configuration

A *golden configuration* is your gold standard for how you will be deploying your SAN infrastructure: a test server with test HBAs hooked up (if you have the cash) and its own test switches.

You can use your gold-standard test box to test faulty HBAs, new versions of drivers, and new configurations without affecting your production SAN. This setup may be costly for some shops, but having a server that's set up exactly the right way and never changed makes impromptu testing quick and painless.

Typical Problem Types

The secret of troubleshooting is being methodical. When you understand the flow of data and the things that interact with its flow, you can figure out what's going on, no matter what the issue is. In this section, I describe the various problems that can arise and why they happen. You can use this section as a reference so you'll know where to look when things go wrong.

Here are the four categories of problems that you'll encounter and need to troubleshoot, along with some examples of each type:

- **Obvious problems**

    Coffee got spilled on a switch.

    Someone pulled a cable out by accident.

- **Phantom problems**

    A sporadic, short-term issue seems to fix itself.

    A bug in an HBA driver causes interruptions in data flow or data errors.

- **Continuous problems**

    Yesterday it worked; today it doesn't; tomorrow it still won't.

    Something changed, and now you need to track down what that something was.

- **Catastrophic problems**

    A combination of one or more of the other three problem types causes a massive outage in your data center. You need to resolve the problem *now*.

Every problem has a particular cause-and-effect relationship. The following sections give examples for each of the preceding categories.

Obvious problems

Tackle the easiest kind of problem first. The smoking switch with the coffee spilled all over it is easy to diagnose and just as easy to solve: Fire the guy who brought the coffee into the data center and then get a sponge.

Obvious problems are . . . well, obvious. They don't really require trouble-shooting, but they do require you to understand their effect on the SAN and what you need to do to put things right. Depending on the component and the specific problem, the fix varies from plugging a loose cable back in to following a detailed procedure.

Broken cables

A broken fiber-optic cable doesn't let any light through it. No light, no data. Most SAN components have this diagnosis process licked, because little light-emitting diodes (LEDs) are next to the ports where you plug in your fiber-optic cables. If light travels through the wire, the LED lights up. No light, no . . . er, light. Unfortunately, you have to look at a switch to see whether the light is on or off. Scanning many switches remotely may be difficult, if not impossible.

 As simple as this process is, a broken cable may not be obvious. The cable itself is dumb, so the problem could be the component on either end of the cable. But if you're sure that the cable is plugged in properly at both ends, yet no LEDs are lighted at either end, your problem probably is the cable. An easy way to confirm is to plug either end of the cable into a port that you know works. If the LEDs still don't go on, the problem *is* the cable for sure.

 A rudimentary way to see whether a cable is passing light is to use a flashlight. Shine the flashlight down one end of the cable, cupping your free hand over the other end, and look for the light at the end of the fiber-optic cable (but heed the following warning). I don't guarantee that this method always works, but if you see no light whatsoever, you can safely assume that the cable is snapped in half somewhere.

 Never, *ever* look into the end of a 9μm SM cable. You'll end up frying your eyeballs. (The light generated by these high-powered lasers is invisible to the naked eye anyway.)

Most SAN switches have a management function that can alert you when a port that has a cable plugged in suddenly *goes dark* (no light is being transmitted). This function can be both a blessing and a burden, however. If you're continually changing cabling or rebooting servers, the ports will go light, dark, light, dark, and you'll be alerted every time a transition occurs in the status of the fiber port. But at least you'll know when something changes. On some switches, you can tailor the alert to worry only about ports that transition from On to Off — not Off to On — which may save you a few taps on the shoulder from your SAN management platform.

Tracking broken cabling is the job of all the other components of the SAN, because the cable is just a piece of glass that can't perform an action when it has a problem. Use your SAN switches' alerting functions to give you a heads-up when something seems unusual, such as a cable's being removed from the switch. At the very least, the event will be logged somewhere you can reference to see whether it could be related to your current issue. The log is either in the memory of the SAN switch itself or on a management console that monitors switches for these types of events.

Broken fabric switch

Here, I'm talking about a switch that's physically broken, not a software corruption or configuration that went astray. (I cover those situations in the upcoming section "Continuous problems.")

A good SAN switch has many redundant features, such as dual power supplies and multiple fans. Most switches have a network connection to send Simple Network Management Protocol (SNMP) alerts to your SAN management framework server that monitors the whole SAN. A catastrophic outright failure of an entire switch is unheard of (knock on wood), but it is possible. Your SAN management framework should be able to alert you about power-supply failures, fan problems, ports going bad, or even an outright disappearance of your SAN switch from the rest of the fabric.

The most important thing is that you have a backup of your switch configuration somewhere. If a switch is toast and needs to be replaced, would you know the zoning and port configuration off the top of your head? Didn't think so. For this reason, it's important to have this configuration saved somewhere off the switch itself.

In a single-switch SAN, or one with two switches that aren't directly connected, the configuration of the SAN is isolated to that switch. In other words, all the settings that define what port can see what other port (zoning) and how those ports are supposed to communicate (fabric, point-to-point, loop mode, and so on) are all self-contained on that switch *only*. If you had to replace that switch with one fresh out of a box, you'd have to replace the configuration manually.

Most switch vendors have a command that you can issue to the switch to make it save its current configuration to a file somewhere on your network. The process usually requires a protocol such as File Transfer Protocol (FTP) to log in to a server on your network and save a file that contains all the zoning and switch parameters. Then this file can be restored via a command to the switch at any time (usually, if something goes horribly wrong).

Figure 12-2 shows the two directions that a configuration can go in: dumped to a server for safekeeping or loaded back to a switch to restore a configuration.

In multiple-switch SAN fabrics, the switches share the configuration information, so if you plug a brand-new switch into an existing fabric, it learns the SAN configuration from the other switches. Check with your switch vendor, but most switch manufacturers are adopting this automatic configure process to make adding onto or replacing switches easier.

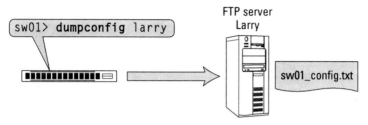

Saving the configuration to an external
server after making changes is a good idea.

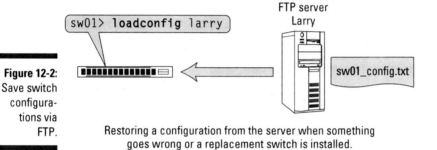

Figure 12-2:
Save switch
configura-
tions via
FTP.

Restoring a configuration from the server when something
goes wrong or a replacement switch is installed.

Figure 12-3 shows how the other switches in a fabric dump the current
config fabric configuration down to a new switch that replaces a fried one.

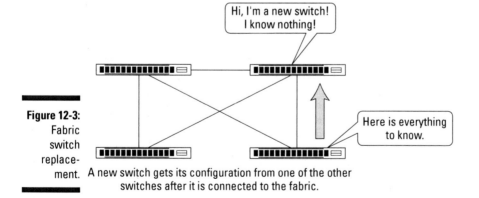

Figure 12-3:
Fabric
switch
replace-
ment.

A new switch gets its configuration from one of the other
switches after it is connected to the fabric.

Broken HBA

A *broken HBA* is a card that doesn't put out light anymore. This problem usually is pretty easy to isolate, because you'll get errors on the server from the HBA's device driver. The HBA may come with software that allows you to test it. If that's the case, use the software to determine whether the card is still operating and whether it can communicate with the device driver out to the SAN.

If the diagnostic software doesn't help, first make sure that the problem isn't a configuration error somewhere.

When replacing a broken HBA, remember this important fact: The World Wide Name (WWN) of that particular HBA is hard-coded to it. Consequently, a new HBA will have a different WWN, which means that the WWN can't see the storage that it originally saw on that HBA. To make a successful swap, you need to add or edit the new WWN to every place in the chain of configuration files/settings where the original WWN was given.

SAN vendors already understand the need to swap HBA cards sometimes because of problems or upgrades. Most cards have a command that you can issue through your SAN management framework or directly to your switches and storage arrays to do the name swap for you. Figure 12-4 shows this option (Swap WWN) being used in a SAN management framework console to give a replaced HBA the same definitions as the original HBA across the switches and storage arrays. (See Chapter 11 for more on SAN management.)

This rename/swap of the HBA WWN needs to be done at both the switch and storage array level if both WWN zoning and Logical Unit Number (LUN) security are being used. Consult your switch and storage vendors on the right procedure; they usually have a simple command that does this job easily. You can also take a peek at the example on LUN security in Chapter 7 for this process.

Broken storage array

Storage arrays are made to be redundant. They usually have multiple power supplies and multiple paths to get from the disk drives to the ports that connect to your SAN. If you have a failed disk drive in your array, look for an LED on the drive or the front of the array that alerts you to a problem. Most larger arrays have a management console that may call for help — literally — by a function called *Dial Home*. This function uses a phone line connected to the array or the management console to call the vendor's support center and log a problem.

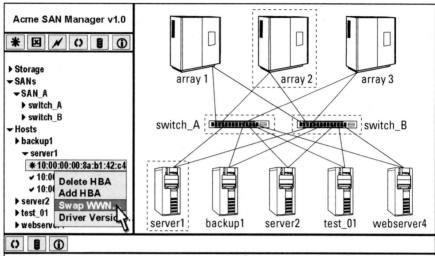

Figure 12-4:
Swap
WWNs
when
replacing
a broken
HBA.

The storage array has diagnostic software that tells you when something fails. It may even report to your SAN management framework, if you have one in place. You can set up your management framework so that a technician is dispatched to repair any hardware-related problems with the storage array.

I recommend relying on technicians to fix broken storage arrays: They have the most expertise.

You could void your warranty if you go poking around with a screwdriver and flashlight yourself. Wait for the tech.

Broken server

Because servers aren't part of the SAN componentry, you're on your own.

Just kidding.

The server's operating system (OS) may be corrupt or unstable for some reason, causing the storage on the SAN to not appear to the server anymore. More often than not, a reboot of the affected server clears up the problem . . . but doesn't explain what went wrong. Closer observation of the server's memory use may be in order to see whether some type of memory leak — done associated with the HBA driver, for example — is causing weird behavior over time.

Check with the HBA's manufacturer for known bugs or recommended updated drivers. Many HBA vendors test their drivers with specific operating system–level patches that you may not be running. Running with HBA drivers or OS patches that aren't tested and certified with your storage vendors can cause major support headaches. Stay certified and supportable by following their recommendations.

Phantom problems

Phantom problems cause sporadic, inconsistent, weird behavior on your SAN — things such as storage that disappears and then reappears on servers, and switches that first lose connections and then reconnect to server HBAs for no reason. Having these problems is almost like having ghosts in your data center pulling plugs and reconnecting them.

Phantom problems are the most difficult to diagnose; because the problems are so random and unpredictable, you don't always have a chance to observe them to figure out the cause.

Faulty HBAs

A faulty HBA can cause the link between your server and SAN switches to go up and down. An HBA should never disconnect its light from a switch for any reason unless the server is in the process of rebooting — when the device driver for the HBA card unloads and reloads, thus resetting the HBA.

HBAs go through a self-test just as most other components do when power is applied to it from the server and/or the drivers are loaded. If the HBA has an immediate fault, the driver either won't load or will load and then gives you a message that something isn't right.

An outright fault is cause to pull out the bad card and replace it. Refer to "Broken HBA," earlier in this chapter, to discover how to swap the WWNs in the SAN configuration when you're replacing a bad card.

An HBA that passes its self-test but still causes problems can be tested further. Replace the HBA (as though it were broken) and then put it in another server that's used for testing. On this server, just read and write to a disk on the SAN, using this suspect HBA continuously, until the problem rears its head. If the problem doesn't follow the HBA, the HBA probably isn't the cause. It could be something else, such as the driver/configuration file or something out on the switches or storage arrays.

Faulty HBA drivers

Drivers are the most common causes of strange problems on a SAN. A *driver* is the software that marries your HBA card to your server's operating system, doing all the communication between it and the storage arrays and switches via the fibre channel protocol.

The manufacturer of the driver tests the HBA to work with a given OS level. If you use the right version of the OS with the specific patch levels requested by the vendor, as well as the right-model HBA and its proper firmware level, everything should work. *Should* work.

Most HBAs also come with a configuration file where settings for your particular type of SAN configuration are placed. These settings, which range from general to specific, give the driver various parameters that affect how it operates. Some entries tell the driver what kind of protocol to use on the SAN; others contain low-level fibre channel timing values that you should never alter unless you have a very particular reason for doing so. Consult your SAN vendor about anything this specific.

After this configuration file is set up, never change it unless something is altered on your server. Changes to the configuration file can really screw up your connectivity to the SAN and the data integrity of your connected storage, so be careful to follow the guidelines of your HBA vendor or SAN vendor. Usually, storage-array and switch vendors worked closely with the HBA vendors to tune their drivers to work better with their particular hardware. Get this specific tuning information for your configuration file from one of those vendors to make the file operate optimally.

Drivers usually work pretty well unless something — such as an OS upgrade or other patch — changed the server's configuration somehow. If you've been running okay forever and something suddenly goes kablooey, don't assume that the problem is the driver. Check the obvious things first, and narrow down the problem from there.

A common issue that pinpoints a driver is a very high input/output (I/O) rate that causes the driver to overload and crash. Many driver problems aren't caused by bugs in the driver but by errors in the configuration file that cause the driver to fail after it has enough work to push it over the edge. The most common culprit is a setting in the file that specifies how many buffers are allocated per LUN. Check with your storage vendor to make sure that these settings are correct from the beginning so that you don't run into a problem after a lot of work is pushed through the HBA.

Heavy testing of these drivers is done by both the HBA vendor and other component vendors, such as the storage and switch vendors. They make sure that everything works together and doesn't alter the data along the path from storage to server.

Fixing a driver issue is as simple as downloading the recommended driver from the HBA vendor's Web site and installing it over the existing one. Just make sure that your SAN vendors approve of that version of the driver before you make things unsupported by their tech support.

Usually, you have to reboot the server for the new driver to take effect. It would be nice to have a golden-configuration setup in this situation, because you can do your own sanity check on the new driver in a test setup before releasing it on your production SAN.

Roll out new driver versions slowly, just to make sure they work properly. When you're confident that the new version doesn't cause any issues, you can deploy it across all your servers in bulk.

Continuous problems

Continuous problems can cause sudden, ongoing problems with your SAN. They typically don't resolve themselves and need to be fixed ASAP to bring things back to normal.

Zoning changes

Zones create the virtual connections between your storage array's fibre ports and your server's HBA cards. They contain the WWNs of the storage array's fibre channel ports and the WWNs of the HBA's ports. (See Chapter 5 for more on zoning guidelines and standards.)

If you suddenly lose connection to your storage array altogether, and you know that the problem isn't cabling or a physical failure of one of the SAN components, checking the zoning information is a good place to start. Zones are grouped into zone sets, only one of which is active at a time. Someone who changes the zone configurations or activates the wrong one will break the connection between the HBA and storage array, thereby causing your problem.

Wrong LUN security

To make sure that only certain LUNs on a given port of a storage array can be seen by a specific host's HBAs, LUN security is activated. If LUN security is changed, it can cause problems on your server, such as making disks disappear or even making the server see disks that aren't supposed to be there. So after you verify your zones, the next step in troubleshooting is checking the LUN security to make sure that the HBA's WWN matches the one assigned to each LUN on the specific port of the array.

Figure 12-5 shows how the combination of LUN security and zoning works to make LUN4 on the pictured array available to the HBA on the server. See how LUN4 is assigned to PORT-2 on the storage array and then to WWN HBA-01? As long as HBA-01 connects via the SAN fabric to that storage port, the server will see LUN4.

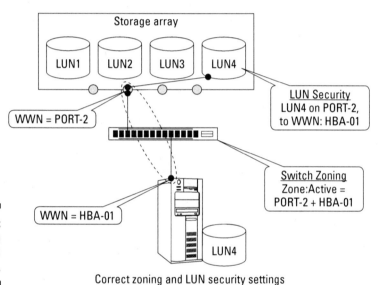

Figure 12-5:
Zoning
and LUN
security.

Correct zoning and LUN security settings

Performance bottlenecks

Using the tools that come with your server's operating system, you can monitor its memory and CPU use. When you know that the server itself isn't experiencing a memory or CPU bottleneck, the next logical thing to check is the I/O subsystem: your SAN.

The performance of the SAN as a whole can cause slowdowns of your application servers. A good storage array comes with software that can show you the amount of I/O your storage array is processing and what various components are doing at any time. A good SAN switch also comes with software that shows how much data is passing through the switch.

Doing performance analysis across your entire SAN with current industry tools takes some coordination, because few products do soup-to-nuts monitoring, especially in real time. Vendors such as EMC (www.emc.com) and Symantec (www.symantec.com) offer SAN management packages that communicate with your SAN components to provide statistics on the system's use of the components and the links among them. Chapter 11 goes into more detail on what SAN management frameworks provide.

Next, you want to look at the storage subsystem itself to see whether it's getting hammered with work. Of the several parameters to view, one of the most important is %Cache Hit Rate. A *cache hit* occurs when your storage array retrieves data from cache memory instead of reading it from the physical disk drives. A high cache hit rate is good: It means that the array is serving data from fast cache memory more than from slower disk drives. A low cache hit rate is bad; it means that performance is suffering because the array needs fetch requests from the slower disk spindles instead of fast cache memory.

Another key performance issue can be the amount of data that's requested from or sent to a given disk in your array. Physical disk drives are mechanical and can transfer only so much data per second. No matter how many switches, fiber links, or HBAs you put between your application server and your array, you can read or write data only at the maximum for that given spindle. For this reason, you should spread your file systems for your servers across multiple disk drives in the array; doing so increases the number of operations that can occur for that file system. Then, and only then, will you need to balance it with more links to support the potential throughput.

Ask your storage-array vendor what other parameters it suggests for monitoring performance. Because so many vendors and models of arrays exist, they vary greatly in operation.

As for SAN switches, you want to look at how much data is transferred between your hosts and storage. All your switch vendors have some kind of software that watches each port on your switch to tell you the percentage of use of that port. On a 4GB-per-second SAN switch (about 400MB per second per port), the theoretical maximum of any port is 4GB. Thus, if you see ports that are in the 80–100 percentage of maximum range, you may be running into a problem like the classic bottleneck pictured in Figure 12-6.

Solve a bottleneck by making the neck of the bottle wider. Look at Figure 12-6: If your host requests data via two HBAs at close to 800MB per second (2 × 400MB per second each), and the disks on the array are available on only one 400MB-per-second port, you have a bottleneck going to that link. The fastest transfer of data across the link from array to switch will always be, at most, about 400MB per second. Adding the second link between the array and the switch removes the bottleneck, thus increasing the potential performance of your SAN (see Figure 12-7).

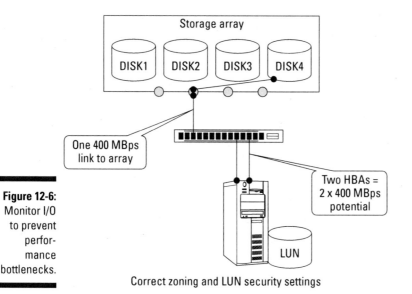

Figure 12-6:
Monitor I/O
to prevent
perfor-
mance
bottlenecks.

Correct zoning and LUN security settings

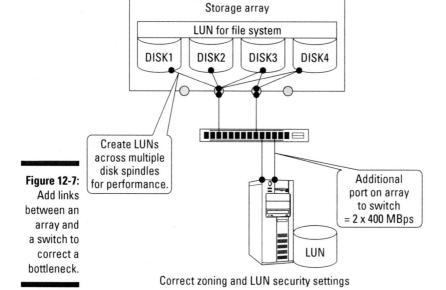

Figure 12-7:
Add links
between an
array and
a switch to
correct a
bottleneck.

Correct zoning and LUN security settings

Tracking performance over time is also a good thing to do. Being able to see trends of your SAN's performance over the past few days, weeks, or months is just as important as seeing it in real time. In Chapter 11, I cover the need to watch your SAN's plumbing to make sure that it isn't overburdened and causing problems that you'll need to troubleshoot later, when someone finally complains.

Catastrophic problems

A *catastrophic problem* causes multiple failures across multiple systems. This type of problem is rare but can happen if you haven't prepared for the possibility. Troubleshooting this kind of problem usually is moot, because it's a series of obvious problems.

Catastrophic problems such as these are why SAN designers build in redundancy and multiple isolated fabrics so that a cascading error can't affect other components of the SAN.

The best way to cope with this type of problem is to build against it. Make your SAN as redundant as possible, using these basic guidelines:

✔ Design your SAN with two separate fabrics.

✔ Make sure that each server has at least two physical HBA cards.

✔ Make sure that each HBA is attached to a separate SAN fabric.

✔ Use fail-over and/or load-balancing software on the servers for your HBAs.

✔ Make changes to one fabric at a time, confirming that the change is successful before making it on the other fabric.

If you follow these basics when you design your SAN, troubleshooting will be less hair-raising; your users probably won't know when something on the SAN breaks, and they won't feel any effect while you're replacing failed components behind the scenes.

Example Scenarios

The best way to learn how to troubleshoot is to go through a scenario step by step and follow the logic to figure out where the problem is. In this section, three scenarios describe a make-believe SAN implementation and insert a mystery problem into it, making your users irate.

You won't find any SAN management framework in these scenarios to tell you about failed switches or arrays or anything else. You need to walk through the whole setup component by component to see whether anything is amiss.

Scenario #1

In Scenario #1, the server used for an accounts-payable application has one HBA called HBA-01. Connected to that HBA is a switch that connects the server to the storage array. The storage array has a LUN called LUN-1 that's assigned to PORT-2 on the array. PORT-2 is connected via fiber-optic cable to the switch. The path to your data looks like this:

> HBA-01➪SAN switch➪Storage PORT-2➪LUN-1

Figure 12-8 shows your expected connectivity.

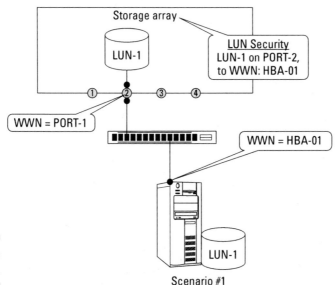

Figure 12-8:
Scenario #1.

The problem

You have everything connected on Monday morning, and you can see LUN-1 on your server. Everything is working fine when you leave at the end of the day. Tuesday morning, you come into the office and find a voice-mail message saying that the accounting office can't access the accounts-payable application.

You spring into action, checking the server to see whether anything is wrong with the volume LUN-1. You log in to the server and notice that there *aren't* any I/O errors on the server's console; it's just plain missing from the server.

By the way, whenever you have a storage volume mounted on a server and something happens that disconnects the volume, the server goes haywire, complaining that it can't access the volume (usually evident in repetitive I/O errors to the volume), and it's very persistent.

Because you don't see errors or the volume either, maybe the volume was never there in the first place. Is that possible?

The investigation

You have a mystery on your hands. What happened to LUN-1? What's changed? Did something break? Did someone make a configuration mistake? The most important thing to remember is that the system worked before, so you know that you had the configuration correct. Now you have to make sure that nothing failed.

If LUN-1 isn't the only volume assigned to this server, and if the other volumes are working fine, the problem can't be the HBA or a cable failure to that HBA. Otherwise, all the other volumes would have disappeared too. But because LUN-1 is the only volume, and it's missing, you have to check the HBA and cabling.

So you check those elements, and the HBA shows a green light, indicating that it's communicating to the switch. For now, you can assume that the cable is okay.

Next, move to the switch and its configuration. Check the logs on the switch for any sporadic connects/disconnects from that server's port. You find one: At 3:00 a.m., it disconnected; then it reconnected at 3:05 a.m. Bingo! Something happened — a clue! Now, what was it?

Go back to the server to see what happened to it around 3:00 a.m. Checking the logs on the server, you find that it rebooted around 3:00 a.m. and was back up and running at 3:05 a.m. That's good. You've correlated the two events.

Checking further in the log, you see the HBA driver loading and scanning for devices; however, it finds none. The server continues along in the boot process and can't mount the file system on LUN-1. Why wasn't LUN-1 found during the HBA driver's scan for storage devices?

What you know so far

So far, you know that the server rebooted at 3 a.m. and that when it did, the HBA reconnected to the switch when the driver for the HBA reloaded correctly. But the HBA couldn't find any disk devices — primarily LUN-1. So the server couldn't mount the file system on LUN-1, and therefore, the accounts-payable application couldn't start up.

The resolution

Because things were working fine up to 3 a.m., when the server rebooted, whatever caused the problem must be on the server itself. Upon reboot, a server reloads its configuration data, so you can be pretty sure that something in the configuration files was changed before the reboot; now the file is wrong and is causing this problem.

If you refer to Figure 12-1 at the beginning of this chapter, you see that the OS and HBA have configuration files that are read once during boot — and that could have been altered.

In this scenario, you investigate the time stamps on the configuration files; sure enough, the HBA's configuration file was changed yesterday afternoon.

Check the time stamps *before* you start editing them and poking around. If the time stamps are very old ones that existed through a previous reboot of the server, you can be certain that they're correct. You don't even need to look at them for troubleshooting purposes; the configuration file is still correct, because it predates the first signs of a problem.

Now you edit your HBA configuration file, scanning each entry to see whether it's correct. (Here's where having a reference printout of your documentation is very handy.) Check the correct settings against what you see onscreen.

You find a typo: AUTO_SCAN=0 instead of the required AUTO_SCAN=1. So you change the setting and reboot the server. The HBA driver loads, and this time it *does* scan for LUNs and finds LUN-1. Everything else works as expected, and your accounts-payable application is back online. Now go find whoever changed that file and smack him (or her).

In this scenario, you see how to locate the problem, correlate the event on the switch with the event that took place on the server (the reboot), and trace through the server's log file to see where the problem first reared its ugly head.

You eliminated the rest of the SAN components, because things were working as they should have been up to the reboot. Checking the time stamps on the configuration files to see whether any changed and having the documentation for the correct settings in the HBA's config file made finding the error very easy. Most important, you didn't go around pulling cables and changing things.

Changes *cause* problems.

Scenario #2

This scenario is a bit more complicated than the previous one. I hope that it gets the point across that correlating information and events helps you narrow the scope of your search for the problem.

Figure 12-9 shows the diagram of your environment for Scenario #2. You have two servers, each with one HBA going to one switch and one storage array. One server gets a single LUN; the other gets two LUNs. (Well, maybe it isn't much more complicated.)

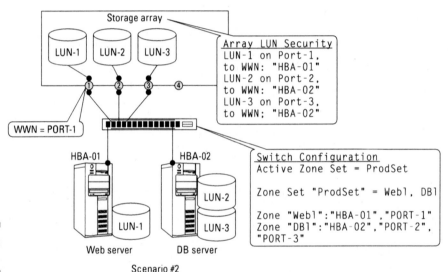

Figure 12-9:
Scenario #2.

The problem

This scenario starts with everything working as expected. As usual, all of a sudden someone calls you to yell about an application that doesn't work anymore. Apparently the database (DB) server pictured in Figure 12-9 lost one of its LUNs: LUN-3. Your job is to figure out why. Like a superhero, you spring into action.

The investigation

Going to the server, you confirm I/O errors, both read and write, on the file system that resides on LUN-3. These errors mean that something is keeping your server from talking to that LUN. The other LUN on the DB server, LUN-2, is still okay, and no other phone calls about any other problems are coming in.

What you know so far

The problem is isolated to one server . . . and to only one of two LUNs on that server. If one LUN is still okay, you know a few things. The problem is *not* the HBA or its configuration file, and it's not the OS's `config` file. These files are loaded at boot time, and because the server has been up all along, these files aren't the culprits. Besides, the little LED on the back of the HBA is lighted up, so it's linked up to the switch.

Move along the path to the next component: the switch. The SAN switch is using WWN zoning, and the zones are listed in Figure 12-9. For the DB server, see the zone called DB1 that contains the HBA's WWN; HBA-02; and the two ports on the storage array, PORT-2 and PORT-3.

Don't assume that this zoning is correct, because it could have been modified erroneously. You need more information on whether this zoning is correct to make LUN-3 appear to this server. Find out what port on the storage array LUN-3 is assigned to and whether it's allowed to be seen on HBA-02. After you have all this information, you'll know whether the configuration is correct from end to end.

The resolution

Checking the configuration of the storage array, as pictured in Figure 12-9, you see that LUN security is enabled and that LUN-2 and LUN-3 are assigned to ports PORT-2 and PORT-3, respectively, and secured to HBA-02 via each port. If you lay everything out logically, you'll get these paths to your volumes:

HBA-02⇨SAN switch⇨Storage PORT-2⇨LUN-2

HBA-02⇨SAN switch⇨Storage PORT-3⇨LUN-3

The switch zoning matches because HBA-02 is allowed to see both ports. The LUN security matches too, because LUN-2 and LUN-3 are assigned to the ports and to the HBA the same way. All the configuration information is correct from storage array to switch and from switch to HBA. So what's wrong?

(You're probably assuming that the cable between the switch and storage port PORT-3 is okay. Just because the configuration is right doesn't mean that the data gets there, however.)

You check the link light on the storage array's PORT-3, and you see that it's dark. Hmm. Did the port go bad? Or did the cable go bad? Most array vendors' diagnostics run all the time, making sure that all parts of the array are operating. If the port itself had gone bad, you'd be able to see the problem by using the array's management tools. The port isn't broken; it's just showing `No Light`. It's time to check the other end of the cable.

The LED next to the switch port where the array's PORT-3 is plugged in is also showing `No Light`, and the little amber failure light is lighted up, too! The port on the switch has failed. A SAN management framework could have alerted you to this problem, but as I state at the beginning of this section, you're working through these troubleshooting scenarios with no such help. (Doing a manual event correlation makes you appreciate the need for something that does this work for you.)

Because you're using WWN zoning on the switch, it doesn't matter what port the cable is plugged into. Unplugging the cable and putting it into a port that works makes the path between PORT-3 and HBA-02 come back to life — and LUN-3 magically reappears to the DB server.

This scenario traces from the application server all the way back to the storage array. Could you have eliminated any of these steps? Yes — you could have checked the cabling and communications first and found the broken port on the switch immediately. A hardware failure that causes only one LUN to disappear from one server is relatively rare, however. This setup has limited numbers of servers and LUNs. In a large SAN shop with hundreds of LUNs, ports, and HBAs, a disconnected storage-array port would be more obvious because it would affect every server using a LUN on that port.

The key to diagnosing this type of multiple-possibility problem is going through the data flow step by step. By going from HBA to switch to storage and comparing the configuration that's in place with what you're observing, you can see rather quickly what doesn't make sense. In this case, everything made sense in terms of configuration, so a hardware issue had to be causing the problem.

Unfortunately, the odds favor a problem that's caused by a human who changed something that was working fine. Doing a sanity check on the configuration eliminates the obvious; then what is left, no matter how bizarre, has to be the answer. This method is the Sherlock Holmes method of mystery solving, and as far as I know, he always solved the crime.

Scenario #3

This scenario goes into the realm of fully redundant fabrics, which guards against catastrophic failures of SAN components. Even though having a LUN disappear from a server is guarded against, however, you still need to figure out what to fix when something breaks.

Figure 12-10 shows the new, fully redundant SAN setup for Scenario #3.

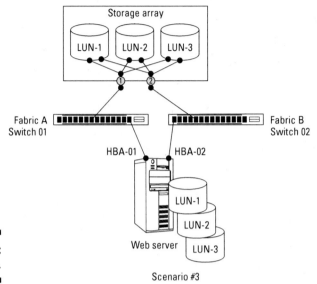

Figure 12-10:
Scenario #3.

The diagram looks much like Scenario #1, but here you have two switches, two HBAs, and the necessary links for everything. The storage array would have its own high-availability features, such as redundant power supplies and Redundant Array of Independent Disks (RAID) to protect against disk failures.

The two HBAs in the server are key because each one talks to its own SAN fabric. Because the two switches aren't connected, they don't share configuration and zoning information. They must be updated separately to make changes consistent between them.

The paths to LUN-1 look like this:

HBA-01⇨Fabric A/Switch-01⇨Storage Array PORT-1⇨LUN-1

HBA-02⇨Fabric B/Switch-02⇨Storage Array PORT-2⇨LUN-1

On the server is some software that knows how to load balance its I/O between the two HBAs to talk to LUN-1. If either HBA gets disconnected from LUN-1, the other HBA takes over all the communication. The application running on this server will never know that an error occurred; it simply continues on just one HBA until the path is restored. When the path comes back and LUN-1 reappears, the software resumes balancing I/O between the HBAs.

The problem

The problems that you encounter with fully redundant fabrics usually are less dire than those involving single attached servers. Because the disk devices don't get completely disconnected from the server's application, you don't have any effect on the users unless you count performance. If you have two connections to the LUN, for example, and then suddenly have only one (if something fails), you may run into a slowdown in performance, but connectivity from server to disk won't be compromised.

In this scenario, you're looking at a performance issue that triggers that nasty phone call from your users.

The investigation

The investigation steps in this scenario are similar to those you would take in Scenario #1. In this case, however, you should make sure that you're looking at the right fabric when you do your detective work. Having documentation is critical because sometimes it's difficult to understand whether Fabric A or Fabric B is having a problem.

First, examine the paths on the server to determine what the problem is — as far as the application sees it. You do this by using the path-management software that the HBAs use to load balance and fail-over the communications between the SAN and the OS.

Make up a generic command for this purpose, and call it `pathstat`. On the server, you run it and get this output:

```
$ pathstat

HBA-WWN    Status Devices   I/O Blocks Errors
-----------------------------------------------------
HBA-01     ONLINE   3         782313     0
HBA-02     ONLINE   2         781902     5

Devices   Paths   Errors
LUN-1      1        5
LUN-2      2        0
LUN-3      2        0
```

It looks as though `pathstat` is telling you that HBA-01 and HBA-02 are talking to the SAN correctly, as you see via the ONLINE entry in the Status column for each HBA. Look at HBA-02's entry, however; it has only two devices compared with HBA-01's three devices. Hmm.

Now look at the Devices list below. LUN-1 has only one path, whereas LUN-2 and LUN-3 have two each.

Taking the error counts into account, you see that the errors listed are for LUN-1 on HBA-02 only.

Now that you know this, you should concentrate on Fabric B, because that's the fabric that HBA-02 is connected to (refer to Figure 12-10). Also, LUN-1 seems to be the only device that's experiencing a problem, because you still have two paths from HBA-01 *and* HBA-02 to LUN-2 and LUN-3.

What you know so far

By using the path-management software on the host, you know that HBA-02 is not seeing LUN-1 correctly. It's still working okay with the other two devices: LUN-2 and LUN-3. This result tells you that both HBAs' links are good all the way through the fabrics to the storage array; otherwise, you'd see problems with the other two LUNs as well.

Furthermore, you can discount a zoning problem because according to the diagram, all the LUNs are assigned through the same ports.

Something is wrong with LUN-1 on that particular HBA. Now ask yourself, "How does a LUN get assigned permission to an HBA?" LUN security handles that task.

You check the LUN security on the storage array. Bingo! The LUN security for LUN-1 to HBA-02 is wrong. Figure 12-11 shows the configuration on the storage array. What's this mystery HBA-05? That's not right.

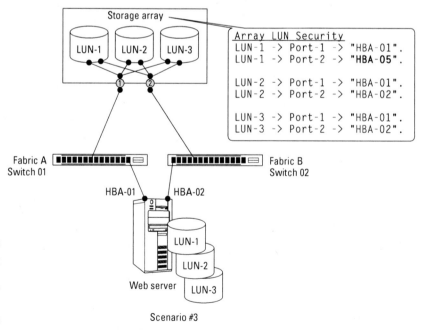

Figure 12-11:
LUN
security
bug.

If this example were in actual WWN format (xx:xx:xx:xx:xx:xx:xx:xx), the error might not be so obvious, so look carefully when double-checking settings.

The resolution

The fix for this problem is putting the correct WWN for HBA-02 into the LUN security configuration on the storage array.

This scenario is a bit different from the previous two because the problem is isolated to a specific LUN that is still accessible to the application, thanks to redundancy software and the second HBA.

This example also shows that you can keep yourself from having to check other components if you know that other paths are working okay. Because LUN-2 and LUN-3 were still using two paths, you knew that the problem couldn't be the HBA itself or the fiber links among the switches, hosts, and array. The problem also couldn't be the zones on the switches, because they don't handle LUN security — just port security between HBA and storage ports.

SNMP: A better way

Simple Network Management Protocol (SNMP) is a way to send alerts across your network from SAN components to a central monitoring console in your data center. Most SAN vendors support this protocol so that your switches, storage arrays, and even HBAs can notify someone about a problem and allow you to skip all this manual sleuthing.

You may overlook this great feature because you're so excited about getting data flowing across your SAN that you forget to configure the SNMP settings right away. But centralizing your monitoring and alerts keeps you from having to look in umpteen places for information on your SAN's status.

Part IV
SAN Management and Troubleshooting

The 5th Wave · By Rich Tennant

AUTO SHOW FOR COMPUTER STORAGE EXECUTIVES

GLOVE COMPAR

In this part . . .

Now that you've built this monster (the SAN) and set it loose on your village (the user community), how do you keep track of it and make sure that it's playing nice? The answer: SAN management— the art of monitoring, maintaining, and documenting your SAN's behavior.

This part also covers the methodical but not impossible task of tracking down and eliminating gremlins — also known as *troubleshooting*. The step-by-step troubleshooting process we follow is much like the steps that are covered in Part II when building the SAN. But here we reverse the process and take the SAN apart to discover how to determine what is broken with a previously healthy SAN.

Chapter 13

Using Data De-Duplication to Lighten the Load

Sometimes people don't exercise or eat right and end up getting fat. A similar situation can happen with data storage. Lazy users who never delete anything make the poor backup administrators' jobs even harder, forcing them to back up useless or duplicate data. Many companies have no formal polices on storing information, so data that the business doesn't really need gets stored, backed up, and even replicated for disaster recovery anyway.

Consider these situations:

✔ Users who never delete e-mails or send e-mails with large attachments to large distribution lists

✔ Users who store multiple copies of the same file because they're not sure which one holds the right changes

✔ Users who download and store MP3 files at work

✔ Multiple duplicate copies of executables like `winword.exe` (the executable file that makes Microsoft Word work) backed up from all the laptops and desktops in the company

All these situations conspire together to waste storage space. As a result, many SAN networks store much more data than necessary, which raises costs. This chapter deals with the general concept of data de-duplication: what it is, how it works, where it should be applied, and the results you should expect.

Understanding Data De-Duplication

In simplified terms, *data de-duplication* means comparing objects (usually, files or blocks) and removing all non-unique or *duplicate* objects (copies). If you look at the left side of Figure 13-1, you see several blocks being stored that are not unique. The de-duplication process removes any blocks that are not unique, resulting in the smaller group of blocks being stored.

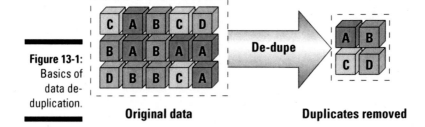

Figure 13-1:
Basics of
data de-
duplication.

Original data   **Duplicates removed**

Benefits of data de-duplication

Data de-duplication is a hot technology in storage because it enables companies to save a lot of money. Using the example in Figure 13-1, you'd need 375 percent less space to store only the unique blocks! Now imagine what that would mean for a large corporation backing up thousands of laptops and desktops every night. Using Microsoft Word as an example (not to pick on Microsoft here, it's just that Word is so prevalent in many companies), think of all the duplicate copies of Winword.exe being backed up every night. (Winword.exe is the executable file that makes Microsoft Word work.)

Even if the company had only 500 desktops, there would be 500 copies of winword.exe. Why in the world are companies backing up and storing so many copies of a single file? If you de-duplicated that one file alone, it would mean a 500:1 de-duplication ratio, and you would use 499 times less storage to store that file. Now extrapolate that to all the files stored in every desktop, laptop, and server across the entire company, and you can see where the savings come from. By implementing a de-duplication solution, companies need fewer disk drives and tapes to store data over time, and they can save huge amounts of network bandwidth when replicating data off-site for disaster recovery.

The basic benefits of de-duplication can be summarized as follows:

- Reduced hardware costs
- Reduced backup costs
- Reduced costs for disaster recovery
- Increased efficiency of storage

You can apply de-duplication in multiple places. Wherever you apply it, de-duplication can affect costs for not only your SAN, but also for your entire IT infrastructure.

Based on a typical enterprise environment running typical applications, you probably could squeeze out between 20 to 90 percent more storage space just by getting rid of duplicate and unnecessary data.

How de-duplication works

Most de-duplication solutions work by

1. Dividing the input data into individual chunks

2. Calculating a hash value for the chunk of data (see the following section for more on what a hash is) and storing the hash in an index

3. Using the hash value of the original chunk of data and comparing it with the hash value of another new chunk of data to determine whether to store or ignore (de-dupe) the new data

The process of data de-duplication can be implemented in several ways. You can manually compare two files and delete the one that's older or no longer needed, or you can use a commercial de-duplication product. Commercial solutions use sophisticated methods (the actual math involved can make your head spin) to find duplicate data. Once you become expert in how it works, if your current line of work doesn't pan out for you, hey, maybe you could get a job at the Central Intelligence Agency.

Most of the data de-duplication solutions on the market today use standard data encryption techniques (see the nearby sidebar) to create a unique mathematical representation of the data in question — a *hash* — so that the hash can be compared with any new hashes to determine whether the data is unique. The hash also serves as the *metadata* (data about data) for the chunk of data in question. The hash is used as an index in a lookup table, allowing you to determine quickly whether any new data being stored is already present and can be eliminated.

TECHNICAL STUFF

Data encryption standards used in data de-duplication

Following are some of the encryption standards that vendors use to de-duplicate data:

- **Data Encryption Standard (DES):** This standard, 56 bits long, is a federal information processing standard (FIPS) that the U.S. government once used to encrypt data.

- **Advanced Encryption Standard (AES):** AES is a complex encryption standard known as a *cipher block*. It can be 128 to 256 bits long and uses a secure key that makes it much more secure than DES, which it has replaced. AES conforms to the FIPS standard.

- **Secure Hash Algorithm (SHA):** The SHA family (SHA-1 to SHA-3) of hashing

algorithms also conforms to FIPS standards and is very secure. The hash lengths start at 160 bits and go all the way to 512 bits. To put that figure into perspective, the mathematical representation of a block of data using SHA-1 would be 160 decimal places!

- **Message Digest Algorithm 5 (MD5):** This standard, 128 bits long, is a common data-security system, and its implementation is fairly simple and robust. The hash is a string of hexadecimal numbers 32 characters long that look something like this: A4BEC893BEE67418975BEAAC53298721. Because each hex character is made of 4 bits (A = 1010, for example), the 32-character string adds up to 128 bits.

Data De-Duplication in the Datacenter

De-duplication can be implemented in one or more locations in the datacenter to help reduce costs. Most de-duplication solutions are focused on reducing the amount of data that needs to be backed up or replicated. Your options include host-based solutions that use the CPU in your servers to reduce data being sent over the network for backup; appliance-based solutions that sit in the network or SAN fabric to reduce the amount of data being replicated for disaster recovery or remote office consolidation; and de-duplication solutions that come as part of other solutions such as Virtual Tape Libraries or NAS file systems.

The process of de-duplication can be applied to either blocks or files. Blocks are used to store data directly on a disk, and files are used to store data in a file system, which is then stored on a disk. When de-duplication is applied at the block level, it can be used for both structured and non-structured data. (Data is structured when it is stored in a database, and it is not structured when it's stored as a file.) When de-duplication is applied at the file level, it simply compares files or the contents of files, and removes duplicates. File-based solutions work with non-structured data such as file shares and home directories.

The de-duplication vendors

The following are a sampling of some de-dupe vendors and where their solutions can be found in the datacenter:

- **Host-based solutions:** These solutions can work on blocks or files and can typically be integrated with the applications. Host-based de-duplication reduces the amount of data moved over the network for backup and can be used to limit the amount of data being sent from remote offices when consolidating backup at a central location. Vendors include IBM, NetApp, EMC, Symantec, Sun Microsystems, Hewlett-Packard, and FalconStor.

- **Appliance-based solutions:** Most appliance-based de-duplication solutions are focused on reducing the amount of data being stored for backup or replicated for disaster recovery. Because they are implemented as appliances, they can be used in almost any storage environment. Appliances eliminate the need to use the CPU in the hosts for the de-duplication process. Some appliance-based de-duplication solutions also include other functionality such as CDP or VTL or even a NAS device. Vendors include Sun Microsystems, EMC, Riverbed, NetApp, Data Domain, Quantum, Sepaton, and FalconStor.

- **Storage-based solutions:** Storage-based solutions deal with blocks and are implemented as a native disk target. Some of the solutions are application-integrated via scripts; others focus strictly on moving data over the wide area network (WAN) or are replication-focused. Vendors include EMC, Hitachi Data Systems, Hewlett Packard, NetApp, Copan, FalconStor, and Pillar.

How data gets de-duplicated

The most common methods used to de-duplicate data are

- File-based compare and compression
- File-level hashing
- Block-level hashing
- Sub-block-level hashing
- Delta versioning, which I call "nodupe," or not duplicating in the first place

Each method is described in detail in the following sections.

File-based compare and compression

Using the file system to compare two files to see if they are the same (as shown in Figure 13-2) is the simplest and least costly method to eliminate duplicates.

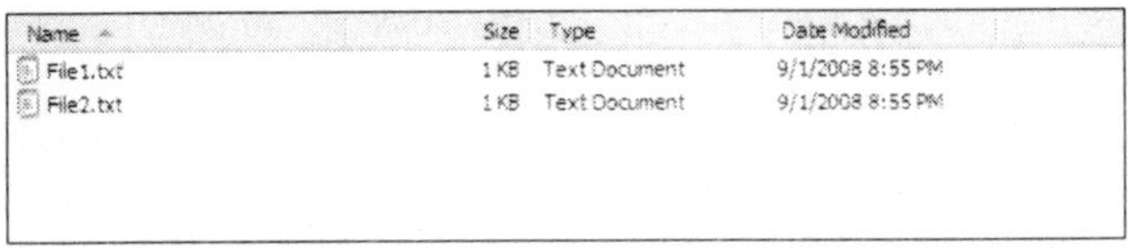

Figure 13-2:
Comparing
files.

Name ▲	Size	Type	Date Modified
File1.txt	1 KB	Text Document	9/1/2008 8:55 PM
File2.txt	1 KB	Text Document	9/1/2008 8:55 PM

You can usually determine if the file is a duplicate by comparing the file meta-data (metadata is the information that describes the data, or in other words, the data *about* the data), which is stored as the file name, file size, and the modification data and time.

An example of this method is comparing the name, size, type, and data-mod-ified information of two files with the same name being stored in a system. If all these parameters match, you can be pretty sure that the files are dupli-cates, and one can be deleted. Although this method isn't as foolproof as the formal data de-duplication solutions, it can be done with any operating system, can be scripted to automate the process, and is free.

If you add a simple off-the-shelf free file-compression solution (such as tar, zip, and so on), you can probably get at least a 2:1 to 3:1 de-duplication ratio, which comes out to over 50 percent less data to move, store, and back up. The results may not be as dramatic as the more complex solutions, but again, who can argue with free?

File-level hashing

More intelligent file-level de-duplication methods use a *hash*. (A hash is a math-ematical representation of data.) File hashing creates a unique mathematical hash representation of files and compares hashes for new files with the origi-nals. If a hash match occurs, the files are the same, and one can be removed.

Some host-based software solutions use these techniques to reduce wide area network (WAN) requirements for centralized backup of remote servers. Intelligent software agents running on the host (desktop, laptop, workstation, or servers) use file-level hashing to send only new unique data over the net-work to the central site.

Some of these solutions are not as intelligent and send all data changes to the central site first, where it is then de-duplicated so only unique data is stored at the central site. Either method is fine to save disk space at the central site, but the first method also reduces network requirements. The tradeoff is more

CPU cycles on the host to de-dupe first and less network bandwidth, or more network bandwidth and less CPU cycles being used on the hosts.

Most solutions that use a hashing mechanism require an index table (database) to store the hashes so that old hashes can be referenced quickly for matches. These indexes must be very fast (normally stored in fast memory) or handled in such a way that as the amount of new unique data being stored increases, the solution doesn't slow down during the hash lookup and compare process.

Solutions from different vendors use different hashing algorithms, but the basic process is the same in all solutions. In layperson's terms, the process of *hashing the data* means encrypting it in a way that the resulting output can be guaranteed to be unique. (The last thing you want in a de-duplication solution is to have two different pieces of data with the same hash, since that would cause data corruption.)

Most de-dupe solutions use generally available and well-tested methods to encrypt each file or block of data so that the resulting mathematical hash that represents that file or block is guaranteed to be unique from every other file or block's hash. (See the nearby sidebar on encryption standards.)

Block-level hashing

Block-based solutions work on blocks of data, which is the way data is stored on disk; they don't need information about the files themselves or even the operating system being used. Block-level hashing solutions work with both structured and unstructured data, meaning the data can be stored on disk as files (unstructured) or inside the tables of a database (structured). Because block solutions simply hash each disk block and compare that hash with any new block of data being stored, what type of data it is or where it came from doesn't matter.

Every new block of data being stored goes through the de-duplication solution and is hashed. The new hashes are compared with every other hash in the index. If the new data hash matches a hash for a block that's already stored, the new data isn't stored, thereby eliminating duplicates.

Sub-block-level hashing

Sub-block-level hashing methods work exactly the same way as the block-level methods, but at a more granular level. Sub-block-level hashing is the most common method of data de-duplication used today in large enterprises. Because the chunk size can be very small (bit level, in some cases), the results can be dramatic, and because this process is done at the sub-block level, it can be used across any operating system and on both structured and unstructured data.

Sub-block-level hashing works by slicing up *(chunking)* a block of data into a set of sub-blocks at a specific size (in this case, 16KB each) and creating a unique hash for each slice (or chunk), as shown in Figure 13-3.

16KB Data chunk 1	01afdcb435396758223eac
16KB Data chunk 2	0687fe473298accf5b74d3f
16KB Data chunk 3	1239bdeac57b64f3cde71e
16KB Data chunk 4	775aec678bbcae543981ac
16KB Data chunk 5	01afdcb435396758213eac
16KB Data chunk 6	01afdcb435396758123ecc
16KB Data chunk 7	0787fe47329457ac5b74d3
16KB Data chunk 8	23476bea33bce9985bcaf3

Figure 13-3:
Sub-block-level hashing.

Unique data (75%) 128KB

The original file is 128KB in size.

128KB segmented into 8 x 16KB chunks

The file is divided into 16KB chunks.

Each chunk goes through the algorithm, and is assigned a unique hash.

The hashes are stored in an index so they can be quickly compared to any other hashes to determine if a new chunk of data is unique. In Figure 13-4, the hashes for chunk 1 and chunk 5 are a match, so you can confidently eliminate one of the chunks.

16KB Data chunk 1	01afdcb435396758223eac
16KB Data chunk 2	0687fe473298accf5b74d3f
16KB Data chunk 3	1239bdeac57b64f3cde71e
16KB Data chunk 4	775aec678bbcae543981ac
16KB Data chunk 5	01afdcb435396758213eac
16KB Data chunk 6	01afdcb435396758123ecc
16KB Data chunk 7	0787fe47329457ac5b74d3
16KB Data chunk 8	23476bea33bce9985bcaf3

Figure 13-4:
Hash compare to remove duplicates.

Chunks 1 and 5 are the same, so one can be eliminated.

After you remove the duplicate chunk of data, you replace it with its hash as a pointer so the original data can be reconstituted later. That data now consists of the unique data chunks, plus the hash as a pointer to the original data. In Figure 13-5, this block of data was de-duplicated by 16K, minus the hash (metadata) that makes up the pointers.

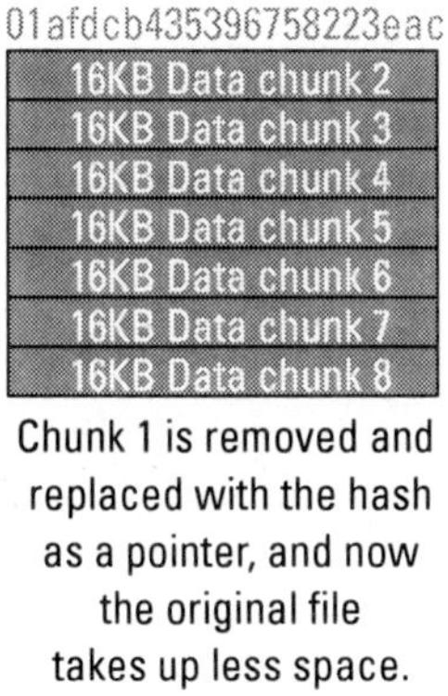

01afdcb435396758223eac

16KB Data chunk 2
16KB Data chunk 3
16KB Data chunk 4
16KB Data chunk 5
16KB Data chunk 6
16KB Data chunk 7
16KB Data chunk 8

Figure 13-5: Chunk 1 is removed and replaced with the hash as a pointer, and now the original file takes up less space.
Data is de-duplicated and stored.

The index table now lists all the hashes, and the hashes point to the unique data, and any chunk of data that was de-duplicated and replaced with a hash pointer. If you need to re-create the original data, the hashes will point to the original data chunks that can be used to re-create the original. In Figure 13-6, the table shows you can use chunk 5 to re-create the original data that was in chunk 1.

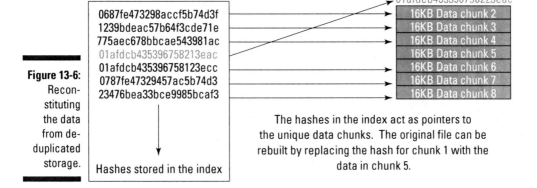

Figure 13-6: Recon-stituting the data from de-duplicated storage.

0687fe473298accf5b74d3f
1239bdeac57b64f3cde71e
775aec678bbcae543981ac
01afdcb435396758213eac
01afdcb435396758123ecc
0787fe47329457ac5b74d3
23476bea33bce9985bcaf3

Hashes stored in the index

01afdcb435396758223eac

16KB Data chunk 2
16KB Data chunk 3
16KB Data chunk 4
16KB Data chunk 5
16KB Data chunk 6
16KB Data chunk 7
16KB Data chunk 8

The hashes in the index act as pointers to the unique data chunks. The original file can be rebuilt by replacing the hash for chunk 1 with the data in chunk 5.

Delta versioning (no-dupe)

Not duplicating data in the first place is the cheapest and most effective method of improving SAN storage efficiency. How do you *not* duplicate data? You monitor the data to make sure data is being stored and moved as efficiently as possible.

Many backup applications have versioning capability, which you may have heard called *incremental* or *differential* backup. (See Chapter 9 for more information on backup methods.) Some backup software (Tivoli Storage Manager is a good example) always uses the versioning method to speed backup. You do a full backup the first time, and from then on, only the changes are stored.

More intelligent file- and block-based monitoring solutions monitor data as it is being stored or replicated, and only store or move the *delta* changes that occur. A delta is an offset of the original data. As an example, take a Microsoft Word document. Suppose that you create a document and save it.

That night, the document gets backed up with all the other files. The next day, you reopen the same document, change a single word, and save it under a different file name. The new file is a version of the first file because the files are basically the same, but the new information in the document (the word you changed) is a delta to the original. If there were a way to monitor the blocks that stored the file as it was written to disk, you would know that the file only changed slightly.

A file-compare de-dupe method would fail here because the file names are different. A backup solution would back up the entire file again, because it looks like a different file to the backup software than the original. Even a file-level hashing solution would probably fail, because the file would be offset by the new data and a new hash would occur. If you needed to replicate the file for disaster recovery, you would also still need a lot of network bandwidth.

Only a delta versioning solution or a full sub-block-level hashing solution would be able to de-duplicate this file:

- **Block-level delta versioning:** This method works by monitoring updates on disk at the block level and storing only the data that changed in relation to the original data. Block-level delta versioning is how snapshots work. Each snapshot contains only the changes to the original data.

  Block-level delta versioning can also reduce data replication requirements for disaster recovery (DR) purposes. Suppose that your company wants to keep the remote data up to date every 6 hours, so you have to replicate changes to the DR location every 6 hours. If a block of data on disk at the local site is updated hundreds of times during the time delta between the last replication and the new one, using a delta versioning solution, only the last update to the block needs to be sent. Delta versioning can greatly reduce the amount of data traveling from the local site to the DR site.

- **Sub-block-level delta versioning:** This method is the same as the block method, but works at the byte level and can be many times more efficient in reducing duplicate data than even block-level versioning. This type of versioning is also known in the industry as *microscanning* (see Figure 13-7).

Replication with Microscan

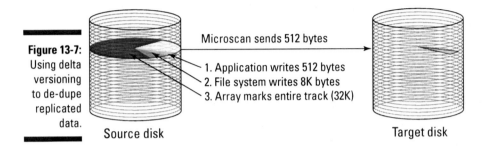

Microscan sends 512 bytes

1. Application writes 512 bytes
2. File system writes 8K bytes
3. Array marks entire track (32K)

Source disk   Target disk

Figure 13-7:
Using delta
versioning
to de-dupe
replicated
data.

In Figure 13-7, using the earlier Microsoft Word example, because you changed only a single word, you probably only need a single 512 byte disk sector to store the changes to the original file. If you used an array-based replication solution to replicate the file for disaster recovery, you would need to replicate an entire 32K disk track (that's the level of granularity that many array-based solutions use). Even a file-system-level monitoring solution would need to replicate the entire 8K write.

Microscan delta versioning monitors changes at a more granular disk sector level (a disk sector is only 512 bytes), so even though the file system needed 8K to write the data, only the 512-byte changed delta would need to be replicated.

Open system servers (Windows, Unix, and Linux) format disks into sectors of 512 bytes. A block of data on a Windows server usually takes up eight 512-byte sectors for each 4KB block of data being stored. Because one of the smallest updates to a disk usually occurs at the sector level, if only one sector is updated, why mark the entire block as updated? A sub-block delta versioning solution that monitors updates at the sector level is eight times more efficient than one that simply tracks block updates, and it can be up to 64 times more efficient for data replication than some array-based solutions that use 32KB tracks as the smallest monitored update.

An update to a single 512-byte sector on a solution that tracks updates at the 32KB track level would need to send the entire track, which represents a lot of *white space* (unused but allocated space) and can be an inefficient use of network bandwidth and storage.

Solutions that monitor the data being updated at a file, block, or sub-block level and store data more efficiently to reduce white space have an advantage over hash-based de-duplication solutions that use hashing methods. Although hashing normally provides better results in reducing the amount of storage required for a particular dataset, because the data is stored as a jumble of mathematical hashes and indexes, you have to reconstitute the data before using it again for your applications.

The reconstitution process to get the data back into a usable format can take a long time in some solutions; test the solution before making a purchasing decision to be sure. However, in delta versioning solutions like snapshots and microscanning, the data is always in the native format of the application and can be used immediately.

In-band versus out-of-band data de-duplication

In-band means the data is de-duplicated *before* it is stored on disk, and out-of-band means the data is stored *after* it is stored on disk.

A holy war is going on in the storage industry about which method of data de-duplication holds the most benefit for the end user. (The same fight is being waged over the methods of storage virtualization; you can read more about that war in Chapter 15.) The war is about *when* the actual de-duplication process takes place:

- ✔ **In-band:** The in-band camp believes that its method is better because it requires users to purchase very little storage. Although the process may cause some overhead to the application while the data is being stored, the benefits of needing less disk space up front outweigh the negatives of the performance hit.

- ✔ **Out-of-band:** The out-of-band (also known as *postprocess*) camp believes that its method is better because it first does no harm. Although more storage may be required up front to act as a *data cache* (a holding area for the data before the de-duplication process is performed), the minimal extra disk requirements outweigh the negative performance effect of doing the de-duplication processing while the data is being stored.

Both camps are right; each method has positives and negatives. The vendors you choose will be more than glad to talk to you about how their methods are better than the other vendors' methods.

In the long run, keep the following information in mind:

- ✔ As your organization grows, the scalability of your solutions becomes more important.
- ✔ When it comes to data de-duplication solutions, the out-of-band method has a better track record in scalability.

Some solutions can perform data de-duplication based on a policy you create. These more-intelligent systems allow you to specify how and when the process should occur, which gives you the opportunity to tune the system to your needs. Some applications have no performance issues and may benefit from in-band de-duplication; others may benefit from a concurrent process, in which only a little extra disk space is needed in the data cache and the data is de-duplicated as soon as possible. For applications such as databases, however, a better choice — one that alleviates performance issues — is a de-duplication process that occurs after the data is stored.

Using Data De-Duplication in a SAN

How you use these techniques to find duplicates in a SAN environment depends on whether your solution de-duplicates data by hashing files or blocks or simply monitors deltas of your data to ensure it is being stored as efficiently as possible.

Files: Honey, I shrunk the files

Most file-based de-duplication solutions use either the delta versioning or file-level hashing technique. Using a file delta versioning solution, you can look inside the files, pull out only the unique data, and store the unique data in conjunction with a link to the original file. The de-duplication solution would store the updates as delta versions of the original file.

Delta versioning has an advantage over hash-based de-duplication in that no reconstitute process is required to get your data back. The data is simply stored more efficiently. As a result, you can shrink the storage required to hold changes to your files and still recover data very rapidly. Snapshot technology is a form of delta versioning.

Some solutions on the market strictly hash entire files and don't bother to look into the file for redundancies. These file-level hashing solutions usually work at the file system level of the operating system. Many of them are implemented as host-based software and are simple to use and deploy.

Blocks: Been there, stored that

The cool thing about block- and sub-block-level hashing is that they can find and remove redundancies in data that otherwise would be considered to be unique.

Think of it this way: In an original document, you probably have multiple instances of the same word. (Consider this chapter to be a document. How many times have I used the words *document* and *hashing* so far?) If you use a hashing algorithm to weed out duplicate information, you probably can even reduce the size of the original.

Why chunk size matters

Size does make a difference in some cases. The size of the chunks of data being hashed to find uniqueness can have a large impact on the speed of the de-duplication process and its results. Some de-duplication vendors use a fixed chunk size to simplify the de-duplication process, make it fast, and keep the size of the hash index to a minimum. By fixing the size of the chunks of data being processed, you can minimize the size of the index and therefore make lookups really fast, but you may miss some opportunity to get a higher de-duplication ratio. Some vendors make up for this missed opportunity by using standard compression after de-duplication, and the results are fairly good.

Hashing with large chunks

Figure 13-8 shows a simple block-based hashing solution with a fixed chunk size of 4KB. Every 4KB chunk sent into the hashing algorithm as an input has a unique output. Even if a single bit or block in the chunk changes, the output remains unique for the entire chunk, and the output hash is always the same size for every chunk of data.

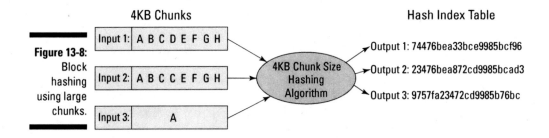

Figure 13-8: Block hashing using large chunks.

The result of the solution shown in Figure 13-8 is that three hashes are stored in the index and all 12KB of data is stored on disk. Because every 4KB block comes out as unique, no de-duplication takes place. Using this chunk size, de-duplication would occur only if another 4KB block showed up with the exact same data as any of the three inputs.

Hashing with small chunks

Now take the data inputs from the preceding section and drop the chunk size from 4KB to 512 bytes. As you see in Figure 13-9, the index grows quite a bit, with eight hashes instead of one for every 4KB of data. So for the three inputs, now you have 24 hashes, with each hash representing one of the 512-byte chunks of each input. But look at what you can actually de-dupe! Because you shrank the hashing-algorithm chunks to sub-block level, you can actually de-dupe within a block, not just across blocks.

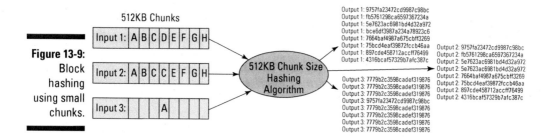

Figure 13-9:
Block
hashing
using small
chunks.

Following is the result of this process:

- ✔ All the outputs for input 1 are unique, and each object must be stored.
- ✔ Two of the objects in input 2 match, and one can be removed (the C block).
- ✔ Seven of the objects in input 3 match, and six can be eliminated; one of the objects matches an object in input 1 and also input 2, and can be removed (the A block).

The results for de-dupe are much better now, because you need to store only one section of blank space from input 3 and one each of blocks A through H (see Figure 13-10).

Stored Results Using 4KB Chunks = 12KB

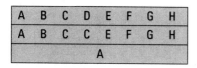

Stored Results Using 512-byte Chunks = 1 x 4KB block and 1 x 512 byte sector

Figure 13-10:
Storing the
results.

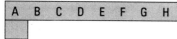

Simply by dropping the chunk size from 4KB to 512 bytes — which is the size of a disk sector and one of the smallest updates you can write to a Logical Unit Number (LUN) — you reduce the space required to store the same amount of data from 12KB to 4608 bytes. The de-dupe ratio for this example is about 2.6:1.

The trade-off is the size of the index table and the number of entries required. As you see in Figure 13-11, fewer hashes are required when you use larger blocks; therefore, the index table will be smaller and faster. On the other hand, your de-dupe ratio is not as efficient when you use larger blocks.

Always ask your vendor whether its solution is tunable based on your policies, so that you can determine whether you want to use more disk space and fewer hash entries to get a faster solution, or use less disk space and more hash entries to get a solution that is a bit slower but generates much better de-dupe ratios. Creating a policy is especially useful for solutions that work out of band; because performance is less of an issue (the backup job is already complete) you can use more time but get a better de-dupe ratio by using smaller chunks.

Hash Updates to Index Table Using 4KB Chunks = 3 Entries

Hash Entries in Index Table Using 512-byte Chunks = 24 Entries

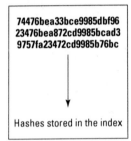

Figure 13-11:
Hash index table entries using different data chunk sizes.

What about hash collisions?

A hash collision isn't a traffic accident, but it could have the same ramifications for your business. A *hash collision* happens when the resulting hashes for two unique chunks of data are the same. Data de-duplication finds redundancy by hashing blocks of data and comparing the hashes to determine whether two data blocks are the same or unique. In this example, two similar inputs would have the same output, and the compare operation would determine that because the two inputs are the same, one can be deleted. The problem with a hash collision is that if the two inputs are different but the output is the same (hash collision), and one of the inputs is deleted, you could lose data.

The following examples involve the MD5 hashing algorithm, which uses a 128-bit hash made from 32 hexadecimal digits. The resulting hash for two matching blocks of data is the same. To keep things simple, the examples use letters of the alphabet.

Example 1: Hash match, data is redundant

In this example, you input two letters (two As) into the algorithm:

> Hash for Letter A = A4BEC893BEE67418975BEAAC53298721
>
> Hash for Letter A = A4BEC893BEE67418975BEAAC53298721

The resulting hashes match, so the letters are duplicates, and one can be eliminated. Everyone's happy.

Example 2: Hash match, data is unique (hash collision)

In this example, you input two letters (A and B) into the algorithm, and the resulting hashes collide:

> Hash for Letter A = A4BEC893BEE67418975BEAAC53298721
>
> Hash for Letter B = A4BEC893BEE67418975BEAAC53298721

Because the hashes match, the algorithm thinks you can eliminate one of the letters, but that would result in the loss of data. The algorithm is in error.

The probability of a hash collision actually happening using 128-bit hash is virtually nil, so you should not worry. As an example, compare the probability of a hash collision with other ludicrously unlikely events:

- ✔ The chance of a killer asteroid striking our planet at any given minute and wiping out most life on Earth is roughly 1 in 10^{13}, so it's more probable than a hash collision.

- ✔ Using a combined hash of MD5 and SHA-1, the possibility of a hash collision is about as likely as purchasing eight consecutive winning lottery tickets. So while you're counting your money while you wait for the asteroid to hit, you can be reassured in the fact that at least your data is safe. In other words, chill out about hash collisions.

The simple fact that hash collisions are possible, though, causes de-duplication vendors to trash the competition, trying to scare you away from Vendor A and Vendor B because they may lose your data. Although the probability of a hash collision in solutions from any of the de-dupe vendors is very low, it is still a statistical possibility that it could happen.

As the size of any de-duplication repository increases, so does the statistical probability of a hash collision, however small. (I think you have about a 50/50 chance of a hash collision when your de-duplicated repository is holding 16 trillion petabytes, where a petabyte equals 1000 terabytes.) Vendors take many precautions to ensure that hash collisions don't happen, however; some of them run compare operations down to the bit level just to make sure that everything is cool before they store data.

Why Data De-Duplication Is Important

Data de-duplication goes a long way toward reducing data storage costs by making storage much more efficient. Data de-duplication solutions can be implemented in many places, with data backup and archives being among the most important. The more data you have, and the longer you need to retain it for business reasons or regulatory purposes (known as the retention schedule), the better results you see from your data de-duplication solution.

Figure 13-12 shows a sample dataset of 20TB (terabytes) being backed up over 5 weeks, with typical data growth and change rates.

If you use a traditional backup solution to back up the data to media (disk or tape) with no de-duplication, as shown in Figure 13-12, you'll need to store more than 101TB of data in only 5 weeks.

Now consider a solution that de-duplicates the same amount of data. As you see in Figure 13-13, the media requirements drop significantly while still conforming to the same retention schedule. (*Retention schedule* is the technical term for how long you need to keep data around before you can overwrite it with new data.)

Why De-dupe Is Important: Without De-dupe

Sample parameters:
Data volume = 20TB; 2% growth, 3% change weekly
Retention = 5 weeks

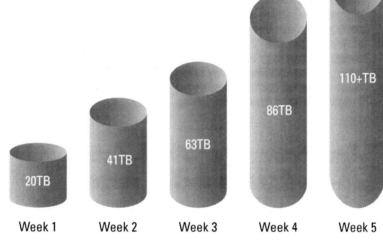

Figure 13-12:
Media require-ments for backing up 20TB of data without de-duplication.

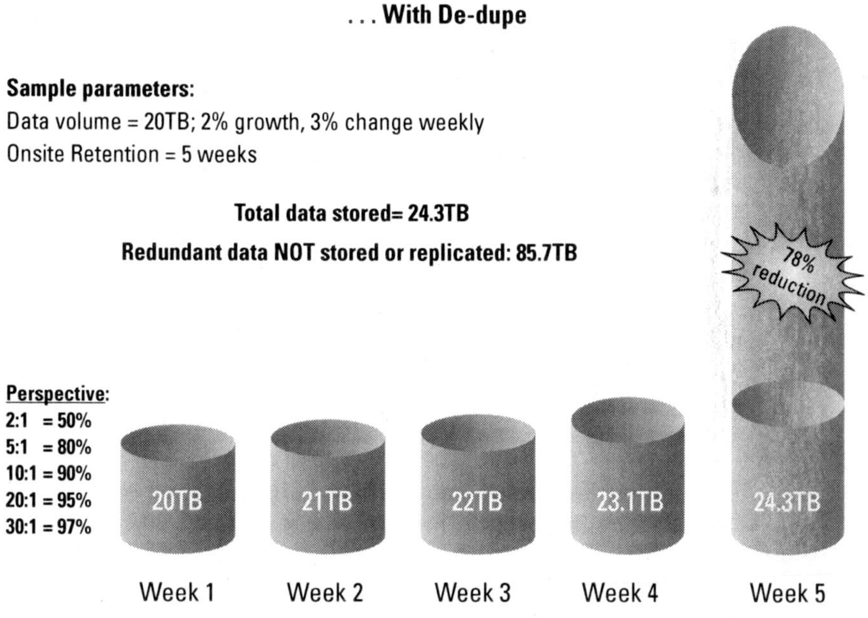

20TB — Week 1
41TB — Week 2
63TB — Week 3
86TB — Week 4
110+TB — Week 5

. . . With De-dupe

Sample parameters:
Data volume = 20TB; 2% growth, 3% change weekly
Onsite Retention = 5 weeks

Total data stored= 24.3TB

Redundant data NOT stored or replicated: 85.7TB

78% reduction

Figure 13-13:
Media require-ments for backing up 20TB of data with de-duplication.

Perspective:
2:1 = 50%
5:1 = 80%
10:1 = 90%
20:1 = 95%
30:1 = 97%

20TB — Week 1
21TB — Week 2
22TB — Week 3
23.1TB — Week 4
24.3TB — Week 5

When to Use Data De-Dupe (And When Not To)

Data de-duplication is best applied when it doesn't affect the performance of your production applications or the process you're trying to complete, such as backup. Using de-duplication in backup applications can save a lot of money that you'd otherwise have to spend for media, but using de-dupe *during* backup may not be such a great idea, especially if you need to reduce your backup windows while saving money on media. (See Chapter 9 for more information on backup windows.) This section focuses on which applications benefit the most from data de-duplication.

Applications for which data de-duplication makes sense

Data de-duplication solutions work best wherever their results can save the company some money. De-duplication has the greatest impact in three areas:

- Data backup
- Data replication
- Data retention

Why? If you de-duplicate data for your clients, you don't need to send as much data over your LAN (local area network) or WAN (wide area network) for remote-office consolidation and data backup. If you store less data at the local site because the clients send less data to the SAN, you don't need to replicate a lot of data or store a lot of data for disaster recovery.

In the following sections, I tackle these areas in a bit more detail.

Data backup

Backup is the killer app in a SAN and also one of the best places to apply data de-duplication. In fact, backup is where most vendors focus their de-duplication solutions. Almost all VTL solutions include data de-duplication.

With client-based solutions, you have to have at least one full backup, but from then on, nothing moves if nothing is changed, and only the changes move when they do occur. When all the changed data is stored in the SAN, you can send all of it to an appliance for further de-duplication or back it up (using your existing backup software) to a VTL that can de-duplicate your data globally, so that only a single instance of each chunk is stored.

Some solutions that work at the client may still need to send duplicate files to a central appliance before the duplicate files are eliminated; others are more intelligent and communicate with the client to ensure that the only objects sent are those that don't already exist at the central site. Make sure that your solution is in the latter category; otherwise, you may end up spending more than necessary on WAN bandwidth for remote client backup.

Data replication

One of the highest expenses for data replication is the WAN bandwidth needed to move all data changes to a DR site. (You can find more information on DR in Chapter 6.) The more data you have to replicate, the more bandwidth you need to move it. Many companies try to reduce their costs by replicating only specific mission-critical datasets or by using lower-bandwidth links and living with the amount of time it takes to get the data to the other side.

When companies need to move massive amounts of data for disaster recovery, it makes a lot of sense to de-duplicate the data so it can be replicated more efficiently using a less costly network. Delta versioning solutions work great for reducing the amount of data that has to be moved and still enable you to recover your applications very rapidly for DR.

Data retention

Long-term archiving is another wonderful opportunity to lower storage costs by storing only one instance of everything in the archive. Suppose that you need to keep data around for 5 weeks (as shown in Figure 13-12, earlier in this chapter). Would you rather have to buy 101TB worth of tapes or just a bit over 24TB to store the same amount of data?

VTL solutions with de-duplication provide a great way to store your data on disk in de-duplicated format for long periods. If you need to conform to regulatory requirements and store your data in immutable format, make sure that your solution also can store data in WORM (Write Once Read Many) format.

WORM tape is a good solution for compliance; it takes no power, can hold a great deal of data, is removable, and is fairly inexpensive.

Applications for which data de-duplication doesn't make sense

Frequently accessed production databases are the worst place to use data de-duplication. Imagine trying to keep performance up while each write operation to the database disks must be preceded by a hash process to store the new data, and each read request must be preceded by an operation that reconstitutes the data so that the application can use it. Not a good idea. Use deduplication on the database when you back it up and leave production alone.

De-Duplication in Action

Consider an example of de-duplication in action. A company has a fairly large central datacenter and two or three remote offices. It can't afford to build its own DR site, so it outsources that function to a third-party provider by renting rack space at a major telephone company. Because the provider charges by the square foot of floor space, as well as by the amount of data being sent and stored in the rack, data de-duplication would be a perfect way for the company to save money.

The company ended up with a complete solution that did the following:

✔ The host-based software enabled client-side versioning so only very small deltas of the company's data had to be moved over the network to the central datacenter.

✔ Because the data was versioned and not hashed, the data was stored in native application format locally for instant recovery by using snapshots with based delta versioning and microscanning.

✔ After all the data was captured (including the deltas) at the central datacenter, it was backed up to a Virtual Tape Library that included hash-based de-duplication of all the data to remove redundancies between files and blocks. The VTL was able to store all its data in a de-duplicated format on disk in only 5 percent of the original space (achieving a dedupe ratio of 20:1 with the VTL).

✔ After everything was globally de-duplicated for efficiency, the company was able to replicate it to another datacenter using 1/20th of the bandwidth previously needed.

✔ The solution operated so efficiently and reduced so much complexity and cost, the company was able to provide a much better service level agreement (SLA) for data availability for all its applications and platforms (even remote offices, laptops, and desktops) and across all physical and virtual servers, so everyone was given a raise, and they all lived happily ever after. (Don't you love a happy ending?)

Chapter 14

Continuous Data Protection

. . . .

. . . .

*I*n this chapter, you find out how to use recent innovations in data protection to make protecting your data easier and more efficient. Continuous data protection enables you to shift your focus from backing up your data to recovering data faster and more efficiently and, perhaps, avoid the possibility of data loss all together.

Understanding What Continuous Data Protection Is

With CDP *(Continuous Data Protection)*, your data is always protected, so you don't need to do backups. CDP can protect every write to a disk, so it's one of the only solutions that can protect your applications from any data loss and can rapidly recover your applications from disk. Because everything is continually protected to disk instead of tape, CDP greatly enhances your recovery point objective (RPO) and recovery time objective (RTO).

Continuous Data Protection (CDP) is one of the more interesting recent advances in SAN technologies for backing up data. With traditional backup solutions, the backup process is performed once or twice a day at the most, and therefore can only provide the ability to recover data to one or two specific points in time. A traditional backup process can take a long time to complete, because it has to move data from one place to another (either to tape or another disk). CDP is different than backup, because there is no backup process, and there is no bulk data movement that must occur. CDP is just always on, like a service.

The amount of time it takes for the backup job to complete is called the *backup window*. During a normal backup job, data is read from production disks and then backed up to either a disk or tape target. Because it has to access production storage, a traditional backup can affect the performance of production applications while the process is running. This is why most backups are scheduled to run at night during the backup window when less business is being conducted, and the impact can be minimized. Because time is a critical factor in today's always-on data centers, the backup window and backups in general are becoming more of a problem for many organizations. Solving the backup problem by using CDP is what this chapter is about.

How CDP Makes Storage Work Like a Database

I know you didn't buy this book to become a database expert, but since CDP relies on some of the same principles that databases use to protect data efficiently and reliably, I need to cover some basic database concepts. If you have worked with a database application, you probably understand the concept of a *transaction log* and a database file. If not, don't worry, I try to explain how a database works in simple terms.

A database update can be made up of several read and write operations bundled into a *transaction*. A transaction is completed fully or not at all. For example, suppose you want to take some money out of an ATM, but you are on vacation in Europe and your bank is in the United States. The bank associated with the ATM you are using requires the money be transmitted to a European entity before dispensing in the ATM machine. This entire process is done as a single transaction; if any part of the transaction fails due to a network failure between where you are and your bank in the United States, the transaction is rolled back as though it never happened.

The ability of the databases involved in this complex transaction to recover from errors is a good thing for you and your money. The ability to roll data backward or forward to ensure that transactions are completed properly is called *atomicity*.

For database solutions to protect themselves from issues, database transactions must be *atomic*, that is, the data must be updated in such a way that if the update fails, the update to the data can be *rolled back*, or removed. If any part of a transaction fails, all other parts of the transaction must be rolled back. The CDP process also relies on this fundamental database principal to roll changes back to a point in time.

When writing data to disk, most relational databases use a discrete function called *transaction logging,* or *journaling writes.* Before data is written to the database, all writes are stored in a transaction log (journal) until the entire transaction is completed. The transaction log is like a temporary staging area where all information is held until everything checks out. Once everything is completed properly, the information in the staging area (transaction log) is applied to the database and stored. Because the log holds every update to the database, the transaction log file gets bigger over time.

Database administrators have control over the size of the transaction log files and when they are *committed* in the database. (A transaction is considered committed when it is written from the log file to the database file on disk.) The larger the size of the transaction log, the more data it can hold and the longer you can go back to recover any changes. After all the completed transactions in the transaction log are committed to the database, space is freed in the log for more transactions.

To protect against losing both the transaction logs and the database, best practices are to keep the transaction log areas on physical disks separate from the database itself. In addition, since writes to the transaction log are usually random in nature, they are usually stored on faster, higher-performing disks than the disks for the database itself.

 A CDP and database best practice is to use RAID 1 or RAID 10 for the CDP journal or log, and RAID 5 for everything else. Databases can be recovered from the data in the logs if required, so this is why you keep the database and the log separate.

Now that you have a basic understanding about how databases work, you can apply that new knowledge to how CDP solutions work.

CDP data journaling

As mentioned, when data is written to a database, it always goes into the log, or journal, area first, until the entire transaction is complete. This way, if the transaction fails for any reason, the information can be rolled back without affecting the database. CDP solutions do the same thing for updates to disk drives. In a CDP solution, all updates to the disk are split off and written to both the primary LUN and the CDP journal area at the same time, as shown in Figure 14-1. This ability to multiplex writes to both the CDP journal and the production storage is the job of the write splitter agent. (A *multiplexed write operation* simply means writing to both places at the same time in one operation.)

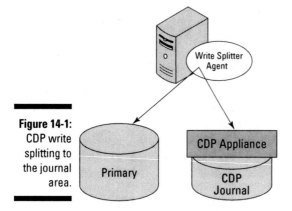

Figure 14-1:
CDP write
splitting to
the journal
area.

The CDP journal captures and holds all the updates in the sequence in which they were written. If the journal is large enough, it can store all updates that occur to the disk for days at a time. (You find out how to size the CDP journal later in this chapter.) Because all the updates are held in the journal in the same time sequence in which they occurred, you can "rewind the writes" from the journal back to the production disk to any point in time.

Splitting the writes

For CDP to do its thing, you need to capture and protect every write that goes into the SAN for a protected server, and store all the writes from that server in the CDP journal. The process of getting every write to the journal is called *write splitting*. The process of getting the writes to the journal can be performed in a number of different ways. You can use a host-based write splitter agent on the server itself, or use an appliance connected to the fabric switches to mirror all writes to the journal.

You can also buy more advanced switches that can perform the write split function in the fabric itself. (Cisco SANtap is an example.) Some storage arrays can copy data directly to a journal using firmware functions in the array (like Hitachi Shadow Image software in a Universal Storage Platform array) and by simply using a host-based logical volume manager to mirror the writes over the SAN or an iSCSI connection to the CDP appliance.

The write split process can occur in two ways:

- ✔ In-band, which means the write split happens in the primary data path. (The fabric appliance can be an in-band solution.)
- ✔ Out-of-band, which means the write split happens outside the primary data path.

Each approach has benefits and trade-offs.

CDP solutions that use host-based write splitters use a software-based host agent to split writes off to the journal, so they can recover only writes that were performed by that specific application or server. Host-based write splitting is considered an out-of-band approach. (Refer to Figure 14-1 for an example of a host-based write splitter.)

CDP solutions that use fabric-based write splitters at the SAN fabric level capture all writes by all applications attached to the SAN, and usually use functionality in the SAN switches themselves to split off and route all protected writes to the CDP journal (see Figure 14-2). Oddly enough, fabric-based splitting is also considered an out-of-band approach because the primary write is not intercepted; it is just copied by the SAN switches and routed to the CDP solution. Cisco's SANtap solution is an example of a fabric-based write splitter.

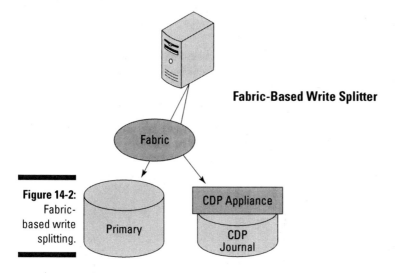

Figure 14-2:
Fabric-based write splitting.

Appliance-based write splitting captures all writes going through the appliance and splits them off to the CDP appliance (see Figure 14-3). This solution removes the write-splitting function from the servers or the SAN switches. Using an in-band appliance means all the writes must go through the appliance before being stored in the primary array. The need to go through an appliance may cause concern for some because the appliance is in the primary data path. These appliances can usually be clustered to alleviate these concerns. Appliance-based splitting in the data path is considered an in-band solution. Using an in-band method may have some advantages though, such as the ability to simply mirror data to any storage, which would ease refreshing storage technologies and reduce downtime when migrating data!

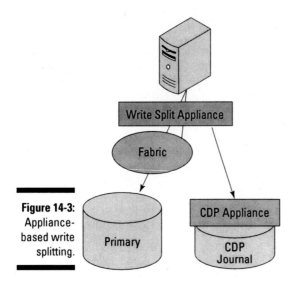

Figure 14-3:
Appliance-based write splitting.

Using the storage array to split off writes allows the CDP solution to sit beside the array and out of the primary data path. Also, using array-based write splitting (see Figure 14-4) can be simpler and cheaper than having to buy proprietary write splitter blades for your SAN switches, and eliminates the load of splitting writes from the server. (A *blade* is a SAN switch component that is inserted into a slot in the switch chassis and performs a specific function.) Some storage arrays (from Hitachi, Sun, and HP) have the ability to connect to external storage, so you can use the internal array copy functions and hook up the CDP solution external to the array.

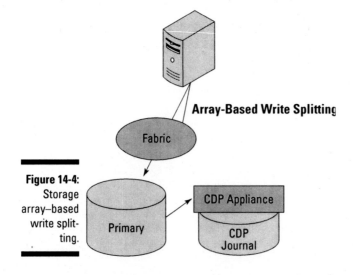

Figure 14-4:
Storage array–based write splitting.

CDP makes everything different

One major advantage of CDP solutions versus traditional backup methods is the ability to create a consistency group across entire applications. (A *consistency group* is a group of LUNS that are recovered together at the same time.) Many applications have multiple tiers or components that need to be recovered to the same point in time, and the ability to create a consistency group across storage platforms and application servers can simplify the recovery of complex applications. CDP solutions usually are implemented as appliances that attach to both the SAN fabric and the network, so they can accept write splits of data from both SAN-attached servers and non-SAN-attached servers. Being able to capture writes from anywhere means you can create a CDP consistency group across all the servers that make up an entire multitiered application, as shown in Figure 14-5.

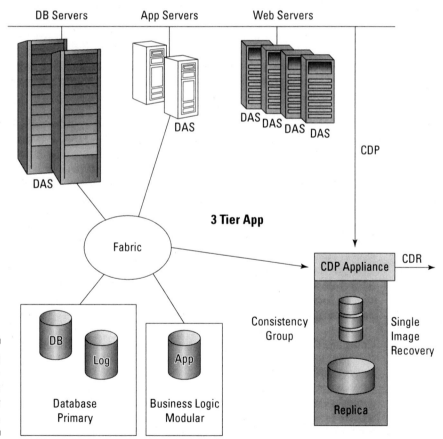

Figure 14-5:
Cross-platform consistency grouping.

Figure 14-5 depicts a typical three-tier application where the application has multiple components, or tiers: a database tier, an application logic tier, and a Web server tier. Multi-tier applications typically can also use a tiered storage environment within the SAN, where the database gets its storage from fast and expensive enterprise storage arrays, and the application logic part of the application uses a less expensive modular array. The Web front end to the application is usually not even connected to the SAN, so it uses its own internal direct attached storage (DAS) in the server itself. The other servers use their own DAS storage to hold the servers' operating system.

If one of the components in the application fails, it's fairly easy to stop the entire application, recover the failed component using traditional methods (such as tape backup), and then start the application back up at a specific point in time that matches either the time of the backup or where the other components in the application were at the time of the failure.

For the application to recover from a disaster in which parts of the application may have been stopped at different points in time though (sometimes known as a *rolling disaster*), you need to bring up all the parts of the application at the same point in time. This can be a difficult undertaking and is one of the reasons why disaster recovery can be so hard for large complex applications that have many components or rely on data updates from other applications.

To recover these complex applications when using regular tape backup, each part must be recovered individually from a backup tape, and then someone must coordinate bringing up each component of the application in the proper order. Even if you use snapshot technology in the arrays or on the servers, you need to make sure that each component was snapshot at the exact same time for data consistency since the components of the application span multiple storage arrays and server platforms. This type of coordinated snapshot usually requires an external atomic clock mechanism.

Some companies have to go through complex and expensive *application interoperability* studies and *critical records analysis* of their data to create a coordinated recovery process for complex applications. Consultants can charge tons of money for this type of study. But CDP can make recovery of complex applications a simple process.

Using the CDP appliance as the external atomic clock that coordinates everything at the fabric and network levels, you can implement write splitters in the fabric and at the hosts to capture all the writes to a central journal (shown as the replica to the right in Figure 14-5) and create a consistency group across all the tiers of the application. When the CDP solution says go, it talks to the agents on each host, tells the agents to put everything into hot backup mode, flushes system memory and file system caches to disk, and then stops all writes.

Once all the data is synchronized to the CDP appliance, the CDP solution can take a snapshot of all the pieces of the application at the same time (shown as the snapshots labeled M, T, W, for Monday, Tuesday, and Wednesday, respectively). Because everything was snapped at the same time, everything can be recovered at the same time automatically. Simple. If the CDP solution also supports data replication, the snapshots can also be replicated to a disaster recovery site so that even in a major disaster, all the components of the application can be recovered to the same point in time at the disaster recovery site.

Sizing a CDP journal

A CDP journal is like a movie camera. When you press the record button on the movie camera, you are capturing everything that happens in front of the lens. After you press the stop button, you can rewind the tape and "go back in time" to review what you just recorded. The bigger the tape, the longer you can record, and the longer you can go back in time. So just as a database can recover itself by replaying the updates stored in the database journal over the last good backup, a good CDP solution can recover the production storage to a known good point in time by rolling back to just before the problem occurred.

The size of your CDP journal determines the length of time you can store any updates to the disk, and therefore how many hours or days you can roll back to should something go wrong. You need to know the following when sizing a CDP journal:

- ✔ **Time:** How far back you want to recover
- ✔ **Average write rate:** How much data is written in a given time
- ✔ **Number of servers to protect:** This is the division factor

Suppose you have 10 database servers that you would like to protect for 2 days to any point in time. You gathered the SAN statistics for these servers by collecting historical write information in the SAN switches, and you know the write rate across all 10 servers averages to about 100MB/second through the SAN.

You can create a formula from these three statistics to average the size of the journal on a per server basis based in gigabytes required per hour of protection. (*Note:* You need to multiply the average writes by 3.6 to convert megabytes per second to gigabytes per hour.)

The formula for average journal size per server is

```
(write rate average x 3.6) x (time in hours to journal) / (number of servers)
```

For example:

```
100MB/s x 3.6 = 360 GB/hour x 48 hours = 17280GB / 10 = 1728GB per server
```

To store two days' worth of writes across 10 servers that are writing data at 100MB/second for 2 days, you will need about 17.3TB worth of disk space for the journals. If you divide that number by the 10 servers, you get about 1.7TB per server for 2 days worth of protection to any point in time. That's a lot of disk space, which is why CDP journaling can be expensive for many applications and why CDP is best used for the most critical servers, where any data loss is a problem.

Using the preceding formula, you can see that storing only the last 2 hours in the journal requires 720GB for all 10 servers [(100 × 3.6) × 2] which comes to 72GB per server. Sizing the journal for the last 2 hours and using hourly snapshots allow you to recover to the last good write, and up to any hour after the first 2 hours from a snapshot.

Some CDP solutions (like from FalconStor) get around the storage requirement issue by using snapshots in conjunction with CDP journaling. These solutions simply journal the last few hours of data and then use snapshots on a periodic or hourly basis. If you do a good job monitoring your applications, you will probably notice within a few hours when something is wrong, missing, or broken, so you can recover from the journal or the snapshot.

If you want to use CDP journaling because you want a recovery point objective (RPO) of 0 (no data loss), you most likely want to get to the last good write, and not something from 2 days, 6 hours, and 23 minutes ago. If your CDP solution has the ability to take periodic snapshots in conjunction with journaling all writes, you can use the snapshots to recover from a consistent point really fast, or just use the journal to roll back to a recovery point right before the incident occurred.

Most snapshot solutions can handle about 255 snapshots per LUN, and since snapshots usually use storage space efficiently, you can use the snapshots with the CDP journal to go back in time to the last few hours, and also any hour within the last 255 hours (about 11 days). You can lengthen the time between snapshots to get about 30 days' worth of recovery points, which is an awesome solution to replace tape backup for both data recovery and longer term data archiving.

Best Practices for Storage When Configuring CDP Solutions

When using CDP technologies, where the data journal and any full copies of the data are stored can affect recovery time, and even whether the data can be recovered at all. CDP journals should be treated just like a database journal and stored separately from the primary data. If the solution you choose can leverage a different storage array than your primary array, that is even better.

In a CDP solution, the journal area is created on separate disks apart from the production data. All data writes or updates written to the primary disks are written simultaneously to the CDP journal. This is why CDP recovery is similar to database recovery. All data writes from your applications are written to the journal area away from your production data. A copy of the writes exists in the journal exactly as they were written to the production LUN. If a problem occurs or someone deletes data by mistake, the CDP journal can recover or roll back the production data to a known good point in time just before the delete occurred.

If the journal had been stored on the same disks as the production LUN and you lost the disks, you would also lose the journal. To make sure that the CDP journal can run at the same speed as the production disks, some CDP solutions use the same storage array as the production LUNs, as shown in Figure 14-6.

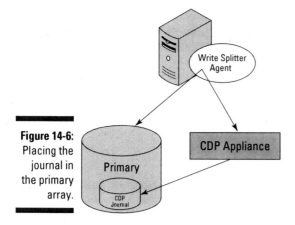

Figure 14-6: Placing the journal in the primary array.

With the journal on disks of the same speed as production disks, the CDP journal can keep up with production writes. The trade-off is that if the production array goes south, you can't recover anything. In these circumstances, having a tape backup of everything still makes a lot of sense.

If your CDP solution is fast enough to keep up with the primary writes, you should always place the journal external to the primary array, as shown in Figure 14-7.

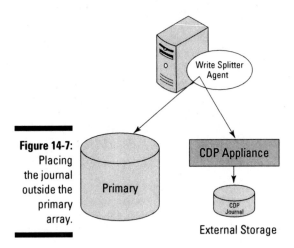

Figure 14-7:
Placing the journal outside the primary array.

Some CDP solutions use the memory in the CDP appliance as a fast write cache so they can keep up with those expensive monolithic storage arrays from EMC, Hitachi, IBM, HP, Sun, and others. Being able to keep the journal on less expensive external storage also makes the CDP solution less expensive to buy and implement.

The Truth about Near CDP and True CDP Solutions

Continuous data protection is different than normal backups. In the following examples, you will see how different data protection solutions — traditional backups, snapshots, near CDP, and true CDP — recover data to a known good point in time, and how each method differs.

Example 1: Recovering a database with traditional backup

Most databases are self healing in most circumstances, in that they can use their transaction logs to either roll the database back to the last known good update or roll the log forward into the database to the last good stored, complete atomic transaction.

For example, consider a financial database that tracks all updates to the stock market. Millions of updates occur all day long to the database, and when the market fluctuates, updates can happen so fast that the database must perform over 100,000 I/O operations per second (100,000 IOPS). Consider what would happen if during one of those moments, a malicious hacker breaks in and in a split second causes the deletion of a massive amount of data, and the database crashes.

Assume that during that second, one of those 100,000 transactions was you sitting at your desk selling 10,000 shares of stock for $100 a share through your broker. (Nice chunk of change!) When the crash occurred, word immediately got out that a hacker broke into the stock exchange and deleted huge amounts of financial information. This news causes a panic, and the market plunges, causing the value of your stock to drop by 50 percent. (I know, this sounds more like a Tom Clancy novel, but bear with me; I'm getting to the point.) The way the database in this scenario was protected would have a profound effect on what happens to your critical transaction!

Simply using normal database capabilities and data protection methods, the database administrator could probably recover most of the data by doing a tape restore from the previous night's backup and applying any saved data in the logs to recover forward to the last good transaction that occurred right before the attack. The news would get out that all is well, and you would cross your fingers and hope that your transaction was one of those that was saved and recovered from the logs.

So that's a pretty good example for traditional backup with database recovery. But what if all the data in the database log files were also deleted by the hacker? In that case, the database administrator could recover only the data to whatever was contained in the most recent backup. Since the last backup was probably done last night, in this example your transaction of selling those 10,000 shares at $100 would be lost, and you would now be the proud owner of 10,000 shares of stock worth $50 instead of $100, and would be out $500,000! Not good. So what would happen if the database was protected by snapshot backups?

Example 2: Recovering a database from a snapshot

Since snapshots happen so fast and no copy operation really occurs (only the metadata [pointers] are captured in the snapshot; see Chapter 10 for more on snapshot backups), snapshots can be taken more frequently than traditional backups, which means you can protect your data more frequently. In the stock market scenario in the preceding section, if a snapshot was taken right after your transaction, your transaction data would not have been lost and you would be $500,000 richer. If the snapshot was taken just before the attack, however, you would be right back in the same boat as before. Snapshot solutions usually max out at about 255 snapshots per LUN. This is where CDP comes in. Continuous protection provides many more recovery points than just snapshots.

The benefits of CDP are most apparent when even the smallest amount of data loss could have a high financial impact on you or your company.

Example 3: Recovering a database using near CDP

Near CDP, unlike regular CDP, does not journal *every* write. The protection is not continuous but periodic at very short time intervals. In most cases, near CDP solutions create an up-to-the-second Point-in-Time copy (snapshot) of the data, and store those frequent snapshots in a separate pool area or journal. If something happens, near CDP solutions can recover the data to any *second* in time. For many applications, this is good enough. But for database applications that can perform hundreds or thousands of I/O operations or transactions per second, a near CDP solution cannot recover the transactional data that occurred within the second. If you were writing 100,000 transactions per second and using a near CDP solution, you would still lose 999,999 transactions. Let's hope the folks at the stock exchange used the right solution for the job.

Example 4: Recovering a database using true CDP

True CDP solutions capture and record every write and split off those writes into a journal. Because *every* write is captured, *any* write can be recovered to *any* point in time. True CDP solutions can work at the sub-second level and provide a view for all the writes that occurred within the second. Recovery can be to any individual write operation within the second. If the stock market database was protected using a true CDP solution in the scenario, all the data would be completely protected, and there would be zero data loss. All transactions that occurred to the exact point in time right before the hacker whacked the data would be recoverable, even if the entire database and all the transaction logs were lost.

CDP versus Snapshots

Where CDP is like a movie camera, capturing everything that happens at all times, snapshots are like pictures, where information is captured at a point in time (see Figure 14-8). The concept of snapshots and near CDP versus true CDP has huge implications for data recovery for critical databases. If you delete a file on a disk by mistake, you can easily use a snapshot to recover back to a point in time before the deletion occurred. Because near CDP can take a snapshot every second, you can recover to the exact second before the deletion, which is pretty darn good. But if you need to recover to the level of a single transaction (such as your stock purchase) for an application writing at 100,000 transactions per second, you need true CDP.

Figure 14-8: CDP versus near CDP and snapshots.

CDP: Rewind to *any* point in time   Snapshot: Select *a* point in time

Snapshots can sometimes have an advantage over CDP solutions that do not have the ability to integrate with the applications they are protecting. Most snapshot solutions come with an intelligent application agent or script that runs on the server they are protecting to record the snapshot event. The agents can force the application into a *hot backup mode* (see the chapter on backup for more on this), which flushes any in-memory or cached transactions to disk and pauses any new writes to the disk while the snapshot process takes place.

Because the snapshot takes place with the full knowledge and cooperation of the application, all the data in the snapshot is in a consistent state. There is no need for file system checks or recovery processes when using the snapshot to recover. Some CDP solutions also have this ability to work with the application (check with your vendor), but others simply track writes only at the disk level, and because they are not "application integrated," recovery from the CDP journal may require an application or file system consistency check prior to being able to bring the application back online. So in some instances, snapshot recovery can be faster than CDP recovery, but the trade-off is data loss. Some CDP solutions get around the consistency issue by using a generic marker that adds an entry into the CDP solution through an agent or a script whenever the database does a checkpoint.

Using CDP to Eliminate Backups

Think about this: If every write from an application is being captured and protected in a CDP journal, isn't that much better than running a backup job to tape every night? The answer is absolutely yes! But to use CDP as a replacement for backup, you need to consider the following:

✔ Backup implies a full copy of your data, so you need to be sure your CDP solution can also create and access a complete replica, or R1, copy someplace else.

✔ Tape backups are also sometimes used to ship data off-site for disaster recovery. If you want to replace tape all together, you need to be sure that your CDP solution can also efficiently replicate your data to another site. If the solution can combine CDP for recovery and data de-duplication to reduce storage and WAN costs, then you have nirvana.

Most CDP solutions available today have the capability to replicate data to a disaster recovery location. And as the technology matures, vendors are realizing that although more storage may be required, having a full copy available locally can be a good thing from a recovery standpoint.

Even if you are protecting every write of a specific LUN in a journal, the journal would never usually contain a copy of every sector of a disk. For example, suppose that something happens to the first disk sector, known as sector 0. It would look like someone erased the disk, even though the disk would be missing only one sector. Sector 0 is usually touched only when the disk is formatted, so it would never have been updated and stored in a journal. Even though only a single sector would be missing, the journal would be useless, and you would need to recover the disk from a full backup, which would probably be on tape. When CDP needs to recover a full disk, it relies on either the primary disk or a replica (R1) copy for the data not stored in the journal.

If the data is not available in the primary disk due to a disk failure or other error, recovery is not possible. This is why having a full copy stored separate from the primary storage array makes a lot of sense; that copy should be local, if possible, so the WAN network would not be required for recovery.

Five things to know about CDP

Having a CDP journal is nice, but it's not a full backup. If you lost any data on the production LUNs that was not captured in the journal, you would not be able to recover. With CDP solutions, you need another complete copy of your data somewhere.

To keep up with all the writes, the disks used for the CDP journal usually need to be just as fast as your production LUNs. Some CDP solutions can bypass this requirement by using memory caches or other proprietary innovations. Make sure you know how your CDP vendor accomplishes this task.

Some CDP solutions can only journal writes and do not keep a full copy of data locally, in what is known as a replica, or R1, copy. Not having a full local *copy* available to recover data means the CDP solution cannot be used as a real backup.

Some CDP solutions integrate with your applications and some do not. If the solution does integrate with the application, the application can "see" the journal and use it for valid recovery points. If the solution is not integrated, the best you will get is crash recoverability from the journal.

True CDP solutions enables zero data loss, but the journals can be expensive and take up a lot of disk space, so CDP should be used on top-tier mission-critical applications that require a very stringent service level. Most other applications would be fine with backup to a disk-based or tape-based recovery solution using a VTL (Virtual Tape Library) or snapshots. If the CDP solution can journal and also do snapshots, then you get the best of both worlds.

In Figure 14-9, you see that a bad sector in the primary LUN is causing the application to fail. Since there is no copy of that bad sector in the journal, the CDP solution cannot be used to recover the data.

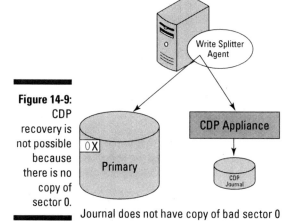

Figure 14-9: CDP recovery is not possible because there is no copy of sector 0.

Journal does not have copy of bad sector 0

In Figure 14-10, the same bad sector is causing an issue, but now you can recover the primary LUN from the copy of the bad sector located in the R1 copy. Because the CDP solution is not only journaling every write, but also mirroring all the data to a local R1 copy, the solution can be used as a full replacement for backup. If any data is deleted, or even if the primary disk goes completely bad, the data is still available for recovery.

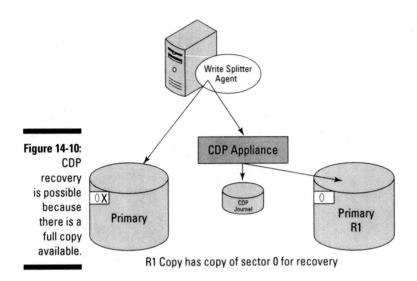

Figure 14-10: CDP recovery is possible because there is a full copy available.

R1 Copy has copy of sector 0 for recovery

This solution requires more disk space, but most companies can afford a single copy to protect mission-critical data. In fact, since the CDP solution also protects from corruption and deletion, the company can probably reduce copies that are being stored as business continuance volumes (BCVs) and even provide more recovery points at a cheaper price by using less expensive storage to hold the copy on a less expensive storage array. (A BCV is a storage-array-based full copy.)

Using CDP to Simplify Recovery and Reduce Costs

If the CDP solution can also replicate data, then it can even replace array-based data replication or shipping tape offsite, simplifying the datacenter even more.

CDP solutions that also replicate data can be a boon to many IT administrators because you can use the same solution not only for backup but also for disaster recovery. Since every write is protected in the journal, every write can also be replicated to an off-site location for recovery. This capability can provide complete disaster tolerance for mission-critical applications and enable a more cost-effective solution for disaster recovery compared to traditional methods.

You can combine CDP (Continuous Data Protection) and CDR (Continuous Data Replication) to provide a complete solution for both backup and disaster recovery. What a paradigm shift for most companies! Most companies are still using tape-based backup, or perhaps have moved to a Virtual Tape Library (VTL), which uses disks instead of tapes for recovery. Tape backup is still pretty slow. A VTL makes disks look like tapes to the backup software, and makes backup and recovery faster, but a VTL still requires backup software to move the data from the production application over the LAN or over the SAN to the VTL.

Since backup usually runs only once a night, it provides only a single recovery point per day. Even VTL requires a fairly long recovery process before an application can be brought back online. Also, the data still needs to get off-site for disaster recovery, so someone will still need to create a tape to send off-site.

With the combination of CDP solutions that provide an R1 copy and CDR, no tapes are required for backup. All data is continually protected, so recovery can be to any point rather than just last night. With CDR, all the data is also continually replicated to the DR site, so no tapes are required to ship data off-site.

Continuous Data Replication (CDR) implies continuous, which is similar to array-based synchronous replication, but CDR, just like array-based asynchronous replication, can also be periodic. Data is simply stored in the journal and periodically updated to the DR site based on the policy you create. Some CDR solutions don't have the same stringent data fidelity capabilities as array-based synchronous replication, but they are also much cheaper to implement. Hey, there are always trade-offs!

One of the main benefits of using a CDP solution with CDR is the ability to use unlike storage at the remote site for recovery, as shown in Figure 14-11. Using array-based replication for disaster recovery, you usually have to buy the same expensive storage that you use in production. Because the intelligence for CDR replication can be appliance based and reside outside the production storage arrays on the appliance, you don't need to buy a similar array at the DR site. You can use the expensive and highly reliable storage at the production site, and less-expensive storage at the DR location. Some CDP solutions, such as the one from FalconStor, also include storage provisioning, data de-duplication, encryption, and virtualization so you can even use less components for DR, and the CDP solution can be used as the primary storage for the remote site.

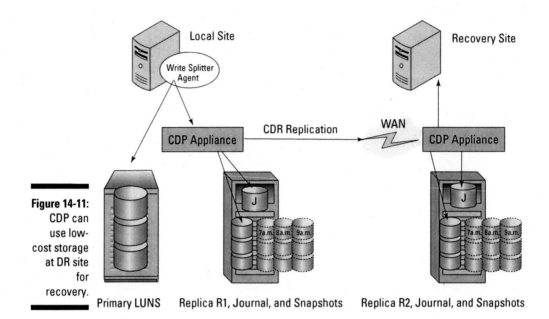

Figure 14-11:
CDP can
use low-
cost storage
at DR site
for
recovery.

Primary LUNS   Replica R1, Journal, and Snapshots   Replica R2, Journal, and Snapshots

In Figure 14-11, the local production site could use an expensive monolithic storage array, and the disaster recovery site could use less expensive SATA storage. By moving the data replication intelligence out of the storage array and into a fabric-level CDP appliance, you can eliminate all the licenses for replication solutions, such as SRDF, Universal Replicator, TrueCopy, PPRC, MirrorView, and any other array-based replication solutions. CDP can make storage a commodity. Although your storage vendor may not be pleased, you can save huge amounts of money by making backup and DR much more efficient.

Knowing Your CDP Vendor

I hope this chapter helped you in your understanding of how CDP works, and how you can use it to save your company money and make your life simpler in the long run. The last thing you need to know is who makes the CDP solutions and how to contact them. To make sure your vendor can provide the capabilities you require to meet your goals, you can create an RFI (see Chapter 16) and gather information from multiple companies so you can make an educated decision. Once you narrow down the vendors to a few, have them bring their solutions into your shop so you can thoroughly test them as a proof of concept (POC). Remember, vendors are always changing or being bought as the industry matures and consolidates. In the following, I list the vendors in alphabetic order:

- ✔ **Asigra:** www.backup-technology.com
- ✔ **Atempo:** www.atempo.com
- ✔ **BakBone:** www.bakbone.com
- ✔ **CommVault:** www.commvault.com
- ✔ **EMC:** www.emc.com
- ✔ **FalconStor:** www.falconstor.com
- ✔ **HP:** www.hp.com
- ✔ **Sun Microsystems:** www.sun.com
- ✔ **Symantec:** www.symantec.com

Chapter 15

Everything You Ever Wanted to Know about Virtualization

In This Chapter

▶ Understanding the meaning of virtualization

▶ Knowing why virtualization is a good thing

▶ Exploring how virtualization is used

*I*f you've been anywhere near the computer industry in the last few years, you have come across the term virtualization. Everyone talks about it, but not many understand why there is so much buzz about it. This chapter covers what storage virtualization means, how and where it is used, and how you can take advantage of it in your company to reduce costs. Since this book is about SAN storage, I cover server virtualization only briefly and direct most of the chapter's focus on storage virtualization and its uses.

Understanding What Virtualization Is

If you look up the term *virtualization* on the Internet, you will get thousands of results covering multiple areas of interest. You can find everything from virtual people (known as avatars) and virtual stores (ever shop on eBay or Amazon?) to virtual places (such as online gaming worlds).

When it comes to technology, many companies have overused and overhyped the term virtualization, which has led to confusion. Simply put, *virtualization* means abstraction. The virtualization solution abstracts the underlying details and complexity of whatever it is virtualizing. As an example of how confusing the marketing of virtualization can be, some companies that perform simple RAID functionality (see Chapter 2 for more on RAID) in their storage arrays sometimes market their solutions as a virtual array, simply because the RAID component *abstracts* multiple underlying physical disks into looking like a single device. RAID technology is available in almost every storage array, so even though some abstraction is involved, marketing a simple RAID array as a virtualization solution is not really ethical. Just to confuse matters even more, some storage arrays do provide virtualization functions! To understand what a true storage virtualization solution does, you need a proper definition of the term.

When we talk about storage virtualization, and tell you that a device is a storage virtualization device, what do we mean? Well, since we are focusing on storage here, we should go to the source for everything storage, which is the SNIA (Storage Networking Industry Alliance) at `www.snia.org` to get a proper definition.

The SNIA defines storage virtualization as follows:

1. The act of abstracting, hiding, or isolating the internal functions of a storage (sub)system or service from applications, host computers, or general network resources, for the purpose of enabling application or network independent management of storage or data.

2. The application of virtualization to storage services or storage devices for the purpose of aggregating functions or devices, hiding complexity, or adding new capabilities to lower level storage resources.

In other words, when you virtualize storage, you group together multiple heterogeneous storage arrays that normally have their own proprietary methods of creating and provisioning LUNs, tying them together into a virtual pool of storage. You can now use a single method to create and provision a LUN from any part of the pool. See Figure 15-1.

So when you hear the term *storage virtualization,* most people will be referring to pooling different storage resources together and then creating LUNs for servers from the pool.

Figure 15-1:
Pooling
multiple
physical
storage
devices to
create a vir-
tual LUN.

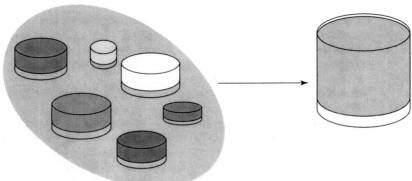

Exploring the Types of Virtualization

Almost everyone has heard of the term *virtual reality,* which means you are not really here; you just think you are. And anyone who has seen the movie *The Matrix* will remember the phrase "there is no spoon," which was a reference to the fact that in the matrix (which is the life you *think* you know to be real), reality is actually all in your mind.

Virtualization in the computer industry is similar in concept. You take physical devices, abstract their functionality, and make them just "seem" real to the end user. In reality, the virtual devices are images of a real entity, but they act, look, and feel like the real thing. Virtualization simply "abstracts" complex real objects into simpler virtual objects. The goal of virtualization is to make things simpler to manage.

Virtualization can be of benefit in many places. For example, since no one person knows everything about everything, most datacenters are divided into multiple layers of administration. People with different skill sets are then asked to perform different administrative functions. There are network administrators who manage the IP network services, server and application administrators who manage database and application services, and storage administrators, who handle all the zoning and provisioning in the SAN. These administrative functions can be divided into multiple administrative layers in a datacenter, as shown in Figure 15-2.

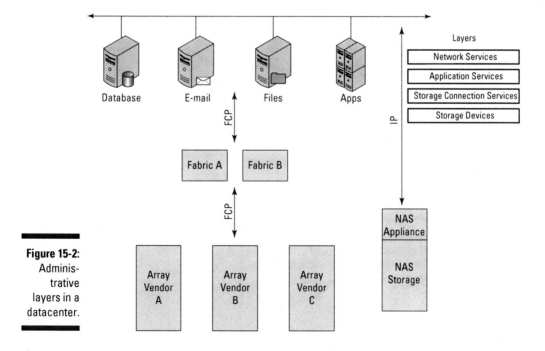

Figure 15-2:
Administrative layers in a datacenter.

Because the goal of virtualization is to simplify things, the idea is to virtualize the different layers and physical elements by abstracting the physical devices into virtual pools of devices, so they would be simpler to manage, as shown in Figure 15-3.

The clouds in Figure 15-3 represent the virtualized pools of devices. In the figure, all the layers in the datacenter are virtualized (except the network layer) to simplify administration of the individual devices. The servers are virtualized using server virtualization, and then a virtual abstraction layer (the cloud in the middle) is placed between the virtual servers and the storage layer. The virtual abstraction layer has the intelligence to turn the individual storage devices from the different vendors into individual storage pools, with each pool providing a different function. All the same physical components are reused, and the fibre-channel protocol is still used for all communication between the devices.

In the datacenter pictured in Figure 15-3, you would need only three administration consoles: the network administrators console, one console to administer the server "cloud," and one console to administer the virtual abstraction layer, which controls the storage pools. The administrators would be shielded from the complexities of all the different elements being managed in the pools.

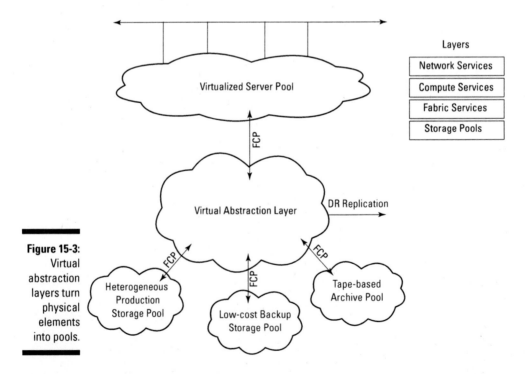

Figure 15-3:
Virtual abstraction layers turn physical elements into pools.

Implementing Virtualization in a Datacenter

Virtualization can be implemented in one or more areas, or layers, in the datacenter. As you can see in Figure 15-3, virtualization can simplify things in at least four administrative layers in a datacenter :

- ✔ Network layer
- ✔ Compute layer (servers)
- ✔ Fabric layer
- ✔ Storage layer

The *network layer* is where the clients connect to the servers. The *compute layer* consists of the servers themselves and the applications that run on them. The *fabric layer* is where all the SAN switches are located and where any SAN appliances would be connected. The *storage layer* is where the disk and tape drives hang out, usually in a storage array or tape library.

As shown in Figure 15-4, we can break these layers down even further to show exactly where virtualization can be implemented based on the flow of data from a client writing data all the way down to an underlying storage.

In Figure 15-4, the client communicates over the local area IP network (LAN) to get access to the applications running on the servers. The applications running on the servers access block storage devices called a LUN. The LUNs are presented to the servers from the storage device through the fibre-channel fabric switches to the host bus adapters in the server.

The operating system in the server creates a file system on the LUNs, and the application is brought up. In the example in Figure 15-4, virtualization can be added at any or all of the different layers to introduce simplicity or provide enhanced functionality.

Following the chain, let's see where virtualization can be used. Let's start with the network layer and work our way down. For example, you can use a Cisco switch to create a virtual LAN (VLAN) from the clients to the servers over the network to simplify access to the servers. You can then virtualize the servers themselves using a hardware-based virtualization solution such as Egenera or Virtual Iron or even blade servers from HP or IBM.

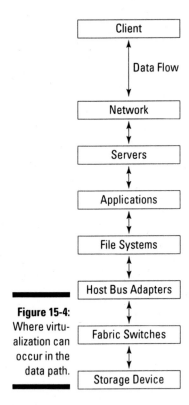

Figure 15-4: Where virtualization can occur in the data path.

At the same time, you can create multiple software-based virtual servers to run on the blade servers using software such as VMware or Microsoft Virtual Server. You can then tie in another virtual layer for the applications by adding clustering or application-level virtualization solutions (such as Microsoft cluster server, Polyserve from HP, or Oracle RAC).

Inside the virtual servers, you can use a virtual file system such as Veritas volume manager (VxVM) to create virtual volumes across the LUNs being presented over the SAN. At the fabric layer, you can tie together all the different storage arrays through the switches and provide thin provisioning to the servers by using a fabric-based storage virtualization appliance such as FalconStor network storage servers (NSS), or the SAN Volume Controller (SVC) from IBM. Inside the storage arrays themselves, you could virtualize the LUNs across all the disks in the array by using a storage array such as an HP Enterprise Virtual Array. You could also use an HDS Universal Storage Platform (USP) array to attach less expensive virtualized SATA storage as external disks to the array.

This example is extreme, because rarely are all these solutions used together. However, using virtualization, each layer in the datacenter can be made more efficient and simpler to manage.

A single virtualization solution can be deployed at a single layer, or virtualization solutions can be combined for added functionality. Another example of virtualization inside a server at the HBA layer is the use of *path failover* (sometimes called *filter driver*) software on the servers in your SAN. The path failover driver virtualizes (abstracts) the connections (paths) to your storage array over the SAN fabric and enables your operating system to failover to the other path if one goes away.

As you can see in Figure 15-5, the path failover driver virtualizes the paths to the primary disk for this server. The server sees only a single disk even though two paths exist to the same disk. If one of the paths fails, the driver simply enables the I/O operations to travel down the surviving path. In this way, the path failover driver provides a simple virtualization function at the server or host level. Many path failover software solutions can provide up to 32 paths per LUN to further increase performance.

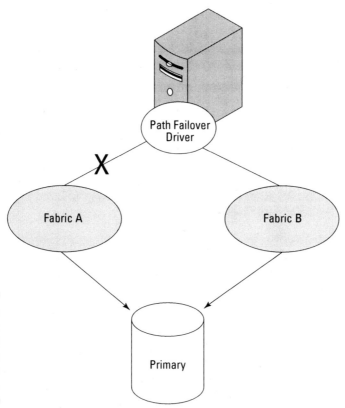

Figure 15-5:
Path failover
drivers
provide a
virtual path
to disk.

Virtualization solutions can be applied almost anywhere, but in a SAN, they typically reside either in the servers, in the SAN fabric, or in the storage arrays themselves. Network layer virtualization is used in IP networks and can be used to virtually combine multiple physical network interfaces together into a single larger virtual interface or even tie together multiple complete physical networks into a virtual LAN. Since server virtualization is a hot topic right now, though, I will cover that briefly.

Server virtualization

Server virtualization enables an abstraction layer between the physical server hardware and the virtual server instances running on that hardware. Each instance or virtual server shares all the I/O hardware, including the network ports, CPU, and memory resources of the physical server. The ability to use multiple virtual servers on a single physical server enables consolidation of computing resources in the datacenter.

Following are some of the benefits of server virtualization :

- ✔ Lower costs by reduced physical server requirements for production and DR

- ✔ Simplified server management and enhanced server reliability through advanced functions of the virtualization solution such as failover

- ✔ Greening of the datacenter by reduced floor space, power, and cooling requirements

- ✔ The ability to rollout new applications faster by reducing the complexity of installing the new servers that are needed to support the applications

- ✔ Lower cabling and infrastructure costs by enabling the sharing of multiple virtual connections over fewer physical connections

- ✔ Simplified disaster recovery through the ability to bring applications up at the DR site virtually on fewer servers

Server virtualization has been around for a long time. For decades, mainframe computers have been using a form of server virtualization known as logical partitions (LPARs). The mainframe partitions its physical resources into logical partitions to run different jobs at the same time, enabling better utilization of that very expensive hardware. Some newer server virtualization solutions use physical hardware to make it easier to partition or virtualize. Server vendors like Sun, IBM, and HP produce servers that are partitioned physically and virtually to provide massive scalability in less footprint. Domain servers such as the Sun E10K, logical partition servers (LPAR) such as the IBM P690, and *blade servers* from HP like the HP BladeServer are replacing less capable standalone servers in the datacenter.

Some vendors who provide hardware-based server virtualization are

- ✔ Dell: www.dell.com
- ✔ Egenera: www.egenera.com
- ✔ Hewlett Packard: www.hp.com
- ✔ IBM: www.ibm.com
- ✔ Sun Microsystems: www.sun.com
- ✔ Unisys: www.unisys.com

Some vendors who provide software-based server virtualization are

- ✔ Citrix: www.citrix.com
- ✔ Microsoft: www.microsoft.com
- ✔ Virtual Iron: www.virtualiron.com
- ✔ VMware: www.vmware.com

An example of some hardware-based server virtualization solutions can be seen in Figure 15-6.

Figure 15-6:
Hardware solutions for server virtualization.

HP BladeServer

Sun E 10K

IBM P690

The *Big Iron* (that's geek slang for powerful servers) shown in Figure 15-6 will enable dozens of applications to run at the same time in less footprint than would be required using traditional servers. The HP BladeServer rack shown uses individual server or storage blades that slide into the rack and are connected over a high-speed backplane; the blades share I/O ports to reduce costs but still provide superior performance. The much more expensive Sun and IBM solutions are well known around the world for being the hardware that makes businesses run. These *domain-class* (DC) and *logical partition* (LPAR) solutions can run multiple computing tasks using different versions of operating systems simultaneously in the same box. These hardware virtualization servers also provide exotic connections such as Infiniband inside the box to ensure massive scalability and fast performance. Many great whitepapers are available from the hardware vendors on server virtualization.

VMware (owned by EMC) is the software-based virtualization solution with all the buzz these days, but Microsoft and other software vendors like Virtual Iron are not sitting still. The simple reason software-based server virtualization solutions are taking off is the ability to turn a single physical server into many virtual servers without having to buy the Big Iron hardware, so you can save money on the hardware to run your applications. A software-based virtual server solution runs on top of any Intel- or AMD-based computer with enough memory.

Once a server is virtualized on top of the physical server, you can move the virtual server between other physical servers by simply dragging the virtual server to another machine (see Figure 15-7). The storage needs to be shared in a SAN, or connected to an iSCSI storage resource. Forget about issues with bringing down applications for hardware maintenance! Virtualization makes maintenance a simple drag-and-drop process.

In summary, server virtualization software makes a single physical server look like many individual servers by abstracting the hardware layer in the server itself. Server virtualization hardware takes a single physical server and stuffs dozens or even hundreds of CPUs in the box, along with powerful hardware abstraction at the firmware level, to provide a robust platform for the virtual servers themselves.

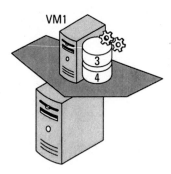
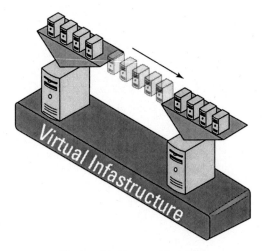

Figure 15-7:
Software-based server virtualization.

Virtual server running on physical server

Moving virtual servers between physical servers

Storage virtualization

Storage virtualization is pretty much the inverse of server virtualization. Where server virtualization abstracts a single physical device and turns it into multiple virtual devices, storage virtualization takes multiple physical devices and turns them into a single virtual device. Storage virtualization can be done at the server layer, the fabric layer, or the storage layer. Storage virtualization can also be done in-band, or out-of-band.

By using storage virtualization, you can

✔ View the entire SAN as one pool or many pools of storage independent of the physical location of the storage devices.

✔ Mask the differences between heterogeneous devices.

✔ Simplify provisioning, control, and management under a single interface.

✔ Centralize all storage volume management on the SAN through a single console.

✔ Dynamically allocate capacity to the applications that need it to any pool of storage based on the type of storage in the pool. (This means you can put data where it's supposed to be based on the cost of the disk in the pool.)

✔ Move data between any device in any pool while your applications are running.

✔ Migrate data from older to newer storage at any time while the applications are running, with zero downtime.

✔ Move the intelligence for things such as data replication into the virtual abstraction layer, which means you can save money because you don't have to buy array-based replication solutions such as SRDF, PPRC, or TrueCopy.

✔ Get better utilization of your storage through things such as thin provisioning and added capacity on demand.

✔ Possibly get other cool features such as data de-duplication, data encryption, or data compression.

✔ Eliminate all physical tapes for backup and use disks for all data recovery, by using virtual tape solutions.

These are just some of the benefits of storage virtualization. You can see many companies are interested in the technology.

The goal of storage virtualization is to enable you to combine multiple individual heterogeneous storage arrays from different vendors into a single virtual storage pool. One of the main benefits of storage virtualization is the ability to use a single console to provision (create LUNs and present them to the servers) storage from multiple vendors using a single console. Instead of having to learn how to provision storage using the interface that comes with an EMC storage array or an HDS array, you can use the same interface for any storage abstracted behind the virtualization solution.

I'm sure you're wondering how storage virtualization works. Storage virtualization uses firmware in hardware or software on a host, switch, or appliance to abstract the underlying physical devices connected to it.

If you look at Figure 15-8, you can see three different storage vendors providing LUNs to a database server through a standard SAN fabric connection. The paths to the LUNs are being virtualized by the path failover driver so the LUNs will fail over between the HBA ports if a port or switch fails. The LUNs are then further virtualized into a volume using the volume manager software running on the server. The LUNs themselves come directly from each vendor's storage array; since they are not virtualized, you would need to use the standard management tools provided by each vendor to create and assign them to the server or buy a third-party SAN management solution that works across different vendors' arrays.

A better way to provide storage to this server would be to use fabric-level storage virtualization appliances attached to the switches. The appliances would be able to create a virtual pool of storage from the LUNs from each vendor's storage array, as shown in Figure 15-9.

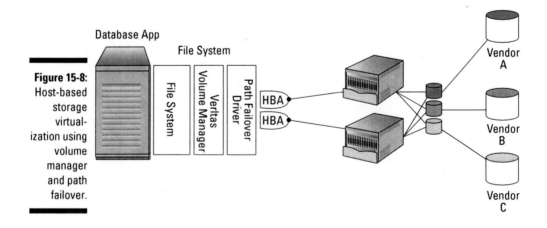

Figure 15-8: Host-based storage virtualization using volume manager and path failover.

Database App

File System

File System

Veritas Volume Manager

Path Failover Driver

HBA

HBA

Vendor A

Vendor B

Vendor C

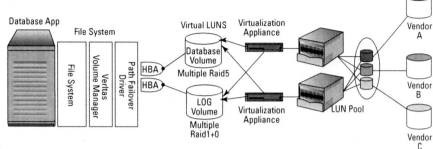

Figure 15-9:
Host-based
storage
virtualiza-
tion using
volume
manager
and path
failover.

Creating virtual disks

Figure 15-9 shows some fabric-based virtualization appliances to pool together the physical LUNs presented by the individual storage arrays, and then uses the appliances to create a virtual LUN for the server. If you look closely at Figure 15-9, you can see that there are separate virtual LUNs for the database and logs volumes for the database server, and that each of the virtual LUNs are built from multiple Raid 5 and Raid 1+0 stripe sets from the pool. The ability of virtualization to provide better performance for SAN-attached devices is covered in a bit more detail later.

Because fabric-based virtualization is transparent to the server, we do not need to remove the host-based volume management or path failover software. The physical disks are simply turned into virtual disks and presented to the server. The server has no idea that these LUNs are virtualized.

Virtual disk

A *virtual disk* is the virtual representation of a physical disk or pool of physical disks. A virtual disk represents block-based storage from the underlying abstracted physical devices.

You can create a virtual disk by

 ✔ *Directly mapping* a physical disk through the virtual abstraction layer and presenting it as a virtual disk

 ✔ Combining multiple physical disks into an *extent pool*, and then mapping out a virtual disk from the underlying pool of storage

Direct mapping an existing LUN as a virtual LUN

The first method of creating a virtual disk — directly mapping (also called *service enabling*) the physical disk back to a host as a virtual disk — may not really seem like virtualization at all, but it is, and direct mapping provides some interesting advantages (see Figure 15-10). If the virtualization solution includes added functionality not present in the original storage array (such

as snapshot or replication capabilities), the new virtualized direct-mapped
LUN inherits those new capabilities from the virtualization solution. Since
the physical LUN is directly mapped as a virtual LUN, the original data on
the original LUN stays in place; there is no need to migrate data into the new
solution for the LUN to be virtualized!

The other great thing about being able to directly map a physical LUN as a
virtual LUN is that you can back things out if you change your mind. Direct
mapping also gives you an easy backout plan if something goes wrong with
the virtualization solution. The LUN gets all these new abilities, and if the
virtualization solution breaks for any reason, you can simply yank it out; your
data is still available. In other words, solutions with direct virtual mapping
capabilities *(service enablement)* provide a fallback method to the way everything was before installation.

Another benefit is the ability to preserve the identity of the original drive, so
you can keep your original path failover software.

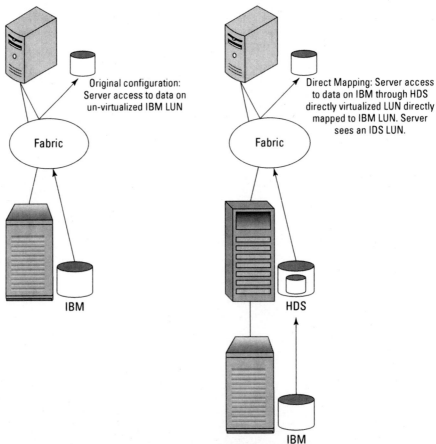

Figure 15-10:
Direct
mapping a
virtual disk.

Few virtualization solutions are available with the capability to directly map a physical disk as a virtual disk. The Hitachi Universal Storage Platform (USP) can do it when attaching a LUN from a virtualized external array. There would be no need to migrate any data from the external array, since all the LUNs could be removed from the hosts, reattached behind the array, and then zoned back in with the hosts. Although the LUNs would now look like Hitachi LUNs, all the data would still be there, and there would be limited changes to the host applications.

This next paragraph is a bit technical but important. By using a direct-mapping virtualization solution, you can even preserve the SCSI inquiry string (the command a server uses to ask the disk array what type of drives they are) so that the hosts will see not only the same data but the same drive type. The only thing that changes is the port connected to the fabric. All the virtual capabilities are present but nothing changes on the original disk. (See Figure 15-11.)

The virtualization solution uses direct mapping (also known as *service enabling*) of a physical LUN to a virtual LUN, so the data already on the LUN does not have to be migrated into a storage pool and can stay where it is. The SCSI inquiry string is preserved, so the host also still sees the LUN as an IBM LUN, which further simplifies introducing virtualization into the SAN. The LUN now gains all the benefits of being virtualized, such as data replication and mirroring, without the risks.

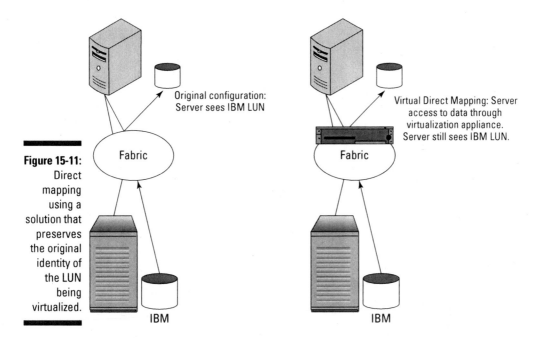

Figure 15-11: Direct mapping using a solution that preserves the original identity of the LUN being virtualized.

Original configuration: Server sees IBM LUN

Fabric

IBM

Virtual Direct Mapping: Server access to data through virtualization appliance. Server still sees IBM LUN.

Fabric

IBM

Extent pool mapping

Creating a virtual disk out of a pool of physical disks is called extent pool mapping. File systems are made up of technical things such as *extents* and *inode structures*, and that all relates to how virtualization solutions technically work. You don't need to know any of the technical stuff to use disk pools though! The virtualization solution does all the hard work for you.

As you can see in Figure 15-12, you can also slice up virtual LUNs from the pool into smaller virtual LUNs. The ability to use virtualization to create any LUN size you want frees the storage administrator from the constraints of the vendor's physical array capabilities.

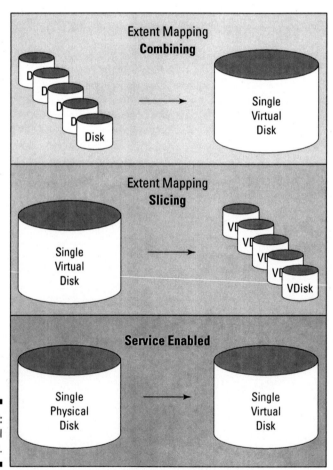

Figure 15-12: Extent pool mapping.

Using virtualization for better performance

Mapping extent pools from physical devices rather than through direct mapping has benefits. Virtual disks that map through extent pools can be spread across many more physical devices than direct mapping. By spreading the I/O workload across many spindles in the pool, you can get better performance from a virtual disk than through a directly mapped LUN.

In Figure 15-13, you can see where multiple physical spindles can be virtualized through the abstraction layer and pooled into a LUN that spans not only a lot of physical spindles but also multiple storage arrays, controllers, and fibre-channel ports. Also, because the virtual LUN is now made up from the extent pool using a virtual volume that utilizes multiple controllers, RAID groups, and even storage arrays, the virtual LUN can be much more fault tolerant than a physical LUN.

Virtual pools of storage can also be divided up by capabilities or cost. Once divided, data can be moved between the pools at any time, even while the applications are running on the servers. The ability to move data at will provides a way to move data between higher-cost production storage and lower-cost backup or archive storage. Moving data between these tiers of storage as the data ages and becomes less relevant to the company is called Information Lifecycle Management (ILM). (See Figure 15-14.)

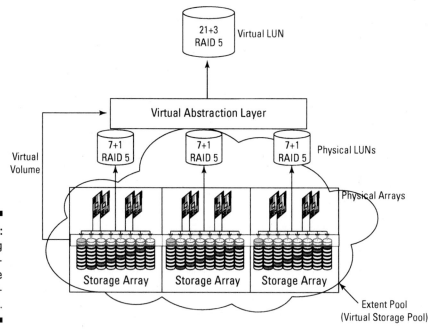

Figure 15-13:
Enhancing disk performance through virtualization.

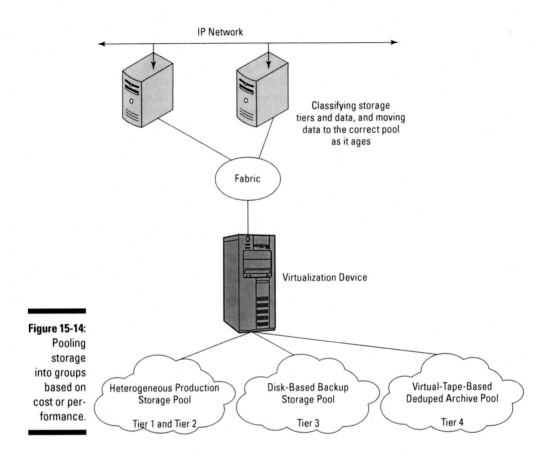

IP Network

Classifying storage
tiers and data, and moving
data to the correct pool
as it ages

Fabric

Virtualization Device

Figure 15-14:
Pooling
storage
into groups
based on
cost or per-
formance.

Heterogeneous Production
Storage Pool

Tier 1 and Tier 2

Disk-Based Backup
Storage Pool

Tier 3

Virtual-Tape-Based
Deduped Archive Pool

Tier 4

Transparent data movement is the holy grail for ILM. For ILM to work, you must be able to easily move data between the different storage arrays in the pools while the applications are running. While the data ages, policies created at the virtual abstraction layer move the data between the different storage arrays, from the most expensive and highest performing, all the way to tape so the data can be archived or removed.

Figure 15-15 shows the different storage devices presenting physical LUNs or tapes through the SAN fabric to the virtual abstraction layer. The physical storage devices are then abstracted into virtual devices, so the host doesn't know or care about the location of the physical devices. Data access is now abstracted from the physical devices. Now we can move the data from the left to the right, from more expensive to less expensive tiers of storage as the data ages, all transparent to the hosts.

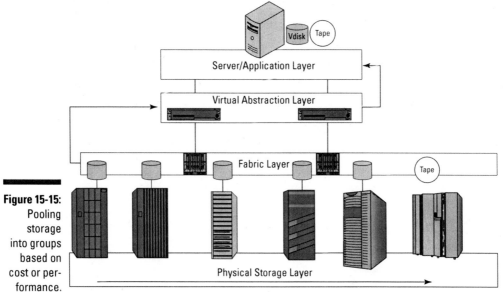

Figure 15-15:
Pooling
storage
into groups
based on
cost or per-
formance.

Transparent Data Movement Over Time

Virtual tape

Virtual tape is not the ability to take multiple physical tape drives and make
them into virtual tape drives. Virtual tapes are created from disks. *Virtual
tape* solutions abstract physical disks and make them look like tape drives
to a server. I know it sounds weird, but think about it. Disks are really fast
random access devices, and tapes are slower sequential access devices.
(Sequential access means you have to access individual files in the sequence
in which they were stored.) If I can make a disk look like a virtual tape,
instead of having to wait for the tape to wind around in circles to get to the
file I want, I simply "seek" to it.

Virtual tape eliminates all the tape movement that slows backup. And since
the writes from the backup are to disks that look like tapes, virtual tape can
eliminate physical tape. De-duplication and electronic replication are now
being used with virtual tape solutions so that data can be stored even longer
on less storage, and once de-duplicated, replicated off-site more efficiently
by using less wide area network (WAN) bandwidth. Figure 15-16 shows how a
virtual tape solution works.

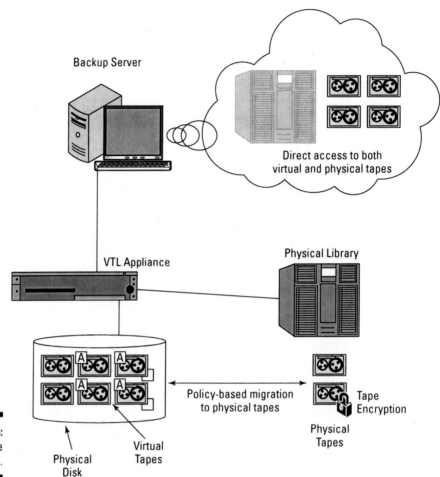

Figure 15-16:
Virtual tape
in action.

The VTL (Virtual Tape Library) appliance connects to physical disks and creates virtual tapes within the physical disks. The virtual tapes are then presented to the existing backup server, which does not see any difference between the physical tapes or the virtual tapes. The physical tape library can even be attached to the VTL so that the VTL can export the virtual tapes to physical tapes when required. Virtual tapes are replacing physical tape libraries more and more as companies move away from tape media as a way to recover data.

In-Band versus Out-of-Band Virtualization

The real war in virtualization has always been about which method is better, in-band virtualization or out-of-band virtualization.

In-band virtualization

Using an in-band virtualization solution, all data flow goes through the virtualization device for both control information and data movement. In-band is the most common form of virtualization used today. In-band solutions are simpler to deploy, easier to use, and less complicated than out-of-band solutions. Since they do not need agents on the hosts, in-band solutions can work with almost any operating system or server platform. (See Figure 15-17.)

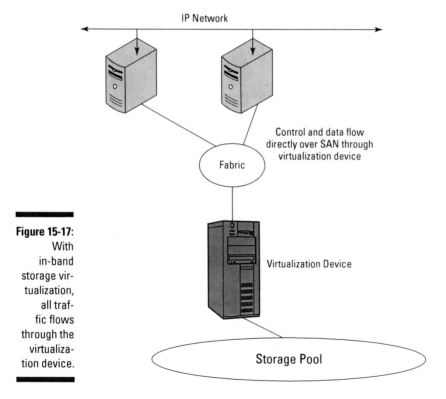

Figure 15-17: With in-band storage virtualization, all traffic flows through the virtualization device.

All of the virtualization solutions I have covered so far in this chapter use an in-band method to abstract the underlying physical resources. This is because in-band is the most common method of virtualization. Virtualization solutions operating at the fabric level use recent advances in fabric switch technology with appliances working with the switches for the control paths. Examples of in-band solutions are DataCore, FalconStor Network Storage Server, Hitachi Universal Storage Platform, and IBM SVC. Others solutions that provide levels of virtualization include 3PAR, Pillar Data, Lefthand, Fujitsu, and XIV.

Out-of-band virtualization

In an out-of-band solution, all data flows directly between the server and the physical storage. Only *control* information travels between the virtualization device and the servers by using the IP-based LAN network. One issue with out-of-band solutions is that they usually require agents on the host, similar to backup agents, which communicate the control information with the virtualization solution. The hosts ask for permission to access the virtual storage mapped by the virtualization device via the control information; when permission is granted, they access the virtual storage pool directly through the SAN. (See Figure 15-18.)

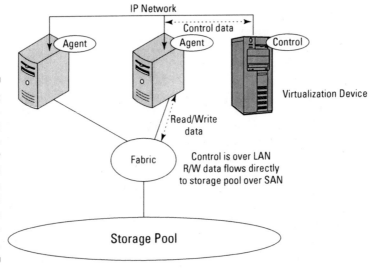

Figure 15-18:
With out-of-band virtualization, only control information is managed by the virtualization device.

Because no read/write data has to travel through the virtualization solution itself, the argument is that out-of-band solutions are much more scalable than in-band solutions. There may be something to that argument, since many of the best-performing virtualization solutions use an out-of-band method.

Following are examples of out-of-band virtualization solutions:

✔ Brocade

✔ Cisco SANtap

✔ EMC Invista (control data is split from write data at the switch)

✔ GRID computing solutions such as Lustre, Platform, and Blue Whale

✔ IBM GFS (global SAN file system)

Some of the in-band solutions can also connect to the storage out of band by going through the switch-based solutions such as Cisco and Brocade.

Dozens of companies provide file-level and NAS-based virtualization solutions, but this book is about SAN, so we will leave that for another book.

The Virtualization Vendors and Where They Play

Virtualization solutions have been a boon for the datacenter manager because they simplify daily operations and reduce costs. You can implement storage virtualization at the host layer, the fabric layer, or the storage layer. Virtualization can also be used in all those layers at the same time and tied together for a true virtualized datacenter. Dozens of companies provide file-level and NAS-based virtualization solutions, but this book is about SAN, so I'll skip those and leave them for another book.

Host-based storage virtualization vendors

Most host-based storage virtualization solutions are software based, and provide volume management or path failover.

Veritas (now Symantec) Volume Manager and EMC PowerPath are perfect examples of host-based storage virtualization solutions. One virtualizes the LUNs it sees into virtual volumes, and the other virtualizes the paths to the LUNs.

The other virtualization software solutions for hosts virtualize the hosts themselves (if you haven't noticed yet, you can use the term *host* and *server* interchangeably almost all of the time). Software-based solutions to create virtual servers include VMware, Microsoft Virtual Server, Citrix, and Virtual Iron.

Fabric-based virtualization storage vendors

Fabric-based virtualization solutions enable you to pool together all the disk arrays from any number of vendors, so they can all be managed from a single console. Instead of having to learn the management interface that came with each vendor's array, you would need to learn only the one that came with your virtualization solution. Fabric-based storage virtualization has an interesting side effect for business: It turns storage into a commodity. On a side note, the only fabric-based solutions that can currently implement direct mapping are the solutions from FalconStor Software.

Fabric-based virtualization solutions are available from many vendors, including EMC, IBM, Sun, Cisco, Brocade, HP, FalconStor, and DataCore. We can include virtual tape solutions for virtualizing tapes at the fabric level. These solutions are available from IBM, Sun, EMC, HP, and Quantum; the following VTL vendors include de-duplication solutions: Dilligent (now part of IBM), Sepaton, FalconStor, and Data Domain.

Storage-array-based virtualization

Virtualization in a storage array was started back in the late '90s by Digital Equipment and IBM, and then Hitachi joined in. Digital was bought by Compaq, and then by HP, so HP now owns one of the original solutions that provided virtualization within the array, the HP Enterprise Virtual Array (EVA). Hitachi took things a step further by enabling true virtualization in firmware with the Universal Storage Platform (USP), which enabled the connection and virtualization of externally attached storage. Both devices are shown in Figure 15-19.

The HP EVA was one of the first storage arrays that provided some sort of storage virtualization. The idea was to use virtualization in the controllers so that any write operation to the disks was spread out across as many spindles as possible (a spindle is an industry term for a disk drive). If you stripe (as in a RAID stripe set) your reads and writes across a lot of disks, your I/O operations can go very fast.

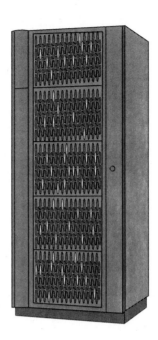

Figure 15-19:
Hardware
solutions for
server virtu-
alization.

HP Enterprise Virtual
Array

Hitachi Universal Storage
Platform

The Hitachi USP is also available through HP as the XP 12000 and 24000, and
through Sun Microsystems as the Sun Storagetek 9990V. The coolest feature
of the USP array is that it can virtualize disk arrays from other vendors that
are externally attached to the array. All you need to do is turn some of the
ports in the array from *targets,* which attach to servers, into *initiators,* which
attach to storage.

The data on any externally attached and virtualized disks comes over intact,
so no data migration into the virtualization solution is required. The data on
the LUNs on the attached array can also be left where it is, and the LUNs can
be directly mapped back to the host. All externally attached disks inherit
the functionality of whatever is inside the array itself, so you can use the
advanced functionality of the higher-end USP on less expensive storage from
other vendors.

So there you have it, everything you ever wanted to know about virtualization as it pertains to SAN storage. Remember that new advances and technical innovations in virtualizing storage become available every day. Keep
reading and searching on the Internet, and I'm sure you will see new and
more amazing things you can do with virtualization solutions. And remember, "There is no spoon."

Part V
Understanding the Cool Stuff

The 5th Wave   By Rich Tennant

EARLY STORAGE SOLUTION

"Configuring it has been a little tougher than we thought."

In this part . . .

This is the part you have been waiting for. Over the years since the first edition of this book was published, there have been major advancements in the technologies used for storage networking. The speed of the storage network has dramatically improved; the storage arrays have gone through major changes to incorporate new capabilities like snapshots and improved data replication. New storage protocols like iSCSI and Infiniband have been introduced, and even the disk drives themselves have matured with new technologies like Serial Attached SCSI (SAS) and Serial ATA (SATA) moving into storage arrays. But the most dramatic advances have taken place in the fabric itself.

Specialized solutions have been developed to work with the devices and data stored in the fabric to improve the backup process by continuously protecting every write operation to disk. The cost of implementing a SAN and data replication for disaster recovery has been reduced by removing any duplicate data being stored. And server and storage virtualization have begun to take hold to simplify management of physical resources and provisioning storage to the applications relying on the SAN. In this part, we cover the awesome technologies of Continuous Data Protection (CDP), data de-duplication, and duplication prevention, and how virtualization is making SAN management so simple.

Chapter 16

Ten Reasons to Use a SAN

In This Chapter

▶ Seeking better storage management and performance

▶ Planning for disaster recovery

▶ Accommodating storage needs and growth

▶ Saving money and resources

*I*n this chapter, I cover the top ten reasons why companies purchase a storage area network (SAN) rather than sticking with the traditional but tried-and-true method of buying large servers with tons of internal disk space. After reading through this chapter, you'll have a good idea about whether implementing a SAN makes sense for your company.

You Want Better Disk Utilization

The number one benefit from installing a SAN is better disk utilization. When all your storage is tied together through a centralized storage network, you gain the capability to manage everything as a single entity. This lets you slice up the central pool of storage resources at the network level and assign that storage more intelligently to the servers that need it. The approach to disk management without a SAN is to buy tons of disks and stick them in huge expensive servers so that you can grow into them. All the disk space that's not currently being used is wasted until you need that space.

Better utilization of disk resources means less disk space is sitting around doing nothing but taking up power and cooling.

Many companies that still use storage internal to the servers — also known as direct attached storage (DAS) — typically report storage utilization rates of 40 percent or less. Those who have implemented SAN technology have reported upwards of 80 percent utilization. Using 80 percent of your storage leaves 20 percent free for growth. This creates a solution that defers future disk purchase needs because what's currently in place is used more efficiently.

Using a SAN also eliminates taking servers down to add disk drives when more space is required. This means that your applications need less planned downtime for normal maintenance. You can see where I'm going here: Installing a SAN can improve your bottom line very quickly.

You Need a Good Disaster Recovery Solution for Multiple Applications

When you have many critical servers in your data center running applications that simply can't go down and need to be recovered quickly if disaster strikes, you definitely need a SAN. Although the upfront costs for implementing a SAN-based disaster recovery solution are high, the benefits can be realized in just a single hour if a disaster happens. The cost of downtime is critical in many organizations. A SAN-based disaster recovery (DR) solution is like having a good insurance policy on your business. (See Chapter 6 for more on DR.)

You Need Better Availability for Your Applications

Those big bad storage arrays in storage networks are built from the ground up to never go down. They use technology, such as *Phone Home* (which I guess comes from the movie *ET*), where the storage array itself makes a call to the manufacturer to report that one of its parts might be going bad. This is very cool stuff. I wish my dishwasher had the same capabilities!

Equipment that you find in a SAN is expensive, but it's built like a tank. For example, the disk drives in Hitachi storage arrays are rated at 2.5 million hours between failures! With a record like that, you'll be retired by the time something goes wrong. Applications fail because of data becoming corrupt when something goes wrong with the disks those applications use. The storage arrays in a SAN use very good data protection algorithms to make sure that your data stays consistent. The best scenario for you is that you forget your SAN is even there. It just works, like the dial tone on your phone.

You Need More Storage Room

If I had a nickel for every time a customer told me the server was full and there was no more room to add disks, I'd be a rich man. I can't figure out why the folks at a company still buy large servers with huge storage bays to add disks inside the server. After the server is full of disks, they go out and buy *another* big server just to add disk space! This is *server creep.* Adding more servers to your environment to simply add disk space is a waste of money.

Installing a SAN to keep storage separate from server resources lets you grow the storage environment independent from the servers, based on your needs.

It would be so much cheaper for your company if all the servers you buy are those really thin (and fast) blade-type servers that are filled with nothing more than a network card, fast CPUs, and tons of memory. All the disks can then be connected externally in the SAN. Using small, thin, fast servers means that you need far less space in your data center to house your servers. All your storage can be allocated to each server through the fibre connection to the storage network. No matter how small the server, you never run out of disk space. If your servers need more space, simply add disks to the SAN and allocate the space to the server that needs it.

Backup Is Taking Too Long

Decreasing the time needed to back up huge amounts of data is also one of the major benefits of installing a SAN. SAN technology like snapshots enables the creation of space-efficient Point-in-Time copies or even full duplicates of your data almost instantly. The snapshots or duplicates can be used as either the backup of your data or as a source for backing up that data to a physical or virtual tape library connected to your SAN. Many backup software solutions have the capability to leverage the functionality of the storage arrays to speed up the backup process for you. (See Chapter 9 for more on backup.)

You're Focusing on Server and Storage Consolidation

If your company has tons of servers located all over the place, with each server having its own internal storage, you have a server management nightmare on your hands. Taking down each server just to add more disk space and to rack mount all those large servers with power-hungry disks inside has to be time consuming and costly. And how frustrating it must be to have to ask for more money to buy new file servers just because yours are running out of disk space.

When you buy a SAN, none of the servers will ever need an internal disk added. You can boot all your servers from the disks located in the storage arrays. You no longer have to buy new servers because you're running out of disk space. You can use your file servers to their fullest potential. Server consolidation saves money for your company. Installing a SAN is one of the enablers of server consolidation.

You've Been Tasked to Save Your Company Money

Implementing a SAN takes money up front. You need to buy all the hardware and software that make it go. The good news is that after your initial investment, the SAN begins paying for itself every day by helping you reduce operational expenses, management expenses, and time.

The head honchos of your organization want your time spent on delivering solutions that help the core business and the bottom line. Keeping the e-mail servers up and running is important, but it doesn't make money for the company. If you can provide a way to keep e-mail running smoothly and to have your storage self-tuning and auto-expanding when room is running out, you can spend your time doing more productive things.

Installing a SAN makes all this and much more very possible. You can help your company survive a disaster by implementing remote-based mirroring solutions with the SAN. You can instantly recover a corrupt database by using the snapshot capability in the hardware of the SAN. Your backup jobs will complete more often without failure and much faster than before. All this helps drive the company's IT (Information Technology) costs down, frees you to do more productive things, and lets everyone sleep better at night.

You Need to Manage Storage for Many Locations from a Central Site

Placing a huge SAN storage box in every one of your remote offices is a costly proposition, but you don't have to use the big boxes for your remote sites. Here's a way to provide storage for all your remote offices by using the standard Internet Protocol (IP) network that's already connected to all your remote offices.

You can use the Internet Small Computer System Interface (iSCSI) protocol to connect to storage over the network. All you need to do is install the free iSCSI driver that comes with your operating system or an intelligent network adapter that enables the use of the iSCSI protocol in hardware. The iSCSI protocol enables block-based access to disk drives over standard Ethernet. This is still considered a storage network, even though you're using a regular IP network for accessing the disks. The disk drives can still be in a SAN in your data center, as long as they can be presented as an iSCSI target (check with your storage vendor to be sure the storage you bought is iSCSI-capable).

As an option, an existing Fibre Channel SAN can be bridged to the Ethernet network through an intelligent appliance or switch, or you can just buy storage that directly supports the iSCSI protocol. As another option to provide simple file-based storage, you can drop in a network attached storage (NAS) appliance at each location or at the central site. NAS devices are built to share and store files over a standard IP network.

For your remote offices that have more than just one or two servers, some vendors offer solutions that enable you to use your network connection to manage the device from your corporate data center. This lets you add storage to servers in remote offices without anyone being physically there.

You Need to Decrease IT Management Costs

As I mention earlier, implementing a SAN is one of the best ways to save your company money in Information Technology (IT) costs over time. The idea here is to do more with less and increase overall efficiency and productivity. I know several companies that have had trouble managing all its servers with direct attached storage even though the companies had many people assigned to the task. Everyone was always busy putting out fires.

In the case of one particular company, there was never enough time to implement new projects because the staff was so busy just keeping what they already had in place running. The outcome of this situation was that the company suffered financially and had to lay off a number of people. Sure, the company saved money in labor costs, but it was left with fewer people to manage the same problem that forced the layoffs in the first place.

The company then bit the bullet and installed a SAN. After all was said and done, just two people were needed to manage all the storage for the entire company. The good news is that these two people now manage 20 times as much storage as the company had in the first place. One person can manage multiple terabytes of storage, a task that took more than ten people before. Everything now hums along nicely with a lot less fire-fighting going on. The SAN implementation ultimately saved the company millions of dollars in annual costs. And the company can be more proactive in driving new applications forward because the storage part is so reliable and flexible. After all, aside from people, a company's data is one of its most prized assets, and storage is where all that data resides. Those in charge of protecting and providing access to that data are some of the most important and highly compensated folks around.

You Need Better Performance for Your Applications

Performance is the Holy Grail of every IT organization.

Moving from internal disks on the server to dual-connected SAN storage can help your applications fly. Look at it like this: An internal disk drive that's connected to one of the latest SATA adapters can run at a maximum of a few hundred megabytes per second. If you connect the same server with dual 8-gigabit SAN host bus adapters, you can get 1600MB per second! And you can easily add adapters to the server or assign more disks in the SAN to increase performance as your needs require. Most SAN drivers support up to 32 host bus adapters in a single server! That's 32 x 8 gigabits per second, or over 25GB per second. That's a heck of a lot faster than a few 100 megabytes per second.

Most SAN storage devices come with tons of cache memory and include algorithms that ensure that your request for data usually comes from cache memory. Because memory doesn't need to move heads and rotate around to find information like a disk drive does, the request for data is very fast. This means that not only is the data request coming over an extremely fast connection, but the request is normally being satisfied out of memory. Getting data from cache memory is thousands of times faster than going all the way down to the disks. Having all that cache in the storage array lets you connect a heck of a lot of servers to a single array without worrying about the performance impact of doing so. Performance with server consolidation is one of the main benefits of a SAN.

Chapter 17

Ten Reasons NOT to Use a SAN

Storage area networks (SANs) aren't for everyone. A storage network *can* pay for itself in a very small period of time, but only if you're in a position to take advantage of everything a SAN has to offer. A SAN may only make sense for your company if you have the right staff, budget, and business requirements to support it. If your storage requirements fall into one of the following ten scenarios, a SAN might *not* be right for you.

You Need Larger File Servers

If all you need is file sharing, then Network Attached Storage (NAS) may make more sense for you. If you require all your servers to have access to the same information at the same time, as is the case with Web servers, NAS is a better solution. NAS allows you to use your corporate network to share data among servers. Access to files based on NAS takes place over a standard Internet Protocol (IP) network. You can create a NAS server from a standard Unix or Windows server by creating a shared folder on the server so others can access that folder over the network. This technique is called a *file share*.

Clients can connect to these file shares over the corporate network, and can share access to the files located in the shared folders. Whereas SANs use the SCSI protocol to access information as blocks of disk space, NAS enables access to storage as files over an IP network. Network File System (NFS) and Common Internet File Services (CIFS) are the protocols used for NAS. The great thing about NAS is that multiple users can have access to the same files at the same time.

NAS provides a way to lock files so only one user at a time can change the information in a file. In a SAN, storage access is based on blocks of a physical disk space; multiple servers can be given access to the same disks within a SAN. However, a SAN has no inherent locking mechanism to prevent data corruption on the disk if two servers try to write to the disk at the same time. Only one server can have access to a disk at a time, unless the servers are configured as a cluster. So for applications, such as Web servers or file servers, NAS is the way to go.

You Only Have a Few Inexpensive Servers

You really see the benefits of a SAN when you have a bunch of servers to hook up to the storage network. A main benefit of using a SAN comes from the centralized management of storage assets. Although companies with dozens or hundreds of servers benefit from this centralized management, managing just a few individual servers is easy enough to do without installing an expensive SAN. You may gain speed and reliability benefits from a SAN for just a few servers, but if you can't justify the cost of the SAN against the needs of your applications, you don't install one. Weigh the costs against the benefits to see whether a SAN investment makes sense for you. The equipment that you need to buy to create an effective SAN can be pricey. For example, even a small SAN solution can cost upwards of $100,000; thus the cost has to be justified. If you have million-dollar servers, a SAN may make sense. If you're running only a few file servers, perhaps not.

You Want to Save Your Company Money This Year

The payback period of a SAN *might* be fewer than 12 months, but look at a lot of factors to see whether this can be true in your case. If your SAN vendor has the capability to give you a return-on-investment (ROI) report based on the solution you're considering, have the vendor prepare such a report.

Many of the cost benefits of a SAN come from the reduction of operational expenses over time. You do get advantages such as less floor space, reduced power consumption, reduced manpower requirements, and increased application uptime. But if you're not growing your business that fast — and you're not planning any layoffs soon because of the reduced manpower requirements — then the payback time will be longer. Depending on your environment, you can calculate the payback period between 12 to 18 months for a large SAN. Just installing the switches and running the cables can cost a lot of money. The storage itself is usually the least expensive part of the SAN.

You Want to Use the Latest and Greatest Solutions Available

Everyone likes new toys. This, however, isn't the main reason to install a SAN. Sure, SANs are way cool and allow you to have access to better ways to protect your corporate data. They even offer increased uptime for your servers and better disk utilization. But installing a SAN simply to have the greatest technology isn't the way to go. You need to consider complex issues, including the costs. If you're getting by just fine with your current disk solutions, then by all means continue doing what you're doing.

You Need a Disaster-Recovery Solution for a Single Application

If your disaster-recovery requirements are for a single application, then using a software-based solution might be more cost-effective than a hardware-based solution that uses a SAN. Plenty of software solutions are available that can create effective, host-based disaster recovery. And this software can cost a heck of a lot less than putting in a SAN just to use the storage array to move your data between locations. Software-based recovery solutions run on the servers that contain the data to be replicated; they use your corporate network as the transport medium to mirror the data from your primary server on another server placed at your recovery site.

You Want a SAN but Don't Have the Budget

Face it, SANs cost money — sometimes not a lot of money (comparatively speaking), but most of the time you have to make a major investment in infrastructure to install a SAN. You need to buy switches, run fiber-optic cabling, train your staff, buy expensive optional licenses for all the cool stuff that SANs can do, and (finally) pay someone to hook it all together. After a SAN is in place, the ongoing costs are minimal and you'll save money down the road.

But if you don't have the budget to buy everything up front, you might want to think about alternatives to installing a SAN. Perhaps just stay the course for now, and keep an eye out. When the cost of doing nothing exceeds the cost of installing a SAN, then you can proceed.

You Use Gigabit Ethernet on Your LAN

If you currently use Gigabit Ethernet, you might be better off using some of the new Internet Small Computer System Interface (iSCSI) solutions on the market today. Solutions that use iSCSI can move data in blocks (working much like disk drives) over the network from the server to a disk drive connected to an iSCSI bridge. Network cards that have iSCSI capabilities can make your corporate network work much like a SAN: Your servers can connect to disk drives (even Fibre Channel disk drives in a SAN) over the network as if they were locally attached to the server with a SCSI cable.

Gigabit Ethernet is just about as fast as a Fibre Channel SAN for moving data back and forth, so long as you use the new network adapters that use a Transmission Control Protocol/Internet Protocol (TCP/IP) Offload Engine (TOE). The TOE removes all the hard network interrupt traffic work from your server's CPU. All the operations that have to go through the TCP/IP stack are offloaded to the hardware in the network card (rather than being implemented in software); they run by using your server's CPU. Removing the network processing from the server makes moving things across the network much faster. Using iSCSI is a much lower-cost solution than creating a storage area network with Fibre Channel.

Everything Already Runs Fine

Despite all the buzz about SANs, if your configuration is already hunky dory, you probably don't really need one. And even though using a storage area network will save you money over time, the initial capital expense might not be worth the cost benefits over time if everything is already running smoothly.

You know you don't need a SAN if three or more of the following issues apply to you:

- ✔ You're not running around frantically trying to fix problems that constantly pop up. (I call this activity *fire-fighting.*)
- ✔ You currently have more than enough disk space in your servers.
- ✔ Your servers are operating at peak performance, and no one is complaining.

✔ You never have to go out and buy servers because you're running out of disk space.

✔ Floor space isn't an issue for you; you have plenty of room for growth.

✔ Your storage needs don't seem to be growing very much on an annual basis.

✔ You're not experiencing outages because of storage-related issues.

✔ You run mostly Web applications, and the information is mostly static.

✔ No regulations force you to keep years' worth of data available online.

✔ Your backups are running fine, and you have plenty of time to complete them.

✔ You have a good disaster-recovery plan, and all your data will be safe if a disaster occurs that wipes out everything within 100 miles of your production site.

If most of the items listed here are true, then installing a SAN is probably overkill for you.

You Need to Back Up Multiple Remote Offices over Slow Links

Connecting multiple remote offices so you can consolidate backup is another place where the new iSCSI solutions can be a real benefit. NAS is also a good solution for access to remote applications but doesn't provide the same block-based disk access to remote storage and tape that iSCSI provides. Although an iSCSI network (which I also mention in Chapter 8) is still considered a storage network, it's not the same as the typical SAN solutions out there that use optical cables running the Fibre Channel protocol.

Backing up data in remote offices is a common problem for companies. Sometimes resources in the remote offices lack personnel who know how to use the backup solution. Take a retail chain, for instance, with hundreds (or even thousands) of stores located across the country. Each store might have its own network and servers but still not have anyone around who's technical enough to make sure that all the data gathered every day at the store is safely backed up. Each day's receipts might have to be sent back to the home office so inventory needs can be scrutinized and suppliers can be notified.

Some companies have found a way around this issue by using a central server or mainframe computer located at the central office; all the remote locations have *dumb terminals* that can only access the data on that central server. This makes backup a snap because no data is ever located at the remote offices. But what about large insurance companies and financial insti-tutions that have *really* large amounts of data gathered every day at the local office? With hundreds of brokers located around the country gathering client data on their laptops, perhaps with a server or two located in the office that provides access to corporate e-mail, how do you back up all that stuff?

One solution that works is to use the server in the office as a file server, to which all laptop users connect when it's time to store their data. The server is then connected via the corporate IP network, using both a network card and an iSCSI card. The network card connects clients to the server; the server uses the iSCSI card to connect to a tape library located at the central office. The tape library is connected to an iSCSI bridge, which is also con-nected to the corporate LAN through the iSCSI bridge. Each server at every remote office sees the tape library as if it were connected locally. No Fibre Channel SAN is needed for this connection.

For this solution to be effective, you need backup software that allows shar-ing of tape resources. Most backup software vendors have this capability. You'll also have to do an initial full backup, which could take a while over the slow links on a wide area network (WAN). After the full backup of each remote office is complete, then you need run only differential backups. Because a differential backup backs up only the changes since the last differ-ential backup, only a small amount of data needs to be pushed over the WAN for each remote server.

You Need to Replicate Your Data for Disaster Recovery but Can't Afford Fast WAN Connections

This is a common problem. The most expensive part of data-replication solu-tions is the money you have to pay to lease network connections between your buildings. For those of us without deep pockets, this can be an issue. One way to accomplish remote copy of data is to use the *CTAM (Chevy Truck Access Method)*. That's right, *Chevy truck,* although you could use a Pontiac sedan or even a van to accomplish the same task. Here's the deal: You back up your servers to tape, throw the tapes in the back of a vehicle, and trans-port them to your remote site. In the event of a disaster, you restore the tapes to the new servers that you just bought and get back to work. It might take a week or two for you to get back to business as usual if you use this method, but hey, you get what you pay for.

Part VI
The Part of Tens

The 5th Wave   By Rich Tennant

SNOW GLOBE DATA STORAGE

Okay, let's shake this thing and see what we come up with.

In this part . . .

Ah, The Part of Tens. The two chapters in this part give you ten reasons to use a SAN and, believe it or not, ten reasons not to. (A SAN is not the answer in some situations.)

Index

• S •

• *V* •

Bonus Chapter

Outsourcing SAN Solutions

*N*ot that crazy about implementing and operating your storage area network (SAN) yourself, eh? In this chapter, I cover what other options you have if you don't want to do everything on your own. First, I describe outsourcing your storage infrastructure to a storage service provider (SSP). Then I go over the other options, such as getting a specialized storage consultant to help you implement a SAN. Finally, I show you how you can manage the project yourself by defining your requirements in a Request For Proposal (RFP) document and how to work closely with the many SAN component vendors, each pitching its best-of-breed solutions for your particular requirements.

Outsourcing the Whole Operation

Outsourcing is getting an external company to do something that your own employees would normally do within your organization. Because of financial reasons, time constraints, or simple lack of expertise, you *source* this technology and expertise from *outside* the company — hence, you outsource.

The main reasons companies outsource their storage infrastructures are

✔ The necessary expertise to handle the job is not available internally.

✔ Internal expertise *is* available, but those folks don't have time.

✔ Outsourcing is cheaper than buying hardware and supporting it using in-house employees.

✔ For political reasons, an external third party can cross political boundaries within the corporate structure without offending anyone when dictating new policies.

That last item is a mouthful, but a true mouthful. When you have a shared storage solution such as a SAN, you have to get the buy-in from all the IT groups as to who controls what and who gets how much storage. Nobody likes to share, so sometimes it's better just to give the responsibility to a neutral party so that no one gets preferential treatment.

A typical example of outsourcing is desktop support. Some companies don't want — or can't afford — to maintain their own internal desktop support for their employees' PCs. They pay an external entity to furnish an entire staff to handle help-desk calls, take care of troubleshooting problems, and fix broken PCs or upgrade older desktops to newer models.

By having an external company handle a task, you don't have to have a staff of internally trained people who spend their time on more generic tasks when they can be focused on more business-centric tasks. In the case of desktop support, for example, the tasks involved are not specific to financial, pharmaceutical, or insurance companies; they just involve a bunch of PCs running your company's preferred operating system and applications. Therefore, you should let someone who is good at fixing PCs concentrate on that task. Your employees should focus on running the core business that your company is known for, not scanning for viruses or replacing dead mice all day (the computer kind, not the whiskered, cheese-eating type; that job, you should outsource to an exterminator).

Knowing what outsourcing involves

Outsourcing your storage concerns turns design, component selection, implementation, and ongoing operation and maintenance over to a third party. Not that you don't have any say in these areas, but usually an established outsourcing company already has a consistent, battle-hardened way of providing these services with all the bugs already worked out of the system. Such a company also probably has a switch vendor picked, a storage array vendor selected, and other components chosen and in place ahead of time. Most vendors already have a SAN-based backup solution and offer disaster recovery to a remote location, so you just plug your storage network (which is very simplified compared with a regular one) into the vendor's and use the disk space over a high-speed link.

This complete outsourcing is both good and bad. Because you're paying someone else to do all this work for you, you don't have to get involved with design, setup, and management. The flip side is that because you give up control, you may be paying for inferior design, implementation, and operation. You can always yell later, but it's best not to have matters come to that point. The best way to protect yourself is to understand how the outsource company supports your SAN. Take a tour of its facilities and check it out.

Get references from other customers. As with any other transaction of this nature, see whether other clients are as satisfied as you intend to be. You don't pick the first plumber that you find in the phone book; you usually ask friends and colleagues about who does good work. The same goes for trusting your data to someone else.

Working with a Storage Service Provider (SSP)

A *storage service provider* (SSP) provides external services for something that a company typically does itself. SSPs can provide cost savings (equipment, training, personnel, maintenance), time, and expertise within the customers' business.

The day-to-day management can be done by your staff, using tools provided by the SSP, or you can place a phone call to have the SSP handle it for you. You don't have to lift a finger besides maybe having to plug in a host bus adapter (HBA) card into your server. Heck, an SSP might even coordinate that for you as well, along with your server vendor or even someone to whom you outsource your server support. The possibilities are endless.

The range of support that you get depends on what the SSP offers and how much control you intend to give the outsourcer over your storage needs and server infrastructure.

In terms of hardware, an SSP will house all its storage arrays in a central location. Some storage arrays are more powerful than others; therefore, they have a different cost associated with renting the space on them for your applications. The faster and more reliable arrays are more expensive to buy, so they are more expensive to rent as well.

The site will also have a SAN in place, as well as some telecommunication equipment that links its SAN with yours over a high-speed link. This link attaches to your company's site where the servers are located. The SSP link plugs into your local SAN switches, and then your servers connect to this mini-SAN. This setup is an extension of the SSP's SAN to your server's location except that the storage is located a few miles away.

Figure BC-1 shows a typical SSP's infrastructure.

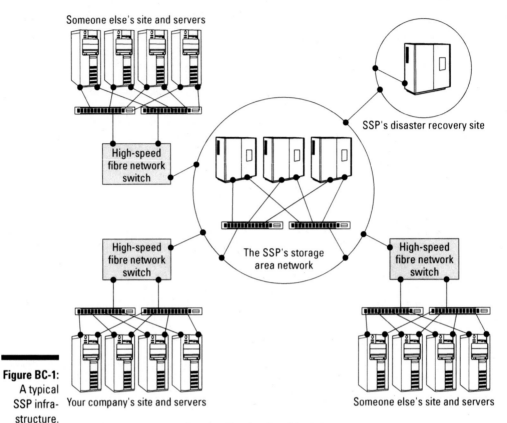

Figure BC-1:
A typical
SSP infra-
structure.

Storage Service Provider Infrastructure

As you see in Figure BC-1, several customers are tapping into the centralized network that the SSP uses to get data to and from its customers' sites. In addition, the SSP has a disaster recovery site of its own to protect customers' data from problems at the SSP.

Getting what you pay for

Typically, SSPs charge by the month for using their storage. For that fee, you get not only storage, but also support and a guarantee of performance for that storage. Ensure that you get what you pay for by making a Service Level Agreement (SLA) with your SSP, covering what your business requires. (For more on SLAs, read Chapter 11.)

Performance

The performance of a SAN from your company's building to the SSP's site usually won't be as good as if you had the storage locally. Most SAN applications don't require 100 percent of the available bandwidth all the time, either. But what if you have an application that does? This situation is where benchmarking your application and putting its needs into the SLA is important.

Because users will be accessing your applications, you need to make sure that they're not upset with the response time caused by accessing the data from a distance. Putting acceptable response times in your SLA will force the SSP to provide a reasonable solution for your application needs. The farther your SSP is from your application servers, the more delay occurs in the communication links and, therefore, in the response time of the applications. Try to pick an SSP that is close to your location — within 50 miles.

Backup

Because your data is over at the SSP's facility, it makes sense to back it up there. But because the SSP hosts many companies besides yours, how do you know whether it's treating your backup with the care that your business demands? Your SLA should clearly state when and what should be backed up, as well as how often. You also want to specify how long your data is kept and what time is needed to restore a file after you request it.

The SSP's data center may be hosting thousands of terabytes (TB), and your data is just awash in an ocean of bits. You're paying big bucks to have your data available and protected, though, so don't skimp on this section of the SLA.

Randomly request file restores at least monthly, even when restores aren't necessary, to test the SSP's operation — and to confirm to yourself and your management that you made a good choice with this SSP.

Disaster recovery

Does your SSP have a good disaster recovery (DR) plan? How does the SSP intend to get your business back up and running if an outage destroys your SSP's data center? Remember that the SSP services customers besides you, and those customers have the same concerns. Have you reviewed the SSP's DR plan? Does it look reasonable? What does your SLA say about disasters — yours *or* the SSP's? Because you're entrusting the company to protect your data, DR is one of the most critical parts of the SLA to review with your storage provider. *Your* company could go under if the SSP has trouble recovering from a disaster or internal failure. (See Chapter 6 for more information about disaster recovery.)

Storage management

When you let the SSP handle the storage management or allocation of storage from its SAN to your servers, always anticipate a lag in response to requests. Expect a string of phone calls, an online form or some paperwork to fill out, or a meeting that needs to take place before your server sees that extra 10GB of space. For some customers, that situation is fine; they won't mind the wait, or they appreciate the provider's methodical process of checking for any issues or errors. Some industries can't tolerate such lags, however; they need their disk *now*.

The SLA should thoroughly explain the process and the turnaround time for a new request. Any request not serviced in the specified period means you can start yelling, but until then, you must sit and wait for the SSP to follow its internal procedures to grant you space.

Data security

Because an SSP houses not only your data, but also the data from many other companies, you want to make sure that others can't see your proprietary information (and they don't want you to see theirs, either). To guarantee that the documents containing the details on your company's new product don't accidentally show up on one of your competitor's servers, your SSP has to have a policy in place that defines how it secures your data from everyone else's.

Your SSP should have a set-in-stone policy on how it allocates storage to a customer's servers, directly addressing how it intends to keep would-be hackers from grabbing disk resources that aren't theirs. This book outlines the Logical Unit Number (LUN) security and zoning techniques (see Chapter 7) used to secure a specific LUN to a specific server's HBA on the SAN. These actions should be outlined in the SSP's policies on data protection. If they aren't, the SSP needs to provide you a clear explanation of how it intends to secure your data from unauthorized access. Some providers offer a form of certification ensuring that no servers except the ones you explicitly define can access your data.

Along with these security guarantees, any changes to the configuration requested by you or someone in your company should have a clear verification process to ensure that the right people are requesting the change and that the change is an appropriate one to make. Requests such as making changes in the middle of the day or reassigning an already assigned LUN to another server are the kinds that commonly lead to problems. The SSP should follow the rules that you define for your organization to keep both your own people and the SSP from violating data-integrity concerns.

Testing the SSP's security procedures is a good idea. If you set a policy that no changes are to be made during business hours, for example, make a request to have something changed during business hours. See what the provider does. Does it compare your requests with the policies and deny the change, or does it just go ahead and make the change?

Compensation for outages

When an SLA is breached, keep good documentation on what happened, when it happened, and how long the problem lasted. Just as when you're complaining about a home cable-television service outage, tell the SSP that a server lost connection or that a restore took too long to come back, and you should get some money back for the trouble. An SLA is a legal document that, if breached, can mandate that you receive monetary compensation for your troubles. All these financial penalties should be outlined in the SLA itself or in the contract you sign with the SSP.

Considering Alternatives to Outsourcing

Besides giving your storage infrastructure to an external company, two popular options are storage consulting and partnering with your storage component vendors to build your SAN. In the following sections, I discuss these options.

Storage consultants

Bringing in consultants who are experts in designing and building SANs is a middle ground between doing it yourself and outsourcing the whole thing. Instead of putting your storage off-site at an SSP site, you keep everything yourself. The people who implement the solution, however, aren't part of your existing staff.

Look to the consultants as been-there-done-that resources you can learn from. Your staff should work closely with them and allow as much experience to rub off as possible, because consultants won't always be around to assist. (Just don't rub too hard; you could cause a rash.)

Consultants can step into the process at any point, but I advise getting them involved as early as possible. They'll understand the SAN implementation better and offer more insight if they can make suggestions early, before bad ideas become the foundation of the project.

This book isn't titled *Selecting Consulting Firms For Dummies,* so I won't get into picking who should help with your SAN. But I *can* say that references are the best way to gauge whether a specific firm or consultant can provide the level of quality that you expect.

First ask each consultant you interview for the requirements of a previous project and the final design implemented; then ask how the design covered the requirements. Make sure that you also throw in a few "Was this the cheapest way to do this?" questions. Consultants are paid very well for their expertise, so don't let them skirt easy questions that they should be able to answer.

When you define the work that consultants will be doing, set some milestones about what you expect to be completed and when. The basic milestones of a SAN implementation using consultants from start to finish are

- Requirements gathering
- Design review (matching requirements to the proposed design)
- Hardware procurement
- Implementation
- Migration of applications
- Verification of migrated data
- Knowledge transfer
- Transition to local resources

Each of the preceding milestones shouldn't look new. These steps follow the beginning life cycle of any large project: understanding what you need, drawing it out, buying it, putting it together, showing management that it works, and then taking it over internally from the consultants who built it.

The consultants take your list of requirements and then run with the whole project. They collect tons of information on how you do things now and how you may want to streamline or expand your current methods of storage.

After you review what the consultants find, they put together a solution for you to critique and approve. This process may be repetitive, but ideally, not too many iterations go by before you're satisfied. (Ahem . . . consultants *are* getting paid by the hour, so be careful that they're offering their best ideas up front.)

When you feel content that a proposal will accommodate your needs and your budget, you give the consultants the okay to purchase the hardware to begin building the SAN. They may even do all the setup themselves. If they subcontract that work out to a storage vendor, they'll manage the vendor for you while your staff concentrates on business.

After the hardware is purchased and installed, the consultants should begin getting your staff involved with how the system works, how it's set up, and how to manage it. Remember that the consultants won't be around all the time; sooner or later, you'll be on your own with the SAN. Your staff needs to take the time to transfer knowledge from the consultants so that they can step right in when it's time to take over from the consultants.

If you want something done right . . .

Do it yourself — at least part of it. No hard-and-fast rule says that a SAN must be conceived, built, and maintained by either you or an external entity. You can always share the responsibilities and tasks by *partnering*. Your IT organization and the vendor(s) team up to achieve the common goal of building a usable SAN infrastructure.

This model is the most common one used for implementing a SAN, because the work involved is spread across more people, each one focusing on what he or she does best. Using this virtual team method (described in more detail in the next section) and working closely with your external vendors usually is the best approach to creating a SAN that your organization (and, you hope, your boss) can be proud of.

 When you partner, you are in charge of the project. That's good and bad: good because the implementation is under your control; bad because it's up to you to make sure that things are moving along smoothly, which is work. It's better to be in charge than out of the loop completely, though. Also, because you're closer to the SAN setup than you would be with consulting or outsourcing, you get to be part of the decision-making process and feel more involved.

Partnering: The virtual team approach

Your virtual team should be comprised of key personnel from your staff who have a say in what the SAN does and engineers from each vendor who specialize in the products that they're proposing. Think of the team as an equation:

Your IT Organization + Vendor 1 + Vendor 2 + Vendor 3 = SAN

Suppose that you have Windows NT, Solaris Unix, AIX, and Linux. You need someone who can cover your organization's platforms as an advocate for making the SAN work for that platform. That person should, at the very least, understand the operating system and the applications that currently run on it. The rest is up to the vendor to educate that person about how its products can help out.

The major benefits of partnering with your vendors are

- A more gradual learning curve for your staff
- Cleaner transitioning of SAN operation responsibilities to internal staff
- Better understanding of the SAN versus a totally outsourced solution

✔ Greater cost efficiency than consulting provides

✔ More chances to fine-tune the solution based on ongoing lessons learned

The only downside to partnering is the investment of time, because your staff works directly with the SAN vendors the whole time. Some items can be left to vendor personnel (they come in, install hardware, and plug things in), but the best time to learn is during this side-by-side, techie-to-techie time.

Consulting doesn't give you this level of understanding; consultants tell you what you need to know and usually not much else.

One of the nice things about partnering is that you feel as though you're in touch with the project, which makes for a lot of enthusiasm among your staff about being part of something new. The best thing is that your staff members don't have to do all the work; they're learning on their own, taking on the SAN gradually without even realizing it. Consider the setup free training as well. Your staff members aren't being asked to understand everything tomorrow, as they would if the whole project were being done internally.

Deciding Whether to Outsource

The decision to manage the SAN internally or to sign up an external vendor isn't easy. Because so many variables play into making the decision, you should look at what you miss by going in one direction versus the other.

The downside of outsourcing

Before you skip to the section "The upside of outsourcing," understand that *downside* doesn't mean the worst. You must weigh all the good and bad things that can happen and then rank what's most important to you, your organization, and your company as each item relates to your SAN implementation.

There are no right answers — only upsides and downsides to be aware of while you consider outsourcing.

Cookie-Cutter Solutions, Inc.

One common situation arises when an external vendor comes in and implements your SAN: The vendor may be so used to "dropping a box" into a data center and calling it a SAN that it doesn't address any of *your* problems with the solution. I call this situation the *cookie-cutter process*. In the cookie-cutter process, the vendor just takes the same plan it used last week for company XYZ (and the week before that and the *month* before that) and uses it as your *custom* solution. The solution looks like every other cookie the vendor bakes — yet you'll be charged for a radical, customized solution specifically tailored to your needs.

The best way to fight this possibility is to ask to see some references and some previously implemented designs. Have the vendor point out the specific reasons why it did what it did. If the vendor can't explain, it doesn't know what it's doing . . . in which case you should move on to a vendor that *does* know.

Reviewing everything that vendors are implementing and having them link their solutions back to your initial list of requirements can help keep vendors honest.

Keep an eye out for extras that you didn't ask for. These items raise the price and probably don't help you solve the problem you're looking to solve. (See "Telling the vendor what you require," later in this chapter, for more information on conveying your needs to the outsourcer.)

"Acme SAN Outsourcers, please hold . . ."

One reason why you outsource your SAN is because your own people don't have the time to put it together. The company that you're paying to take care of it had *better* have the time to talk to you. Even if you have a contract promising prompt service, as everyone knows, that promise doesn't always fly when you drop a dime at 2 a.m. to call about a problem.

Check whether the outsourcing firm has the requisite staff and expertise to handle your service levels for your internal customers. Then check its references again to understand what the firm does to train its people on all aspects of SAN design, operation, and so on. Think of this process as interviewing everyone in the company when you're deciding which vendor to hire to work on your SAN.

You're paying vendors to provide you something that works. If it sounds as though you can't trust a vendor to help you, find one that can before you get yourself into a contract that you can't get out of.

The upside of outsourcing

Outsourcing a SAN project gives you many benefits. Among them: You don't have to do all the work, and you get focused experts with new ideas looking at your specific situation. This fresh, objective approach is a very healthy way to see your environment from a new angle, which may uncover even more issues than you already know about.

Throwing the whole project over the fence to an external group, however, is like giving a total stranger your checkbook and saying, "Okay, now go redecorate my house." You should provide clear requirements, guidance, and feedback so that you end up with something that fits your needs. If the requirements are clear and logical, the solution that the vendor proposes should be clear and logical too. A Request for Proposal (RFP), which I discuss later in this chapter, is the key to defining those needs.

Screening Vendors

The process of finding the right vendors to source your SAN from is an interesting process. You have to be able to determine what your business wants to accomplish, put it down on paper, and then decide which vendors are meeting those objectives and which ones are trying to snow you.

This cat-and-mouse game starts with the RFP, or Request for Proposal, document. Your vendors hope it ends with a sale, and you hope for a SAN that meets your needs. Keep that last sentence in mind, and you won't go wrong.

Writing a Request for Proposal document

Many vendors complain that their failed attempts at a project are the client's fault — that expectations weren't realistic or weren't defined properly and clearly. Assumptions were made, and you know how assumptions turn out. The best way to lay it all on the line for your external vendors and consultants is to create a document that dots the i's and crosses the t's on your SAN solution.

This *Request for Proposal (RFP)* document is a list of demands that you make for a solution that your company requires. The RFP lists your requirements for a project or business need; vendors then use that document to develop a solution featuring the products and services that they sell.

A vendor's reply to an RFP can range from "Yeah, we can help you" to a weeklong conference at its corporate headquarters (a free trip known as a *boondoggle*) to describe the proposed solution in detail with presentations, handouts, dinners, drinks, free shirts, golf games, and so on. You'd be surprised what some vendors will do to earn your business. Just don't select a solution based on the boondoggle. Stop daydreaming about playing Pebble Beach, and make sure that the solution fits your needs. Remember — those ethics officers at Corporate HQ are watching you.

Listing your demands

Like the kid in the toy department who holds his breath until he gets the toy he wants, you should exercise your power when working with vendors — on a much more professional level, of course. You do have the power to get what you want, provided that you clearly explain what you expect to get.

Stating the SAN's requirements to your internal organization and your external vendors, whether those vendors are consultants or outsourcing firms, is critical when you paint the picture of what you want to accomplish. Everything that you hope the SAN will provide is built on this foundation of needs.

Describing your environment

First, you need to describe what your company is, what it does, and what it needs in terms of business functionality. Example: "We are a financial services firm, handling billions of dollars a day for the top 50 banking institutions in the world." A statement like this should immediately pique the interest of those reading it; it makes them realize that your company is a serious player demanding a solution that works $24 \times 7 \times 365$ — no excuses accepted.

Next, define what your current computing environment looks like. List each of your locations, the types of servers residing there, the operating system versions used, the type of storage used, and the backup tactics that you employ (a tape drive per server or a shared library?).

Telling the vendor what you require

Now create your wish list. Make it good but not unrealistic. State any new visions that senior management has stated to your IT organization, such as disaster recovery plans, zero-downtime backup solutions, centralized management of all storage, multimedia services, or video on demand. This wish list is what the vendors or consultants will try to accommodate with their SAN solutions.

Your wish list is a 30,000-foot overview, not techie talk. That conversation will come later, after you're selected a few vendors that sound as though they understand your vision and can walk the walk.

Setting limits on the solution's scope

The most common failure in an RFP is neglecting to define when enough is enough. A vendor can reply with a 100 percent viable solution — but it costs ten times as much as you're willing to spend. As long as you're realistic in your requirements, a solution is out there. Just make sure that you put a dollar cap on it so that you don't price a vendor out of a solution. Vendors can always make compromises within your budget, so set the expected cost up front to keep from flipping your wig when you get the quote. As you do when buying a car, don't go in there holding out your checkbook. Be conservative about how much you expect to pay — and stick to your guns. Vendors want your business; they'll figure out how to stay within your budget.

Time is another important definition in the scope of the project, especially for consultants and professional-services engagements, which are charged on a time and materials basis. Do you expect to have the project done (to a certain point) in three months? Six months? A year? State that in your RFP so that the quote will reflect the people hours that have to be factored into the project plan. If your company has multiple sites, geographically dispersed, some travel time and expense may also have to be factored in.

Also, specify when the project must go from being run by the vendor to being internally run. If you're proposing a phased approach to the project, make sure to state that fact as well.

Make sure that internal projects that relate to the SAN have well-established timeframes and expectations. Things need to line up; otherwise, you'll be caught with a business rollout without any storage to connect to it. You may need 50TB of storage for 200 hosts, for example, but want to start with 2TB and five servers on Day 1. The costs will differ depending on how the project expands over time, especially if leasing rates are involved, with the possibility of swapping out existing computing infrastructure for new technology. Vendors can be quite creative when they know that they may reap future business with a customer, so make sure to note that possibility up front so that the vendors can crunch numbers and make their solutions look very attractive.

Deciphering the replies

Reading an RFP is an art. You must fully understand what you asked for in the RFP in the first place and then see whether the answers match the questions.

When you have an RFP that looks good, the next round is a chalk talk to find out how the vendor can really help you in the long run. In a *chalk talk*, you invite the SAN vendor to give a more technical overview of its solution. The vendor representative usually has a presentation with diagrams or maybe gets crazy on a whiteboard, drawing out some ideas. Then you can discuss the proposed solution. This dialogue is essential so that you can narrow down and weed out any misconceptions or confusion in the proposal. (**Bonus:** You may be able to learn a lot for free by asking questions.) You'll also find out more about your own environment, because vendors will ask in-depth questions about it, invoking a philosophical discussion about why you do what you do with your current gear. The vendor rep will fill you in on who else she's seen in your predicament and how she addressed those issues. It can be quite eye-opening to realize that your firm uses baling wire and bubblegum when your competition uses duct tape and zip ties to solve the same problems. But I digress.

Make sure that the proposal describes the vendor's plan to implement it. Does the plan have a timeline, and is that timeline the same as your expectation? Can the plan be done more quickly for less money? You want to see where this schedule aligns with yours in terms of the intended dates of purchase, delivery, implementation, and turnover.

Narrowing down the choices

After you craft your RFP, seek vendor bids, and choose the likely winner, here's one final bone to chew on: Can this vendor deliver what you want? Before you sign on the proverbial dotted line, make sure that you're comfortable with the answers to these questions:

> ✔ **Is the vendor financially stable?**
>
> Translate that question as "Will the vendor be around for the life of your SAN?"
>
> ✔ **Have you checked with its closest competitor?**

> You can make the best deal by having your first- and second-choice vendors compete for the same business. One of them has to break and pull out of the deal at some point, so you could make out with a great deal on a SAN implementation that would have cost twice as much if you hadn't asked the other guy to show his face.

Holding a reverse auction

If you're comfortable with any of the solutions proposed your final vendor choices, you can allow them to make the final decision on price for you. You accomplish this task with a reverse auction. In a *reverse auction,* the vendors submit their lowest bids to your company as "best and final" prices. This way, you accept that all the vendors' solutions meet your technological requirements; you're just looking for the cheapest overall price. Think of a reverse auction as a regular auction in which the *lowest* price wins. Doing the deal this way keeps any favoritism out of the picture. (Boondoggle? What boondoggle?)

Support makes the sale

Here's a real-life story from an unnamed vendor. A vendor goes into a bar . . . no, that's not the one.

A vendor goes on a sales call to a large customer. The salesperson and a systems engineer are in the conference room with several technical people (plus a high-level CEO type), and they begin the song and dance about their product. When they start talking about their great support structure and claim that they get the experts on the phone with the customer within 15 minutes (no matter what!), the CEO chuckles and says that this claim is nonsense. "Even your competition doesn't make wild claims like that, and they're twice as big as you guys," the CEO states. He excuses himself to talk to someone out in the hall and comes back near the end of the presentation.

Suddenly the systems engineer's cell phone rings, and he excuses himself from the room to take the call. A minute later, the CEO's cell phone rings. The caller is the SE from the presentation, calling from a phone in the hallway.

When the CEO left the room, he did so to call the vendor's help desk. What he said was this: "Hi. I don't have any site ID or customer number or anything; I just got your product, and I'm having some trouble. I need someone who can help me out. Here's my cell-phone number. Goodbye." The vendor's help desk paged an engineer (the systems engineer who was in the meeting) and had him return the call — all within five minutes. The CEO was so impressed that the company ended up buying the product. True story. No, really!

Picking a Winner

Lots of ideas can look good on paper, and some sound better when they're delivered by a skilled wordsmith, but don't get snookered by pretty graphics and glib rhetoric. Before you commit to a vendor, remember that anyone can promise you the moon but give you a plate of green cheese. After all, vendors are salespeople who want to sell you something — and in some cases, something you don't need. Be careful to understand the offer and match it to what you *do* need.

On the flip side, however, perhaps you've found a gem of a vendor that's looking out for your future needs. You have to weigh the need and the desire to get the right solution. Some final points should make you confident you're picking the right vendor:

✓ **Make sure that the solution meets your needs.**

Ask questions. It's your nickel, so make sure that things make sense. If you don't understand the answer, ask the question again. There are no stupid questions. It's the vendors' job to sell their wares, so make them earn your business. (Boy, are my friends in sales gonna kill me when they read this paragraph.)

✔ **Use one of your lifelines before you need to.**

Test your support infrastructure. Before you buy anything, call the vendor at 3 a.m. to see what happens. You should know what the support structure is before you decide to depend on it for your problems. Testing it is your due diligence.

✔ **See how flexible the vendor is about changes in technology.**

SANs may start small, but they grow at an unknown rate. You need to know how flexible your vendors are in adapting to these changes and scaling the solution accordingly. Ensure that they change directions and offer other solutions that still interoperate.

Also verify how quickly the vendor supports new technology. If you have more than one vendor, do the vendors cross-certify one another's products when those products come out? Cross-certification shows tight partnering, which helps you when you need to get something fixed. The less finger-pointing that goes on, the better for your SAN (and for your personal sanity).

WITHDRAWN